AF867772

17th ANNUAL TCL/TK 2010 CONFERENCE

Chicago (USA)
11-15 October

Conference Proceedings

TclA Publications

©Copyright 2009 Tcl Association
All Rights Reserved
No part of this publication may be reproduced, stored in a retrieval system or transmitted in any form, or by any means electronic, mechanical, photocopying, recording or otherwise without the prior consent of the publisher. Individual authors retain full re-distribution rights for their contributions to these proceedings.

ISBN: 978-0-578-07483-2

Thanks to Gerard Sookahet for the design of, and permission to use the Tcl 2010 conference logo.

Cover art by David Sky downloaded from
http://commons.wikimedia.org/wiki/File:Chicago-Illinois-USA-skyline-day.jpg

Special thanks to Dawson Cowals for designing
the Tcl Association logo.
For graphic design or web development consulting
please visit him on the web at
http://www.dawsoncowals.com/

Table of contents

17th ANNUAL TCL/TK 2010 CONFERENCE
Chicago (USA)
11-15 October

Being Webbed

Wed October 13, 2010 11:00-12:45

TclA Publications

WubTk - Tcl/Tk Apps Anywhere

Steve Landers and Mike Doyle
Buonacorsi Foundation

steve@digitalsmarties.com
mike@iomas.com

Abstract

WubTk is a new implementation of Tk that is layered on jQuery in a browser. It allows development of web applications in Tcl using a familiar Tk-like API.

This paper describes the conversion of an existing biomedical visualization program to WubTk, enabling it to be deployed in a browser. It also describes a custom iOS App that provides a more native look and feel on devices like the iPad and iPhone.

The paper also positions WubTk with respect to Tk (including enhancements beyond the Tk API) and discusses planned new features.

Background

WubTk is a new Tk implementation that maps a subset of the Tk API onto the jQueryUI [1] widgets running in a browser. In terms of the Model-View-Controller (MVC) design pattern [2], the Model and Controller execute in the web server (in Tcl code) and the View executes in the browser (in Javascript code).

The goal of the WubTk project is to provide a Tk-like API that uses a browser as a "display device". So, rather than mapping Tk commands to X11 or Win32 or Cocoa (as does the default Tk implementations), WubTk maps onto the jQueryUI widgets (although it could use any Javascript-based widgets). Instead of using "wish myapp.tcl" the developer runs "wubtk myapp.tk" and connects to the local host from a browser.

The work is being driven by Steve Redler (steve@sr-tech.com) and his customer needs, with development work largely being done by Colin McCormack (colin@chinix.com). Steve was initially inspired by Roy Keene's tkweb project [3] but WubTk has gone much further.

The API is “Tk-like” in the sense that there is no intention of implementing all of Tk, just the parts appropriate for web applications and which map conveniently onto jQueryUI features.

Development priorities are driven by the needs and interests of the developers and early adopters. While it would be nice if WubTk scripts could also be guaranteed to run on Tk, this isn't seen as essential. The goal is more to ensure portability of Tk skills rather than portability of scripts.

The History

The desire to build interactive web applications in Tcl/Tk isn't new.

In 1995 Eolas released a version of WebRouser, an applet-enabled web browser based on Eolas' enhanced version of NCSA Mosaic that could run Tcl/Tk scripts using Eolas' WebWish Tcl plugin. WebRouser and WebWish were presented in the cover story in the February 1996 issue of Dr Dobb's Journal [3].

In 1996 Jeff Hobbs produced a "proof of concept" Tcl plugin for Netscape following a visit to the Tcl group that was then at SunLabs. Jacob Levy (part of that group) produced the first Tcl/Tk plugin for Netscape and Laurent Demailly worked on the 2.0 implementation [5]. Version 3.0 [6] can still be installed in Firefox and Internet Explorer.

In 1998-1999 Mark Roseman and his team at TeamWave software implemented ProxyTk, a Java applet user interface toolkit for Tcl [7]. The small Java applet (50k bytes in size) runs in a user's browser to provide the user interface, and communicates with a Tk-like API running in a Tcl web server. Unlike the two previous browser plugin examples, with ProxyTk, the application was split between the user interface running in the browser and the application Tcl code running on the server, with an efficient protocol connecting the two. ProxyTk was ahead of its time, and showed the way forward for Tcl/Tk web apps (i.e. a client / server solution), the application was split between the user interface running in the browser and the application Tcl code running on the server, with an efficient protocol connecting the two. ProxyTk was ahead of its time, and showed the way forward for Tcl/Tk web apps (i.e. a client / server solution) but unfortunately it was swallowed in a corporate takeover and never reached its full potential.

All of the above solutions have the disadvantage that they require a plugin. In many organisations, it isn't possible for the user to install plugins in the standard operating environment (SOE) and so a solution that leverages components that don't require installation is desirable.

In 2003 Roy Keene wrote TkWeb [8], an attempt at rendering Tcl/Tk scripts using HTML. And around the same time Wilfred J. Hansen published a technical note about Rendering Tcl/Tk Windows as HTML [9]. Both of these were experiments aimed at proving the practicality of retaining the Tk API while rendering Tk widgets in a browser by generating HTML.

In 2006 Tom Poindexter developed Æjaks [10] – which "combines the server-side Ajax-based windowing system, Echo2, with the powerful simplicity of the Tcl language" . Æjaks is a thin layer over Echo2 [11] , a Java and Javascript-based platform for building interactive web-based applications. It translates Echo2 objects into Tcl objects, accessible behind a Tk-like object interface. Æjaks is a very capable system, and definitely one to consider for Tk based web development. But it does have a downside: the Tcl interpreter used is Jacl (an alternative implementation of Tcl 8.0 written in Java). Thus many recent developments in Tcl aren't available, although Jacl is currently being overhauled and this situation should improve significantly in time.

The other consideration with Æjaks is that, although Echo2 provides excellent cross-browser compatibility and uses modern Javascript techniques, it doesn't have the same amount of community acceptance or contributed widgets as other Javascript Web frameworks – in particulary jQuery and jQueryUI.

jQuery [12] is a cross-browser JavaScript library designed to simplify the client-side scripting of HTML. jQueryUI is a library that "provides abstractions for low-level interaction and animation, advanced effects and high-level, themeable widgets, built on top of the jQuery.

Both jQuery and jQueryUI have a significant and growing community of developers and users, and present an obvious choice for developers of rich, interactive web applications. The question is how best to leverage them from Tcl? The answer is to combine the approach of TkWeb (i.e. generating html) with the power and simplicity of jQueryUI.

The result is WubTk - a Tk-like API that maps Tk commands to jQueryUI widgets.

The Design

WubTk is (as the name indicates) implemented on top of Wub, a web server written in Tcl [13]. Although it isn't tied to Wub specifically, Wub was used because of its support for rapid prototyping, extreme configurability and advanced features (including HTTP 1.1 persistent connections and support for generating jQuery from within Tcl).

Each WubTk instance is run in a separate interpreter within the Wub server. The WubTk script is interpreted by the same Tcl interpreter as is running Wub, thus the application developer has access to all the features the latest Tcl provides.

Each WubTk instance has a persistent state, in that the per-instance interpreter is retained between requests from the browser. When the Wub "human" module recognises an individual user session it will crate a unique "human" cookie for the instance. Just like online stores with shopping carts (where a user accessing a store from the same browser twice will see the same shopping cart contents) so also with a WubTk intance. The current instance can be explicitly deleted from within the WubTk script by calling the "exit" command.

The WubTk API is intended to be as close to Tk as is practical, but with no guarantee as to preserving either the syntax or semantics of the existing Tk implementations. As stated previously, the goal of WubTk is to ensure portability of Tk skills and (in particular) to make those skills relevant in the Web 2.0 and mobile Internet world.

There are a number of differences with Tk, which can be categorized as follows:

- features that have already been implemented
- features that aren't yet implemented
- features that most likely won't be implemented because there is a conceptual mismatch with the client/server web world
- enhanced features that could be implemented as a shim over Tk
- convenience features relating specifically to the browser environment
- features that leverage jQueryUI functionality

Features already implemented include the button, select, combobox, checkbutton, radiobutton, label, scale, entry, text, wm, image, grid, frame, toplevel and notebook widgets.

Note that grid is the geometry manager for WubTk. In this alone it is of enormous value in that it frees the programmer from the constraints of the HTML/CSS Box Model.

Feature that aren't yet implemented include a large part of the canvas functionality. Some preliminary work has been done by Steve Redler on implementing some canvas features on top of the Tcl to SVG package [14]. This has been used, for example, to port Arjen Markus' Plotchart package [15] to WubTk, providing temperature charts from plant sensors in a factory automation product.

Features that most likely won't be implemented, or will be implemented in a different form, include the Tk event facility. It just doesn't make sense to have a low-level event mechanism that requires a round trip from the client to the server for each event (e.g. the interaction between a listbox and a scrollbar). A better approach is to abstract the event handling into two categories:

- one for user interface events to be handled between widgets in the browser
- another for application events that would be passed back from the browser to the application running on the server (more akin to the standard Tk event mechanism)

There are a number of enhanced features already implemented including the gridding option on each widget, used instead of the grid command:

```
entry .entry -textvariable ::entryvar -grid {2 1 -sticky nsew}
```

Another enhanced feature is the ability to grid an image directly, rather than needing to create a label to reference that image, and the -url flag to specify a URL for the image to load.

```
image create photo .image -url /images/logo.gif
```

Yet another is that the frame widget can take a label, and display a border around the frame. Examples of frames can be seen in the application described later in this paper. Each of these features could be implemented as a shim for standard Tk at some stage.

There are a number convenience features related to the browser environment. These are particularly useful when prototyping new widgets, or to add new behaviour to existing widgets.

For example, the following shows how to add Javascript functionality to a Tk button using the -js option:

```
button .size -text "Video size" -grid {3 2} -command VidSize -js {
      $('grid_3_2').onclick = function() {
          // do something useful in JS when button is clicked
      }
}

proc VidSize {} {
     # do something useful in Tcl when button is clicked
}
```

The -style option can be used to inject CSS to the definition of a widget. The CSS is specified as a Tcl dictionary, as follows:

```
button .stop -text "Stop it" -grid {1 1} -command StopIt -css {
      position absolute top 50% left 50% text-align center
}
```

The other convenience features are browser related widgets, including html, cookie, and upload. The html widget is used to inject HTML when the page is rendered, typically to specify a widget in HTML and CSS. For example, to define a widget to display a video using the HTML5 video element:

```
html .movie -grid {4 0 1 3} -text {
     <video src='/path/to/movie.m4v' controls autoplay></video>
}
```

The "wm header" command can be used to inject markup into the page header. The following adds a no-cache directive to the page:

```
wm header . {
    <meta http-equiv="Pragma" content="no-cache">
}
```

And finally, there are new features that leverage jQueryUI functionality, in particular new widgets such as accordion and toolbar, but with many more to come.

An Application - Biomedical Visualization

As an exercise in familiarising the authors with the WubTk features, an existing Tcl/Tk application was adapted to run under WubTk.

Vis is a biomedical visualization application developed by a team led by Mike Doyle in 1996. It comprises a Tcl/Tk front-end application communicating with a back-end Java Anatomical Server (MultiVis) using a socket connection and a custom textual protocol.

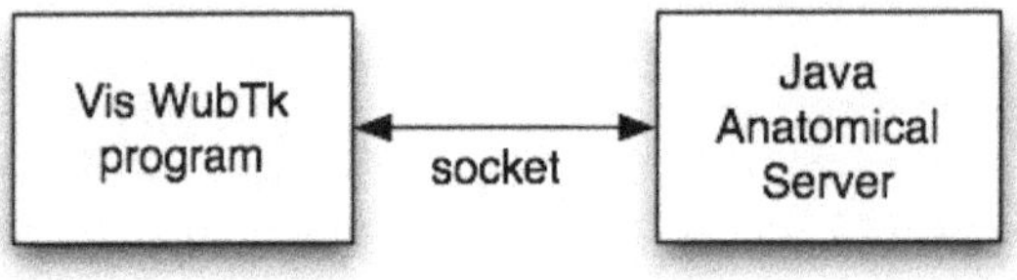

The Vis user interface comprises an image display, with a series of popup menus underneath it to control the view orientation parameters sent to the anatomical server. On receiving the parameters, the Anatomical Server constructs a GIF image and returns it (base64 encoded) to the Vis program, which displays in a label widget.

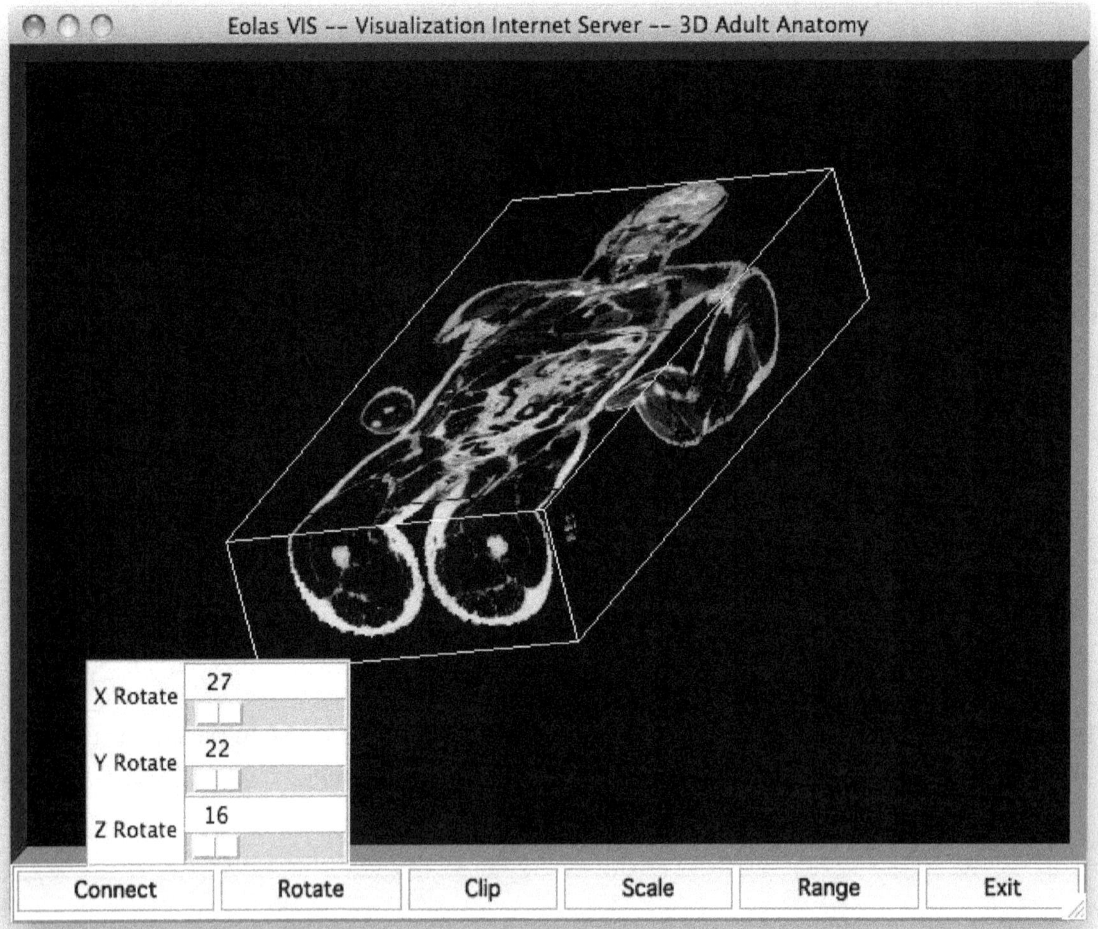

In the above screenshot, the Rotate menu (containing scale widgets for X, Y and Z rotation) is displayed after the user has clicked on the "Rotate" button. Likewise there are scale widgets for Clip, Scale, and the X, Y and Z ranges.
To gain experience in WubTk, a new Vis program was implemented that communicates with the Java Anatomical server using the existing protocol.

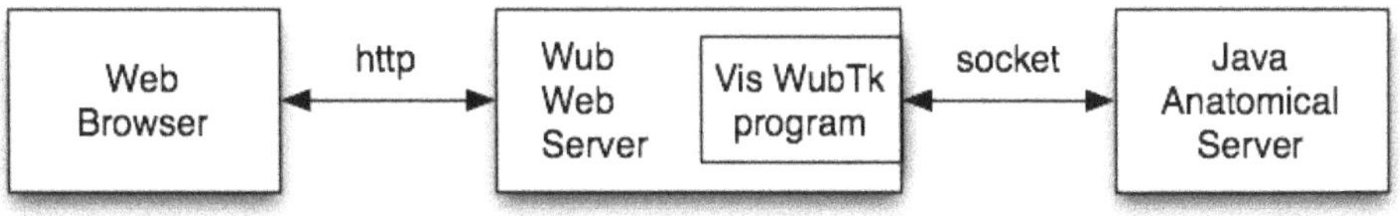

The layout of the new user interface was straightforward and resembles the old Vis Tcl/Tk program, except that popup menus aren't used, since they don't fit well with the browser user interface model.

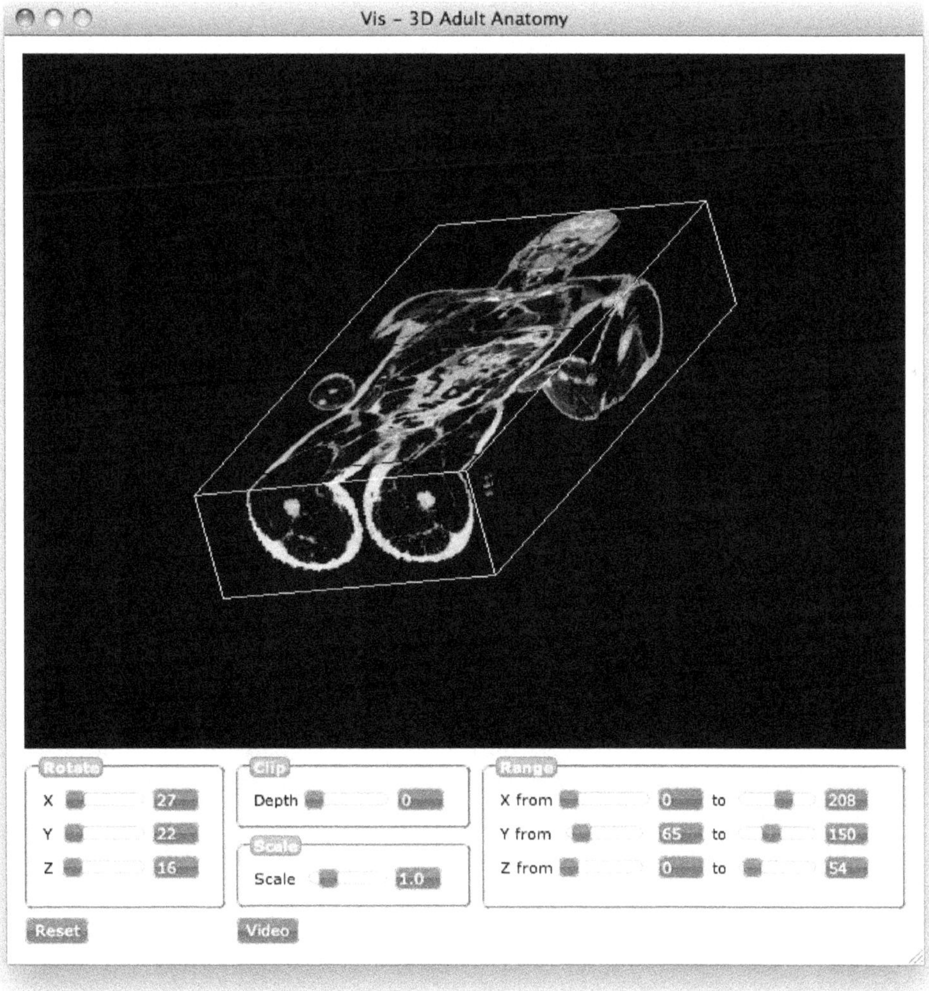

The image is displayed centered in a label, since the image size is smaller than the width of the page . Note the frames with text labels (i.e. Rotate, Clip, Scale and Range) similar to Ttk (a.k.a. Tile) labelframes.

The markup for this page is remarkably similar to a Tk program. For example, the following code was used.to define the Rotate frame

```
frame .rotate -text Rotate -grid {1 0 2 1 -sticky ns} \
              -style {height 9em}
label .rotate.xl -text "X" -grid {0 0} -style {padding-right 5px}
scale .rotate.xs -variable ::rotateX -from 0 -to 360 \
              -grid {0 1 -sticky nsew} -width 5em
entry .rotate.xe -textvariable ::rotateX -width 3 -grid {0 2}

label .rotate.yl -text "Y" -grid {1 0} -style {padding-right 5px}
scale .rotate.ys -variable ::rotateY -from 0 -to 360 \
              -grid {1 1 -sticky nsew} -width 5em
entry .rotate.ye -textvariable ::rotateY -width 3 -grid {1 2}

label .rotate.zl -text "Z" -grid {2 0} -style {padding-right 5px}
scale .rotate.zs -variable ::rotateZ -from 0 -to 360 \
              -grid {2 1 -sticky nsew} -width 5em
entry .rotate.ze -textvariable ::rotateZ -width 3 -grid {2 2}
```

Note the text ("Rotate") in the frame command options, the -style option to set the height of the frame and the use of -grid. Another point to note is the specification of width in ems on the scale commands. But otherwise this markup should be very familiar to a Tk programmer.

The declaration of the label and associated image widgets is a little more complicated.

```
image create photo .image -url /images/logo.gif

label .display -background black -image .image -borderwidth 0 \
          -grid {0 0 1 3} \
          -style {
               display          table-cell
               vertical-align   middle
               text-align       center
               width            650px
               height           512px
          }
```

The image command uses the -url option to set an initial value. This is later updated when the first anatomical image is returned from the server.

The label command includes some (arguably) tricky CSS to both set the size, and ensure the image widget is centered within it. Surprisingly, centering an image in a label (or rather, a HTML div) is a Frequently Asked Question in the HTML/CSS world.

Rather than force the WubTk programmer to remember this, it would make sense to add a flag to the label widget to indicate vertically centered contents, as a partner to the existing -justify

flag. This is an example where WubTk might reasonably diverge from Tk, although it would be quite feasible to provide a WubTk package that could hide or support the additional features when using Tk.
Once the user interface was specified, the next step was to start adding actions in response events in the user interface (such as moving a scale widget or typing in an entry widget). Like with standard Tk, this is done by adding traces on global variables that are set by the scale. So, in the following example, the .rotate.xs scale sets the global variable rotateX, as does the .rotate.xe entry widget.

```
label .rotate.xl -text "X" -grid {0 0} -style {padding-right 5px}
scale .rotate.xs -variable ::rotateX -from 0 -to 360 \
              -grid {0 1 -sticky nsew} -width 5em
entry .rotate.xe -textvariable ::rotateX -width 3 -grid {0 2}
```

Then a trace is added to the rotateX variable to trigger the execution of a Tcl procedure when the variable's value changes:

```
trace add variable ::rotateX write do_rotateX
```

The do_rotateX procedure sends the value of rotateX to the Anatomical Server using the exiting protocol and awaits a response. It is important to remember that this code executes in a real Tcl per-instance interpreter running in the web server.

Here we encounter the first of the conceptual design issues that differs between a web application and a traditional Tcl/Tk application. Because the web application may be serving multiple users, it isn't reasonable for the Vis application to wait for the response from the back-end server. So a more appropriate approach is to suspend the Http request from the browser and resume when the data arrives from the back-end server. In Wub this is quite straightforward:

```
[Httpd Suspend $r]
```

and

```
[Httpd Resume $r]
```

where $r is the dictionary containing the request from the browser (a standard Wub data structure).

The fact that changing a widget in the browser can trigger Tcl functionality in the server means that complex data integrity rules can be implemented in Tcl.

For example, in the original Vis application the Range menu allowed the user to specify the minimum and maximum values for each range, and to constrain these so that the minimum is less than or equal to the maximum (and vice versa). This was achieved by implementing a megawidget using customized scale widgets on a canvas, as shown in the left screenshot following:

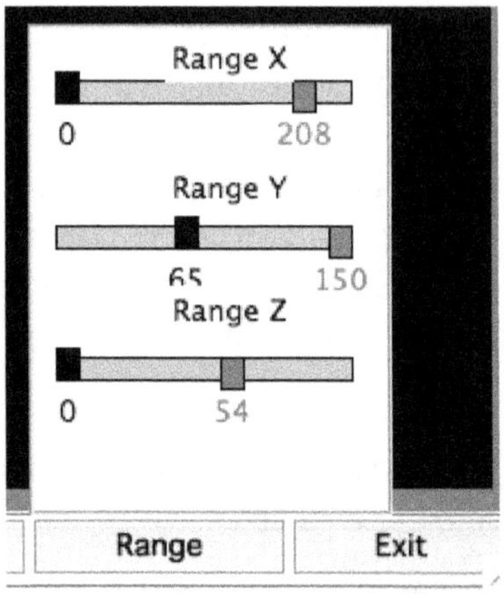

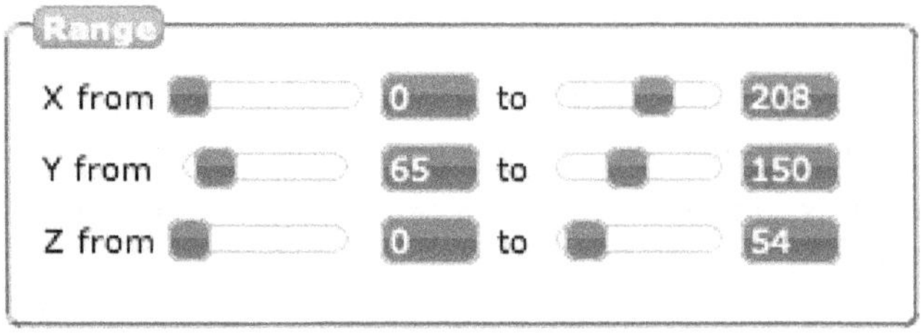

In the WubTk Vis application (shown on the right), this is achieved using the standard scale widgets in a frame and by adding checks to the trace command on the associated variables:

```
trace add variable ::rangeXmin write do_rangeX
trace add variable ::rangeXmax write do_rangeX

proc do_rangeX args {
    global rangeXmin rangeXmax
    if {$rangeXmin > $rangeXmax} { set rangeXmin $rangeXmax }
    if {$rangeXmax < $rangeXmin} { set rangeXmax $rangeXmin }
    sendToBackendServer
}
```

The experience of reimplementing Vis using WubTk has proven that the approach combining Tcl and a Tk-like API with a Javascript-based user interface running in a browser is a practical and productive way of building web applications.

Getting Mobile

Mobile computing is the fastest growing area of IT. The market penetration of Internet-connected devices like SmartPhones and Tablets is significant and growing. Having a web-based Tk implementation makes it feasible to use these and other portable devices as "displays" connected to a server running Tcl application code. For networked applications this is, in many ways, a better solution than installing and maintaining an application on each device.

For some platforms, in particular iOS (iPhone/iPad) this is currently the only way to develop applications in Tcl/Tk for these devices. And increasingly, these devices are optimized to support Javascript, CSS and HTML (in particular, through WebKit-based browsers such as Safari and Chrome). So the performance of web applications is often indistinguishable from native applications.

The Vis application has been tested from the iPhone and iPad, and works just fine. Thus it is perhaps the first Tcl/Tk application for iOS.

The following shows Vis running on the iPad and iPhone simulators:

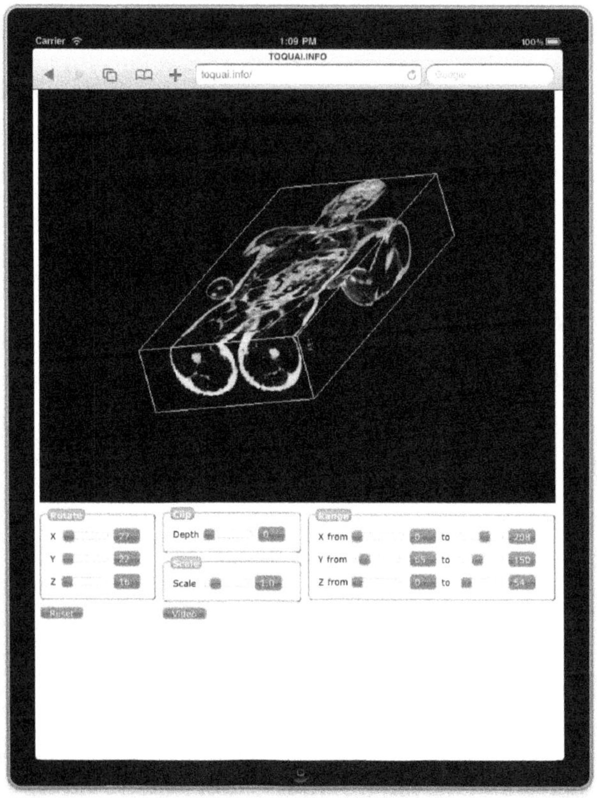

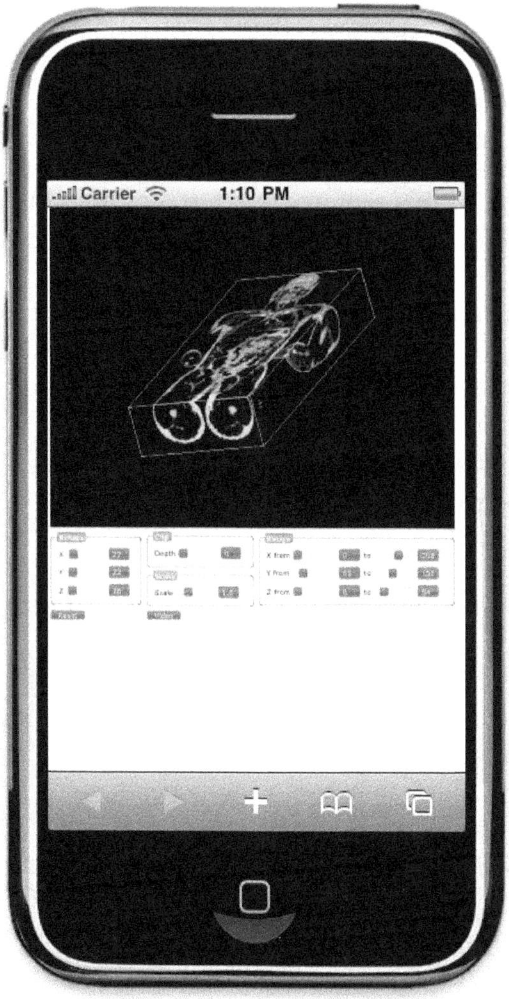

WubTk apps on such devices can be improved by leveraging mobile and/or Apple-specific CSS markup.

For example, the viewport tag can be used to properly fit the page content to the device screen:

```
wm header . {
      <meta name="viewport" content="width=device-width,
                        initial-scale=1.0, maximum-scale=2.0,
                        user-scalable=yes"/>
}
```

There are several Apple-specific tags that can be used to make a web application's behaviour more like a native application:

- apple-touch-icon - specifies the icon used when the user adds the app to the home screen
- apple-touch-startup-image – the application splash screen

- apple-mobile-web-app-capable – enables full screen mode so the browser location bar and controls aren't visible
- apple-mobile-web-app-status-bar-style to set the appearance of the status bar in full screen mode

These are only an intermediate solution to getting full native application look and feel. To achieve that requires two further steps – a generic embedded browser app for WubTk and a mobile device theme.

An app has been produced for iOS and ones for Android and even traditional desktops like Linux, OSX and Windows will follow: one for each platform that WubTk applications are to be deployed on.

The iOS WubTk app (called Toquai, pronounced tokay) is a native iOS Objective-C application that wraps a full-screen UIWebView (i.e. a Webkit browser without the location bar, controls and status bar).

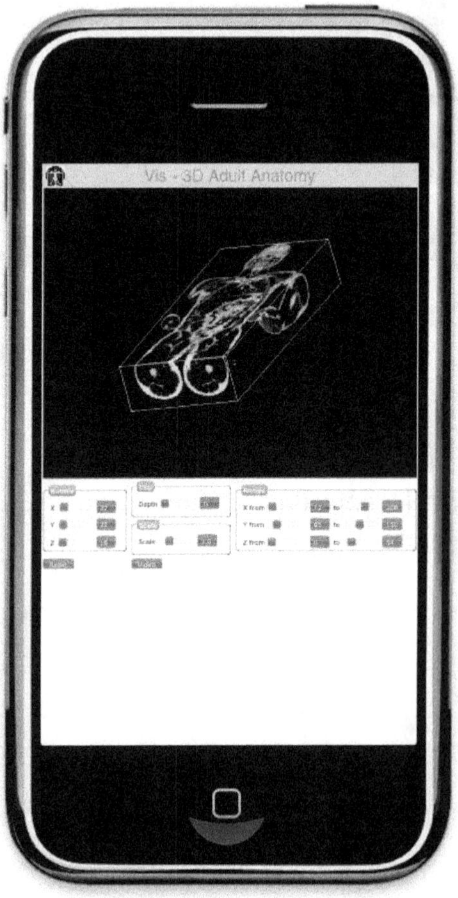

The screenshot to the right shows Vis running via Toquai on an iPhone.

The user can add an application by dragging a URL over the Toquai icon on the iPhone/iPad home screen. Toquai then adds a new application-specific icon to the home screen. When the application icon is clicked it invokes an instance of Toquai connected to the application URL.

Toquai registers as a custom URL handler with iOS, so that a URL prefixed by "tok:" causes Toquai to be invoked and passed that URL. When Toquai is creating a home page icon for a WubTk application, it is just creating a link, such as "tok://vis.bionetlab.org" - the image and splash screen for the app come from the WubTk application itself.

There are several advantages to this approach:

Firstly, Toquai is generic, doesn't include application code and so doesn't need to be updated when an application is updated. Once Toquai is installed on a device it can present a choice of available applications simply by visiting a web site. Clicking on a link to an app will cause the app to be installed, as described above.

Secondly, platform-specific content can be served out of Toquai's local storage rather than retrieved each time an application starts. In effect this will be a separate cache from the browser cache, so that libraries like jQuery and jQueryUI, and platform specific CSS will be less likely to be retrieved from the web (since it won't be flushed from the browser cache). This will potentially decrease the start-up time on slower devices or connections. Of course, Toquai can still update these locally cached copies if the versions in its cache don't match those on the web.

Thirdly, and perhaps most importantly, Toquai allows calls from the Javascript of an application into functionality provided in Objective-C (and vice-versa). This functionality will include encryption and authentication code, which is inherently insecure if implemented in the Javascript layer. By moving these functions to external code, they are kept safely out of reach from malicious code executing in the browser's address space.

The last piece of the puzzle is mobile-device specific theming.

The initial approach investigated was to use a platform specific package such as iWebkit [16] to create a more native look and feel. iWebKit substitutes more appropriate CSS when a web page renders on a mobile device. For example, checkbuttons are transformed to iPhone switches in the following before and after example:

But iWebKit also requires different markup (i.e. it isn't totally CSS based) and so a fully themed approach (i.e. CSS only) was considered a more appropriate cross-platform solution.

As mentioned earlier, jQueryUI is themed, and includes a facility called "ThemeRoller" for creating new themes [17]. One approach considered was to use to produce specific themes for each mobile platform supported.

However before this could be implemented the jQuery Mobile was announced [18]. jQuery Mobile is a "Touch-Optimized Web Framework for Smartphones & Tablets". It provides a single user interface system across all popular mobile platforms, including iOS, Android, BlackBerry, Windows Phone, Symbian and Palm WebOS. It includes t;ouch-optimized layouts and UI widgets; and ThemeRoller-based designs.

Since jQueryMobile availability was announce for late 2010, and jQueryMobile appears to provide exactly the features needed by WubTk on mobile devices, the decision was made to wait and integrate jQueryMobile as soon as it is available.

This further vindicates the decision to base WubTk on a popular platform like jQueryUI.

Getting Funky

HTML5 [19] and CSS3 [20] are becoming mainstream, and are going to significantly change the way web applications are developed. WubTk is well positioned to take advantage of this, allowing a Tk-like API to be easily combined with advanced HTML5 / CSS3 markup.

It was previously mentioned that the WubTk html command can be used to inject HTML when a page is rendered, typically to specify a widget in HTML and CSS, and an example of including an HTML5 video element was shown. This could be expanded to use CSS3 transforms to animate the display of the video element

```
html .movie -grid {4 0 1 3} -text {
        <video src='/path/to/movie.m4v' controls autoplay></video>
        <style type='text/css'>
                video#movie {
                        -webkit-transition: all 0.5s;
                        -moz-transition: all 0.5s;
                        -o-transition: all 0.5s;
                }
        </style>
}
```

Transformations can also be specified dynamically. For example, the "Video Size" button in the Vis application causes the video to be display in reduced size, over the top of the anatomical image. The video display can be skewed using the following jQuery command:

```
$('movie').style.webkitTransform = "skew(4deg, 10deg)";
```

Other transforms are available for alternative browsers such as Firefox.

The screenshot on the right shows the video in a skewed sub-window overlaying the image.

This only begins to scratch the surface of what can be done by combining Tk, jQuery, HTML5 and CSS3, but hopefully demonstrates the power of the facilities now accessible to the Tcl/Tk programmer through WubTk.

The HTML5/CSS3 train is coming, and developers can either get on board or get run over – but it can't be ignored.

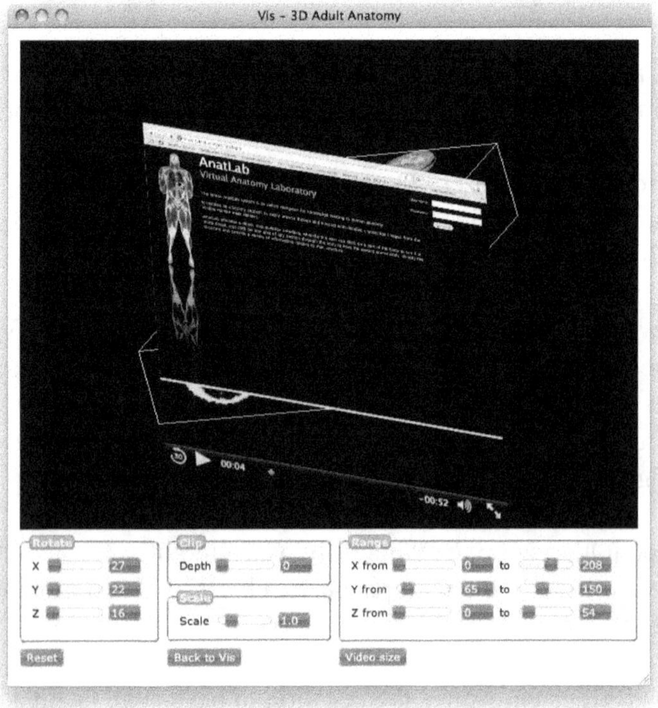

Summary and Conclusion

WubTk validates the design direction of using a Tk-like API for building web apps. The combination of Tk, jQuery, HTML5 and CSS has allowed modern web features to be utilised by Tcl/Tk developers without losing the productivity that Tk is well known for.

WubTk allows Tcl/Tk programmers to apply their skills to the web and mobile domains, providing the first practical implementation of Tcl/Tk for deploying applications on iOS.

And further, it ensures the many advancements in web technology such as jQuery, HTML5 and CSS3 can be leveraged by Tcl/Tk developers.

While the current implementation is a proof of concept that will be optimised (or even replaced) over the next year, nevertheless it has already proven practical in the development of a number of web applications, including the example shown in this paper.

The technology described in this paper is covered by at least U.S. Patent 7,599,985, and other pending patents. Interested parties should contact Eolas Technologies Inc. for licensing of these patents.

References

[1] jQueryUI – http://jqueryui.com/
[2] Model-View-Controller – http://en.wikipedia.org/wiki/Model–View–Controller
[3] TkWeb - http://www.rkeene.org/projects/tkweb/
[4] WebRouser – Dr Dobb's Journal, Issue #244, February 1996
[5] Levy, J. A *Tk Netscape Plugin*. Proceedings of the Fourth Annual Tcl/Tk Workshop. July, 1996. http://www.usenix.org/publications/library/proceedings/tcl96/full_papers/levy/index.html
[6] Tcl/Tk Plugin Version 3 – http://www.tcl.tk/software/plugin/
[7] Roseman, Mark *Proxy Tk: A Java applet user interface toolkit for Tcl.* Proceedings of the Seventh Annual Tcl/Tk Conference, February 2000 http://www.usenix.org/events/tcl2k/full_papers/roseman/roseman_html/
[8] TkWeb – http://www.rkeene.org/projects/tkweb
[9] Hansen, Wilfred J. *Rendering Tcl/Tk Windows as HTML*. Proceedings of the Tenth Annual Tcl/Tk Conference, July 2003 http://www.tcl.tk/community/tcl2004/Tcl2003papers/rendering.doc
[10] Æjaks – http://aejaks.sourceforge.net/Aejaks_Home
[11] Echo2 – http://echo.nextapp.com/site/echo2
[12] jQuery – http://jquery.com
[13] Wub – http://wiki.tcl.tk/wub
[14] Tcl SVG – http://wiki.tcl.tk/TclSVG, http://wiki.tcl.tk/4534 and http://wiki.tcl.tk/4940
[15] PlotChart – http://wiki.tcl.tk/plotchart
[16] iWebKit – http://iwebkit.net
[17] jQueryUI ThemeRoller – http://jqueryui.com/themeroller/
[18] jQueryMobile – http://jquerymobile.com
[19] HTML5 – http://en.wikipedia.org/wiki/HTML5
[20] CSS3 – http://en.wikipedia.org/wiki/CSS3

All web references as at September 2010.

A Tcl Web Framework

(*A*rnulf's *T*cl *W*eb *F*ramework)

ATWF

Abstract

ATWF a [Tcl] web framework is a work in progress, which started about 3 years ago with a brain storming wiki page [ToW Tcl on WebFreeWay]. The ideas collected at that page with a lot of feedback from the community were the base for further investigation. Inspired from a payed work project using [PHP]'s [Zend framework] I decided to convert as a starting point the basic parts of that framework nearly 1:1 into [Tcl]. The very first pre-alpha version is now handling the first requests. It has some adaption to [Tcl] constructs, but the rest is nearly identical to the original version.

Contact Information

Arnulf P. Wiedemann

Email: arnulf@wiedemann-pri.de

Tcl Wiki: http://wiki.tcl.tk/apw

Germany Prittriching

1 History (Collecting Ideas)

In May 2007 I started a wiki page named [ToW Tcl on WebFreeWay] inspired through the (comp.lang.tcl) discussion on "Tcl on Rails". I had some thoughts on how to make that (or at least a part of it) happen.

As I was thinking about some Tcl tools to help me create some personal web pages, I thought that could be the starting point of going deeper in that area. Knowing nothing about "[Ruby] on Rails" [RoR] at that time, I had some contact with it through downloading it and looking for some of the features.

My idea was to build something using [Tcl]/[Itcl]/[TclXML]/[TclXslt] and [starkit]s for use with [Apache] 1.3 and [Rivet] or [tclhttpd] or [wub].

It was not my intention to just clone [RoR], but to build some [Tcl]-ish framework and get a little bit inspired from [RoR].

I was asking for features which are useful. My direction at that time was to build some generators to make it easy to build at first simple web pages and later on web pages with more comfort.

My Idea was to have a [XML] structure (maybe similar to a [XML]-Schema specification) and to use that to generate [XSLT] templates, which then can be filled. But that is an additional feature besides "normal" [HTML] files. I was also thinking about a little tool which helps you defining [CSS] files. Another tool would be a simple generator, which uses a [XML], [XSLT] and [CSS] file and generates the [HTML] file (that's very easy using the tools already there, but for beginners that might be hard). I also thought to have as one of the databases a [starkit]/meta DB and I thought some of the tools or all should be in a [starkit] to make it easy to install and start. There should be also included one of the [Tcl] [http] servers to be able to generate a small application to begin with minimal effort.

During the discussion I decided to use [MVC] (model/view/controller) concepts and to have additional layers below model, view and controller and to allow template [HTML] forms which are "preprocessed" by [Tcl] (on the server side) using for example the following syntax:

<% some code %>

or:

<%TCL some code %>

and to let [Tcl] build the final [HTML] output on the fly when called via some cgi-bin script interpreting the above parts within <% ... %>.

I was also planning to have a TK GUI which represents the file system structure of the views, templates etc. as a tree so you can navigate and open the files in a text widget or with your favorite text editor. But in case you only wanted to maintain the structure using the GUI, it should be possible to directly edit the files (containing for example the templates) within the file system.

I wanted to put the commands/application for maintaining the structure (the scaffolding) into a [starkit], to make it '''very easy''' to start with the tool, just download the kit file, open a new app and start building the structure and filling in the templates.

After having had a more detailed look at [symfony] [http://www.symfony-project.com/], [propel] [http://propel.phpdb.org/trac] and phing [http://phing.info/trac/] (the [PHP] analog on to [RoR]), I did like some of the stuff they provided for example having [XML] files for storing all the information and for automatically having the possibility to validate all input.

I didn't like that the application(s) was/(were) too big and on some places too complicated, but I thought, if one would strip down that and also have a look at [RoR], that would be the right direction to go.

After having a short look at [AOLserver] ADP, I found that the package had too many hard wired features, which could make it hard for programmers to be flexible.

[Wtcl] used to many calls in my opinion (but that is a question of taste :-))). I wanted to get a generator, which makes the "low level stuff" and produces files which can be modified, if one is not satisfied with the generated stuff.

By the way, the ideas for templating for [RoR] and [symfony] are after all very similar, I think both have been influenced by the [Apache] Torque project (for [symfony] I know it).

I had a closer look at [YAML]. Nevertheless I was thinking to use a GUI to generate the [XML] files with minimal input from a user and only if you wanted to make special things you would modify and not create the [XML] configuration files.

At that time I thought, one advantage is, that there exist a lot of [Tcl] tools to work with [XML] files and using [XSLT] makes it easy to convert it and using [XSD]-SCHEMA allows you to verify input easily. Not that I was fixed to [XML] but at least there was no [Tcl] Parser for [YAML] and the existing C-parser is not easily integrated to [Tcl]. I have looked at it and it is not easy (not difficult but a lot of work) to write a [Tcl] native parser for [YAML].

2 Template Formats

At that point there was some discussion about the format of the templates to build the final [HTML] or [XML] pages.

One of the discussed formats looked like:

```
<!-- Begin of document --->
<h1><%= @page.title %></h1>
<p class="pageDescription"><%= @page.description %></p>
<hr>
<div id="pageText"><%= @page.text %></div>
<p class="pageAuthor"><%= @author.name %> (<a href="mailtto:<%= @author.email %>"><%= @author.email
%></a>)</p>
<!-- comments
<table border="0" width="300">
  <tr>
    <th bgcolor="green">Comments (<a href="<%= :SCRIPT_NAME %>?action=add">add a comment</a>)</th>
  </tr>
  <% foreach |entry| @comments %>
    <tr bgcolor="<%= cycle values="#dedede,#eeeeee" advance=false %>"><td>
      posted by <%= escape(@comments.author{entry] => :name) %> on <%= date_format("%e %b, %Y",
@comments[entry] => :date) %><br />
      <%= escape(@comments[entry] => text) %>
    </td></tr>
  <% foreachelse %>
    <tr><td>No records</td></tr>
  <% end %>
</table>
<!-- End of document --->
```

After all the discussion my conclusion was, the ideas of [symfony], [RoR], [Smarty] seem to be relativly similar in using the [MVC] concept, having an abstraction from the data source, using a generator to convert an input template in some format be it [HTML], [XML] whatsoever with spread in [Tcl] code to generate (at least for the 3 systems mentioned) [HTML] output.

In [RoR] they have something like "abstract" calls to the data sources with the [CRUD] (Create, Read, Update and Delete) layer, which is differently implemented for each data source for example by having the calls as abstract virtual calls in a base class, which must be implemented by derived classes.

My preference was the spread in code should not only be able to handle one static input of the data source, but to be able to make additional requests to the data source for getting additional input to handle. The data source should be accessed via the abstract [CRUD] interface (shortly described above), the generators should be able to handle different kinds of templates (i.e. [HTML], [XML] ...). There should be controllers, which handle the requests (actions) in calling generators for producing the output. The output is driven by the use of templates (the views) which describe how the output has to be formatted and by use of [CRUD] requests for getting the appropriate data.

As [HTML] and [XML] have both the < ... > tags there is no problem in parsing the stuff, if no validation of the semantic is done, the validation could be done by some different program which could be added to the tool later. For other stuff [WAP], [Postscript], [TeX] etc. one would need a closer look to see, if that is also possible with the same generators or with different ones (at least parsers for the input).

Then I had the idea of doing the templating the other way around and let the template be some [Tcl] code which is called like a preprocessor and produces output (for example a [HTML] page):

An example could then look like:

```
<%= {
 <!-- Begin of document --->
 <h1>} ; <%= {[@page getTitle]} ; <%= {</h1>}
<%= {<p class="pageDescription">} ; <%= {[@page getDescription]} ; <%= {</p>}
<%= {<hr>
 <div id="pageText">} ; <%= {[@page geText]} ; <%= {</div>}
 <%= {<p class="pageAuthor">} ; <%= {[@author getNname]} ; <%= {(<a href="mailtto:}
   <%= {[@author getEmail]} ; <%= {">}
<%= {[@author getEmail]} ; <%= {</a>)</p>}
<%= {<!-- comments -->
 <table border="0" width="300">
  <tr>
     <th bgcolor="green">Comments (<a href="} ; <%= {[set SCRIPT_NAME]}
      <%= {?action=add">add a comment</a>)</th>
  </tr>}
set rows [@comments getRows]
foreach entry $rows {
 <%= {<tr bgcolor="}
   <%= {[cycle values "#dedede,#eeeeee" advance false]}
   <%= {"><td>
         posted by} ; <%= {[escape [[[@comments getEntry] getAuthor] getNname]]}
   <%= { on } ; <%= {[clock format [clock scan [[@comments getEntry] getDate] -format "%e %b, %Y"]}
   <%= {<br />}
   <%= {[escape [[@comments getEntry] getText]]
   <%= {</td>
  </tr>}
}
if {[llength $rows] == 0} {
  <%= { <tr><td>No records</td></tr>}
}
<%= {</table>
 <!-- End of document --->}
```

“@page”: the @ marks it as a "page" object (from the model of that application).

“getText”, “getAuthor” etc. are methods of that object, which return the field value of the appropriate field of the current row of the object.

“<%=” is a proc which is returning its argument "<%= {hallo}" returns "hallo" or if it starts with "[" is evaluating the argument "<%= {[@page getTitle]}" returns the title field contents of the current row of the page object.

The “escape” proc would do the [HTML] escaping.

The generator knows what to do with the results (for example it just outputs them to the client using the result as a [HTML] page).

During that discussion there had been a very interesting suggestion from Jean-Claude Wippler [jcw] [Templates and subst] called “substify”. I was sure that would be a good approach for a template syntax (and an implementation was already there).

With that a solution for templating was found, so the next point was a database abstraction layer. For that I planned to use [nstcl]. After a closer look at it, it seemed to have all the features needed. Nevertheless an additional layer would be needed to separate object relations from database table relations.

3 Implementation Start

After that discussion, which ended in May 2007, there was no progress until December 2008 because I was working on 3 other Open Source projects [itcl-ng], [ntkwidget] and [ReportingTools]. And only a few small parts of code had been implemented at that time.

Finally in April 2010 I got back to that ideas and started a project called [ATWF] (A Tcl Web Framework).

As implementation language I did choose [itcl-ng], for the Db layer I did choose [tdbc] from Kevin Kenny [kbk] to be able to connect to/working with databases.

Then in payed work we were looking for a web framework and [Tcl] was not an option because of not enough people in the project environment were familiar with [Tcl].

So we choose [PHP]'s [Zend framework], as the tool, as one colleague had already experience with it in other projects and others did at least know [PHP]. Looking at that, a lot of features seemed to be very interesting i.e. [MVC] concepts, possibility to overwrite all the defaults provided by the framework, big flexibility in processing a request etc.

I started building some classes for the DB abstraction layer based on [tdbc] using ideas from [PHP] [Zend framework]

I first had the idea of only using some ideas from [Zend framework] and building my own framework completely from ground up. But very soon I noticed that I was adding very similar code to my version from the [Zend framework] code and on the other side there were already a lot of interesting features for driving the handling of a request ready in [Zend framework].

[PHP] code with the use of [PHP] class system (on which [Zend framework] is based) and objects looked very similar to [Tcl] code when using [Itcl] as object system. So I finally decided to use the original code and to convert it very close to the original into [Tcl] Code. By doing that I would be able to use all the features, [Zend framework] had already tested and decided to be useful during their development phase.

I have reimplemented a big part of Db package of the [PHP] [Zend Framework] in [Tcl] within 2 weeks by replacing the [PDO] layer used in [Zend framework] by [tdbc]. Simple selects/inserts/updates/deletes were possible with that, but there was still a lot of work in debugging and testing that part.

In ATWF the identical syntax for the DB interfaces is used as in [Zend Framework]. This is mostly the '''model''' part of [MVC].

After that I implemented a big part of the controller layer also by reimplementing the equivalent sources from [PHP] [Zend Framework] in [Tcl]. By doing that, a bigger part of '''controller''' of [MVC] concepts was done (needs still a lot of testing) so the missing part of [MVC] was the '''view''' part.

For generating web pages, I decided to use [Templates and subst] the “substify” proc from Jean-Claude Wippler [jcw] (this was a part of the '''view''' part of [MVC]).

The first version of the '''view''' part was done in 2nd half of April 2010. The first request using apache2 and cgi-bin was routed and executed and produced a [HTML] page with data from a mysql database, as expected.

Now there were about 30.000 lines of [Zend Framework] converted to [Tcl]. The total number of lines of [Zend Framework] (of the used version 9.3) is about 140.000 lines and about 27.000 lines thereof are targeted to [PDF] handling.

Implementation continued and at beginning of May 2010 there were about 55.000 lines rewritten and the first web pages using apache 2.2.15 and rivet 2.0.0 were running including context switch between [HTML] and [XML] output depending on a "format=..." parameter.

The [HTML] respective [XML] page context is generated using [Templates and subst], which means there is a .html or .xml template with inserted [Tcl] statements and the "substify" proc is generating the real page to be sent to the client.

4 Differences in the Implementation

There were only 4 places, where I have used a different approach to [Zend framework] for implementation.

1. *Database adapters*: as I just had experimented with Kevin Kenny's [kbk] [tdbc] I found that [tdbc] is a suitable replacement for the [PDO] DB adapters of [Zend framework].
2. *Arrays*: all the [Zend framework] classes are derived from an array class and nearly all collections of variables are based on [PHP] arrays. I found the equivalent in [Tcl] are [dicts], which Donal Fellows [dkf] has provided. And as most of the array uses in [Zend framework] are key/value pairs, [dicts] are optimal for that part,
3. *Views*: Generating [HTML] or [XML] code using [PHP] code parser in the view part, which could also handle [HTML]/[XML] code intermixed with escaped [PHP] code was not possible for the equivalent [Tcl] part. But for that I had already a replacement the „substify“ procedure from Jean-Claude Wippler [jcw]. It was easy to replace that part of the view mechanism of [Zend framework] with the „substify“ proc call and some additonal code in ATWF.
4. *Namespaces*: [Zend framework] uses a 1:1 relationship between directory structure and class name architecture. Class names are built from directory path names by replacing the path delimiter (normally a „/“ character) by an underscore („_“) character. That inhibits the use of underscore characters within class name parts. As [Tcl] has already a [namespace] feature I replaced the generation of class names with underscores for the directory parts by using of the [Tcl] [namespace] „::“ syntax and thereby the normal syntax for [Tcl] [namespace]s. Using that approach, I think the idea of the namespace philosophy is much more visible in the ATWF implementation.

5 General Structure of an Application

ATWF uses - as does the [Zend framework] - the [MVC] (Model/View/Controller) technology. This can also be seen in the directory structure used for an application/ project.

A Project in [Zend framework] has the following general layout in the file system:

```
application
    configs
    controllers
    models
    layouts
    views
    modules
        module1
            controllers
            models
            layouts
            views
        module2
            controllers
            models
            layouts
            views
        :
        :
public
```

6 Building of URLs for the Requests

URL's for sending a request are built as follows:

....../<module name>/<controller name>/<action name>?<parameters>

- <module name> the name of the module can be empty
- <controller name> the name of the controller (default name index)
- <action name> the name of the action (default name index)

7 Contents of the Application Directories

A controller has a corresponding [Tcl] script in the *controllers* directory with the same name and in that script for every *action* there must be a method with the name <action name>Action i.e. IndexAction for the index action.

The *models* directory normally has a *DbTable* subdirectory and in that directory a DbTable class for every table in the DB used by the project.

The name for a DB Table person is "::Model::Dbtable::Person", if no module name is used, otherwise the module name is prepended as namespace in front of that name "::Module1::Model::Dbtable::Person"

The *views* directory normally contains a scripts directory, which contains a directory for every controller with the name of that controller and in there a [Tcl] script for every action for that controller. These scripts are either templates for a [HTML] page or for a [XML] page with mixed in [Tcl] code, which is executed and replaced when applying the "substify" procedure on that template.

The *layouts* directory normally contains .css etc. files, which drive the layout of a page, so the contents in the views directory and layout in the layouts directory are separated.

8 Bootstrapping

The bootstrapping starts with an index.ttml file, which bootstraps the application. The following steps are performed:

1. scanning of the application.ini file
2. calling of setOptions (which is:)
3. initializing standard resources:
    - Db
    - FrontController
    - Layout
    - Locale
    - Modules
    - Navigation
    - Resource
    - Router
    - Session
    - Translate
    - View
4. For Application::Resource::Resourcebase setBootstrap is called (always)
5. call FrontController for handling of the request

9 Work Flow for a Request

The general work flow is: the *controller* calls an action, the *action* uses the *models* and eventually gets data from the DB using the "DbTable" class for the needed table(s). It processes the result sets and hands the result over to the *view* part. Then the *view* part is called running the rendering code and producing the wanted page and during that part calling the „substify" procedure for getting the processed [HTML]/[XML] template and producing the *response*. The *dispatcher*, which is driving the controller/action/view part, is then sending the response back to the requester.

The dispatcher is part of FrontController and does the following steps:

- setRequest
- setBaseUrl
- setResponse
- for every plugin call method setRequest
- for every plugin call method setResponse
- initialize router
- router setParams
- initialize dispatcher
- dispatcher setParams
- dispatcher setResponse
- while not dispatched
    - for every plugin call method routeStartuo
    - router route
    - for every plugin call method routeShutdown
    - for every plugin call method dispatchLoopStartup
    - while to be dispatched
        - setDispatched true
        - for every plugin call method preDispatch
        - if request is not completely dispatched continue
        - dispatcher dispatch request
        - notify plugins of dispatch completion in calling postDispatch
        - if request is dispatched break
    - end of to be dispatched
    - for every plugin call method dispatchLoopShutdown
    - if returnResponse return the response
    - else: response sendResponse

When the dispatcher is dispatching a request, it determines the controller and the action from the request using defaults for module, controller and action, if the request has no values for these.

In the action method within a controller the output to be rendered is passed to view object.

If not inhibited by the controller, the view object is called and executes method render which produces the rendered output by also calling "substify" proc on the way and stores the output in the response object.

When calling sendResponse that output is passed back to the sender of the request.

10 Current Status

Right now the first requests sent from an [apache] server using [rivet] for forwarding a request to [ATWF] are running and giving back the requested results. An earlier version was also handling [wub] from Colin McCormack [CMcC] requests, this has to be adapted for the current version again. And I also had a version handling cgi-bin requests, to be adapted too.

Unfortunately there is nearly no demo available at the moment.

11 Todos

There are the following items on the todo list:

- Test suite
- Complete integration into the 3 server types: Apache, wub, cgi-bin
- Prepare alpha version
- Demos
- Documentation
- Look for parts which can be made more Tcl'ish
- Decide which other parts of [Zend framework] are needed/interesting to take over
- Take care of feedback to the alpha version

17th ANNUAL TCL/TK 2010
CONFERENCE Chicago (USA)
11-15 October

Core Internals

Wed October 13, 2010 14:00-15:45

TclA Publications

Adventures in TclOO

Donal Fellows,
University of Manchester

Abstract

I have been working on a number of small projects that use TclOO in fairly complex ways, and this paper will cover some of them. In particular, it will look at its use for building more advanced APIs in the areas of interfacing to the HTTP protocol for use with REST services, for mapping relational databases into Tcl, and for supporting metadata on TclOO objects themselves.

This paper is a collection of write-ups for some small projects in Tcl that I have been working on in the past year that all leverage the TclOO object system[1]. The first is a wrapper for the standard http package that makes it easier to write clients for particular types of web services, the second is a way of representing the contents of a relational database in Tcl and interacting with it, and the third is a mechanism for adding extra information to classes and their contents.

Note that the first package described here is actually implemented so as to be usable in Tcl 8.5, whereas the other two both require Tcl 8.6.

Simple REST Interface

Representational State Transfer[2] (or REST) is a way of providing services over the web in a way that works well with the fundamental architecture of the web. In particular, it focuses on the use of standard HTTP verbs[3] (including whether or not they are supposed to be idempotent) and resources characterized by URLs that can be retrieved in multiple formats (with content negotiation to decide which format to use). For example, a collection of pizzas might be represented by the URL `http://example.org/pizzas`, that you would do a normal GET of to get a list of URLs as some format like HTML, XML, JSON, YAML, Tcl list, S-expression, etc. A URL such as `http://example.org/pizzas/pepperoni` would represent each pizza on the list, and you would be able to GET that URL to get a detailed description of the pizza and remove the pizza from the list by doing a DELETE on the URL. A pizza of known name would be created or altered by doing a PUT on its URL, or a POST could be done on the collection of pizzas to create a new one (of the chef's choice); the response would be an HTTP redirect to the newly created pizza.

There are many ways to interact naturally with a REST web service – it is even feasible to just treat one as a collection of plain web pages – but the standard Tcl http package does not make this particularly easy. Key things like handling of HTTP verbs, redirects and content negotiation are concealed behind an interface that both conceals critical features and reveals much of its implementation. That's where my REST support code comes in.

Code and Discussion

It simply consists of a TclOO class that provides methods that implement each of the common HTTP verbs required for RESTful service interaction (GET, PUT, POST and DELETE). These methods in turn delegate their behaviour to a worker method that takes care of the nitty gritty details of things like redirections. It also makes it much easier to specify an alternate preferred set of content types for a particular request (e.g., so you could get a directory either as a listing of its contents or as a zipped archive).

For the GET method, since it is common to not provide an entity with this method, it does a join on the arguments provided with "/" as a separator, adding these on to the base URL set in the constructor. This is then passed straight on to the fundamental DoRequest method, which is a bounded loop that performs basic requests using the standard http library until success or a recoverable failure is reached. The actual decision of what to do about a particular redirect is taken by another method, OnRedirect.

```
method DoRequest {method url {type ""} {value ""}} {
  for {set reqs 0} {$reqs < 5} {incr reqs} {
    if {[info exists tok]} {
      http::cleanup $tok
    }
    set tok [http::geturl $url -method $method \
        -type $type -query $value]
    if {[http::ncode $tok] > 399} {
      set msg [my ExtractError $tok]
      http::cleanup $tok
      return -code error $msg
    } elseif {[http::ncode $tok] > 299
        || [http::ncode $tok] == 201} {
      try {
        set location [dict get [http::meta $tok] Location]
      } on error {} {
        http::cleanup $tok
        error "missing a location header!"
      }
      my OnRedirect $tok $location
    } else {
      set s [http::data $tok]
      http::cleanup $tok
      return $s
    }
  }
  error "too many redirections!"
}

method OnRedirect {tok location} {
  upvar 1 url url
  set url $location
  # By default, GET doesn't follow redirects; the next
  # line would change that...
  ###return -code continue
  set where $location
  set len [string length "$base/"]
  if {[string equal -length $len $location "$base/"]} {
    set where [string range $where $len end]
    return -level 2 [split $where "/"]
  } else {
    return -level 2 $where
  }
}
```

```
method ExtractError {tok} {
  return [http::code $tok],[http::data $tok]
}
```

With the aid of the above methods, the definition of the general method for handling GET requests is just this:

```
method GET args {
  return [my DoRequest GET $base/[join $args "/"]]
}
```

The equivalent for other HTTP verbs is very similar, though with additional arguments defined due to the need to control how values are uploaded.

Usage

In subclasses of this general REST support class, I can just do a read/write accessor method like this:

```
method status {{status ""}} {
  if {$status eq ""} {
    return [my GET status]
  }
  my PUT status text/plain $status
  return
}
```

You don't get much easier than that without adding in code to directly work with a WADL file published by the service, and that's not so commonly published for REST services.

This was used to rapidly prototype an interface for a service I was developing. That service had a very large service API (42 methods, most of which have renderings as both SOAP and REST styles simultaneously) so the use of a testing tool was vital. While I already had an existing (non-Tcl) infrastructure for checking the SOAP interface[1], I needed something I could work with for the REST interface. In particular, I needed to be able to build things up piece-by-piece so I could check what I was doing as I was doing it. By turning a reasonably complex sequence of operations with the http package into a simple method call, it made

[1] I also uncovered a few problems with the Tcl-WS[4] packages, subsequently fixed of course, when trying to do this in Tcl.

it much easier for me to focus on the debugging of my service and it also allowed me to very rapidly throw up a GUI (thanks, Tk!) for the purposes of demonstration.

Object Relational Mapping

When a database is used with Tcl, it is most common to do this by simply issuing SQL queries and statements to the database using one of the many existing interfaces. Indeed, TDBC[5] is a standardization of these interfaces to promote best practices in database access so that it can become easier to write cross-platform code that works with many databases. However, using such interfaces still requires the script author to understand SQL[6]. One way to relax this requirement is to map a database as a collection of classes and objects; the classes correspond approximately to the tables in the database schema and the objects to the rows in those tables. This is a common approach in many languages[7][8][9], especially where there are strict static types, and often involves a complex compilation step that generates the classes and queries from the database. But I wanted to see how much I could do in an entirely dynamic way while leveraging TclOO and TDBC to do the difficult parts for me. It turns out you can do a lot!

I opted in this work to make objects that reflected the database rather than the reverse, this being driven largely by the fact that databases tend to have more detailed information about relationships between tables and columns (plus the types of the columns) than is actually required for Tcl. After all, Tcl is quite happy with almost anything as a value. Because of this, my aim is to have a package of TclOO classes such that it could be told to attach to a TDBC database connection and have a class created for each (non-metadata) table. Constructors would correspond to the use of SQL queries or inserts, and individual columns would map to methods that read and write the values inside the corresponding columns. There is an explicit one-to-one mapping between table names and class names, and between the names of columns and methods; the unexposed support methods have names that it is wholly unreasonable to use as column names.

Code and Discussion

The ORM package is composed of four classes that represent the overall database, a table in that database, and two that represent different types of row.

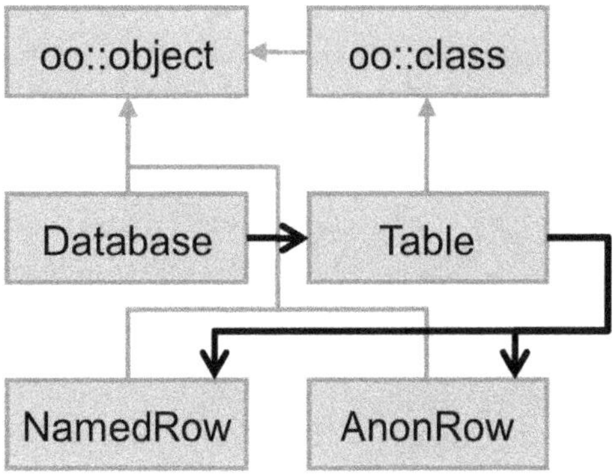

Figure 1: ORM class diagram

Figure 1 shows how the classes related to each other (the standard TclOO classes are included in green for clarity). The blue links indicate inheritance, and the black links indicate where one class is responsible for creating instances of another.

The Database class encapsulates the whole database, or rather the TDBC connection, and it acts as a collection of tables. It also generates the particular table classes with the help of introspection on the database.

```
oo::class create ORM::Database {
  variable db tableClasses dying
  self {
    variable classes
    method ClassFor {category default {class ""}} {
      if {$class ne ""} {
        set classes($category) $class
      } elseif {![info exists classes($category)]} {
        return $default
      }
      return $classes($category)
    }
    forward classOfTables \
        my ClassFor table ::ORM::Table
    forward classOfNamedRows \
        my ClassFor namedRow ::ORM::NamedRow
    forward classOfAnonRows \
        my ClassFor anonRow ::ORM::AnonRow
  }
  constructor {databaseHandle} {
    set db $databaseHandle
    oo::objdefine [self] export GetRowClass
```

```
    $db transaction {
      dict for {table ?} [$db tables] {
        dict set tableClasses $table \
            [my MakeAMappedTable $table]
      }
    }
    oo::objdefine [self] unexport GetRowClass
  }
  destructor {
    set dying "dying"
    foreach tbl $tableClasses {$tbl destroy}
  }
  method transaction script {
    $db transaction {uplevel 1 $script}
  }
  method tables {} {
    dict keys $tableClasses
  }
  method table {table args} {
    if {![llength $args]} {
      return [dict get $tableClasses $table]
    }
    tailcall [dict get $tableClasses $table] {*}$args
  }
  method MakeAMappedTable {table} {
    [[self class] classOfTables] create $table \
        [self] $db $table
  }
  method GetRowClass {type} {
    [self class] classOf${type}Rows
  }
}
```

The Table class is the core of the ORM package as it contains almost all of the complexity. In particular, the constructor uses introspection on the underlying database table to discover not just the collection of columns, but also their natures. Unlike most object-relational mapping technologies, we do not need to do much to handle the types of the columns (though the current prototype does ignore SQL NULLs) but the nature of columns is still important because it is important to use primary key and foreign key information to manage the mapping between tables; that enables the transparent following of links between tables, coupling row objects together smoothly. (This sample code omits much to keep things short.)

```
oo::class create ORM::Table {
  superclass oo::class
  variable db dbHandle table sql id2obj idColumn \
      columns foreignKeyMap
  constructor {mappedDB connection tableName} {
    set db $mappedDB
    set dbHandle $connection
    set table $tableName
    set pkinfo [$connection primarykeys $table]
    set fkinfo [$connection foreignkeys -foreign $table]
    if {[llength $pkinfo] == 1} {
      set idColumn \
          [dict get [lindex $pkinfo 0] columnName]
      oo::define [self] superclass \
          [$db GetRowClass Named]
    } else {
      set idColumn ""
      oo::define [self] superclass \
          [$db GetRowClass Anon]
    }
    array set id2obj {}
    dict for {c info} [$connection columns $table] {
      if {$c eq $idColumn} {
        set name "ORM.Access.ID"
        set target {}
      } else {
        lappend columns $c
        set target [my GetFKTarget $fkinfo $c]
        if {[llength $target]} {
          set name "ORM.Access.Linked"
          lassign $target targetTable targetKey
          dict set foreignKeyMap $c $target
        } else {
          set name "ORM.Access.Simple"
          set sql(update,$c) \
              [my MakeUpdateOfRowColumn $c]
        }
      }
      oo::define [self] forward $c my $name $c {*}$target
      oo::define [self] export $c
    }
    set sql(query,all) [my MakeQueryForAllRows]
    if {$idColumn ne ""} {
      set sql(query,byID) \
          [my MakeQueryForRowByIdentifier]
      # etc...
    }
  }
  unexport create new
  method GetFKTarget {descriptor sourceColumn} {
    foreach fkDesc $descriptor {
      dict with fk {
        if {$foreignColumn eq $sourceColumn} {
          return [list $primaryTable $primaryColumn]
        }
      }
    }
  }
  method MakeQueryForRowByIdentifier {} {
    format {SELECT * FROM "%s" WHERE "%s" = :id} \
        $table $idColumn
```

```
    }
    # etc...
    method findById {id} {
        if {![info exist id2obj($id)]} {
            $dbHandle foreach -as dicts $sql(query,byID) row {
                set id2obj($id) [my MakeRowForId $row $id]
                break
            }
        }
        return $id2obj($id)
    }
    method foreach {varName script} {
        upvar 1 $varName v
        $dbHandle foreach -as dicts $sql(query,all) row {
            set id [dict get $row $idColumn]
            if {![info exists id2obj($id)]} {
                set id2obj($id) [my MakeRowForId $row $id]
            }
            set v $id2obj($id)
            uplevel 1 $script
        }
    }
    method MakeRowForId {rowDictionary identity} {
        tailcall my new [namespace which my] \
            $rowDictionary $identity
    }
    method MakeRowWithoutId {rowDictionary} {
        tailcall my new [namespace which my] $rowDictionary
    }
    method mappedDB {args} {
        if {![llength $args]} {return $db}
        tailcall $db {*}$args
    }
}
```

Database rows are represented by subclasses of the two row classes. One is for rows where we have a mapped identity, and the other is for rows where that was not possible (e.g., because the primary key consists of multiple columns). I show just one of these classes here; the other is a stripped-down version of it.

```
oo::class create ORM::NamedRow {
    variable contents tbl id
    constructor {table row identity} {
        array set contents $row
        set tbl $table
        set id $identity
    }
    destructor {
        $tbl RemoveRow $id
    }
    method ORM.writeback {column value} {
        tailcall $tbl SetRowColumn $id $column $value
    }
    method ORM.Access.Simple {c args} {
        if {[llength $args]} {
            lassign $args value
            set contents($c) [my ORM.writeback $c $value]
        }
        return $contents($c)
    }
    method ORM.Access.Linked {c targTbl targCol args} {
        if {[llength $args]} {
            lassign $args value
            # Error checking elided for clarity
            set cls [$tbl mappedDB table $targTbl]
            set otherId [set [info object namespace $value]::id]
            set contents($c) [my ORM.writeback $c $otherId]
            return [$cls findById $contents($c)]
        }
        $tbl mappedDB table $targTbl \
            findById $contents($c)
    }
    method ORM.Access.ID {c} {
        return $contents($c)
    }
}
```

Usage

To show how this mapping might be used, let us consider a simple order database. Each order has its ID, of course, and a description of the order, and it also has references to the customer who is paying for the order and where it is to be dispatched to. They are linked as in Figure 2.

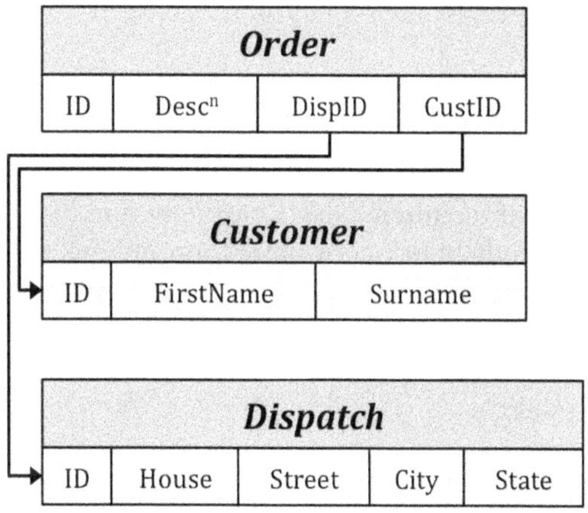

Figure 2: Order dispatch database schema

Specifically, this table definition is used for this example:

```
CREATE TABLE customers(
    id          INTEGER PRIMARY KEY,
    firstname   TEXT,
```

```
  surname          TEXT)
CREATE TABLE dispatch(
  id               INTEGER PRIMARY KEY,
  house            INTEGER,
  street           TEXT,
  city             TEXT,
  state            TEXT)
CREATE TABLE "order"(
  id               INTEGER PRIMARY KEY,
  customer         INTEGER NOT NULL,
  dispatch         INTEGER NOT NULL,
  description      TEXT,
  CONSTRAINT fk_customer
    FOREIGN KEY (customer)
    REFERENCES customers(id)
    ON DELETE CASCADE,
  CONSTRAINT fk_dispatch
    FOREIGN KEY (dispatch)
    REFERENCES dispatch(id)
    ON DELETE CASCADE)
```

To print out a listing of the contents of this (admittedly very simple) database with ORM, you would just need to write code like this:

```
set conn [tdbc::sqlite3::connection new "mydb.sqlite3"]
ORM::Database create db $conn
db table order foreach ordr {
  puts "Order #[$ordr id]"
  puts "Customer: [[$ordr customer] firstname]\
      [[$ordr customer] surname]"
  puts "Address: [[$ordr dispatch] house]\
      [[$ordr dispatch] street]"
  puts "Address: [[$ordr dispatch] city],\
      [[$ordr dispatch] state]"
  puts "Description:\n\t[$ordr description]"
  puts ""
}
```

The fact that the order class's customer and dispatch methods both return objects on queries is deduced automatically from inspection of the foreign key constraints, together with the way that they map to primary key columns in the other tables.

Annotations

The third of these short "adventures" is into adding metadata to TclOO classes through annotations. The aim of this is to allow all declarations in a class, together with the overall class itself, to have extra information added to them that was not originally envisaged as part of the TclOO specification. The key goal of this is to allow the definition of new annotations simply by creating an appropriate subclass (the instances of the class being created automatically during the annotation process).

The inspiration for this is the annotation mechanisms present in Java[10], C#[11] and Python[12], where they serve many purposes. However, I have not focussed on adding annotations to overall individual objects so far because of the wider variety of ways in which objects are created in practice, relative to classes.

Code and Discussion

The core of the annotation system is an array in the package's namespace that maps from class names to the collection of annotations on things related to that class. That collection is implemented as a dictionary (keyed by the name of the annotation) to a list of annotation objects with that name on that class.

A lookup command is provided to search the collection of annotations; this command is integrated into Tcl's info command:

```
proc oo::InfoClass::annotations {
    class {annotation ""} args} {
  upvar #0 ::oo::Annotations::classInfo info
  set class [uplevel 1 [list namespace which $class]]
  if {$annotation eq ""} {
    if {![info exists info($class)]} return
    return [dict keys $info($class)]
  } elseif {
    ![info exists info($class)]
    || ![dict exists $info($class) $annotation]
  } then {
    return -code error \
        "unknown annotation \"$annotation\""
  }
  set result {}
  foreach h [dict get $info($class) $annotation] {
    try {
      $obj describe result {*}$args
    } on error msg {
      return -code error $msg
    }
  }
  return $result
}
```

Insertion of an annotation into the array is done by the combination of a unknown-command handler that builds the annotation when necessary, and rewritten versions of the definition commands that add in the current accumulated annotation set to the array once it is determined what the annotations actually apply to.

The unknown handler is this:

```
proc DefineUnknown {cmd args} {
  if {[string match @* $cmd]} {
    try {
      variable subject [lindex [info level -1] 1]
      variable currentAnnotators
      lappend currentAnnotators \
          [Annotation.[string range $cmd 1 end] new \
          "class" {*}$args]
      return
    } on error msg {
      return -code error $msg
    }
  }
  # Use some knowledge of how TclOO really works...
  tailcall ::oo::UnknownDefinition $cmd {*}$args
}
namespace eval ::oo::define [list namespace unknown \
    [namespace which DefineUnknown]]
```

The definition commands are spliced like this:

```
namespace eval RealDefines {}
apply [list {} {
  foreach cmd [info commands ::oo::define::*] {
    set tail [namespace tail $cmd]
    set target ::oo::Annotations::RealDefines::$tail
    rename $cmd $target
    proc $cmd args "
      ::oo::Annotations::ClassDefinition $tail {*}\$args
      tailcall [list $target] {*}\$args
    "
  }
} [namespace current]]
```

This is supported by the ClassDefinition procedure:

```
proc ClassDefinition {operation args} {
  variable currentAnnotators
  if {![info exists currentAnnotators]} return
  variable subject
  variable classInfo
  try {
    foreach a $currentAnnotators {
      set name [$a name]
      $a register $operation {*}$args
      if {
        ![info exists classInfo($subject)]
        || ![dict exists $classInfo($subject) $name]
      } then {
        dict set classInfo($subject) $name {}
      }
      dict lappend classInfo($subject) $name $a
      set currentAnnotators \
          [lrange $currentAnnotators 1 end]
    }
  } on error msg {
    foreach a $currentAnnotators {$a destroy}
    return -level 2 $msg
  } finally {
    unset currentAnnotators
  }
}
```

The final part of the annotation package is the base annotation classes themselves.

```
::oo::class create annotation {
  unexport create
  variable annotation Type Operation
  constructor {type args} {
    set Type $type
    my MayApplyToType $type
    my RememberAnnotationArguments $args
  }
  method MayApplyToType type {
    throw ANNOTATION \
        "may not apply this annotation to that type"
  }
  method MayApplyToOperation operation {
    throw ANNOTATION \
        "may not apply that annotation to this operation"
  }
  method RememberAnnotationArguments values {
    set annotation $values
  }
  method QualifyAnnotation args {
    # Do nothing by default
  }
  method name {} {
    set name [namespace tail [info object class [self]]]
    return [regsub {^Annotation.} $name @]
  }
  method register {operation args} {
    set Operation $operation
    my MayApplyToOperation $operation
    my QualifyAnnotation {*}$args
  }
  method describe {varName} {
    upvar 1 $varName v
    lappend v $annotation
  }
}
::oo::class create classannotation {
  superclass annotation
  method MayApplyToType type {
    if {$type ne "class"} {next $type}
```

```
  }
}
```

A major class of annotations are those that are used to provide simple descriptions of parts of a class definition. To support this basic use, a class of annotations that are such descriptions is also given:

```
oo::class create Annotation.Describe {
  superclass oo::Annotations::classannotation
  variable annotation Operation method
  method MayApplyToOperation operation {
    if {$operation ni "method forward constructor"} {
      next $operation
    }
  }
  method QualifyAnnotation {name args} {
    if {$Operation eq "constructor"} {
      set method "<<constructor>>"
    } else {
      set method $name
    }
  }
  method describe {varName {name ""}} {
    upvar 1 $varName result
    if {[llength [info level 0]] == 3} {
      dict set result $method [join $annotation]
    } elseif {$method eq $name} {
      set result [join $annotation]
      return -code break
    }
  }
}
```

Usage

To use the annotations now, all you would need to do is put them on the definition, like this:

```
oo::class create foo {
  @Describe This method simply prints its arguments
  method bar args {puts $args}
}
```

After that, the annotation would be read by just using the introspection mechanism:

```
puts annotations:\t[info class annotation foo]
puts describe:\t[info class annotation foo @Describe bar]
```

Which would print out this:

```
annotations:   @Describe
describe:      This method simply prints its arguments
```

The second could have been written without the final "bar" argument, in which case it would have returned a dictionary with one entry for each method it applied to.

Just subclassing the Describe annotation class creates specialist types of description. For example, to create one just for describing side effects you might do this:

```
oo::class create Annotation.SideEffects {
  superclass Annotation.Describe
}
```

We can do the same for results, except that this time we do not want them to apply to constructors (where the result is ignored if it isn't an error):

```
oo::class create Annotation.Result {
  superclass Annotation.Describe
  method MayApplyToOperation operation {
    if {$operation eq "constructor"} {
      throw ANNOTATE "not on a constructor"
    }
    next $operation
  }
}
```

Annotations can also be extended so they can refer to individual arguments to a method:

```
oo::class create Annotation.Argument {
  superclass Annotation.Describe
  variable annotation method argument
  constructor {type argName args} {
    set argument $argName
    next $type {*}$args
  }
  method describe {varName {name ""} {argname ""}} {
    upvar 1 $varName result
    if {[llength [info level 0]] == 3} {
      lappend result $method
    } elseif {$method eq $name} {
      if {[llength [info level 0]] == 4} {
        lappend result $argument
      } elseif {$argument eq $argname} {
        set result [join $annotation]
        return -code break
      }
    }
  }
}
```

These are applied in a completely analogous way:

```
oo::class create foo2 {
  @Describe          This has many annotations attached
```

```
  @Argument x        Ignored.
  @Argument args     To allow any number of arguments
  @Result            None.
  @SideEffects       Prints to stdout.
  method bar {x args} { puts foo }
}
```

If we introspect simply, we get a list of all the annotations that are present:

```
puts [info class annotation foo2]
```

This will print:

```
@Describe @Argument @Result @SideEffects
```

Future Work

I would like to be able to work further on the REST package so that it is better able to handle supporting the wide range of RESTful APIs found out there. In particular, the current http package creaks at the seams rather when pressed into use for this as it makes a number of assumptions that do not hold when dealing with APIs for computer consumption rather than for human consumption.

For the ORM package, I think it needs some more work so that it becomes even more natural to use before it can be considered suitable for use. In particular, there are problems with whether a row should be deleted when its corresponding object is destroyed, and also with just how eagerly objects should be created to represent database rows. After all, the aim is to make working with an *existing* database as natural as working with Tcl.

The annotations work is interesting and may lead to new things being added to TclOO in the future, though it is (as of the time of writing) significantly incomplete in that it is very awkward to create class-level annotations. This is a consequence of the fact that interceptors for the annotations are all hooked off the TclOO definition subsystem. It's also arguably the case that the axes on which annotations are currently looked up are in the wrong order (currently the order is class, annotation name, method name, etc). Some work is clearly needed in this area.

The interesting thing that can be learned from other languages though is that using annotations can lead to an interesting way for a system of objects to interact with a framework such as a web front end or GUI. This is an area where I feel I have only scratched the surface.

References

[1] Fellows, D. et al, *TIP #257: Object Orientation for Tcl*, in Tcl Improvement Proposal series, Tcl Core Team, 2005–2008.

[2] Fielding, R., Taylor, R., *Architectural styles and the design of network-based software architectures*, University of California, Irvine, CA, 2000.

[3] Fielding, R. et al, *RFC 2616: Hypertext Transfer Protocol – HTTP/1.1*, in IETF Requests for Comments series, The Internet Society, 1999.

[4] Lester, G. et al, *Web Services for Tcl* package, hosted on Google Code at `http://code.google.com/p/tclws/`, 2006–2010.

[5] Kenny, K. et al, *TIP #308: Tcl Database Connectivity (TDBC)*, in Tcl Improvement Proposal series, Tcl Core Team, 2007–2008.

[6] Date, C., *A guide to the SQL standard*, Addison-Wesley, Boston, MA, 1986.

[7] Bauer, C., King, G., *Java Persistence with Hibernate*, Manning, Greenwich, CT, 2006.

[8] Roos, R., *Java Data Objects*, in Computing Reviews, vol. 45, no. 4, pp. 202, 2004

[9] Bächle, M., Kirchberg, P., *Ruby on Rails*, in IEEE Software, vol. 24, pp. 105–108, IEEE Computer Society, Los Alamitos, CA, 2007.

[10] Buckley, A. et al, *JSR 175: A Metadata Facility for the Java™ Programming Language*, in Java Specification Requests, 2002–2004.

[11] Gunnerson, E., *A Programmer's Introduction to C#, Second Edition*, Springer, New York, NY, 2001.

[12] Smith, K. et al, *PEP 318: Decorators for Functions and Methods*, in Python Enhancement Proposals series, Python Software Foundation, 2003–2004.

A bytecode assembler for Tcl

Ozgur Dogan Ugurlu[*]
University of San Francisco, San Francisco, CA
`dogeen@gmail.com`
Kevin B. Kenny
GE Global Research Center, Niskayuna, NY
`kenny@ge.com`

Abstract. Tcl, like most dynamic languages, operates by compiling its programs to an intermediate language ("bytecode") that is executed by an interpreter. This paper presents an assembler for the Tcl bytecode language. Prior to the development of the assembler, a Tcl program could generate bytecode only from Tcl scripts (or from C code using unpublished interfaces in the Tcl core). With the advent of the assembler, a Tcl script can generate specified bytecode directly. This ability should enable readier experimentation with compile-time optimizations, with targeting other languages onto the Tcl bytecode engine, and with trading off Tcl's dynamic nature for speed of execution. Some of the challenges faced in developing the assembler are presented, and some preliminary observations about the performance that can be gained from assembly code are made.

1 Introduction

Tcl, like most dynamic computer languages, interprets its programs in two phases. In the first phase, the code is compiled to an intermediate language ("bytecode"), and in the second, a virtual machine interprets the bytecode produce the program's results. The translation of Tcl commands to bytecode happens late in the proceeding – usually at the first time that a procedure is called, or even later – and the bytecode compiler is extremely conservative. For instance, it is careful to preserve source code for recompilation in the event that a core command like `[set]` or `[for]` is redefined while the code is executing. Because of this conservatism, the bytecode is often not as efficient as it might be. Moreover, since evaluating Tcl scripts is at present the only means of generating bytecode, it is difficult for people to experiment with different compilation strategies or with targeting other languages into Tcl's bytecode interpreter.

This paper presents an assembler that will aceept an abstract representation of bytecodes in a Tcl-like syntax and prepare them for evaluation in Tcl. This assembler is the first time that bytecode has been exposed at a user level (even in C!) and is expected to open the door to experimentation with the engine.

Section 2 presents a brief overview of Tcl's bytecode language. Section 3 discusses the internal programming interfaces that support the compilation of scripts and expressions, and how they are adapted to processing assembly language. Section 4 presents the assembly language notation in brief. Section 5 discusses some of the problems that the assembler must solve in order to generate code that will execute safely in the execution engine. Section 6 goes into more detail about potential uses of a bytecode assembler, including some estimation of the performance difference between handwritten assembly code and Tcl. Section 7 discusses the work that remains to be done, and Section 8 presents some conclusions.

* Research sponsored by the Google Summer of Code, 2010

2 How Tcl bytecode works.

The Tcl bytecode interpreter is an abstract stack machine, akin to Forth or PostScript. All of its instructions work by moving operands to and from an operand stack. The commonest instructions move constants and variables to and from the stack, or remove operands from the stack and replace them with results. For example, the Tcl code:

```
set x [expr {$x * 2}]
```

might compile to bytecode like:

```
load x; # move $x to top of stack
push 2; # push "2" on top of stack
mult;   # multiply top two stack
        # elements. Replace with
        # product.
store x;# put top of stack in $x
pop;    # discard top of stack
```

As the just-in-time compiler is processing a script to produce bytecodes, it tracks what distinct constants are present in the script, and places them in an array of Tcl_Obj pointers called the "literal pool." (There is one instance of the literal pool per bytecode compilation; in practice, this translates very nearly to one instance per procedure.) The `push` instruction, in the actual bytecode, contains the index in the current compilation's literal pool of the constant to be stored on the stack.

In a similar way, the compiler maintains a table of local variables known in a procedure. A variable whose name is known at compile time can be addressed by index into the local variable table: the `load` instruction in the bytecode above gives the variable's index in the local variable table. In addition to these tables, there are several other tables that can be addressed, that hold auxiliary data for complex instructions, "exception ranges" (which describe the locations to which break, continue, and errors will divert control flow in a given block of code), and commands. Commands are present in order to identify places where code must be recompiled if the definition of a command changes on the fly, (for instance, if user code redefines or overloads a core Tcl command).

Most of the bytecode instructions come in multiple varieties. First, there are usually two sizes of operand: 1-byte (useful for short indices into the literal pool and the constant table) and 4-byte (for when the tables grow large enough that one byte will not suffice). In combination with these, instructions that operate on variables generally come in scalar (for when an operand is completely known at compile time – and known to be local to the procedure), array (for where an array name is known, but the array key is not), stack (for when a scalar's name cannot be determined at compile time, for instance for Tcl code like `[set $x]`), and array-stack (the most complicated case, used to access dynamically named or non-local arrays) variants. A few instructions also allow for immediate data operands as opposed to having all their data on the stack.

Control transfers take the form of jumps and conditional jumps `jumpTrue` and `jumpFalse`. The latter consume an operand from the stack and decide whether or not to jump based on whether or not its is equal to zero. There is also an `invoke` instruction that calls a Tcl command, `break`, `continue` and `done` instructions that escape an inner context to an outer one (using the exception range table to determine where to go), and a set of operations for returning and throwing errors.

Most if not all of the math operations and built-in functions in expressions have bytecode instructions that support them; all of these instructions work by consuming some number of operands from the stack and producing a single result.

In addition, there are highly complex operations that manage things like `[foreach]` loops and `[dict update]` blocks. These instructions frequently reference elaborate data structures stored in the "auxiliary data" arrays.

All told, there are about 150 different instructions in the bytecode engine. More get added with every Tcl release.

For a more comprehensive explanation of Tcl bytecode execution, see [LEWI96].

3 How compilation works.

Tcl scripts are compiled as late as possible: generally, for instance, a procedure body is compiled when the procedure is first invoked. A script is compiled by breaking it apart into commands (and comments, which are ignored), breaking the commands into words, and breaking the words into tokens (which may be constant strings, or variable, command or backslash substitutions). The parsing interfaces that the compiler uses are also exported at the C level from the Tcl library.

Code generation is orchestrated in a data structure called a `CompileEnv`. This structure manages a group of dynamically resizable arrays that hold the bytecodes, the literal pool, the local variable table, the exception and command ranges, and so on.

When a script is being compiled, if the compiler encounters a built-in command that has a "compilation procedure" associated with it, it invokes the compilation procedure, passing it the arguments to the command (in a `Tcl_Parse` structure) and the compilation environment. Commands such as `[if]` and `[for]` will then invoke the parser recursively to parse embedded expressions and scripts.

Because of Tcl's dynamic nature, a parse error in an individual command does not prevent the entire script from being compiled. Instead, code is inserted to invoke the uncompiled form of any command whose compilation procedure reports an error. If something changes before the direct invocation is called (for instance, the command is redefined), the direct evaluation will still succeed.

The fact that there is a fallback to direct evaluation means that not all commands' compilation procedures can handle all cases. In complicated situations, a compilation procedure can "throw up its hands," and defer the problem to run time. This technique is necessary, for instance, to handle unbraced expressions, where the correct parse cannot be determined until the results of command and variable substitution are known.

The assembler fits into this structure by defining an `[assemble]` command in the `tcl::unsupported` namespace. This command's compilation procedure emits inline code into the bytecode of the script that contains the `[assemble]` call. In the event that the assembly code cannot be parsed, the run-time command creates a fresh `CompileEnv` and tries again at run time. Only this second attempt will report an ultimate failure.

4 The assembly language

The assembler uses the same parser as Tcl itself, so the assembly language has the same fundamental syntax as Tcl. Because the assembly language is simpler, several things that can appear in a parsed Tcl script (namely, variable and command substitutions, and {*} expansion) simply are reported as errors. Comments, separation of commands with semicolons and newlines, joining of lines with terminal backslashes, and quoting all follow exactly the same rules as Tcl, so the syntax of assembly code should be familiar to a Tcl programmer.

Since the compilation environment is shared between the assembly code and the containing script, local variables and the current namespace are the same for both. The sharing of the compilation environment also allows for mixing of languages, as we shall see below.

Each 'command' in the assembly code represents a single bytecoded instruction. As a convenience to the programmer, one source instruction may map into a choice of bytecodes, so the assembly programmer need not worry about the correct choice of operand sizes and addressing modes.

A few "operations" are provided that do not correspond to bytecode instructions. The most significant of these are `label`, which defines a symbolic name for the current instruction pointer, so that jump instructions can refer to it, and two language-mixing primitives, `eval` and `expr`.

When `eval` appears in the source text, its operand (which must be a constant string) is interpreted as a Tcl script, by calling the Tcl script compiler recursively in the same compilation environment. Of course, the script can share the same variables and appears in the same namespace as the assembly code. (The result at runtime is that nothing is consumed from the stack and the script's result is pushed to the stack.) Similarly, `expr` results in compiling a Tcl expression (again, a constant string) and pushing its result to the stack.

This language mixing means that code can be written in the language most appropriate to the problem. Where a given source notation is particularly convenient (for example, infix expressions), the programmer can simply switch languages. The power of all three notations (arithmetic expressions, Tcl scripts, and bytecode assembly) is captured in a single package. (To be fair, this idea was anticipated in the compiler for the L programming language [BONI06].)

Literals and variables are added to the local tables as they are encountered, and a symbol table is maintained of jump labels. The assembler runs in a single pass; jumps to undefined labels are emitted as 4-byte jumps (because the jump displacement is not known in advance) and the address of the jump target is filled in when the label is encountered.

5 Challenges faced with the assembler

Fitting the assembler into the Tcl compilation system, which was not designed for user extension, involved some interesting challenges. Among these were stack management and the possibility of instructions for which correct code cannot be generated.

5.1 Stack management

Tcl's execution system preallocates space for the operand stack, so that individual push and pop operations do not need to check for stack overflow. The way it does this is that each bytecode sequence is expected to assert the maximum number of operands that it can put on the stack. In assembly code, which shifts operands onto and off the stack freely interspersed with jumps, this depth can be difficult to determine.

Moreover, assembly code that unbalances the stack could crash the interpreter quite easily. For these reasons, we decided early on that the assembler will require a comprehensive analyzer for maximum stack consumption and for stack safety. It works according to the following outline:

1. It partitions the program into a series of "basic blocks": segments of code that are executed sequentially without jumps. Any appearance of a jump in a program ends the basic block in which it appears; any appearance of a label begins a new basic block, since the label is at least a potential jump target.

2. As code is generated, the checker updates the stack requirements of the basic blocks. It tracks three numbers: the high water mark (the maximum number of

stack elements that the block may have pushed), the low water mark (the minimum stack depth – which may be negative if a block of code begins by consuming operands), and the net effect (the difference between the stack depth on entry to and exit from the block).

3. After all code is generated, the checker begins at the entry to the assembly program, and visits basic blocks in a depth-first traversal of the control flow graph. Each basic block has zero, one or two successors: zero if it is a return (or, in some cases, a break, continue or error); one if it ends with an unconditional jump or execution falls off the end without jumping, and two if it ends with a conditional jump (the succeeding block, and the jump target). As it walks the graph, it uses the net effects to compute the stack depth on entry to every block other than the first.

4. If a block in the traversal is already visited, the stack depths are checked for consistency. If a block can be arrived at by two different paths through the code that have different net effect on the stack, an error is reported. If a block is not visited, its stack depth on entry is recorded and its successors are visited recursively. The low water mark is also examined, to guard against rogue assembly code underflowing the stack. The high-water mark for stack consumption is also tracked.

5. Once all blocks have been visited, low and high-water stack commitments are known. The stack depth at the end of the exit block is the net effect on the stack of the assembly code. It is enforced that assembly code, like any other Tcl command, leaves a single result on the stack.

Since stack effects are monitored closely, and since the assembler generates no unchecked memory addresses (a program, for instance, cannot access outside the bounds of the literal pool or local variable table), it may turn out that the assembler always generates “safe” code in the sense that it will not cause pointer smashes in the Tcl interpreter. Nevertheless, until we have more user experience with it, the plan is to have it remain in the `tcl::unsupported` namespace. (Translation: If it breaks, you own both pieces.)

5.2 Impossible instructions

There are several situations in which a sequence of assembly code will contain an instruction for which it is impossible to emit correct code. The first of these occurs if the [assemble] command is invoked at runtime, and an operation tries to use a local variable table slot for a previously unseen variable. The LVT is not resizable, and therefore the variable cannot be converted to a slot number. (Another case that arises is that the 'increment' instructions, puzzlingly, require the variable to be in one of the first 256 slots of the LVT because they lack 4-byte variants.) Finally, it is possible that a programmer simply inserts a reference to a namespace-qualified variable that cannot appear in the LVT.

In all of these cases, the correct thing to do is to put the variable name on the stack and then use a stack-based operation to manipulate it. The problem is that for array operations, the correct order of operations is that first the variable name and then the key should be pushed; for stores, appends and increments, there is an additional operand that must also follow the variable name. Since it isn't possible to “go back in time" and insert the push of the variable name when it was actually needed, the next best thing is to generate code to reorder the stack to put the operands in the correct sequence even when the variable name arrives late. This will result in silently generating additional instructions, but will at least yield correct code.

We have not yet attempted to deal with impossible instructions, and instead report errors when they are encountered. (It is generally fairly simple to code around the problems by inserting the stack operations explicitly.) The automated recovery from impossible instructions may be implemented by the time you read this.

6 What's the assembler good for?

An assembler is of primary use as the backend of a compiler, either a compiler for a new language, or object-code transformations on Tcl itself (for optimization, code instrumentation for profiling and callgraph analysis, and so on. Having the assembler available within the Tcl system allows bytecode to be generated from a very-high-level language such as Tcl, rather than needing to resort to C code that is intimate with Tcl's execution system.

6.1 Performance and benchmarks

The chief reason that people have been interested in an assembler is performance. The dynamic nature of the Tcl language has made it difficult to generate really good code from it. (Too much can change between compilation and execution). The problem of radical language change on the fly substantially limited early attempts such as [ROUS95] to compile Tcl to machine code, even after heroic attempts ([ROUS97]) to use type inference to constrain the problem. Assembly code can bypass all the expensive runtime checks that are needed to ensure that compiled code remains valid even in the face of such radical changes.

Other languages, as well, can target the Tcl execution engine, and in fact, several other languages have been designed ([SAH94], [BONI06]) that constrain the dynamic nature of Tcl to achieve better performance while still targeting the same execution engine.

The folklore in the Tcl community has predicted that optimization at the bytecode level is likely to give disappointing results. The bytecodes, the pundits have said, are close enough to being precise counterparts to Tcl commands that little room for modification of the code sequences is actually available. Of course, without an assembler, there was no way to test this hypothesis. Given the assembler, we can attempt a benchmark to test how much we can improve a representative Tcl script by hand optimization.

Let's examine a Tcl script to compute Stanisław Ulam's "3n+1 function" [WEIS??]. The script is fairly simple, performing a handful of mathematical operations (albeit in a quite chaotic manner).

```
proc ulam1 {n} {
    set max $n
    while {$n != 1} {
        if {$n > $max} {
          set max $n
        }
        if {$n % 2} {
          set n [expr {3 * $n + 1}]
        } else {
          set n [expr {$n / 2}]
        }
    }
    return $max
}
```

Figure 1. on the following page gives an overview of the generated bytecode. Contrary to the expert opinion (which one of the authors [Kenny] of this paper used to share), there appear to be several opportunities to optimize it. (Some other possibilities can be found in [KENN02].)

First, we can observe that there are various bits of completely useless code. For instance, in block L111 at the bottom of the chart, there is a sequence – in straight-line code – that simply pushes a zero onto the operand stack and pops it off again. This sequence can be removed entirely without ill effect. (There are perhaps similar cases elsewhere in the flow.)

It is tempting to consider further optimizations such as tail merging and common subexpression elimination. Let's start by examining the code flowing into block `L103` just below the centre of the diagram. Both the earlier blocks end with `store n`. It would be tempting to place a single `store n` at the head of `L103` instead.

Unfortunately, without further information about the program, it's also incorrect! The problem is that an variable trace can determine (through the error stack, if by no other means) what command caused it to fire. If there is a trace present on the variable n, then at least one execution path will present the wrong calling command to the trace.

That said, few Tcl programs ever attempt to establish traces on procedure-local variables. While it is challenging to prove that local variable traces are possible (commands could get redefined, or other traces could set them), a programmer – and certainly an assembly programmer – can make such assumptions with impunity. So let's start moving code around, beginning with that offending `store n` instruction.

When the instruction is moved as suggested, there is then a straight-line sequence:

```
store n
pop
load n
```

This is another sequence with an obvious optimization: remove the second two instructions (and add the load to the bottom of block `L0`). Popping the value that we just stored, only to load it back again, is another thing that simply wastes time.

If we continue propagating similar changes through the flowchart, we eventually realize that – if we assume there are no traces on local variables – we can simply keep their values on the stack, and use deep stack accessors to bring them to the top at need. This technique is almost precisely parallel to doing "frame pointer omission" in compilers targeting x86 hardware ([OSTE07]) in that it gains performance by keeping local references stack-relative, and that it makes debugging (either with conventional debuggers, or with Tcl's traces) much more challenging.

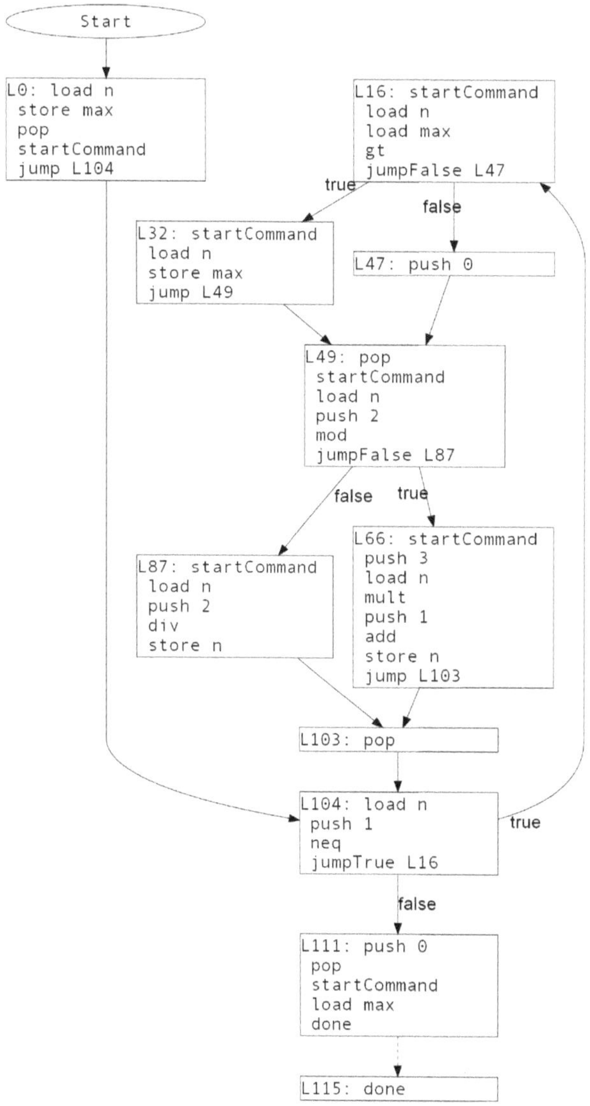

Figure 1. Flowchart of 'ulam1'

Nevertheless, let us proceed, with more enthusiasm than caution to revise the code so that `n` is at top of stack on entry to each block, and `max` is the next on the stack. Loading `n` is then simply `dup`, while loading `max` is `over 1`.

Figure 2. shows the transformed code. The only really tricky bit is the translation of `set max $n`. Readers are invited to verify for themselves that the codeburst in block `L24` has the desired effect.

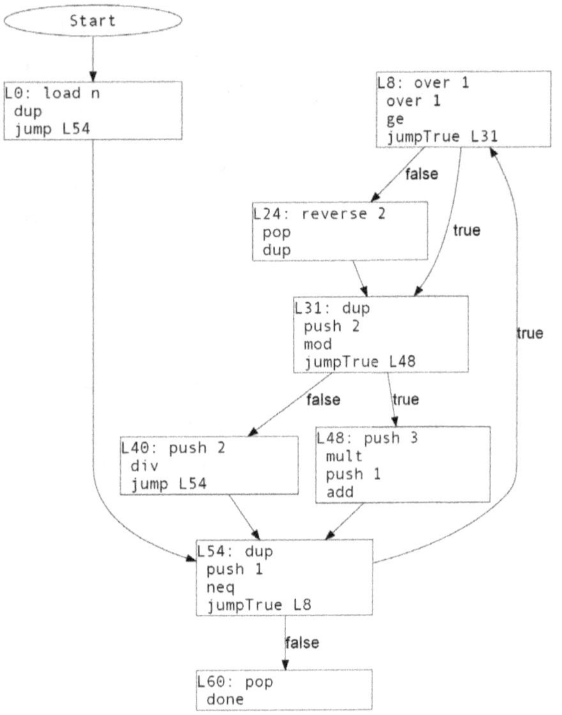

Figure 2. Hand-optimized version of 'ulam1'

What have these transformation achieved? They've roughly halved the size of the code (from 116 bytes down to 61). To see whether they make a difference in speed, we run the Tcl version and the assembly version on an unloaded 2.6 GHz Core 2 machine, and turn the two procedures loose on the first 30000 integers. For the given test case, in the best of ten runs, we find that the Tcl version takes 1.46 seconds, while the assembly version takes 1.00 seconds. While a 32% improvement in run time is not spectacular, it is surely something that could be worth pursuing for code "hot spots" that are the speed-determining steps of an application.

6.2 Targeting other languages

As mentioned earlier, making bytecode assembly available at the Tcl level makes it much easier to integrate other bytecode-targeting languages such as L or Rush. It would be an interesting experiment to see whether a language not originally designed to interoperate with Tcl could be retargeted to the Tcl virtual machine using a bytecode translation layer. Identifying missing features in the Tcl virtual machine might not only make it able to target more languages, but also give ideas how to improve its performance, stability or footprint for Tcl itself.

6.3 Bytecode rewriting

In addition to optimization, bytecodes could be rewritten to add functionality such as tracing. By replacing operators like `add` and `mult`, it might even be possible to do things like expand the semantics of mathematical operators, perhaps producing an [expr] that operates on complex numbers or other extensions beyond the integers and floating-point numbers. Tcl has a rich heritage of allowing the programmer to redefine the language to suit the needs of the moment. Rewriting object code is simply another place to insert hooks to do so.

7 Work yet to be done

The assembler described in this paper is still very much at the "proof of concept" stage. It still only emits about two-thirds of the bytecodes that the Tcl engine has (although some of remaining ones are of questionable utility, and a few exist only to support legacy bytecodes loaded with `tbcload`.) Finishing the set looks fairly straightforward.

To solve the conundrum that the "impossible operations" pose, some more powerful instructions for stack rearrangement may be needed. Adding them to the Tcl engine seems sensible, and there appears to be consensus among the maintainers that they would be useful for other purposes.

Finally, before the object-to-object transformations mentioned in the last section can be done in earnest, the Tcl disassembler has to be modified to produce code that can be assembled again. (Until now, it's been intended for display, not for machine processing, and it's accumulated various hard-to-parse accoutrements.)

8 Conclusions

The Tcl bytecode assembler has been a very frequently-requested feature, despite the fact that the Tcl pundits have frequently pooh-poohed it as being of less benefit than programmers think. Now that it is a reality, it seems to be at least potentially worthwhile (even without hacking in the bytecode engine, 30-40% speedups can be seen by rewriting in assembler code), and it will at least now be possible for assessments of its capability to be founded in science, rather than speculation.

The experimental source code is available on a feature branch in the Tcl repository, if other investigators want to examine it. To retrieve it, the command:

```
cvs -d:pserver:anonymous@tcl.cvs.sf.net:/cvsroot/tcl checkout \
        -r dogeen-assembler-branch tcl
```

will retrieve the branched source tree (a modified Tcl 8.6 HEAD). User documentation, when prepared, will also be placed in that source tree.

References

[BONI06] Bonilla, Oscar; Tim Daly, Jr. and Larry McVoy. "The L programming language: or, Tcl for C programmers." *Proc. 13th Ann. Tcl/Tk Conf.*. Naperville, IL: Tcl Association, October 2006. <http://www.bitmover.com/lm/papers/l.pdf>

[KENN02] Kenny, Kevin B.; Miguel Sofer and Jeffrey Hobbs. "Tcl bytecode optimization: some experiences." *Proc. 9th Ann. Tcl/Tk Conf.*. Vancouver, British Columbia, Canada: ActiveState, September 2002. <http://www.tcl.tk/community/tcl2002/archive/Tcl2002papers/kenny-bytecode/paperKBK.pdf>

[LEWI96] Lewis, Brian T. "An on-the-fly bytecode compiler for Tcl." *Proc. 4th Annual Tcl/Tk Conference*. Monterey, California: USENIX, July 1996. <http://www.usenix.org/publications/library/proceedings/tcl96/full_papers/lewis/>

[OSTE07] Osterman, Larry. "FPO." *Larry Osterman's Weblog*. Redmond, WA: Microsoft, March 2007. <http://blogs.msdn.com/b/larryosterman/archive/2007/03/12/fpo.aspx>

[ROUS95] Rouse, Forest R. and Wayne Christopher. "A Tcl to C compiler." *Proc. 3rd Ann. Tcl/Tk Conf.*. Toronto, Ontario, Canada: USENIX, July 1995. <http://www.usenix.org/publications/library/proceedings/tcl95/full_papers/rouse.ps>

[ROUS97] Rouse, Forest R. and Wayne Christopher. "A typing system for a multiple-backend Tcl compiler." *Proc. 5th Annual Tcl/Tk Workshop*. Boston, Mass.: USENIX, July 1997. <http://www.usenix.org/publications/library/proceedings/tcl97/full_papers/rouse/rouse.pdf>

[SAH94] Sah, Adam; Jon Blow; and Brian Dennis. "An introduction to the Rush language." *Proc. 2nd Tcl/Tk Workshop*. New Orleans, LA: Computerized Processes Unlimited, May 1994. <number-none.com/blow/papers/rush_tcl94.pdf>

[WEIS??] Weisstein, Eric. "Collatz problem." *MathWorld.* : A Wolfram Resource, .

<http://mathworld.wolfram.com/CollatzProblem.html>

Cookfs

New VFS driver for standalone binaries
Wojciech Kocjan, BitRock S.L.
http://sourceforge.net/projects/cookit/

Abstract

Cookfs is an open source VFS for Tcl written in C and Tcl. It is designed to achieve better compression ratio compared to Mk4 VFS and ZIP archives. It also offers configurable compression algorithm – currently zlib and bz2, with plans for lzma in the future.

It's also designed to be used in Tclkit-like applications. Cookit project shows how cookfs can be used for this purpose.

Introduction

Historical background

Tcl is the first (and probably the only) language that has a solution for providing Tcl runtime and Tcl/Tk based application as single executable file. This requires embedding additional files inside the executable in a way that the Tcl I/O mechanism can access them. Tcl 8.3 supported this functionality internally and version 8.4 started exposing Virtual FileSystem (VFS) API and allowed creating additional VFS drivers that provided means of accessing files – listing them, getting/setting information and opening for reading and/or writing.

This brilliant move allowed a way for multiple solutions such as TclPro's prowrap[1] binary, TclKit[2], freeWrap[3] and eTcl[4] to offer standalone Tcl interpreter binaries. These solutions also provided mechanisms for embedding Tcl/Tk based applications by putting all scripts and resource files into a single binary.

These technologies base on either ZIP archive format (prowrap, freeWrap and eTcl) or Metakit archive (TclKit). ZIP was chosen as it is a standard for storing one or more files in a single archive. Metakit is a complex, but efficient generic database engine that can be easily

---

[1] http://www.tcl.tk/software/tclpro/doc/TclProUsersGuide14.pdf

[2] http://www.equi4.com/tclkit/

[3] http://freewrap.sourceforge.net/

[4] http://www.evolane.com/software/etcl/index.html

adapted to store multiple files in a single archive. Metakit based solution is called Mk4tcl and aside from TclKit it was also adopted by commercial offerings such as Tcl Dev Kit[5] from ActiveState.

Why cookfs?

Cookfs is a similar solution – its main goal is being able to store multiple files in a single archive, focusing on standalone binaries and packaging of large Tcl applications as a single file. The main difference between approaches is that cookfs is focused on creating an efficient solution to specific problems – packaging Tcl scripts and various types of payload.

Tcl applications can contain large number of small files – around 1-5 kB. Mk4vfs and ZIP based solutions compress each file individually. Both of these filesystems use zlib for compression. Cookfs uses the same algorithm by default, but also supports bzip2.

Cookfs compresses large files individually, but groups and packages small files together. This can greatly reduce size for files such as `pkgIndex.tcl` files that usually have very similar contents. Cookfs also groups such files by their name so all `pkgIndex.tcl` files are usually compressed in the same chunk.

Cookfs can also be used to package additional payload that is not related to Tcl – such as installers that might store very big files, but can also contain small files. Of course all other solutions also allow you to do this, but cookfs stores this kind of data more efficiently due to file grouping. One example might be packaging the Joomla[6] application on Linux along with all of its prerequisites – Apache, PHP and MySQL. Such payload consists of 9000 files, 4000 of which are smaller than 1 kB and another 3000 files which are smaller than 5kB. Compressing such files individually is inefficient and therefore cookfs provides much better results at compressing such data, which is shown later in the document.

A very important benefit compared to other solutions, especially mk4vfs is that cookfs offers better memory management. Cookfs does not consume more than specified amount of memory when reading files from an archive. It is also possible to copy files directly to archive and avoid storing them in memory. This makes reading from and writing to an archive memory efficient even for very large files – such as hundreds of megabytes.

Cookfs also offers ability to choose between lower memory consumption and faster read access – configuring page cache can speed up reading process at the cost of more memory depending on which is more important for a particular application.

---

[5] http://www.activestate.com/tcl-dev-kit

[6] http://www.joomla.org/

How and where to get it?

Both cookfs and cookit projects are hosted on SourceForge as cookit project and is available at http://sourceforge.net/projects/cookit/.

Cookit binaries for Microsoft Windows, Linux and Mac OS X can be downloaded from SourceForge files section. They are located in cookit folder: http://sourceforge.net/projects/cookit/files/cookit/. Cookfs source code can be found in cookfs folder: http://sourceforge.net/projects/cookit/files/cookfs/. Latest source code can also be found in cookit Subversion repository under `cookit` and `cookfs` folders respectively.

Cookfs can either be used from a standard Tcl distribution – such as ActiveTcl – or using cookit standalone binaries. In the latter case, cookfs is already loaded in the main interpreter and nothing needs to be done.

For any other case, cookfs needs to be built from source code and installed. The build procedure follows well known standards:

- we need to run configure script first, providing `--prefix` and `--with-tcl` flags that provide path to installation and where Tcl libraries can be located; currently required Tcl version is 8.6 and configure script will mention this if older version is provided; in addition to this, tclvfs package is also required – typically it is installed with all ActiveTcl distributions
- next step is to run `make` to compile the package
- finally `make install` command will install cookfs to specified Tcl distribution

Using cookfs

Now that cookfs is available, using it is very similar to other virtual filesystems. In order to load it all that is needed is to run:

```
package require vfs::cookfs
```

Mounting an archive is as easy as doing `vfs::cookfs::Mount`, specifying path to archive and Tcl's local mount point. Cookfs archives often end with `.cfs` suffix. Both locations can be the same. For example:

```
vfs::cookfs::Mount /tmp/archive.cfs /tmp/archive.cfs
```

Next we can perform operations on */tmp/archive.cfs* and all subdirectories and those will be performed on cookfs archive. The command returns `fsid` (filesystem identifier), which can be used by other cookfs commands.

In order to unmount it we need to call `vfs::unmount` providing local mount path. For example:

```
vfs::unmount /tmp/archive.cfs
```

All typical operations such as file copying work without any issues. For example we can open a file for writing, store something in it, close it and read it afterwards. Unmounting the archive and mounting it again using same or different Tcl process will also allow us to read the file. In generic, cookfs archives can be read from multiple processes or threads, but only one process or thread can write to a cookfs archive at a time.

Please note that due to nature of cookfs it is essential to unmount it before exiting – otherwise index information will not be stored and archive will not be readable.

Additional options can be passed while mounting an archive. These options have to be specified before archive name and local mount point. The syntax is as follows:

```
vfs::cookfs::Mount
    ?-readonly? ?-compression none|zlib|bzip2?
    ?-pagesize bytes? ?-pagecachesize count?
    ?-smallfilesize bytes? ?-smallfilebuffer bytes?
    archive local
```

- flag `-readonly` tels cookfs to mount an archive as read only and is needed if a file cannot be written to – such as in standalone binaries. For example:

  ```
  vfs::cookfs::Mount -readonly \
      /tmp/archive.cfs /tmp/archive.cfs
  ```

- type of compression to use can be specified using `-pagesize`. Currently three values are accepted – `none`, `zlib` and `bzip2`. First does not perform any compression, second uses zlib library and last uses bz2 library. The default is `zlib`, which is very fast and offers good compression ratio. It is also used by ZIP and Mk4 based virtual filesystems.

- option `-pagesize` specifies maximum size of a page. It defaults to 256kB and should not be changed by default. Details on pages are described in next sections. This only affects files that will be written to archive as files already stored in the archive will not be modified in any way.

- number of pages that will be cached can be specified using `-pagecachesize` option. It defaults to 8, which means maximum of 2MB memory usage. In order to speed up reading from archive it can be increased. For example:

  ```
  vfs::cookfs::Mount -pagecachesize 64 \
      /tmp/archive.cfs /tmp/archive.cfs
  ```

- options `-smallfilesize` and `-smallfilebuffer` specify maximum size for small files as well as buffer for queuing small files' writes to disk. This mechanism is described in more details in next sections.

Cookfs provides feature to store all changes in a filesystem in memory. Command `cookfs::writetomemory` enables writing changes to memory. It accepts `fsid` parameter, which is returned by `vfs::cookfs::Mount` command. For example:

```
cookfs::writetomemory $fsid
```

This option can also be enabled by specifying `-writetomemory` flag when mounting an archive – for example:

```
vfs::cookfs::Mount -writetomemory \
    /tmp/archive.cfs /tmp/archive.cfs
```

When this option is enabled – during or after mount – any changes to this archive are not saved to disk. They are discarded whenever archive is unmounted or process exits. This can be used for running legacy scripts that require writing data to its relative location or as temporary file storage.

It is also possible to use a separate file for saving changes to an archive. Command `cookfs::aside` can be used for this and accepts `fsid` followed by path to file to store changes. For example:

```
cookfs::aside $fsid ~/.myapplication/updates
```

Changes in aside file persist across mounts of a filesystem and therefore can be used to store updates to standalone binaries or archives stored on read-only media such as CD or DVD disk. Aside file does not have to be specified at mounting time – it is possible to specify aside file after archive is mounted and changes in aside file will be visible immediately.

In current cookfs version only creating aside archive for read-only archives works properly. In order to create an aside file for read-write archives it is recommended to do:

```
vfs::unmount /path/to/archive.cfs
set fsid [vfs::cookfs::Mount -readonly \
    /path/to/archive.cfs /path/to/archive.cfs]
cookfs::aside $fsid /path/to/aside-changes.cfs
```

Cookfs provides a function for copying files directly to archive – this is mainly meant for performance issues. Command `cookfs::writeFiles` takes `fsid` returned by `vfs::cookfs::Mount` followed by list consisting of 4 elements for each file – path relative to archive, source type, data and file size. It bypasses Tcl I/O mechanisms for writing to an archive and uses cookfs functionality directly for faster writes. Currently only two types of source – `file` and `data`. For the first one, data specifies name of the file to copy from, for second one data is binary data that should be used as file contents.

For example in order to copy `/etc/passwd` as `passwd` and add a text file `textfile` to archive, we can do:

```
cookfs::writeFiles $fsid \
```

```
    passwd file /etc/passwd {} \
    textfile data {Hello world}
```

This will create those two files within cookfs archive and this operation will bypass writing those files to VFS layer.

Cookfs is used for storing Tcl libraries and scripts for standalone applications inside cookit. It is a proof of concept of using cookfs filesystem to create standalone binaries, similar to Tclkit. Cookit is described in more details in next sections.

Cookfs archives can be built using TABS (Tcl Automated Build System)[7]. It is a tool for building Tcl standalone applications and/or archives based on set of targets and predefined jobs. The wrap job by default uses mk4vfs archives, but providing -driver cookfs flag allows building cookfs based archives. For example:

```
target sample.cookfs -body {
    runjob wrap \
        -output sample.cookfs \
        -driver cookfs \
        -copy [list sample.vfs .]
}
```

This defines a target called `sample.cookfs` that creates cookfs archive by copying contents of `sample.vfs` directory to it. We can also use it to build cookit-based binaries by doing:

```
target sample.exe -body {
    runjob wrap \
        -binary cookit.exe \
        -output sample.exe \
        -driver cookfs \
        -copy [list sample.vfs .]
}
```

Tutorial on using TABS can be found at http://www.endorser.org/blog/tcl/tools/21-tabs.

Cookfs also introduces an idea of packages. These are regular cookfs archives that store libraries or packages in its `lib/` subdirectory. Currently tools such as TABS can be used to automatically add such a package by doing:

```
target sample.exe -body {
    runjob wrap \
        -packages pkg/sqlite3-win32.cfspkg \
        -binary cookit.exe \
        -output sample.exe \
        -driver cookfs \
        -copy [list sample.vfs .]
```

[7] http://sourceforge.net/projects/tabs/

```
}
```

With current solutions such as Mk4 VFS adding one or more packages requires mounting and copying it at VFS level. With cookfs design it is possible to copy entire archive by appending compressed data without decompressing and recompressing files. The only action that needs to be done is to add appropriate items to updated archive's index. When cookfs will provide APIs to merge archives packages will allow much easier creation of applications and will speed up process of building large binaries by reusing already compressed building blocks.

Overview and design

Cookfs consists of three basic elements – pages, file index and VFS layer.

- pages mechanism stores actual file contents and provides storage for filesystem index. It is the lowest layer of the filesystem. It allows storing multiple pages (chunks of information) along with compressing them. It provides API for adding a page, getting a page and storing index information by other parts of cookfs.
- File index provides means for importing and exporting file structure. It also provides API for getting, setting file information and listing file structure. Indexes also keep reference of pages that are used for storing a specified file.
- VFS layer provides way to access cookfs archive contents as regular files in Tcl and from Tcl's C API. It leverages pages and file index for storing file contents and its metadata.

Cookfs and file grouping

Ability to perform smart file grouping is one of most important features of cookfs. Whenever a file is to be added to a cookfs archive, its size is checked if it is smaller than small file limit. Threshold for files that should be grouped can be specified by `-smallfilesize` flag when mounting a cookfs archive and defaults to 32kB, which will be used for all examples in this section. Also, page size will be assumed to be 256kB.

Files that are larger than specified limit use up 1 or more pages to store only specified file. For example when writing a 100kB file, its contents will be stored in a newly created page and this page will only store contents of this file. Uncompressed size of this page will also be 100kB, however compressed page size will vary on compression ratio. As soon as file is written, information on this file is added to cookfs index – specifying page index and size of data in this page.

For a 1200kB file, its contents will be split in a total of 5 pages – storing 4 pages of 256kB and last page will store remaining 176kB. This information is added to index – specifying 5 pages, their order and sizes of each page.

For each small file that gets added to an archive, it is first added to a queue of small files – it is not immediately stored in cookfs archive. Files waiting on small files queue are written to disk when cookfs archive is about to be closed or queue has reached its size limit. By default queue size limit is 4MB, which means that after total size of all files in the queue exceeds 4MB, they are written.

The algorithm for grouping small files in pages in pseudo code below:

```
# initialize empty list of files for next page be added
set filelist [list]

foreach file [lsort ... $pendingFileQueue] {
  set newFilelist [linsert $filelist end $file]
  if {[pagesize $newFilelist] > $pagesize} {
    # add current list of files to page
    addNewPage $filelist

    # update indexes
    updateIndex $filelist

    # initialize empty list of files for next page
    set filelist [list $file]
  }  else  {
    # new file list does not exceed size, keep it
    set filelist $newFilelist
  }
}

If {[llength $filelist] > 0} {
    # add current list of files to page
    addNewPage $filelist

    # update indexes
    updateIndex $filelist
}
```

First files are sorted by their file name and then added to archive – called `pendingFileQueue`. List of files (`filelist`) to be added to next page is also created as empty list. List of all pending files (`pendingFileQueue`) is then iterated on.

If size of file currently iterated over (`file`) combined with `filelist` is larger than page size, files in current `filelist` are added as new page – cookfs indexes are updated and `filelist` is set to only file currently iterated over.

After iterating over `pendingFileQueue` is complete, if there are any files in `filelist`, they are added as new page.

Whenever a page is created – during iteration or afterwards – cookfs index gets updated to reflect that particular file's contents is now stored in specific page at specific offset and having specific size.

Cookfs pages

Cookfs archive stores contents of all files in pages. Each page is a chunk of binary data and cookfs consists of any number of pages followed by cookfs metadata – information on size and checksum of each page and index binary data. Limit for a single cookfs page size is 2GB (2^{31}). Limits of page size are specified when mounting a cookfs archive and are enforced in VFS layer. When specifying page size to an existing archive, existing pages will not be affected by newly set up limits.

The concept of pages is very generic – it allows the following operations to be performed on it:

- `add` *`binaryData`* – add specified data as new page and return its index
- `get` *`pageIdx`* – get data of specified page
- `length` – returns number of pages
- `index` – get cookfs index
- `index` *`newData`* – set cookfs index
- `delete` – save all changes and delete specified page object

Commands above are actual Tcl methods that can be invoked on pages. While these are not all the operations available, these are the ones needed for cookfs VFS layer to work.

Page indexes are integer numbers starting from 0 up to `[length]-1`. Invoking `add` returns new page index, which can then be used to `get` pages. Pages can only be added – they cannot be deleted or changed. At first glance it may strike you as major drawback, but in fact real-life experience clearly indicates that the user far more often adds files to the archive than removes them. The assumption is that if cookfs archive has multiple updates it is better to create it from the beginning, which is also explained in next section.

Index information is a binary data that is stored in cookfs metadata. It is handled by separate part, which is able to import binary index data and export it when writing to a cookfs archive. Additional information on cookfs indexes can be found in next section of this document.

All pages are stored as binary data and are not modified in any way by cookfs paging mechanism. Pages can be compressed, though – in this case `add` and `get` operate on uncompressed data and handle compression internally when reading from disk or writing to disk. It's worth mentioning that in all cases every page is compressed independently and all get operations are performed on a complete page.

Cookfs stores pages content followed by index and pages metadata:

Cookfs pages are one or more pages, stored one after another. Pages do not contain any metadata about themselves and/or their relationship to any files in the VFS.

Pages are followed by metadata, consisting of index and information on sizes and checksums of all pages. Metadata contains enough information to locate all pages, index by just knowing the index of end of cookfs archive.

Cookfs archive can also be preceded by any data – such as platform-specific binary, which is used to create standalone applications. Archives are located at the end of a file or can be found by specifying location of end of archive, in case the archive is followed by additional information, such as digital signature or another type of VFS.

When an update is performed on existing archive, file is truncated to remove metadata and new pages are appended straight after last page. When the cookfs archive is closed, new metadata is appended at the end of the file.

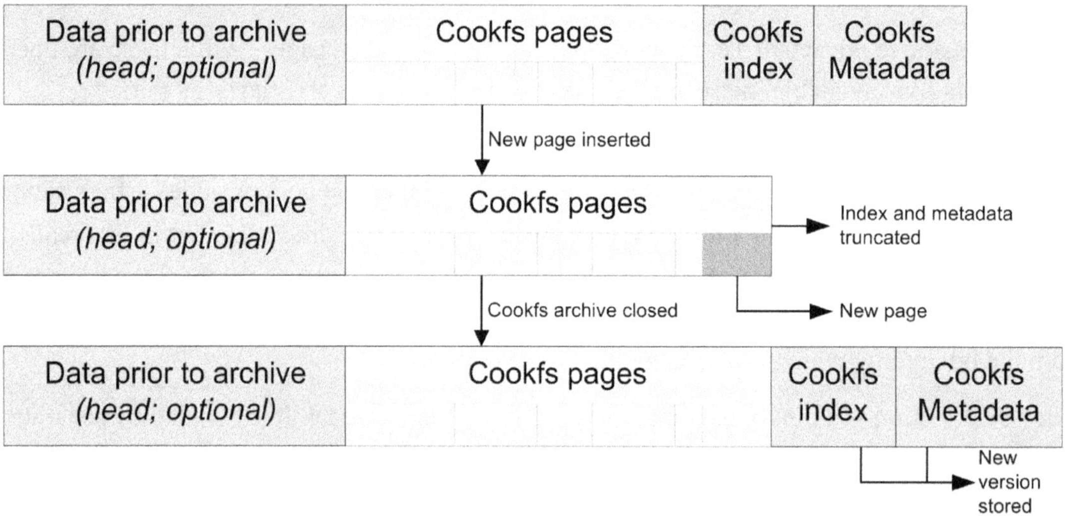

Cookfs caches pages that are read up to specified amount of pages. This is especially useful for small files, in which cases a page can be accessed very often. This allows tuning between smaller memory usage and better performance. Further sections show how increasing cache reduces overall time for reading files.

While concept of pages is generic, cookfs uses them only for storing files. Large files can be stored in multiple pages – for example 10MB file can be stored in 40 chunks of 256kB each. Smaller files might be stored entirely in a page. Files under 32kB are usually grouped and stored in a single page. Information on which pages are used by which files is stored in the index and VFS layer is responsible for splitting files into pages when adding or updating files.

Cookfs is also fully using 64bit offsets, which allows it to store more than 4GB of data. The only limitation is that cookfs can handle up to 2^{31} pages, which allows storing up to 512TB with page size of 256kB.

Cookfs pages mechanism is currently implemented in C, although a limited implementation in Tcl also exists.

Index and directory hierarchy

Cookfs index stores information about directory structure of cookfs archive. It maintains information about archive's directory structure by storing a tree of files and directories in the archive.

Similar to pages, index part provides set of Tcl methods that can be invoked on indexes. Below is a subset of these:

- `get` *`path`* – gets metadata about specified entry as Tcl list; for files it returns modification time, size and list of integers – their meaning is described in next section; for directories it returns only modification time
- `set` *`path mtime ?filedata?`* – adds file or directory to index; if `filedata` is not specified, entry is created as directory; otherwise item is created as a file `filedata` is a list of integers, same as the one later returned by `get` method
- `unset path` – removes an entry from index; only files or empty directories can be deleted
- `list` *`path`* – lists all items in specified path
- `export` – exports index as binary data
- `delete` – delete an index object

These are essential commands required for cookfs operations. Index can be created as empty one or by providing data that has previously been saved using `export` method. Paths are specified in the form of `dir/subdir/filename` – for example `lib/tcl8.5` specifies `tcl8.5` entry, located as subdirectory of `lib` directory.

Indexing mechanism automatically detects inconsistencies and throws an error in such cases. This makes it impossible to create file `lib/somefile` and later create another file `lib/somefile/invalidname`.

Indexes are internally stored using tree of hash tables, which represent files and directories hierarchy. Indexes are exported as binary data for storing on file system, where each directory stores its children recursively. For example for a simple directory structure the index would be stored as follows:

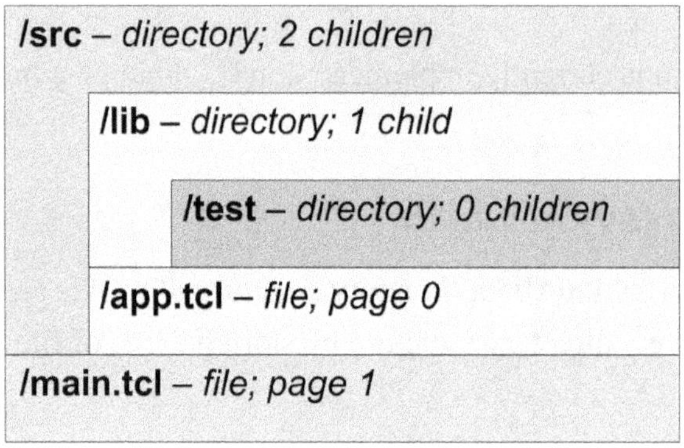

Information about directory `/src` would also store information on `/src/lib` recursively and `/src/app.tcl`. This allows storing the index efficiently. Storing information on all files in a single chunk also aids compressing index, especially when archive contains large number of files.

Cookfs index stores information about all directories and files in the archive. For each directory in an archive, index contains information about modification time and its child items.

For files, index stores information about file size, modification time and list of all pages the file is stored. Information on pages contains index of the page, starting offset in that page and number of bytes used for storing the file. This allows handling all types of files – ones that use multiple pages for their contents, files that use up exactly one page and files that are grouped in a single page.

Index handling is currently implemented in pure C, although a limited implementation in Tcl also exists.

Cookfs and VFS layer

VFS layer is at the heart of cookfs package. It leverages pages and index mechanisms to create an archive based virtual filesystem for Tcl.

Main features are reading and writing files from and to cookfs archive. Reading files is done using special type of channels and they do not read entire file contents in the beginning. As file is read, required part of the file is retrieved from cookfs pages. Pages are also cached, which often causes reading multiple files to reuse cached pages and avoid I/O operations on cookfs archive.

As pages store parts of a file independently, seeking operations are very efficient – when 100MB file is to be read from 80th megabyte, previous 80MB do not need to be read. When compressing entire files, seek operation needs to re-read file from the beginning in order to be able to uncompress from 80th megabyte.

This can be useful for things like seeking in audio files or extracting parts of large file.

Writing files is done using memchan[8] package. Whenever a file is written, its contents are stored in memory. When the file is closed whatever was written to it is saved to cookfs archives, creating new pages if needed. This mechanism is used for all operations that can write to a file - writing to a new file and appending to existing files.

Cookfs also allows adding one or more files to archive directly. This way files are read directly from disk and step of reading entirely into memory is avoided. Writing files directly instead of writing to memchan greatly speeds up copying files.

Whenever new contents are to be added to an archive, a check of file size is made. Large files are added to cookfs archive immediately. Small files are not added to archive immediately, but are queued. They are added when the size of all files is reached or archive is unmounted. By default the size limit for small files is 32kB and limit after which they are added to archive is 4MB.

Small files are also grouped by their file names. This allows files such as `pkgIndex.tcl` to be stored next to each other, usually storing them one after another and in the same chunk. This helps compressing the files as files with similar names usually have similar content.

All files are added to archive index after their contents is added to cookfs pages. Index stores each file's modification time and information on pages storing its contents. This is stored as one or more group of 3 integers - page index, offset from page start and number of bytes. For files that use up entire page offset is 0 and size is the size of a page. For small files this will be the page index, offset of the data and file size.

Cookfs VFS layer supports all filesystem related operations that tclvfs package supports. This includes getting and setting file information, listing files and/or directories in specified path and deleting files/directories. These operations simply reuse index functionalities. Creating directories in a virtual filesystem simply adds them to index.

Even though cookfs allows deleting contents of an archive, this simply removes information from the index, without removing any pages that store particular file's content. This is due to cookfs design. Recreating a cookfs archive from scratch is the best way to remove pages no

---

[8] http://memchan.sourceforge.net/

longer used. This will also copy all files to new archive. In such case small files will be grouped and compressed again, which will also increase effectiveness of compression.

Currently the VFS layer is written in Tcl and leverages tclvfs[9] package. Operations that require reading or modifying information in cookfs index leverage those functionalities using Tcl API that index provides. Writing a file is done as memchan channel that is then added to cookfs after writable channel is closed. Reading files functionality is implemented in Tcl using `chan create`[10] to create script level channels.

Cookit – standalone applications using cookfs

Cookit is a project closely related to cookfs. It is an effort to create Tclkit-like standalone Tcl solution leveraging cookfs as VFS for storing Tcl files and application to run. Currently cookit and cookfs only supports Tcl version 8.6 due to Tcl 8.6 specific features used such as zlib compression.

Cookit binaries contain statically linked Tcl library and have a virtual filesystem appended to them to store additional files – both platform-specific libraries and Tcl scripts. Upon initialization cookit mounts cookfs archive, reads scripts required to initialize Tcl properly. Next if `main.tcl` file is present in the archive, it is loaded and cookit works as a standalone application. If the file is not there, cookit starts interactive shell.

Cookit comes with Tcl compiled statically and only ships libraries that are part of Tcl itself – such as tdbc and TclOO. Microsoft Windows binaries come in two flavors – cookit.exe, a console application (similar to tclsh or tclkitsh) and cookit-ui.exe, version including Tk, similar to wish or tclkit binaries. Windows version also ships dde and registry packages in addition to the default ones.

It is possible to add additional libraries such as Tk or SQLite to a cookit binary by adding them to archive simply by mounting it and copying libraries. Cookfs and cookit plans also include creation and easy adding of ready to use packages – such that SQLite can be easily built and packaged into a cookfs package that can then be used by tools such as TABS as ready to use building blocks.

Cookit binaries do not support reading from or writing to mk4vfs. However, it is possible to simply copy mk4vfs package to cookfs virtual filesystem. As cookfs's main goal is to use cookfs based archives, there are currently no plans to include mk4vfs support by default to cookit binaries.

---

[9] http://sourceforge.net/projects/tclvfs/

[10] http://www.tcl.tk/man/tcl8.5/TclCmd/chan.htm#M22

Building cookit

Cookit build process requires a small set of scripts and source code. Cookit is built automatically by retrieving source code for all required packages and then compiling them – this includes Tcl, cookfs and tclvfs source code. Source code is retrieved from each project's source code repository, such as SourceForge's CVS/Subversion repositories. It currently supports using cvs[11], subversion[12] and GIT[13] source code management solutions. Support for fossil[14] is planned in near future. Paths to each project's source code are embedded in the build scripts.

Afterwards all parts of cookit are configured and compiled – tcl, tk (optionally), tclvfs and cookfs. Finally small piece of code that initializes tclvfs and cookfs is compiled and binary is built.

Next Tcl-only implementation of cookfs is used to build a temporary cookfs binary. It is not compressed in any way and is only used to create final cookfs binary build – which is compressed and created using C-based version of cookfs. This way cookit binaries can be built from any Tcl version – and build system currently supports versions down to 8.3, which can be sometimes found on older versions of operating systems.

From user perspective building cookit is straightforward. Build process below is shown using a Linux machine. Windows machine will perform similar operations. After downloading and unpacking cookit build system from SourceForge downloads page[15] we have the cookit build system ready to go. All commands are done using `build.tcl` or `build.sh` scripts – the latter one is simply a wrapper for `build.tcl` script. Running `build.tcl -help` will print out help on all available build commands and options.

First we need to retrieve source code using `build.tcl retrievesource` command:

```
[ 1/ 3] Retrieve source code for cookfs
    [21:08:37] Retrieving
    [21:08:46] Success

[ 2/ 3] Retrieve source code for tcl
    [21:08:46] Retrieving
    [21:12:32] Success

[ 3/ 3] Retrieve source code for vfs
```

[11] http://www.cvshome.org/

[12] http://subversion.tigris.org/

[13] http://git-scm.com/

[14] http://www.fossil-scm.org/

[15] https://sourceforge.net/projects/cookit/files/cookit/

```
    [21:12:32] Retrieving
    [21:14:17] Success

[21:14:17] Command completed successfully
```

Currently commands to `svn` and `cvs` have to be installed in order to retrieve source code. Future versions of cookit might offer fallback to http based downloads.

All we have to do next is run `build.tcl build-cookit` and a binary will be built. We can also pass `-upx best` option to compress the final cookit binary using UPX[16].

```
$ tclsh build.tcl -upx best build-cookit

[ 1/ 6] Build tcl 8.6b1.2
    [21:22:57] Initializing
    [21:22:57] Configuring
    [21:24:39] Compiling
    [21:28:52] Installing
    [21:29:05] Finalizing

[ 2/ 6] Build cookfs 1.0
    [21:29:05] Initializing
    [21:29:05] Configuring
    [21:29:40] Compiling
    [21:29:43] Installing
    [21:29:43] Finalizing

[ 3/ 6] Build vfs 1.4.1
    [21:29:43] Initializing
    [21:29:43] Configuring
    [21:30:20] Compiling
    [21:30:21] Installing
    [21:30:23] Finalizing

[ 4/ 6] Build cookit 1.0
    [21:30:23] Initializing
    [21:30:23] Configuring
    [21:30:23] Compiling
    [21:30:24] Installing
    [21:30:24] Finalizing

[ 5/ 6] Link binary
    [21:30:24] Initializing
    [21:30:24] Linking
    [21:30:48] Stripping
```

[16] http://upx.sourceforge.net/

```
    [21:30:48] Compressing

[ 6/ 6] Add CookFS layer
    [21:30:57] Initializing
    [21:30:57] Adding temporary VFS
    [21:30:58] Re-compressing VFS
    [21:30:58] Finalizing


[21:30:58] Command completed successfully
```

We can now find our correctly built cookit in directory _output/<platform>/cookit. Since our build took place on Linux x86 machine, cookit is located in _output/linux-x86/ directory.

Cookit build system currently offers stable mechanism to build cookit binaries. Currently only these commands work properly. In the future cookit build system will also offer stable mechanisms to build additional packages – such as tls with embedded openssl, sqlite, tcludp and tclx.

Cookit initialization code

Cookit initialization is similar to other solutions – cookit.c file provides CooKit_AppInit function, which initializes statically linked packages and passes Tcl code that initializes and mounts cookfs archive.

Tcl code that initializes the archive is very small and reads actual code to initialize required libraries from cookfs archive. The code simply creates cookfs pags object and gets first page, which stores entire code to initialize cookfs archive – such page is called bootstrap in cookit project.

Entire Tcl code embedded in C is as follows:

```
static char preInitCmd[] =
"namespace eval ::cookit {}\n"
"load {} Cookfs\n"
"load {} vfs\n"
"proc getCookfsBootstrap {} {\n"
"set ::cookit::cookitpages [cookfs::pages -readonly [info
nameofexecutable]]\n"
"uplevel #0 [$::cookit::cookitpages get 0]\n"
"}\n"
"getCookfsBootstrap ; rename getCookfsBootstrap {}\n"
"";
```

During cookit build process, page 0 is specially created that it combines multiple libraries – Tcl scripts from tclvfs library, Tcl scripts from cookfs itself, creates and registers cookfs mount. Initialization code also checks for existence of `main.tcl` and reads it if the file exists. Bootstrap code only includes essential packages – files such as `main.tcl` are stored as regular files in cookfs archive.

Comparison – compressing sample filesystems

Cookfs was designed to create smaller files by performing grouping of files. Some samples below show what are the differences and also demonstrate how zlib based compression differ from bzip2 both in size factors and time taken to compress and decompress contents of the archive.

Packing is taking a directory structure from a real filesystem and putting it into an archive – this includes time to prepare archive, copy actual contents and finalize the archive. Unpacking an archive means mounting already created archive and copying its contents back to real filesystem. Both steps were done independently of each other not to reuse any information across writes and reads.

For the purpose of comparison, the following VFS technologies have been used:

- Mk4 VFS – most commonly used VFS solution
- ZIP VFS – commonly used format for archiving; zipper package used for compressing archives, `vfs::zip` package used for decompressing
- Cookfs with zlib compression – standard cookfs compression, same as in Mk4 and ZIP; archive compression was done using both writing using VFS layer and direct writing
- Cookfs with bzip2 compression – more efficient compression that takes significantly more time to compress and/or decompress; archive compression was done using both writing using VFS layer and direct writing

The following sample directory structures have been used for measuring size and timing differences:

- TclHttpd 3.5.1 – this is a distribution of TclHttpd package[17] version 3.5.1; it is a relatively small package but commonly put in standalone Tcl/Tk applications; uncompressed size: 460kB
- Tcllib 1.11.1 –Tcllib[18] is a library of commonly used functions in Tcl/Tk – a package that is very commonly embedded in Tcl/Tk applications; only Tcl scripts were used for testing, without compiled helper libraries; uncompressed size: 12MB

---

[17] http://sourceforge.net/projects/tclhttpd/

[18] http://sourceforge.net/projects/tcllib/

- ActiveTcl 8.4 for Linux – typical installation of ActiveTcl 8.4.19.0[19]; uncompressed size: 71MB
- Joomla with LAMP – good example of packaging non-Tcl content into an archive; contains entire BitNami Joomla stack[20] for Linux (along Apache, MySQL and PHP); uncompressed size: 224MB
- Redmine with RubyStack for Linux – largest sample archive; contains entire BitNami Redmine stack[21] for Linux (along with Ruby and all other artifacts) installed on a filesystem; uncompressed size: 535MB

Tests are performed on two platforms – Microsoft Windows and Ubuntu Linux. Both machines have similar configuration – virtual machines using single core, 2GB of memory and 20GB disk drive. Tests were performed when both host and guest operating system were idle. All tests were repeated 5 times and average time was taken as resulting time.

Tclhttpd 3.5.1

First sample is a relatively small package, a minimal subset of Tclhttpd. It shows the difference that cookfs can make even for smaller packages – saving around 20% while still using zlib compression.

Below is analysis of how many files sample file structure included distributed by file sizes. It shows how many files are there in each of size range. Files up to 32kB were treated as small files and are shown in different color on the bar chart.

Size range	Count
>=4MB	0
1-4MB	0
256kB-1MB	0
32-256kB	1
4-32kB	25
1-4kB	18
<1kB	1
Total:	45

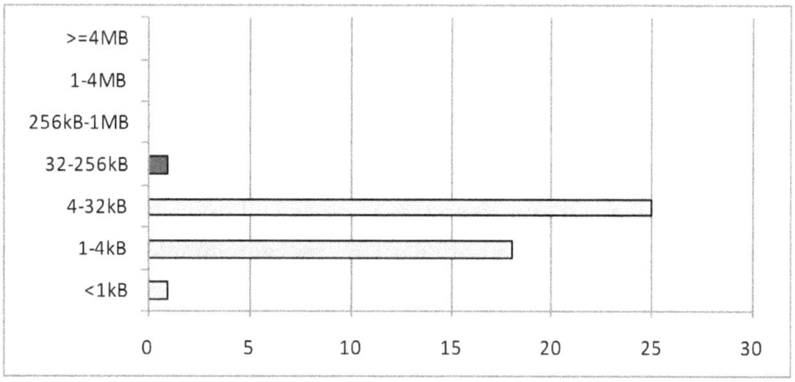

Bar chart below shows differences in archive file size for all types of compression:

[19] http://www.activestate.com/activetcl/downloads

[20] http://bitnami.org/stack/joomla

[21] http://bitnami.org/stack/redmine

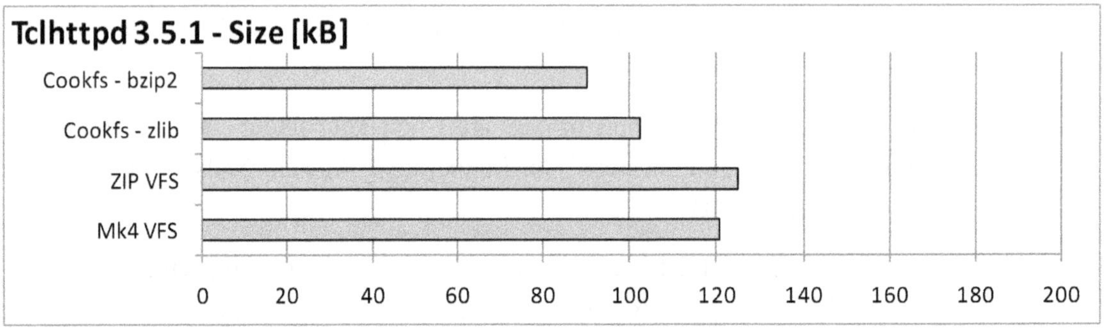

Table below shows sizes and time for each of compression types:

VFS technology	Size [kB]	Linux – Time [s]		MS Windows – Time [s]	
		Pack	Unpack	Pack	Unpack
Mk4 VFS	121	0.2	0.1	0.2	0.1
ZIP VFS	125	0.1	0.1	0.2	0.1
Cookfs – zlib (vfs write)	102	0.1	0.1	0.1	0.1
Cookfs - zlib 16MB (vfs write)		0.1	0.1	0.1	0.1
Cookfs – zlib (direct write)		0.1	0.1	0.1	0.1
Cookfs – zlib 16MB (direct write)		0.1	0.1	0.1	0.1
Cookfs - bzip2 (vfs write)	90	0.2	0.1	0.2	0.1
Cookfs - bzip2 (direct write)		0.1	0.1	0.1	0.1

Time needed to pack and unpack contents of Tclhttpd is small enough that differences are probably due to timing inefficiencies and other factors. However, benefits in size are significant – we can save over 20% of total Tclhttpd size by simply compressing it more efficiently. We can save additional 10% by switching to more optimal compression algorithm.

Tcllib 1.11.1

Tcllib is a set of Tcl libraries that is often embedded in standalone Tcl/Tk applications. This test is meant to illustrate how cookfs could compress scripts very similar to typical Tcl/Tk application.

Below is analysis of how many files sample file structure included distributed by file sizes. It shows how many files are there in each of size range. Files up to 32kB were treated as small files and are shown in different color on the bar chart.

Size range	Count
>=4MB	0

1-4MB	0
256kB-1MB	1
32-256kB	66
4-32kB	277
1-4kB	236
<1kB	458
Total:	1038

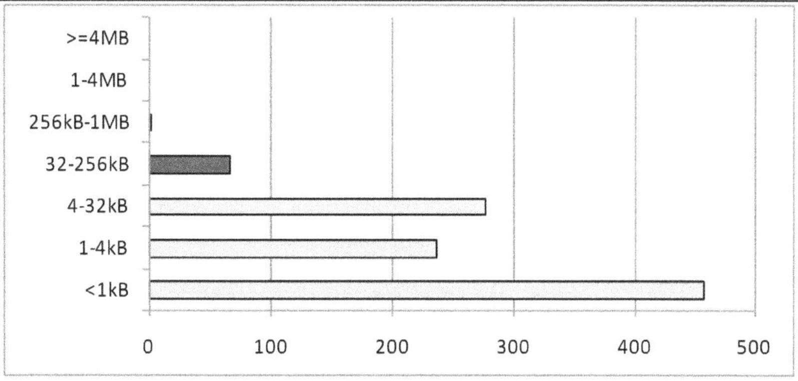

Bar chart below shows differences in archive file size for all types of compression:

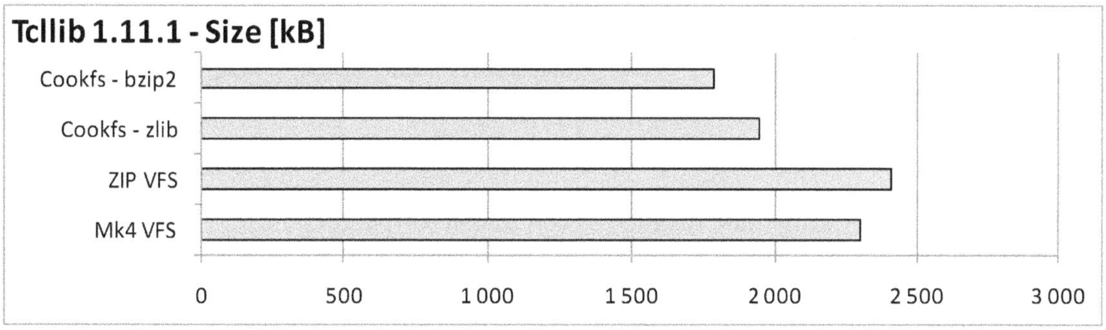

Bar chart below shows differences in time taken to pack and unpack entire contents of the archive on Linux platform:

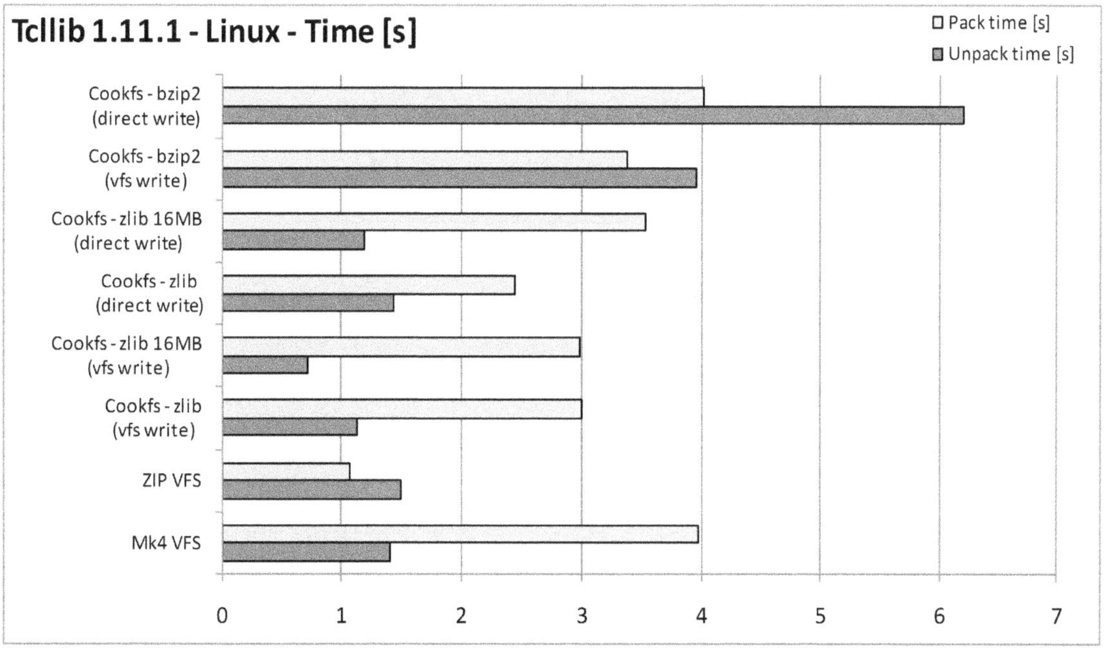

Bar chart below shows differences in time taken to pack and unpack entire contents of the archive on Microsoft Windows:

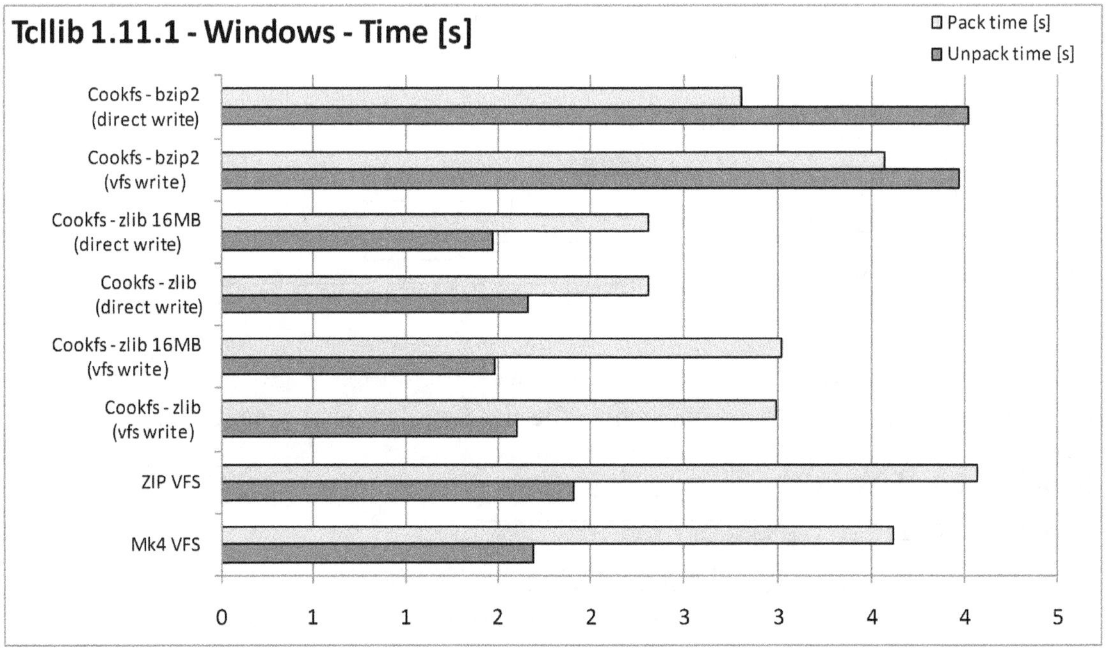

Table below shows sizes and time for each of compression types:

VFS technology	Size [kB]	Linux – Time [s]		MS Windows – Time [s]	
		Pack	Unpack	Pack	Unpack
Mk4 VFS	2 300	4.0	1.4	3.6	1.7
ZIP VFS	2 410	1.1	1.5	4.1	1.9
Cookfs – zlib (vfs write)	1 948	3.0	1.1	3.0	1.6
Cookfs - zlib 16MB (vfs write)		3.0	0.7	3.0	1.5
Cookfs – zlib (direct write)		2.4	1.4	2.3	1.7
Cookfs – zlib 16MB (direct write)		3.5	1.2	2.3	1.5
Cookfs - bzip2 (vfs write)	1 787	3.4	4.0	3.6	4.0
Cookfs - bzip2 (direct write)		4.0	6.2	2.8	4.0

This example shows that cookfs with zlib compression provides faster results in both compression and uncompression than Mk4 VFS. Using direct writes instead of using VFS layer provides additional benefit for packing and using larger cache provides in faster unpacking of the archive. Similar to Tclhttpd, simply using cookfs with same compression provides 15% gain in archive size. Using bzip2 compression provides additional 10% gain at the cost of higher compression and uncompression times.

Difference in time taken to compress and uncompress all of zlib based solutions is similar, although cookfs offers a minor performance increase over Mk4 VFS and ZIP VFS. Using bzip2 clearly takes much longer to complete.

ActiveTcl 8.4 for Linux

This part of comparison is meant to show an archive which contents is mixed – it consists of both large number of Tcl scripts and binary files – multiple binary files as well as all libraries that ActiveTcl provides. The reason version 8.4 was chosen is that it is the last version of ActiveTcl that ships all commonly used libraries by default.

Below is analysis of how many files sample file structure included distributed by file sizes. It shows how many files are there in each of size range. Files up to 32kB were treated as small files and are shown in different color on the bar chart.

Size range	Count
>=4MB	1
1-4MB	10
256kB-1MB	18
32-256kB	205
4-32kB	1573
1-4kB	791
<1kB	1013
Total:	3611

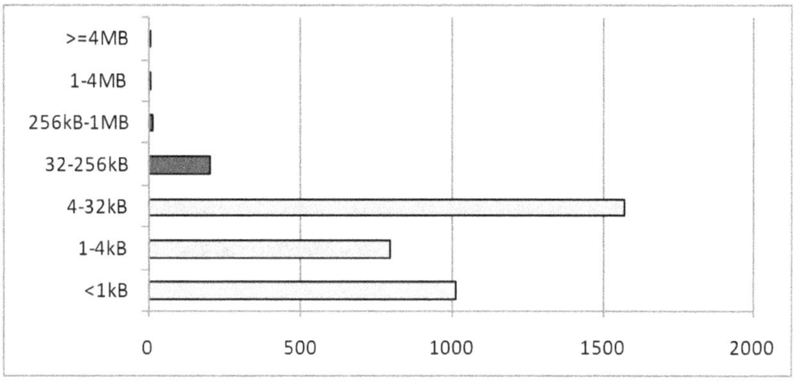

Bar chart below shows differences in archive file size for all types of compression:

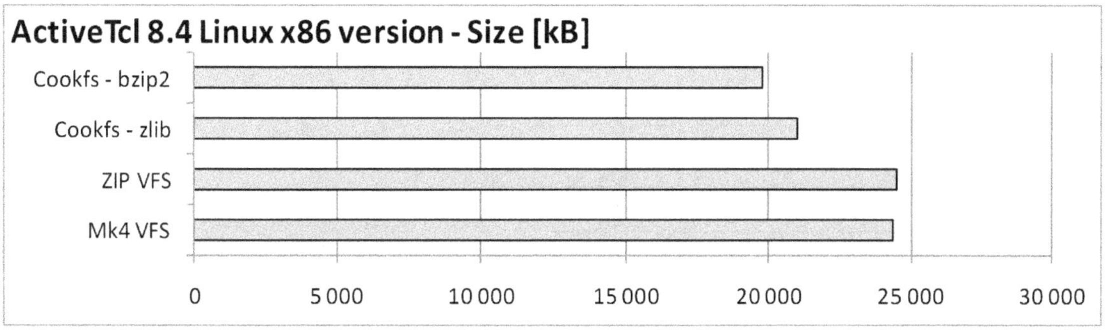

Bar chart below shows differences in time taken to pack and unpack entire contents of the archive on Linux platform:

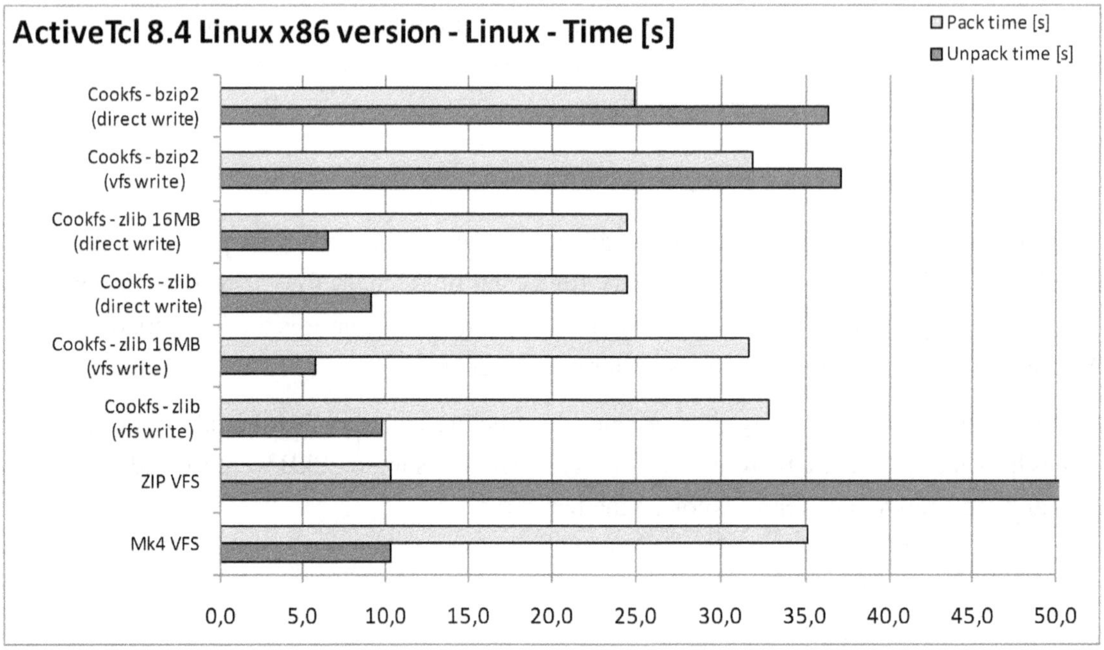

Bar chart below shows differences in time taken to pack and unpack entire contents of the archive on Microsoft Windows:

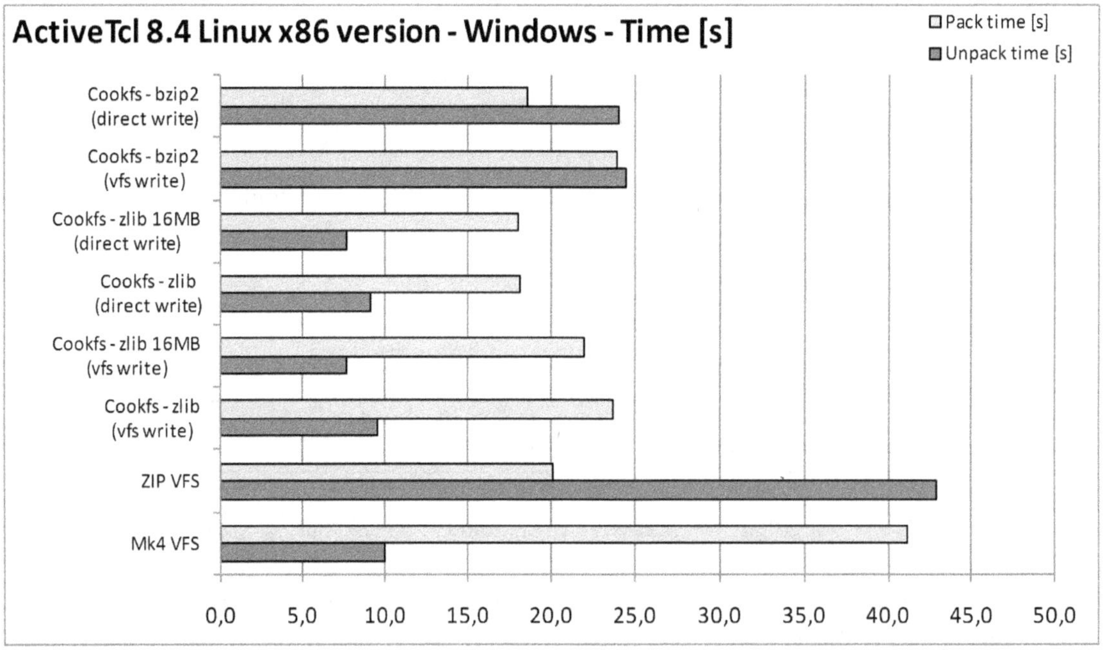

Table below shows sizes and time for each of compression types:

VFS technology	Size [kB]	Linux – Time [s]		MS Windows – Time [s]	
		Pack	Unpack	Pack	Unpack
Mk4 VFS	24 408	35.2	10.3	41.2	10.0
ZIP VFS	24 535	10.3	72.1	20.1	42.9

Cookfs – zlib (vfs write)	21 010	32.9	9.7	23.7	9.6
Cookfs - zlib 16MB (vfs write)		31.6	5.8	22.0	7.7
Cookfs – zlib (direct write)		24.5	9.1	18.1	9.1
Cookfs – zlib 16MB (direct write)		24.4	6.5	18.1	7.7
Cookfs - bzip2 (vfs write)	19 815	31.8	37.1	23.9	24.5
Cookfs - bzip2 (direct write)		24.9	36.3	18.6	24.0

Similar to previous examples cookfs clearly offers better compression ratio with zlib compression – around 15% smaller archive was created. Using bzip2 compression offers additional gain, but only over 5% at a cost of much higher compression and decompression times.

Times taken to compress the archives are similar for Mk4 VFS, ZIP VFS and cookit. The only difference is if cookit is used with direct writes. Unpacking from an archive works much faster with cookit, especially if using 16MB of memory for cookfs cache.

Joomla with LAMP

Next sample contens is a Joomla application along with all Linux x86 binaries needed in order to get it up and running – Apache, MySQL and PHP. The content was extracted from a fresh installation of Joomla using BitNami Joomla Stack[22]. This is first example that does not involve packaging files typical to Tcl.

Below is analysis of how many files sample file structure included distributed by file sizes. It shows how many files are there in each of size range. Files up to 32kB were treated as small files and are shown in different color on the bar chart.

Size range	Count
>=4MB	14
1-4MB	25
256kB-1MB	23
32-256kB	318
4-32kB	2038
1-4kB	1729
<1kB	2892
Total:	7039

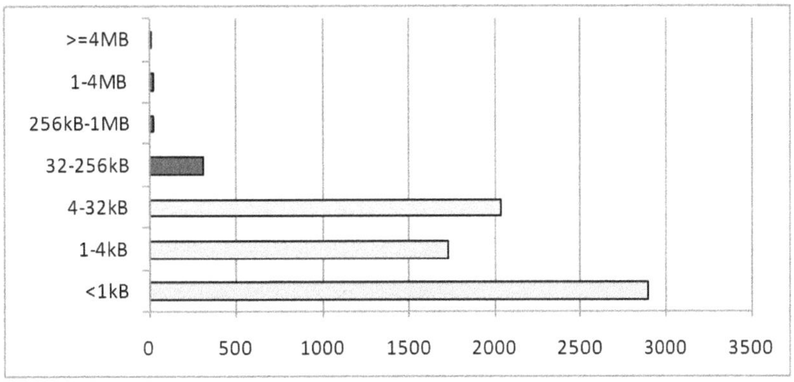

[22] http://bitnami.org/stack/joomla

Bar chart below shows differences in archive file size for all types of compression:

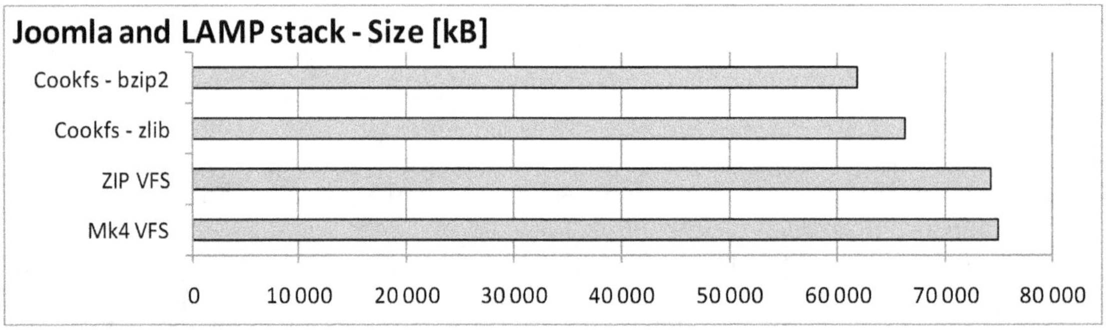

Bar chart below shows differences in time taken to pack and unpack entire contents of the archive on Linux platform:

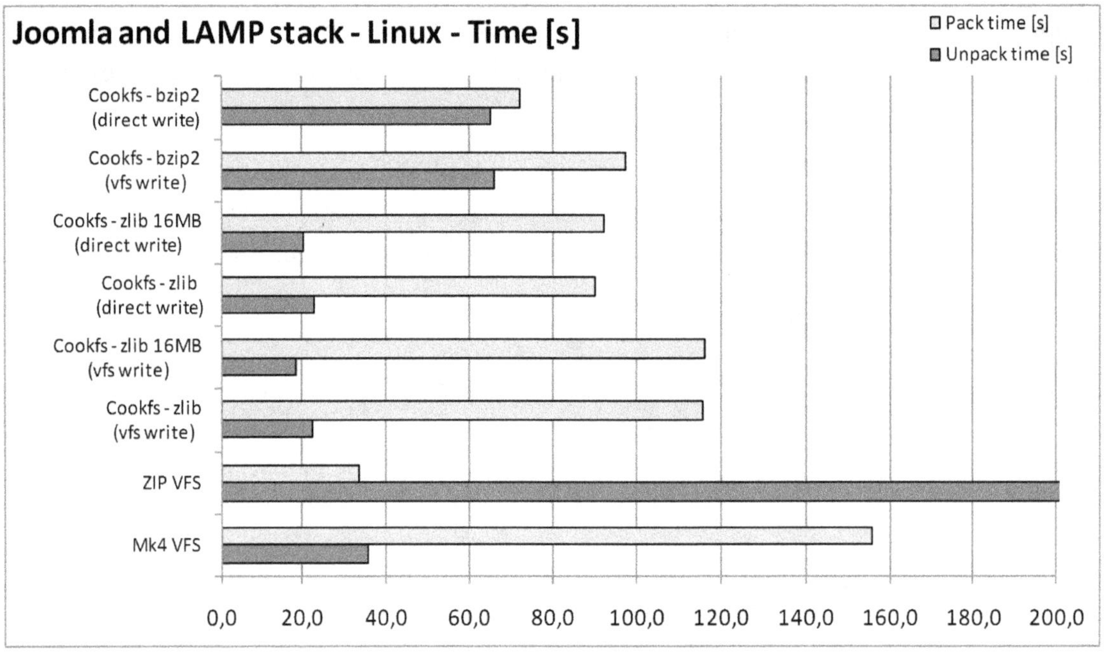

Bar chart below shows differences in time taken to pack and unpack entire contents of the archive on Microsoft Windows:

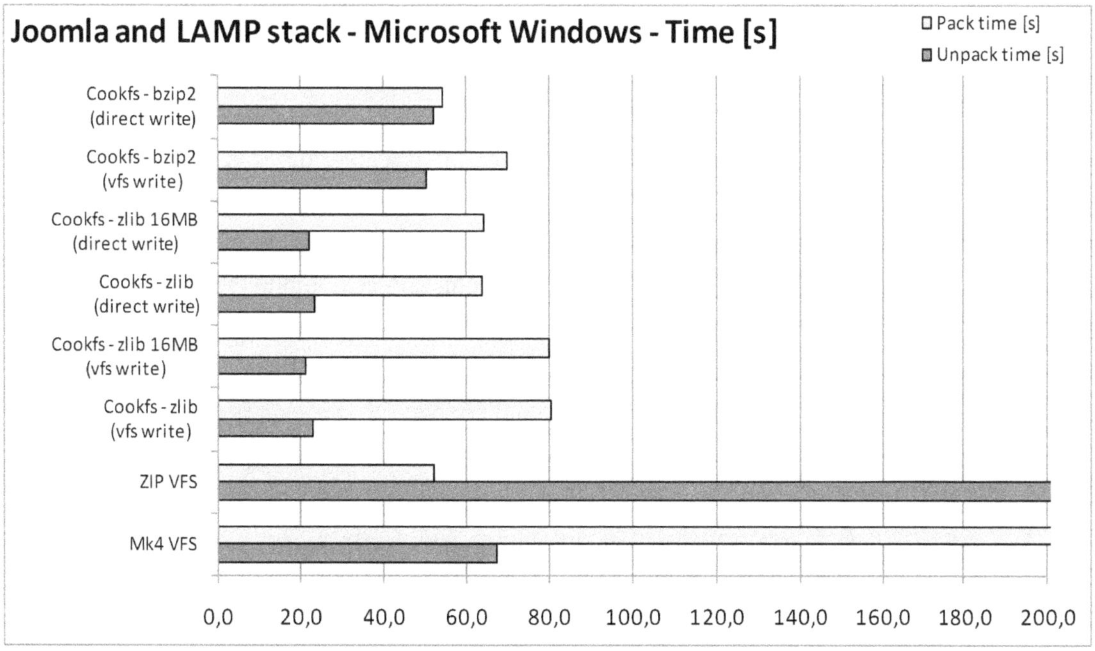

Table below shows sizes and time for each of compression types:

VFS technology	Size [kB]	Linux – Time [s]		MS Windows – Time [s]	
		Pack	Unpack	Pack	Unpack
Mk4 VFS	74 951	155.9	35.4	223.9	67.1
ZIP VFS	74 266	33.5	1263.3	52.1	713.4
Cookfs – zlib (vfs write)	66 260	115.9	22.4	80.4	22.9
Cookfs - zlib 16MB (vfs write)		115.9	18.4	79.9	21.0
Cookfs – zlib (direct write)		90.0	23.0	64.0	23.1
Cookfs – zlib 16MB (direct write)		92.0	20.2	64.4	21.9
Cookfs - bzip2 (vfs write)	61 800	97.6	65.9	69.8	50.4
Cookfs - bzip2 (direct write)		72.2	65.1	54.2	52.1

This example is interesting as it is not strictly related to Tcl – application itself is PHP and majority of size is taken by binaries and libraries needed for it to run.

Cookfs managed to get much better compression ratio – 10% smaller archive than Mk4 and ZIP VFS. Bzip gained another 7% increase, but at a very high cost, especially when decompressing archive's contents.

Mk4 VFS does take a lot of time to compress all the files – it probably is related to the fact that it creates each file individually and stores its index information individually while cookfs and ZIP VFS store this when finalizing archive.

The fact that ZIP VFS is created much faster than any other technologies is intriguing – it seems to outrun each other technology, which might have something to do with how cookfs and Mk4 VFS handle larger number of files. Unpack time for ZIP VFS is also a bit out of order as it is around 50-100 times worse than other technologies, which is probably related to how `vfs::zip` package is written and that it might not be handling very large number of files efficiently as well. However, multiple runs of the test show conducted at different times showed the proportions to other technologies do not change.

Redmine and RubyStack for Linux

This example consists of all applications that are needed to run Redmine application – Apache, MySQL, Perl, Ruby and additional helper applications. Uncompressed size is 535MB, which is a great example for compressing content for installer applications.

Below is analysis of how many files sample file structure included distributed by file sizes. It shows how many files are there in each of size range. Files up to 32kB were treated as small files and are shown in different color on the bar chart.

Size range	Count
>=4MB	17
1-4MB	59
256kB-1MB	138
32-256kB	1229
4-32kB	5753
1-4kB	6563
<1kB	8053
Total:	21812

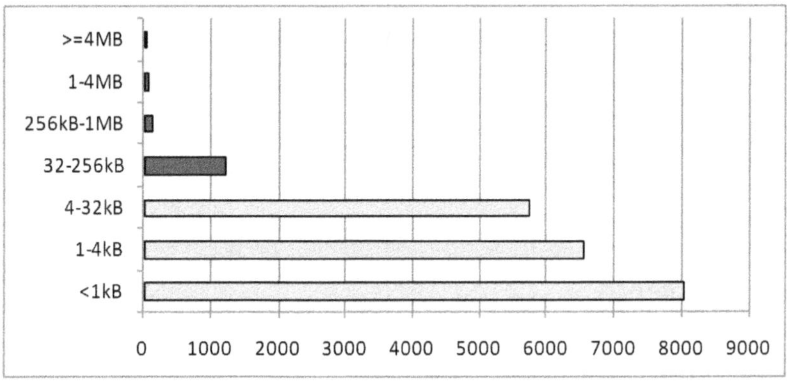

Bar chart below shows differences in archive file size for all types of compression:

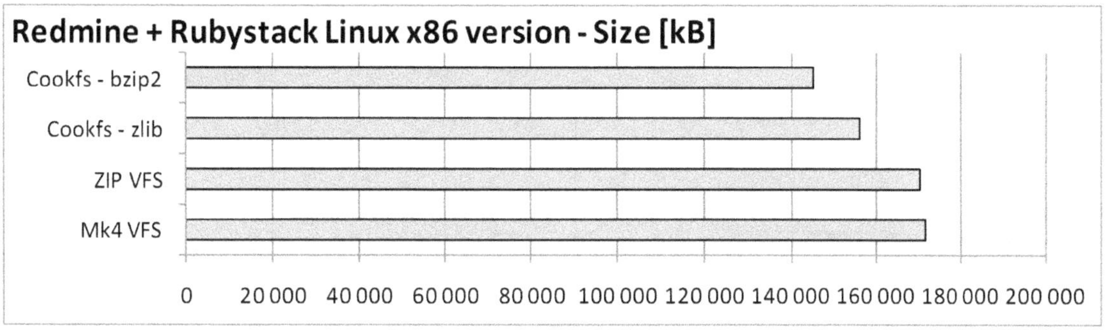

Bar chart below shows differences in time taken to pack and unpack entire contents of the archive on Linux platform:

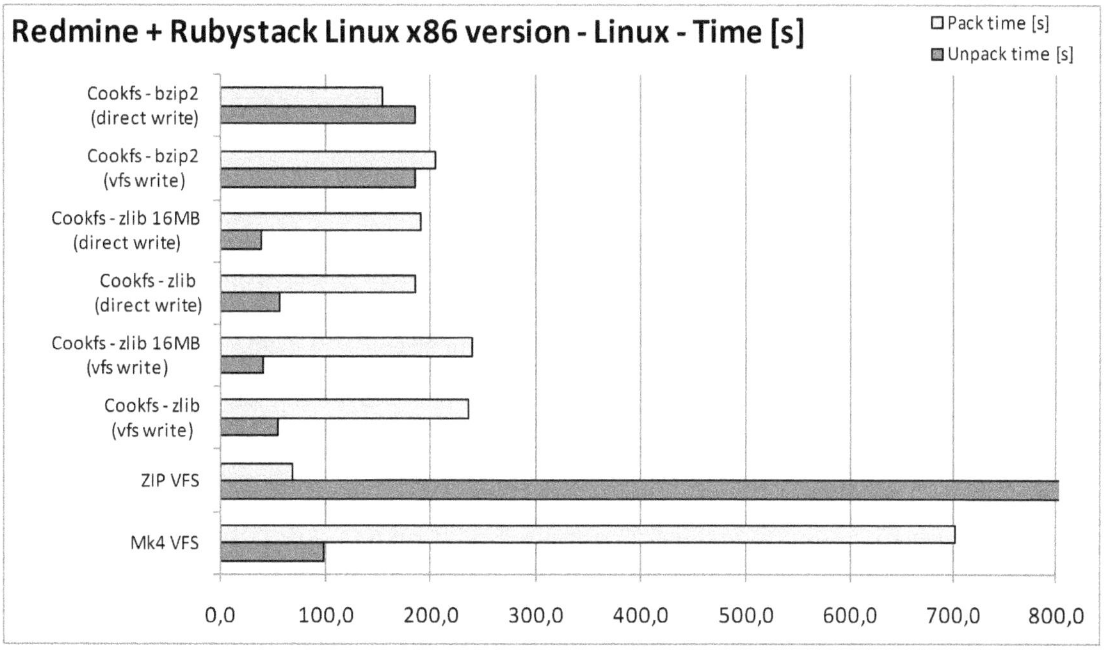

Bar chart below shows differences in time taken to pack and unpack entire contents of the archive on Microsoft Windows:

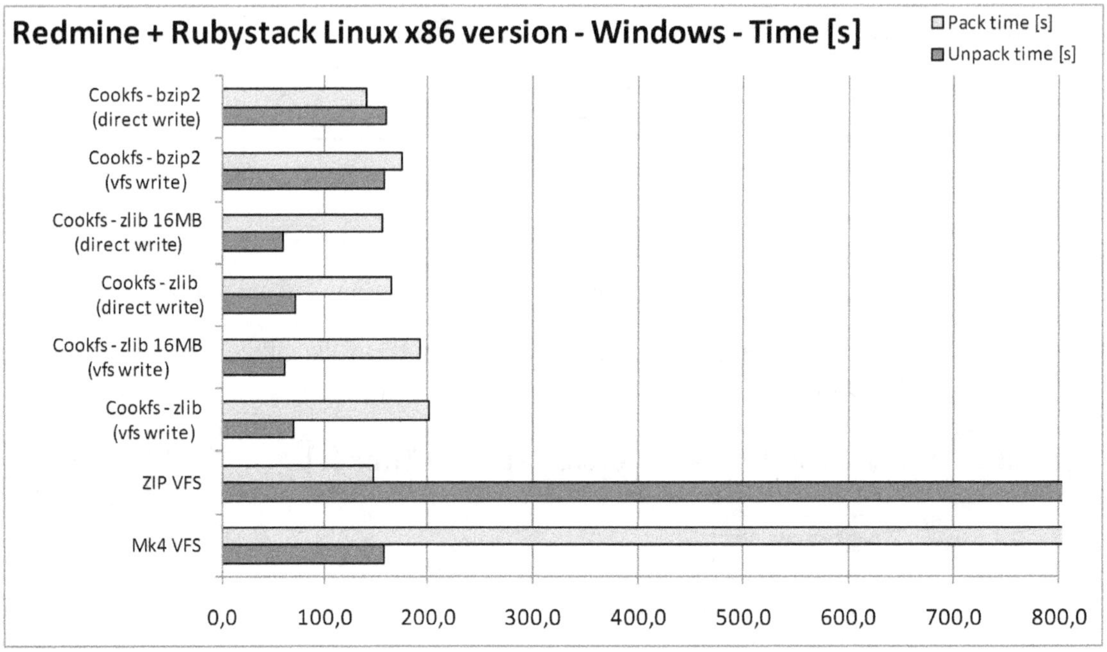

Table below shows sizes and time for each of compression types:

VFS technology	Size [kB]	Linux – Time [s]		MS Windows – Time [s]	
		Pack	Unpack	Pack	Unpack
Mk4 VFS	171 503	701.8	98.4	3650.4	158.3
ZIP VFS	170 306	69.5	1883.9	147.4	1215.6
Cookfs – zlib (vfs write)	156 134	236.4	55.3	201.3	70.5
Cookfs - zlib 16MB (vfs write)		239.1	39.9	192.6	61.1
Cookfs – zlib (direct write)		186.2	57.2	163.7	71.4
Cookfs – zlib 16MB (direct write)		189.9	39.7	155.0	60.7
Cookfs - bzip2 (vfs write)	145 368	203.9	185.3	175.8	158.3
Cookfs - bzip2 (direct write)		153.5	184.9	139.6	159.6

Similar to smaller Joomla example, cookfs managed to compress entire contents most efficiently – although in this case it was only 10% less than Mk4 VFS or ZIP VFS. Using bzip2 compression introduced only a small improvement of 7%. However, cookfs' compression and decompression times for zlib were much better than other ones shown in this example.

What is interesting is that cookfs is able to uncompress the data around 30% faster by using 16MB instead of 2MB for cache. This is especially interesting that archive is over 150MB, so only 10% of its entire contents is cached.

Same as in previous example, Mk4 VFS takes a lot of time to compress archive contents – even an hour on Microsoft Windows. Its unpack time is only a bit bigger than cookfs, unless cookfs.

Similar to Joomla's example ZIP VFS takes much smaller amount of time to compress the data. However its unpack time is also much lower – around 10-30 times slower than competitive solutions in this example.

Current status and future plans

Cookfs project is a reasonably stable and mature solution, therefore it is versioned as 1.0. While it does not currently offer all features that are planned, it can safely be used as VFS for standalone application as cookit project shows.

One of limitations is that cookfs and cookit only support Tcl 8.6 for now. Plan is to allow integration with older Tcl versions, starting with 8.5 and perhaps even supporting 8.4 versions.

Since pages and index mechanisms are complete and written in C, most changes will happen within VFS layer. Those changes will also likely not cause backward or forward incompatibilities. Newer cookfs versions will be able to read archives created using previous versions as well as older cookfs releases will be able to read archives created by more recent versions.

Cookfs currently still has some drawbacks or limitations – one of its bigger flaws is having code partially in Tcl and C, which then causes it to require tclvfs - both C level and Tcl level elements of tclvfs. Currently Tcl scripts handle reading of archive contents. This code will be replaced by creating a channel driver in C. This will speed up reading operations.

Another issue is that for writable channels, they can be implemented in C and without the need to fully buffer file contents before storing it. Files can be written to memory until enough content is written to this channel to create a new cookfs page. This will reduce time and memory usage when writing to VFS using Tcl I/O. It will reduce the difference between writing to VFS and directly using cookfs command.

Using tclvfs for providing VFS layer for Tcl can be replaced by fully implementing VFS at C level, similar to trofs[23] project. Cookfs would then offer a much better alternative to other VFS solutions and its performance would also increase. However, due to large effort to implement it, this is currently a low priority feature.

---

[23] http://math.nist.gov/~DPorter/tcltk/trofs/

Current VFS layer implementation also does not work properly with cookit and multi-threaded applications. Often deadlocks occur when creating a child thread that needs to access VFS during its initialization. This is related to using tclvfs and will no longer be an issue when cookfs provides its own C level VFS driver.

A temporary limitation of cookfs is that if an archive with any pending changes is not unmounted before process exits, data is lost and archive will be unreadable. This can be worked around by adding Tcl exit and/or thread exit handlers to properly unmount archives.

Cookfs will also include additional tools and commands for building applications and ease of archive management. A very useful command would be one that can compact an archive – recreating an archive to prevent wasting space in an archive that had multiple changes, especially file deletions.

In addition to this, cookfs will provide commands for merging one or more cookfs archives without recompressing their contents – by simply adding pages and merging indexes.

Additional feature worth considering as additional tool is being able to unpack large amounts of files more efficiently. Currently files are unpacked in order they are found. A smarter mechanism can order the reads by page indexes to speed it up even more.

Cookit project is currently stable and mature – binaries are available for most common platforms – Microsoft Windows 32bit, Linux 32bit, Mac OS X 32 bit, Solaris x86 32 bit. Cookit build process allows building on most platforms that are supported by configure scripts for each of the components so extending set of platforms should be at most adding platform-specific changes or hacks to allow these platforms to be built.

17th ANNUAL TCL/TK CONFERENCE 2010
Chicago (USA)
11-15 October

WIPS

Wed October 13, 2010 16:15-17:30

TclA Publications

TkRibbon: Windows Ribbons for Tk

Georgios Petasis

Software and Knowledge Engineering Laboratory,
Institute of Informatics and Telecommunications,
National Centre for Scientific Research "Demokritos",
Athens, Greece
petasis@iit.demokritos.gr

Abstract

This paper is about TkRibbon, a Tcl/Tk extension that aims to introduce support for the Windows Ribbon Framework in the Tk toolkit. The Windows Ribbon is a graphical interface where a set of toolbars are placed on tabs in a notebook widget, aiming to substitute traditional menus and toolbars. This paper briefly describes Windows Ribbon framework, the TkRibbon Tk extension and presents some examples on how TkRibbon can be used by Tk applications.

1 Introduction

In this paper TkRibbon is presented, a C extension for the Microsoft Windows operating system that aims to introduce support for the Windows Ribbon framework in the Tk toolkit. The Windows Ribbon framework is a rich command presentation framework that aims to unify traditional multilayered menus, toolbars and task panes into a single, modern alternative graphical element. The Ribbon framework consists mainly of two primary user interface components:

- The Ribbon command bar. This component contains the application menu, a set of standard tabs, a set of contextual tabs (activated by the currently application element that has the focus), and a Help button. TkRibbon currently offers complete support for this interface component.
- A rich contextual menu. There is no support for the time being in TkRibbon regarding this interface component.

An example of a Windows Ribbon can be seen in Figure 1. The Ribbon framework, from the application point of view, can be decomposed into two distinct but dependent development platforms:

- A XAML-based markup language, which describes the controls, their properties and their visual layout.
- A set of COM C++ interfaces that ensure interoperability between the Ribbon framework and the application.

The Windows Ribbon framework is implemented as a COM object, which can be attached to any application window, and taking control of the window upper part (Figure 1) it redraws the window as needed, reacting to user keyboard/mouse input and requests from the application. The Ribbon framework is built around "commands": when the user activates a command (either by pressing a button, selecting an item, etc.), the framework uses COM messaging to communicate the action to the application. In addition, communication with the application can occur in some other cases, i.e. when the framework requests missing information about a control (like a missing or invalidated property). TkRibbon acts as a mediator between the Ribbon framework and a Tcl/Tk application, translating messages into callbacks written in Tcl and Tk virtual events, while "packaging" a Ribbon instance as a Tk widget.

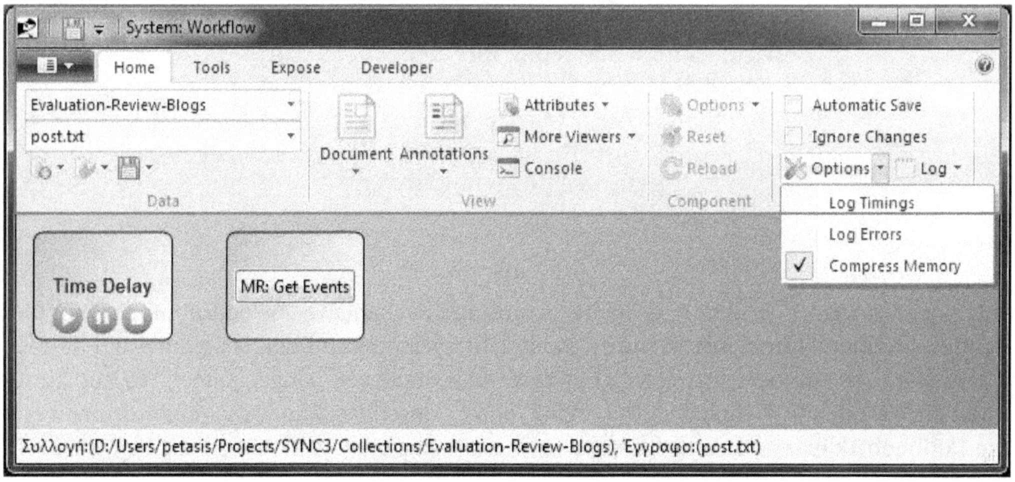

Figure 1: An example of a Windows Ribbon. The marked area is drawn by the Ribbon framework (including part of the window decoration).

The rest of the paper is organised as follows: chapter two presents an overview of how TkRibbon can be used in order to load and display a Ribbon that is contained in a resource DLL. The whole chapter is a running event starting from the XAML markup describing the Ribbon to the loaded Ribbon inside a Tcl/Tk application. Chapter three concentrates on the interaction between the Ribbon framework and the application, through a brief presentation of how a Ribbon requests information from the application, how Ribbon events are communicated to the application and how the application may pose requests to a Ribbon instance. Finally, chapter four concludes the document by reporting on the current status of the TkRibbon extension.

2 Creating a Ribbon

The process of implementing a Ribbon and incorporating it into a Tk application involves three basic tasks: describe the Ribbon controls in XML markup, compile the markup into a resource DLL, and write the code that loads the Ribbon from the resource DLL and handles the interaction between the Ribbon widget and the application. These tasks are illustrated in Figure 2.

2.1 Writing the Ribbon Markup

The first step in creating a Ribbon is, of course, to design it: to decide the tabs, the task panes each tab will have, and the controls that will be placed in each task pane. There is extensive documentation by Microsoft on how Ribbons should be designed in the "Ribbon User Experience Guidelines"[1], while documentation and tutorials can be found at the "Windows Ribbon Framework Developer Guides"[2].

---

[1] The "Ribbon User Experience Guidelines" can be found at:
http://msdn.microsoft.com/en-us/library/cc872782.aspx

[2] The "Windows Ribbon Framework Developer Guides" can be found at:
http://msdn.microsoft.com/en-us/library/dd742866%28v=VS.85%29.aspx

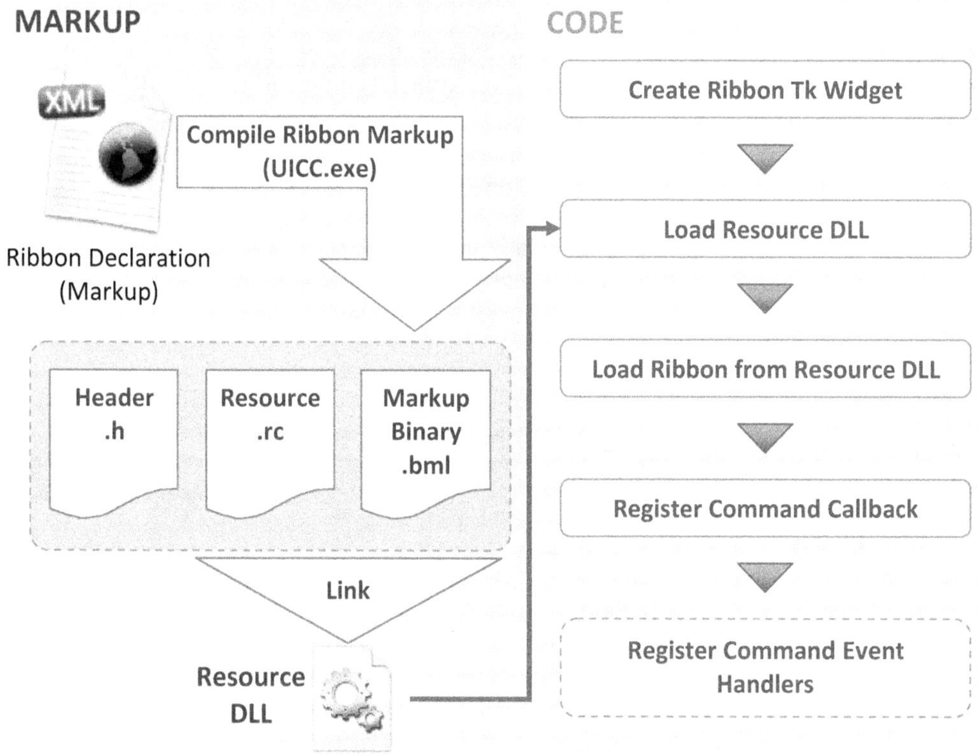

Figure 2: Creating a Ribbon in a Tk application.

Once the Ribbon has been designed, it must be described in XML using the Ribbon markup. The Ribbon XML contains two major parts. The first part defines the commands (with properties like a numeric id, a command name, the command label, tooltip, etc.), while the second part defines the organisation of the Ribbon in tabs, groups inside a tab, and commands inside a group (Figure 3). As an example, let's assume a Ribbon that has a single tab labelled "Home", with a single group labelled "Commands" that contains a single command, of type button, labelled "Exit". The following code illustrates the XML markup that describes this Ribbon:

```
<?xml version='1.0' encoding='utf-8'?>
<Application xmlns="http://schemas.microsoft.com/windows/2009/Ribbon">
  <Application.Commands>
    <Command Name="cmdExit" Symbol="cmdExit" LabelTitle="Exit"
             TooltipTitle="Exit" TooltipDescription="Exit Application..." />
  </Application.Commands>
  <Application.Views>
    <Ribbon>
      <Ribbon.Tabs>
        <Tab>
          <Group>
            <Button CommandName="cmdExit" />
          </Group>
        </Tab>
      </Ribbon.Tabs>
    </Ribbon>
  </Application.Views>
</Application>
```

Figure 3: XML markup of a simple Ribbon, containing a single command button.

For the purpose of the example, we will assume that the XML markup shown in Figure 3 is saved in a file named "ribbon1.xml"

2.2 Compiling the Markup

The XML markup must be compiled in order to be usable in any application, and there is a dedicated compiler for this in the Windows 7 SDK: the UI command compiler (UICC), which can be invoked from the command prompt:

```
uicc.exe ribbon1.xml ribbon1.bml /header:ribbon1.h /res:ribbon1.rc /name:RIBBON1
```

The parameters such as /name: are optional, but it is a good idea to identify each Ribbon with a custom name, instead of the default "APPLICATION_RIBBON", allowing multiple Ribbons to be placed inside a single resource DLL. Once the Ribbon markup has been compiled, a resource DLL can be easily created:

```
rc.exe ribbon1.rc
link.exe /NOENTRY /DLL /MACHINE:X86 /OUT:ribbon1.dll ribbon1.res
```

2.3 The TkRibbon widget

Up to now, there is nothing different in how a DLL containing one or more Ribbons is prepared. However, using any Ribbon from a DLL is somewhat different under TkRibbon, deviating from having to link the Ribbon to the code that uses it. Being an extension for the dynamic language Tcl, TkRibbon implements all the needed middle-ware to load a Ribbon UI from a DLL and interact with it. The main disadvantage of this approach is that interoperability is limited to what has been implemented by TkRibbon, suggesting that some advanced operations (i.e. serialising and restoring button layout changes done by user) are not yet supported.

In order to load and use a Ribbon from a Tk application, the steps shown in the code section of Figure 2 have to be followed. A minimal implementation in Tcl, which loads and uses a Ribbon from a DLL, is shown in Figure 4.

```
package require Tk
package require tkribbon
set ScriptDir [file dirname [file normalize [info script]]]
## The resources DLL containing the Ribbon...
set RibbonDLL $ScriptDir/ribbon1.dll
## Create a Ribbon widget:
set toolbar [tkribbon::ribbon .ribbon -command \
                 onRibbonUpdatePropertyDispatch]
## Load the resources DLL: must be executed at least once for each DLL...
$toolbar load_resources [file nativename $RibbonDLL]
## Load the Ribbon UI from the DLL...
$toolbar load_ui [file tail $RibbonDLL] RIBBON1_RIBBON
## Pack the widget at Toplevel top: ensure expanding is false!
pack $toolbar -side top -fill x -expand false
## Important: The Ribbon will not be drawn, unless the window is
## large enough!
wm geometry . 300x250 ;# The minimum size for showing the Ribbon!
## Events:
foreach event {Execute Preview CancelPreview CreateUICommand ViewChanged
               DestroyUICommand UpdateProperty} {
  bind $toolbar <<on$event>> [list onRibbonEventDispatch $event %d]
}
proc onRibbonUpdatePropertyDispatch {args} {
  puts "onRibbonUpdatePropertyDispatch: args: $args"
};# onRibbonUpdatePropertyDispatch
proc onRibbonEventDispatch {event args} {
  puts "onRibbonEventDispatch: event: $event, args: $args"
};# onRibbonEventDispatch
```

Figure 4: Loading and using a Ribbon from Tcl/Tk.

The result of running the code of Figure 4 is shown in Figure 5. It is interesting to note that elements missing a name in the XML markup specification of the Ribbon were assigned automatically generated names by the XML markup compiler UICC.exe. These elements (tab, group) can be assigned a name through commands: a command must be created for every element (tab, group) and assigned through the "CommandName" attribute to the corresponding XML tag.

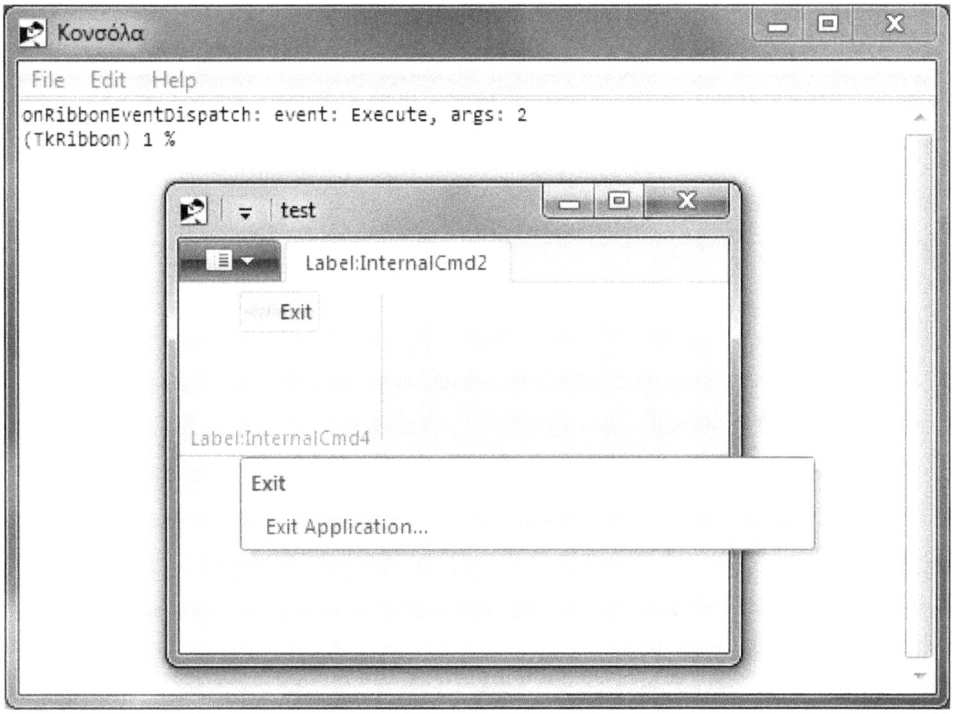

Figure 5: The loaded Ribbon

3 Interacting with a Ribbon

Interaction with an instance of a Ribbon is achieved through two means:

- A callback that can be registered to a widget through the "-command" widget option. This callback will be called each time the Ribbon wants to retrieve a control property from the application and is expected to return a suitable value, according to the control property requested.
- A virtual event of the form <<on*>>, delivered to the Ribbon widget. Events are not expected to return a value.

Controls inside a Ribbon UI are identified by an integer id, assigned by the XML markup compiler (UICC.exe). A mapping between the symbolic names and the assigned numeric ids can be found in the header file (.h) produced by UICC.exe, and is up to the application to map ids to symbolic names, if desired. The contents of "ribbon1.h" are shown in Figure 6.

```
// *****************************************************************************
// * This is an automatically generated header file for UI Element definition *
// * resource symbols and values. Please do not modify manually.               *
// *****************************************************************************
#pragma once

#define cmdExit 2
#define cmdExit_LabelTitle_RESID 60001
#define cmdExit_TooltipTitle_RESID 60002
```

```
#define cmdExit_TooltipDescription_RESID 60003
#define InternalCmd2_LabelTitle_RESID 60004
#define InternalCmd4_LabelTitle_RESID 60005
#define InternalCmd6_LabelTitle_RESID 60006
```

Figure 6: The contents of "ribbon.h", the header file produced by UICC.exe for the markup of our example.

3.1 The widget command callback

The widget callback is responsible for returning the value of various properties associated with controls. There are two main cases where the callback will be called: a) to retrieve properties not defined in the XML markup and b) to retrieve the value of properties that have been invalidated by the application (which is the primary means of changing any control property). The callback can be a Tcl command prefix, while two or 3 arguments will be appended before execution. A typical prototype of such a callback is:

```
proc callback {contol_id property_type {current_value {}} {...}
```

where:

- control_id is the numeric identifier of the control (integer),
- property_type is the type of the property whose value is requested (symbolic, one of UI_PKEY_Enabled, UI_PKEY_RepresentativeString, UI_PKEY_ItemsSource, UI_PKEY_Categories, UI_PKEY_SelectedItem, UI_PKEY_BooleanValue),
- and current_value is the current property value, if such a value exists, expressed in a type suitable for the current property type (i.e. a Boolean value for UI_PKEY_BooleanValue or a Tcl list for UI_PKEY_ItemsSource).

The callback may return an updated value according to the requested property or use "return –code break" to avoid setting a value. The property type UI_PKEY_Enabled is issued by the Ribbon UI in order to retrieve which Ribbon controls are enabled or disabled. Typically, it is called for all controls in a Ribbon, when the Ribbon is loaded, or a tab is raised for the first time. The return value is expected to be a Boolean Tcl value, which if true enables the control under question. The property type UI_PKEY_RepresentativeString is used in order to retrieve a "representative" string to be shown in a control that displays dynamic content (i.e. a combobox). The return value must be a string, whose dimensions will be used to obtain a size for the control under question. UI_PKEY_BooleanValue will be used when the Ribbon widget wants to retrieve the value of a checkbutton or radiobutton Ribbon control, with a Boolean value expected as the result.

The property types UI_PKEY_Categories, UI_PKEY_ItemsSource, UI_PKEY_SelectedItem are related to controls that display a collection of items, such as galleries and comboboxes. The items in collection objects can be separated into categories: the type UI_PKEY_Categories is used to retrieve these categories. The return value can be no categories (through "return –code break"), or a set of categories, specified as a Tcl list of one of the following formats:

```
[list [list categoryName1 ... categoryNameN] {} ]
[list [list categoryName1 ... categoryNameN] [list imageResourceId] ]
[list [list categoryName1 ... categoryNameN] [list imageResourceId1 ... imageResourceIdN]]
```

The three formats differ in the way an image is specified with a category. If no images are specified, no images will be used by the Ribbon widget when displaying the categories. If a single image is specified, this image will be displayed for all categories. Finally, an image can be specified for each category individually: in this case the length of the images list must match the length of the category names list. The image resource id can either be the empty string (no image), or an integer identifier of an image resource contained in the resource DLL of the Ribbon. It cannot be the name of a Tk image.

The property type UI_PKEY_ItemsSource works in a similar way, expecting a similar return value, as a Tcl list of 3 Tcl lists. This property type will be used by the Ribbon widget in order to retrieve the contents (items) of a control showing a collection (a gallery or a combobox). The return value of this property type is as follows:

```
[list [list item1 ... itemN] images-list categories-list ]
```

where:

- images-list can be either the empty list, the resource identifier (integer) of a single image (used for all items), or a list of resource identifiers, specifying an image for each item. In the latter case, the number of items must match the number of image identifiers, and
- categories-list can be either the empty list (when no categories have been specified), a single category name (used for all items), or a list of category names, specifying a category for each item. In the latter case, the number of items must match the number of category names.

Finally, the property type UI_PKEY_SelectedItem is used to retrieve the currently selected item. The return value must be the numeric index in the list of items, with the first index position starting at 0.

3.2 The virtual events bindings

All interaction between the Ribbon widget and the application is performed through Tk virtual events. (The only exception is when the Ribbon widget wants to retrieve the value of the property as described in the previous section.) TkRibbon delivers seven virtual Tk events to the Ribbon widget:

- <<onExecute>>: this event will be delivered when the user has executed a control, i.e. a button has been pressed or a combobox/gallery selection has been changed. The identifier of the Ribbon control can be retrieved through the "%d" code in the binding script. This is the most important event that must be processed.
- <<onPreview>>: this event will be delivered when the Ribbon wants to temporarily apply the current value of the control, in order to show a preview before the user actually applies the value. The identifier of the Ribbon control can be retrieved through the "%d" code in the binding script.
- <<onCancelPreview>>: this event will be delivered when the Ribbon wants to cancel (terminate) a previously requested preview. The identifier of the Ribbon control can be retrieved through the "%d" code in the binding script.
- <<onCreateUICommand>>: reserved for future use.
- <<onViewChanged>>: reserved for future use.
- <<onDestroyUICommand>>: reserved for future use.
- <<onUpdateProperty>>: reserved for future use.

3.3 Widget subcommands

The widget callback and the events are the primary means of the Ribbon framework to retrieve information from the application and notify events occurring in the Ribbon to the application. Communicating in the opposite direction (i.e. the application requesting something from the Ribbon framework) is performed through subcommands of a TkRibbon widget instance. Currently, the following subcommands are available:

- *pathname* **attach**: this subcommand attaches a Ribbon to the Tk Ribbon widget. It is an internal subcommand that is called by the TkRibbon library when a Ribbon Tk widget is created.

- *pathname* **load_resources native-dll-path**: this subcommand loads a resources (or other DLL) into the application. It is a wrapper for LoadLibrary() and requires a single argument, the native full path name of the DLL file to be loaded.
- *pathname* **load_ui module ribbon-name**: this subcommand loads the Ribbon UI named **ribbon-name** from the DLL handle **module**. The DLL handle is the name of the DLL without the path.
- *pathname* **get_property property-type control-id**: this subcommand returns the value of the specified property. **control-id** is the numeric (integer) identifier of a Ribbon control, and **property-type** must have one of the following values: UI_PKEY_Enabled, UI_PKEY_RepresentativeString, UI_PKEY_ItemsSource, UI_PKEY_Categories, UI_PKEY_SelectedItem, UI_PKEY_BooleanValue.
- *pathname* **set_property**: reserved for future use.
- *pathname* **invalidate_state state-property control-id**: invalidates the state aspect of the specified **state-property**, for control **control-id**. **state-property** must have one of the following values: UI_PKEY_BooleanValue, UI_PKEY_ContextAvailable, UI_PKEY_DecimalPlaces, UI_PKEY_DecimalValue, UI_PKEY_Enabled, UI_PKEY_FormatString, UI_PKEY_Increment, UI_PKEY_MaxValue, UI_PKEY_MinValue, UI_PKEY_Pinned, UI_PKEY_RecentItems, UI_PKEY_RepresentativeString, UI_PKEY_StringValue.
- *pathname* **invalidate_value property control-id**: invalidates the value aspect of the specified **property**, for control **control-id**. **property** must have one of the following values: UI_PKEY_BooleanValue, UI_PKEY_ContextAvailable, UI_PKEY_DecimalPlaces, UI_PKEY_DecimalValue, UI_PKEY_Enabled, UI_PKEY_FormatString, UI_PKEY_Increment, UI_PKEY_MaxValue, UI_PKEY_MinValue, UI_PKEY_Pinned, UI_PKEY_RecentItems, UI_PKEY_RepresentativeString, UI_PKEY_StringValue, UI_PKEY_Keytip, UI_PKEY_Label, UI_PKEY_LabelDescription, UI_PKEY_LargeHighContrastImage, UI_PKEY_LargeImage, UI_PKEY_SmallHighContrastImage, UI_PKEY_SmallImage, UI_PKEY_TooltipDescription, UI_PKEY_TooltipTitle, UI_PKEY_Minimized, UI_PKEY_QuickAccessToolbarDock, UI_PKEY_Viewable, UI_PKEY_GlobalBackgroundColor, UI_PKEY_GlobalHighlightColor, UI_PKEY_GlobalTextColor.
- *pathname* **invalidate_property property control-id**: invalidates the property aspect of the specified **property-type**, for control **control-id**. For valid **property** values, please see subcommand **invalidate_value**.
- *pathname* **invalidate_all property control-id**: invalidates all aspects of the specified **property**, for control **control-id**. For valid **property** values, please see subcommand **invalidate_value**.

4 Conclusions

This paper presented TkRibbon, a Tcl/Tk extension written in C++ which allows the use of the Windows Ribbon Framework from Tcl/Tk. Currently, the TkRibbon extension is in alpha state, while the first public release is pending. Despite its alpha state, many features of the Ribbon framework are already supported, while more features are expected to be supported until the first stable release. TkRibbon is hosted at SourceForge, and can be found at http://sourceforge.net/projects/tkribbon/.

A large part of this document has been devoted on how to use the TkRibbon extension in order to use a Ribbon contained inside a DLL, followed by a brief description of the available callbacks, events and widget subcommands. However, a basic understanding of how the Windows Ribbon Framework operates is required in order to understand some the available functionality, especially regarding the various property values.

The `diagram` Package

Andreas Kupries ActiveState Software Inc. 409 Granville Vancouver, BC CA
andreask@ActiveState.com

ABSTRACT

This is a small introduction to the `diagram` Package, a `Tcl` [6] based diagramming language and package inspired by Brian Kernighan's `pic` [1] processor. After a brief history and examples of its use we look into the internals and possibly interesting directions for the future.

1. OVERVIEW

`diagram is` a package for the easy construction of diagrams (sic), i.e. 2D vector graphics, on a `Tk` [7] canvas or other API compatible object. As such it is not a replacement for canvas, but a layer on top which makes it easier to use by abstracting away the minutiae of handling coordinates to position and size the drawn elements. The user can concentrate on the content of the diagram instead.

This is similar to Brian Kernighan's `pic` [1] language for `troff` [2], which is the spiritual ancestor of this package.

The remainder of this paper is structured as follows: In the next chapter an anecdotal overview of the history of this package is provided, followed by a chapter showing examples of the language with their results. After that, in chapter 4, a general overview of its design, implementation, and features is given. Lastly chapter 5 discusses possible applications and future directions for the package.

2. HISTORY

`diagram's` genesis is a long one, although with nothing much happening for long stretches of time.

The original idea was to have a package or tool with which to specify diagrams in writing, instead of having to click through an endless series of dialog boxes for object properties and the like. I had already played with Brian Kernighan's `pic` [1] in the past and wanted something like that. No dealing with absolute coordinates and the pain of minutely positioning objects to get the right alignment.

Nothing came of that for a long time, except that Arjen Markus got infected by the bug and wrote a small proof of concept. He put it up on the wiki first [3], and later put the code into `tklib` [8]. Then after the hassle I had with making the diagrams for last year's paper [14], struggling with the applications `dia and InkScape I` finally had enough motivation to put something together which went beyond a proof of concept.

First I based my work on Arjen's code, but abandoned it because the interface did not feel very smooth or Tclish. Then I tried to to work something out using the Tcllib Word Interpreter package [12], which forced a forthish style. That code became pretty much unusable due to escalating complexity of the internals while trying to fit in vector and point arithmetic. At last I went back to the basic roots of Arjen's code, i.e. using Tcl as the interpreter, and commands as the API. The main trick which got added in this iteration was the use of `namespace unknown handlers` to provide various pseudo-commands, which made the vector arithmetic and other things easy to write without requiring an infinite family of commands.

This third iteration became the code described here, also replacing the original proof of concept in `tklib` [8].

3. EXAMPLES

A few examples of what can be done with `diagram,` from the very trivial to the complex.

The basic shapes can be seen in figure 1.

Figure 2 demonstrates drawing of splines.

Figure 3 shows how most positioning can be done relative to previous elements, without using any coordinates at all.

Tw more examples of such relative positioning are seen in the figures 4 and 5 which place things on the line between two points and at the intersection of 2 lines.

At last a larger example in figure 6, without the diagram description.

4. DESIGN & IMPLEMENTATION

The inner structure of `diagram,` i.e. the set of internal packages and their dependencies can be seen in figure 7. The main division is between a core managing the general drawing state and a package implementing the basic shapes seen in figure 1. The drawing state handled by the core is further split into the processing of element attributes, a database of named directions, i.e. angles, a database of the drawn elements, and the state of the automatic element layout. A supporting package provides commands to construct points and vectors and perform vector arithmetic on them. This is partially a repackaging of `math::geometry,` mainly adding type-tags differentiating absolute and relative coordinates.

Permission to make digital or hard copies of all or part of this work for personal or classroom use is granted without fee provided that copies are not made or distributed for profit or commercial advantage and that copies bear this notice and the full citation on the first page. To copy otherwise, to republish, to post on servers or to redistribute to lists, requires prior specific permission and/or a fee.
Tcl '2010 Oakbrook Terrace/Chicago, IL, USA

```
# -*- tcl -*- tcl.tk//DSL diagram//EN//1.0
proc showcorners {e corners} {
    foreach {c anchor text} $corners {
        circle radius 2 at [$e $c] \
            color red text $text \
            anchor $anchor
    }
}

block {
    down
    block {
        spline right \
            then down [1 cm] left \
            then right
    }
    text {The spline curve ...}
}
move
block {
    down
    block {
        line dashed                  right \
            then down [1 cm] left then right
        spline from [last line start] right \
            then down [1 cm] left then right
        showcorners [last line] {
            1 ne 1  2 nw 2  3 se 3  4 sw 4
        }
    }
    text {... with tangents displayed}
}
```

Figure 2: Drawing of splines

At the language level the public drawing commands are defined in an internal namespace for the lightweight encapsulation of the system's overall configuration. This is modeled after `pic` [1], using variables to hold the default values for various lengths and other attribute values. The core mostly provides the commands to declare such variables, the associated attributes, etc. and only declares a very small set of the language itself. The large majority of the drawing language is then provided by the package for the basic shapes.

Another reason for using a namespace was the ability to implement the special forms of the language (see table 1) via a namespace-specific unknown handler, allowing them for the language without polluting the global namespace and possibly affecting other parts of the application the package is used in.

Encapsulation in a full-blown safe interpreter was considered for the implementation, but ruled out as too restrictive and possibly a premature optimization. As the diagram application package shows, encapsulation in a safe interpreter can be added after the fact, where needed. So this is not something required for the implementation. With the current setup of keeping everything in a namespace a diagram specification is able to access the global and other namespaces should this is needed and.or allowed for a particular application.

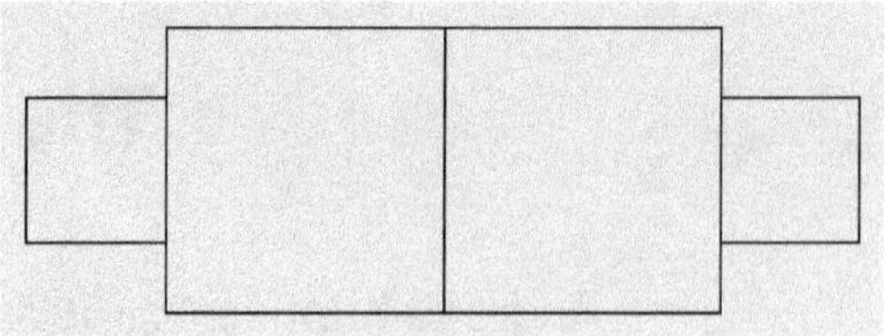

```
# -*- tcl -*- tcl.tk//DSL diagram//EN//1.0

box
box width [4 cm] height [4 cm]
box same
box
```

Figure 3: Relative positioning

5. FUTURE DIRECTIONS

To conclude this document some thoughts on the future of `diagram`, i.e in which directions we can go with it.

1. The package has a variety of possibilities for extension, allowing the implementation of higher DSLs for specific types of diagrams, like mathematical formulas, chemical structures, or visual record descriptions (data types, file formats, ...).

    (a) Diagrams can define their own commands for custom aggregation of shapes or to create new shapes.

    (b) The package's extension APIs enable the declaration of new attributes, elements (shapes), named angles, and commands, the latter either like procedures, or as aliases to to command prefixes. They also allow the registration of command prefixes to call when encountering unknown attributes, enabling special forms for attribute specification.

2. The `dia application` written to work on top of the package[1] currently uses the packages `canvas::snap` [9] and `Tkimg` [5] to produce raster images from descriptions, and `canvas::mvg` [10] to generate `ImageMagick` [16]'s MVG vector format.

    Obviously, any extension of `Tkimg` [5] will automatically extend the number of formats supported by diagram.

    There is also a package, hidden in the `Coccinella` [15] chat application, to dump the contents of a canvas widget to the SVG format. This has not been integrated yet.

3. Both of the converters to vector formats work by using canvas' introspection abilites to determine the items to convert, and their attributes. This has the disadvantage of requiring a canvas widget, therefore Tk, therefore X11.

    So, another direction would be the creation of object classes which are API compatible to canvas, but whose machinery does not require X11. Karl Lehenbauer's `tcl.gd` [17] comes to mind, for example.

[1] Do not confuse it with the X11 based drawing application I mentioned in chapter 2

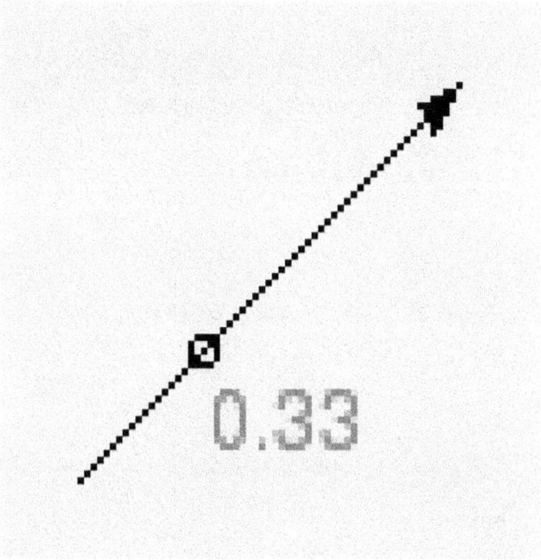


```
# -*- tcl -*- tcl.tk//DSL diagram//EN//1.0

arrow up right
circle radius 2 \
    at [0.33 between \
            [last arrow start] \
            [last arrow end]] \
    text 0.33 anchor nw textcolor red
```

Figure 4: Interpolated positioning

4. As **diagram is** mainly a package, it can be integrated whereever simple 2D vector graphics are required. One example I hope to pursue is integraqtion within the doctools [13], to give writers of manpages access to graphics without having them to leave the environment.

APPENDIX

A. REFERENCES

[1] Brian Kernighan, pic. http://www.troff.org/papers.html

[2] troff http://www.troff.org/

[3] Arjen Markus. Drawing diagrams. http://wiki.tcl.tk/13434

[4] Wolf-Dieter Busch, canvas2mvg. http://wiki.tcl.tk/26859

[5] Jan Nijtmans, tkImg. https://sourceforge.net/projects/tkimg/

[6] Various, Tcl. https://tcl.sourceforge.net

[7] Various, Tk. https://tcl.sourceforge.net

[8] Various, Tklib. https://sourceforge.net/projects/tcllib/

[9] Various, canvas::snap. https://sourceforge.net/projects/tcllib/

[10] Various, canvas::mvg. https://sourceforge.net/projects/tcllib/

[11] Various, Tcllib. https://sourceforge.net/projects/tcllib/

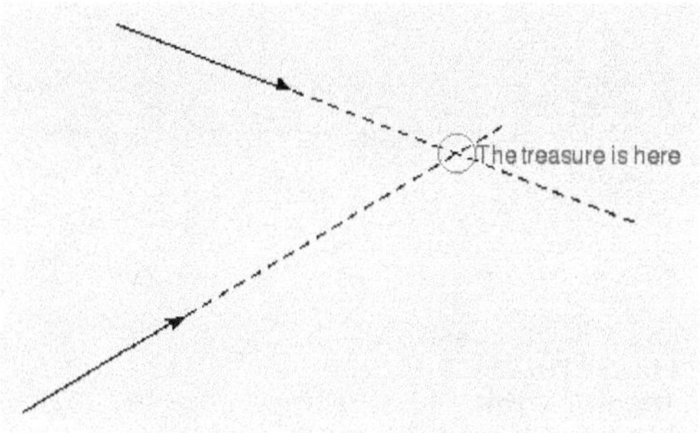


```
# -*- tcl -*- tcl.tk//DSL diagram//EN//1.0

proc extend {s e} {
    line dashed from [$e end] \
        to [$s between [$e start] [$e end]]
}

proc dot {p anchor text} {
    circle radius 10 at $p color red
    text with w at [last circle e] \
        text $text anchor $anchor \
        textcolor blue
}

set A [arrow from [ 0    0] to [by 100 -20]]
extend 3 $A

set B [arrow from [-50 200] to [by 100  30]]
extend 3 $B

dot [intersect $A $B] w {The treasure is here}
```

Figure 5: Computing intersections

[12] Various, Word Interpreter. https://sourceforge.net/projects/tcllib/

[13] Various, Documentation Tools. https://sourceforge.net/projects/tcllib/

[14] Andreas Kupries, Reflected And Transformed Channels, Tcl 2009, Portland. http://www.tclcommunityassociation.org/wub/proceedings/Proceedings-2009.html

[15] Various, Coccinella. http://wiki.tcl.tk/4005

[16] Various, ImageMagick. http://wiki.tcl.tk/12849, http://www.imagemagick.org/

[17] Karl Lehenbauer, tcl.gd. http://code.google.com/p/flightaware-tcltools/

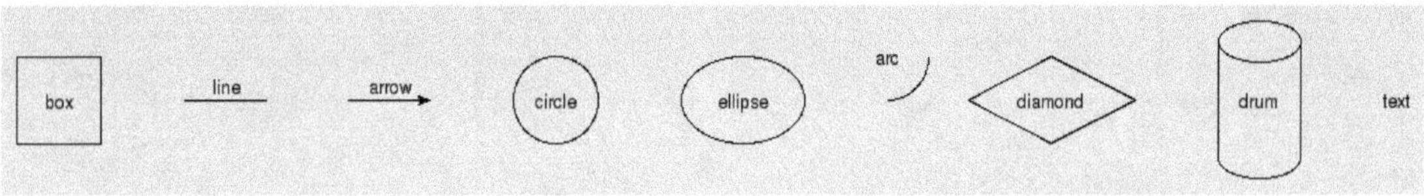


```
# -*- tcl -*- tcl.tk//DSL diagram//EN//1.0

box "box" ; move
line "line" "" ; move
arrow "arrow" "" ; move
circle "circle" ; move
ellipse "ellipse" width [3 cm] ; move
group { arc "arc" } ; move
diamond "diamond" height [2 cm] ; move
drum "drum" ; move
text text "text"
```

Figure 1: The basic shapes

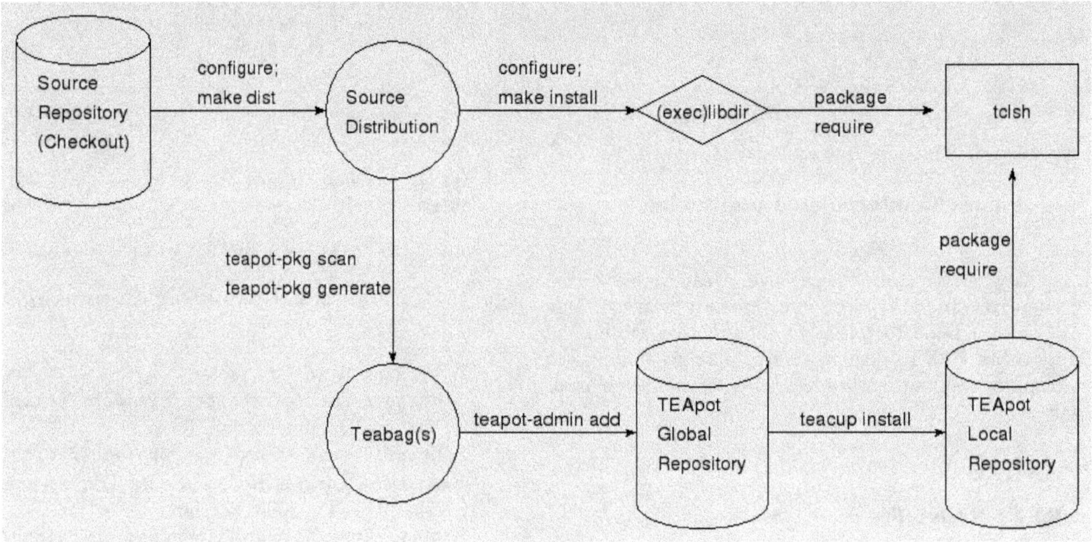

Figure 6: Teapot Dataflow

Syntax	Meaning
named-direction	Tell the layout engine to follow this direction from now on as default for new elements.
number cm|mm|inch|point	Return pixel equivalent for the length. This uses `tk scaling` as basis for the conversion.
number number	Construct an absolute location.
number between *point point*	Construct point by linearly interpolating between two others.
point by *distance direction*	Construct point by moving from the given point a certain distance in the specified direction.
point +|- *point*	Vector arithmetic on two points.
nth shape?corner? *nth* last *shape?corner?* last *shape?corner?* *nth* last ?*corner?* last ?*corner?*	Access to named locations in previously drawn elements.
*element?corner...??*names *pattern?*	Access to named locations in elements.

Table 1: Special command forms

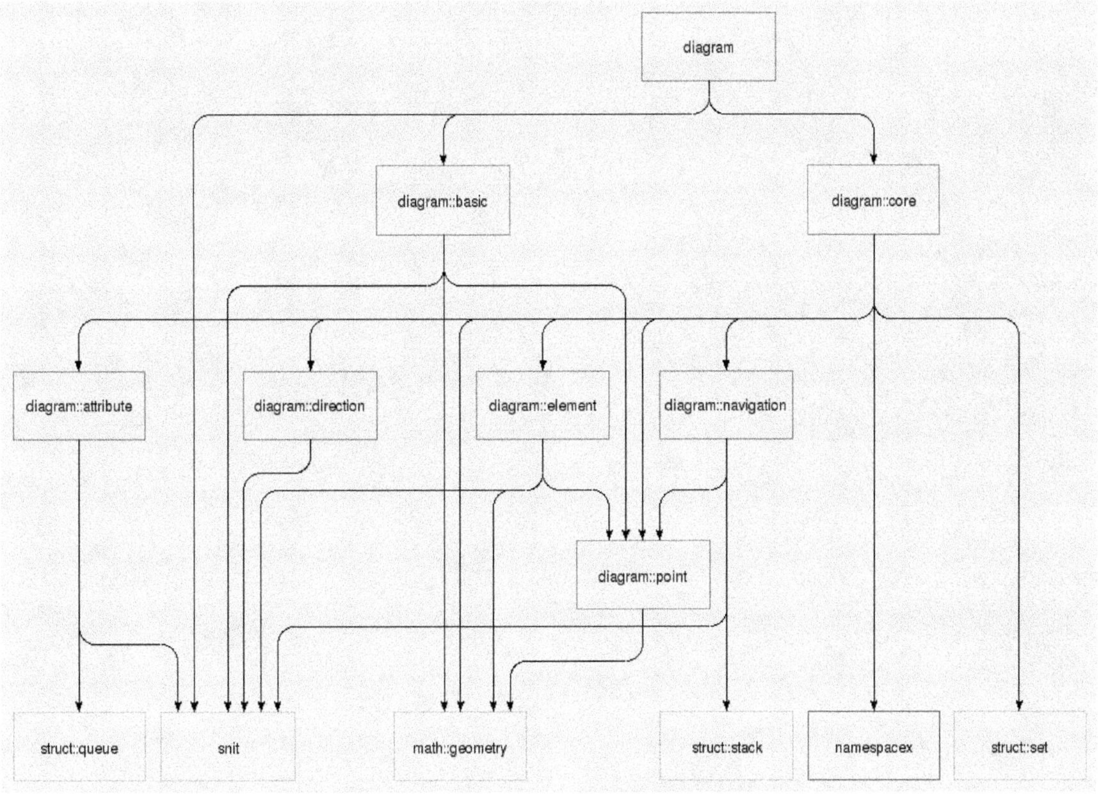

Figure 7: diagram package and its dependencies

17th ANNUAL TCL/TK 2010 CONFERENCE
Chicago (USA)
11-15 October

TCL and the Community

Thu October 14, 2010 09:00-10:45

TclA Publications

Tcl/GSoC 2010

Andreas Kupries ActiveState Software Inc. 409 Granville Vancouver, BC CA
andreask@ActiveState.com

ABSTRACT

As in previous years the Tcl Community took again part in Google's Summer Of Code[1], under the auspices of the Tcl Community Association[2].

1. OVERVIEW

Google's Summer Of Code[1] (short: GSoC) is a global program funded and operated by Google that offers student developers stipends to write code for various open source software projects. The Tcl Community participated again this year, for the third time in a row. As in previous years this participation was managed by the Tcl Community Association[2] (short: TCA) as the mentoring organization, the same organization which runs the US Tcl Conferences.

The main entrypoint to the program for the community itself can be found on the Tcler's Wiki [4].

2. PAST

Starting in 2007, we applied three times, and were accepted two times, with only our very first application not getting accepted by Google. This year was our fourth application and third participation.

Through negotiations by previous program administrators we usually got just shy of 10 slots for our projects[4], with our usual argument the fact that the Tcl Community Association[2] acts as an umbrella for smaller organizations with Tcl related projects. An example for this is the aMSN chat client[3]. The full statistics for the past years[5] are shown in table 1 below.

	2006	2007	2008	2009
Students	630	950	1125	1000
Organizations	102	>130	175	150
Average	6.18	<7.31	6.44	6.66
Tcl	-	-	9	9

Table 1: Statistics of past four years

Permission to make digital or hard copies of all or part of this work for personal or classroom use is granted without fee provided that copies are not made or distributed for profit or commercial advantage and that copies bear this notice and the full citation on the first page. To copy otherwise, to republish, to post on servers or to redistribute to lists, requires prior specific permission and/or a fee.
Tcl '2010 Oakbrook Terrace/Chicago, IL, USA
.

3. PRESENT

Matthew Burke[8], our program administrator of the past years served in that capacity this year as well, with me as backup.

In the slot allocation game/roulette we got seven slots, a loss of two compared to previous years. We considered this to be quite higher than the average, because of Google originally dialing down the total number of slots to 950 in general. In the final statistics[5] we are only average however, as can be seen in table 2 below.

	2010
Students	1026
Organizations	150
Average	6.84
Tcl	7

Table 2: Final statistics for 2010

Our projects for this year are listed in table 3 [1] on the next page, with larger descriptions in the upcoming sections The overall timeline we followed is shown in table 4.

3.1 Base JIT compiler for Tcl

[10] by Guilherme Goncalves
Mentor: Donal Fellows

This project aimed to create a base JIT compiler for the Tcl core, translating bytecodes to (x86) machine code on demand in order to improve the language's performance.

After GSoC's ending, the project still requires several future improvements to be able to land in the Tcl core or be usable in the wild. The first two ideas on the list are: proper register allocation and a finer grained intermediate representation (IR). Currently, the encoding of a very simplified form of the `incr` command requires 51 x86 opcodes, with the current IR this is all done inside a single clause of a switch statement. The idea is to transform this mid-level IR to a lower level one that is closer to a form of a generic-RISC architecture, and then develop and run instruction selection on it. Currently, only toy programs can be tested given the ad-hoc, or inexistent, register allocator, so this is another priority. This second "future" idea is already being developed. Another idea involves the application of another kind of IR, the SSA. It has been used by some known projects: LLVM [18], gcc [19], Jalapeño (or Jikes RVM) [20] and is mentioned as a way to allow some optimizations[21] to take

[1]The same table can also be found at[9]

Student	Project	Mentor
Michael Aram	SCORM Compliant Run-Time Environment for OpenACS	Gustaf Neumann
Andrew Shadoura	OpenStreetMap package and editor in Tcl/Tk	Matthew Burke
Ewa Leszczynska	Themed Tk on Unix	Jeff Hobbs
Ozgur Dogan Ugurlu	Tcl state machine back-end module for XMLVM	Kevin Kenny
Eduardo Santos	OpenACS Abstraction Layer	Colin McCormack
Guilherme Goncalves	Base JIT compiler for Tcl	Donal Fellows
Paraskevi Nikolaidou	MSNP2P refactoring for aMSN	Youness Alaoui

Table 3: 2010 Projects, Students, and Mentors

	February 8	Program announced.
Organizations	March 8	Organization application window opens.
	March 12	Deadline for organization applications.
	March 13-17	Submission review.
	March 18	Publication of accepted organizations.
Students	March 18-29	Discussion of ideas between students and organizations.
	March 29	Student application wind opens.
	April 9	Deadline for student applications.
	April 10-21	Organizations rank and review student applications.
	April 21	Ranking/scoring deadline. Mentor sign-up deadline.
	April 26	Publication of accepted students.
Coding		Community bonding sudents to mentors.
	May 24	Coding period starts.
	July 12-16	Mid-term evaluations.
	August 9	Soft-end of coding. Scrub code, test, document.
	August 16	Hard end of coding period.
Post-Mortem	August 16-20	Final evaluations.
	August 23	Final results announced.
	August 30	Students can begin submitting the require code samples.
	October 23-24	Mentor Summit at Google.

Table 4: 2010 Timeline

place in an efficient manner. Other important improvement is allowing the compilation of non-leaf procedures, which requires a study between the interaction of the JIT compiler and the Tcl VM in order to properly manage the VM state.

3.2 MSNP2P refactoring for aMSN

[11] by Paraskevi Nikolaidou
Mentor: Youness Alaoui

Continuing the series of aMSN projects done in previous summers, this year the current MSNP2P implementation was rewritten to use `snit`[17]. This was done to overcome the problems with the current code base, which was complicated, with code scattered over different files and mixing several different functionalities in the same procedure.

As a bit of background, MSNP2P is the protocol used for P2P data transfers, taking care of webcam video, file transfers, etc.

This rewrite of the current code base will also help with implementing MSNP2Pv2, which is the version used in the latest builds of Windows Live Messenger and supports concurrent login from different locations. Implementing MSNP2P-v2 will in turn enable full support of protocol version 18 and audio/video calls.

3.3 OpenACS Abstraction Layer

[12] by Eduardo Santos
Mentor: Colin McCormack

The basic idea behind this project was to rewrite the server integration of the OpenACS' web framework to use Colin's Wub web server packages, extending OpenACS' portability.

3.4 OpenStreetMap package and editor

[13] by Andrew Shadoura
Mentor: Matthew Burke

A set of packages for the convenient handling OpenStreetMap data was created, both for its storage and rendering into a Tk canvas. On top of that a visual editor for OpenStreetMap data was made, using Tk for the interface and allowing the creation and editing of ways and tags.

Future work may include expansion of the editor's modular approach into a full plugin system.

3.5 SCORM Compliant Run-Time Environment for OpenACS

[14] by Michael Aram
Mentor: Gustaf Neumann

This was a follow-up project to last year's successful SCORM project, which focused on input, export, and presentation of SCORM packages. During the last project it turned out that implementing the runtime environment (RTE) is a relatively big task. As the RTE implemented only the most basic RTE-API functions it was therefore only capable of importing simple packages.

This year's project overcame these limitations, implementing a fully standard conformant RTE according to the minimal compliance level defined by ADL. In future subsequent projects reaching even higher compliance levels, which enable further SCORM features, could be a sensible goal. Also, incorporating newer versions of the SCORM or alternative packaging standards (e.g. SCORM 2004, IMS CC) should be considered.

3.6 Tcl state machine back-end module for XMLVM

[15] by Ozgur Dogan Ugurlu Mentor: Kevin Kenny

Originally planned was the creation of a back-end for the XMLVM bytecode cross-compiler, enabling all languagues producing JVM or .Net bytecodes to be translated to and executed by Tcl.

This project mutated over the summer and became a "Tcl Bytecode Assembler" instead, extending the Tcl core with a command taking a textual description of Tcl bytecodes and creating the executable internal representation.

3.7 Themed Tk on Unix

[16] by Ewa Leszczynska Mentor: Jeff Hobbs

This project first and foremost updated the Qt and Gtk bindings for Themed Tk to work with the latest versions of their respective GUI toolkits. Additionally some shortcomings and general code quality issues in the previous versions of those packages were addressed.

4. FUTURE

For a mentoring organization Google's Summer Of Code[1] is pretty much a year-round operation. Simply look back at the timeline (Table 4 on the previous page).

Next up in this cycle is starting the preparations for 2011, i.e., updating our application[6], restarting the collection of project ideas, and reaching out to prospective students and mentors in general. The last point is one of the more important things to do, not only for us as a mentoring organization, but for the Tcl community at large too, to make a general effort of spreading awareness of Tcl and its community as a viable (and fun) scripting language which doesn't has to hide.

APPENDIX

A. REFERENCES

[1] Google, GSoC.
`http://socghop.appspot.com/`

[2] Tcl Community Association.
`http://www.tclcommunityassociation.org/`

[3] aMSN.
`http://www.amsn-project.net/`,
`http://wiki.tcl.tk/12783`

[4] Google Summer Of Code on Tcl'ers Wiki.
`http://wiki.tcl.tk/25801`

[5] GSoC Statistics. `http://code.google.com/p/google-summer-of-code/wiki/ProgramStatistics`

[6] Tcl Org Application 2010.
`http://wiki.tcl.tk/25802`

[7] Andreas Kupries.
`http://wiki.tcl.tk/26`

[8] Matthew Burke.
`http://www.seas.gwu.edu/~mmburke/`

[9] GSoC 2010 Executed Projects.
`http://wiki.tcl.tk/26114`

[10] Base JIT Compiler, Guilherme Goncalves.
`http://code.google.com/p/tcljit`

[11] MSNP2P refactoring for aMSN, Paraskevi Nikolaidou.
`http://www.amsn-project.net/`

[12] OpenACS Abstraction Layer, Eduardo Santos.
`http://code.google.com/p/portable-nsd/`

[13] OSM/Tk, Andrew Shadoura.
`http://bitbucket.org/andrew_shadoura/tcl-osm/`

[14] SCORM, Michael Aram.
`http://wiki.tcl.tk/26120`

[15] Tcl ByteCode Assembler, Ozgur Dogan Ugurlu.
`http://wiki.tcl.tk/26123`

[16] Themed Tk on Unix, Ewa Leszczynska.
`http://hefka.pl:1027/index`,
`http://github.com/aweelka/`,
`http://wiki.tcl.tk/26122`

[17] Snit's Not IncrTcl. Will Duquette.
`http://wiki.tcl.tk/3963`

[18] LLVM: A Compilation Framework for Lifelong Program Analysis & Transformation, Chris Lattner and Vikram Adve. CGO '04: Proceedings of the international symposium on Code generation and optimization, 2004, ISBN 0-7695-2102-9, page 75, IEEE Computer Society

[19] GNU Compiler Collection Internals – SSA, Free Software Foundation.
`http://gcc.gnu.org/onlinedocs/gccint/SSA.html`

[20] The Jalapeño virtual machine, B. Alpern and C. R. Attanasio and others. IBM Syst. J. vol 39.1, 2000, ISSN 0018-8670, pages 211 – 238, IBM Corp.

[21] Efficiently Computing Static Single Assignment Form and the Control Dependence Graph, Ron Cytron and Jeanne Ferrante and Barry K. Rosen and Mark N. Wegman. ACM Transactions on Programming Languages and Systems vol 13.4, 1991, pages 451 – 490.

17th ANNUAL TCL/TK CONFERENCE 2010
Chicago (USA)
11-15 October

Meta Programming

Thu October 14, 2010 11:15-13:00

TclA Publications

Accelerating Tk Development with Wize 3.1

Peter MacDonald

PDQ Interfaces Inc.

September 14, 2010

1. Introduction

If Tk is to realize growing adoption, it must offer developers a compelling reason to use it. It may seem ironic, but a key issue limiting Tk's growth is complexity. Simple demos may be straightforward, but scaling up to a full-blown applications is a different matter.

Wize attempts to reduce complexity by offering a development environment that lets programmers do more, with less, by providing:

- Code and data validation.
- Abstract GUI creation (layouts, scrollbars, tooltips, bindings, etc).
- Powerful widgets (TreeView, Tabset and shaped widgets).
- Hierarchical Tcl data (Tree).
- A common base of support components.

Wize is built on Tcl/Tk 8.5.9 and Blt 2.5, both of which have been modified extensively. The Wize binary is complemented with a package of Tcl support code (Mod/Gui) that backfills commonly required functionality. Mod deals with everything from tooltips and image management, to debugging, packaging and deployment.

2. Validation

Wize validation involves checking Tcl code for syntax, call arguments and types when run with:

```
wize -Wall script.tcl
```

Wizes validation capabilities are based on **extern** and **type** definitions which provides declarations for all built-ins, eg:

```
extern incr {varName {amount 1}} {Int var Int} I "Increment the value of a variable"
extern source {file args} {. {vopts ?-encoding type?} .} I "Evaluate a file or resource as a Tcl script"
```

2.1 Checking Performed

Validation performs the following checks:

- All code in proc bodies is compiled, including nested switch/if/while blocks.
- Syntax errors are detected, eg. unbalanced braces and quotes.
- Commands called without a preceding proc definition or extern.
- Parameters to static calls are checked for count (and possibly types).
- Virtually all calls to **builtin commands** are validated
- Detection of missing upvar, variable or global statements.
- Data access to all static elements in _ array are checked for pre-initialization.
- A **Declare** statement to specify other arrays to check.
- Any extern argument of **type** code or 'expr is compiled.

2.2 How Tcl is Validated

Validation in Tcl is challenging because the language is highly dynamic. For example, standard Tcl does not normally compile a proc until it is first invoked. Even then, the sub-eval blocks such as while, if and switch are not compiled until they themselves are actually executed.

While this lazy evaluation is a plus in production, it makes detecting problems during development difficult.

Wize overcomes this by providing the option -Wall to forces Tcl code to compile as it is being sourced. Then, in the resulting compilation phase, extensive checks are performed to identify problems.

Errors or warnings from checking are output in a form similar to gcc warning messages.

2.3 How Tk is Validated

Validation of Tk code presents a additional challenges because Tk widgets are normally created as **object-commands**. Sub-commands are then accessed via the object/widget-path. Eg:

```
text .t
.t insert end "ABC"
.t delete 1.1
```

Unfortunately, the use of object/path presents the compile phase with no effective way to perform checking. Maintaining such code afterwards is also problematic. Lastly, text-editors can not effectively provide command completion for Tk calls. This last is truly annoying as Tk widgets are responsible for the vast majority of all command options in Tcl.
To address this, Wize refactors the **Tk widgets** to create a Module command-namespace per widget in ::Tk. Eg:

```
namespace eval ::Tk::Text {
    namespace ensemble create; # ...
    extern insert {win pos str args} I
    extern delete {win pos args} I
    # ...
}
# note: above ensembles get imported from ::Tk to ::
Text new .t
Text insert .t end "ABC"
Text delete .t 1.1
```

Code written in this way can be checked be Wize, and it allows editors (like **Ted**) to support argument completion.

2.4 Array Validation

Elements in arrays can be validated by using Declare. This will report use of any element not initialized, eg.

```
variable pc
Declare pc Array

array set pc { a 1 b 2}

proc foo {args} {
    variable pc
    set pc(c) 1;  # Warns that "c" is uninitialized.
}
```

2.5 Tod Validation

Tod is a simple object extension used in Gui. Wize checks array references to $() for elements not initialized in _, eg.

```
namespace eval ::foo {
  variable _
  array set _ { a 1 b 2 }

  proc sub {_ args} {
    upvar $_ {}
    set (c) $(b);  # Warning is issued for var 'c' undefined.
    $_ bar 1;      # Warning issued for proc 'bar' undefined.
    $_ sub
  }

  # ...
}
```

Note that the dispatch call (eg. bar) is also validated.

---

3. An Introduction to Gui

Gui simplifies the creation of resilient Tk user interfaces using a model similar to that of HTML Markup/CSS/Javascript:

HTML	GUI
Markup	*Layout* a nested Tcl list with tags based on Tk class names
CSS	*Styles* a definition language based on pattern matching rules.
Javascript	*Tcl* contained in the **script** tag.

3.1 Layout

A GUI layout specifies a hierarchical set of tags containing attributes and content-values. Tags are usually just the Tk class name. After the tag can be a +/-: the + flag is used to indicate a child sub-tree. Lastly are the attributes to modify the layout, such as pack positioning and scroll-bars.

Here is a simple GUI layout:

```
{Toplevel + -title "Simple Editor"} {
    {Text - -pos * -scroll *} {}
    {Frame + -pos _ -subpos l} {
        Button Save
        Button Load
        Button Quit
        {Entry - -id status -pos *l} {}
    }
}
```

3.2 Styles

Styles are used in a layout to abstract the use of Tk options such as colors, fonts and images. This avoids hard-coding options which is convenient in small applications, but in larger applications tends to lead to excess complexity. Styles also apply options fault tolerantly such that errors become warnings that are seen only at development time (ie. with -Wall).

```
{Toplevel + -title "Simple Editor"} {

    {style} {
        Button  { -bg DarkKhaki }
        .save   { -bg DarkGreen }
```

```
        .txtwin { -bg Khaki }
        Entry.status { -bg LightGray -state disabled }
        Toplevel {
          @defimages { bled greenball }
        }
        .bsave { -image ^bled -compound left }
    }

    {Text - -id txtwin -pos * -scroll *} {}
    {Frame + -pos _ -subpos l} {
        {Button - -id save -id bsave} Save
        Button Load
        Button Quit
        {Entry - -id status -pos *l} {}
    }
}
```

In a style definition, the dot-prefix patterns will match -id attribute names, while title-case patterns will match tags/widget-class names.

Note that we can define images once in the Toplevel using @deficons and then apply them with image lookups using^.

3.3 Script

Unless prototyping is the end goal, an application usually requires at least some code. This is added with a script tag. Using an -id attribute will setup variables to dereference widgets from within code

- (w,NAME) - The widget.
- (v,NAME) - The -variable or -textvariable.

eg.

```
{script} {
    array set _ { file "" }

    proc Quit {_} { ::Delete $_ }

    proc Load {_} {
        upvar $_ {}
        set fn [tk_getOpenFile]
        if {$fn == ""} return
        Text delete $(w,txtwin) 1.0 end
        Text insert $(w,txtwin) end [*fread $fn]
        set (file) $fn
        set (v,status) "[mc {Loaded file}]: $(file)"
```

```
    }

    proc Save {_} {
        upvar $_ {}
        if {$(file) == ""} { set (file) [tk_getOpenFile] }
        if {$(file) == ""} return
        *fwrite $(file) [Text get $(w,txtwin) 1.0 end]
        set (v,status) "[mc {Saved file}]: $(file)"
    }
}

{Toplevel + -title "Simple Editor"} {
    {Text - -id txtwin -pos * -scroll *} {}
    {Frame + -pos _ -subpos l} {
        Button Save
        Button Load
        Button Quit
        {Entry - -id status -pos *l} {}
    }
}
```

Note that in the above Tk code is written using the widget class command (.ie Text). This is the mechanisim which allows code to be **validated**. Note also the use of **Tod** $_, in providing simple object-like functionality..

3.4 Dialogs and Menus

An application can define dialogs using Toplevel and Menu.

```
{Toplevel + -id tlinput -ns Input} {
    {Entry - -pos _} {}
    Button Ok
}

{Menu + -label Main} {
    {menu + -label File} { x Open x Save }
    {menu + -label Edit} { x Copy x Paste }
}

{Menu + -id mpop -label IO} {
    x Read
    x Write
}
{Toplevel +} {
    style {
        .txt {
            @bind { <Control-g> !tlinput <3> !mpop }
        }
```

```
    }
    {Text - -pos * -id txt } {}
}
```

The following rules apply:

- The first defined Toplevel with no id or the id main will be the main window.
- The first defined Menu with no id or an id of mainmenu will be used as the toplevel menu.

The main Toplevel can use a @bind style to trigger opening Dialogs or Menus. (or use Tk::gui::toplevel from the program).

4. GUILD - the GUI Layout Designer

Guild is a **GUI** layout editor for .gui files.
While Gui files can easily be hand edited, it's not a convenient way to learn which attributes are available for which tags. Guild custom tree editor uses introspection to display which attributes are available for a tag.

Here is a screenshot of Guild in action:

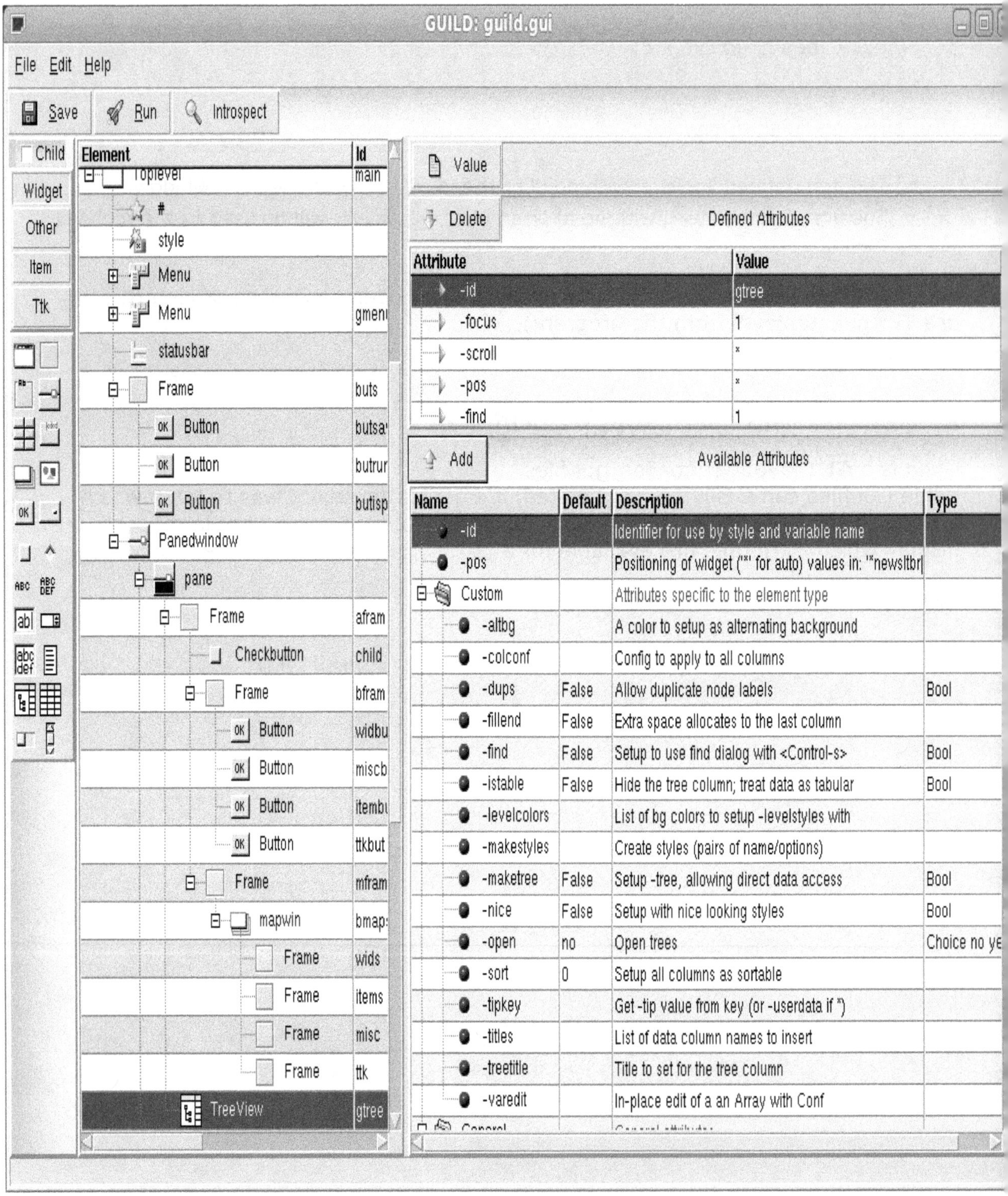
GUILD: guild.gui
File Edit Help
Save
Run
Introspect
Child
Widget
Other
Item
Ttk
Element
Id
Toplevel
main
#
style
Menu
Menu
gmenu
statusbar
Frame
buts
Button
butsa
Button
butru
Button
butisp
Panedwindow
pane
Frame
afram
Checkbutton
child
Frame
bfram
Button
widbu
Button
miscb
Button
itembu
Button
ttkbut
Frame
mfram
mapwin
bmap
Frame
wids
Frame
items
Frame
misc
Frame
ttk
TreeView
gtree
Value
Delete
Defined Attributes
Attribute
Value
-id
gtree
-focus
1
-scroll
-pos
-find
1
Add
Available Attributes
Name
Default
Description
Type
-id
Identifier for use by style and variable name
-pos
Positioning of widget ("*" for auto) values in: "*newsltbr
Custom
Attributes specific to the element type
-altbg
A color to setup as alternating background
-colconf
Config to apply to all columns
-dups
False
Allow duplicate node labels
Bool
-fillend
False
Extra space allocates to the last column
-find
False
Setup to use find dialog with <Control-s>
Bool
-istable
False
Hide the tree column; treat data as tabular
Bool
-levelcolors
List of bg colors to setup -levelstyles with
-makestyles
Create styles (pairs of name/options)
-maketree
False
Setup -tree, allowing direct data access
Bool
-nice
False
Setup with nice looking styles
Bool
-open
no
Open trees
Choice no ye
-sort
0
Setup all columns as sortable
-tipkey
Get -tip value from key (or -userdata if *)
-titles
List of data column names to insert
-treetitle
Title to set for the tree column
-varedit
In-place edit of a an Array with Conf

4.1 Starting Guild

Guild can be started using:

```
wize / Gui/Guild ?file.gui?
```

When started with no file, it prompts for the name of a file. If no file is selected, it asks to insert the application template.

A running application can be modified using <Control-Alt-Shift-2> and selecting Open in Gui Builder from the menu. There you can examine or edit the Gui, save changes, etc.

4.2 Using Guild

Elements can then be inserted by clicking the button icons on the left hand side. This will insert a tag element at the current level, or as a child if Child is enabled. Also, some elements have dialogs.

There is a right-click menu for moving tags around, allowing entire tag trees to be Cut and Pasted.

On the right, attributes can be selected and added with 'Add and then edited. Similarly they be selected and removed with Delete.

4.3 Styles and Scripts

There is currently no style or script editing dialogs. Instead you just click on Value and an editor pops up.

A better way is to just use your normal editor on the .tcl file and then add to the bottom:

```
Tk::gui::create { include myfile.gui }
```

For styles it is best to execute or run the program and use <Control-Alt-Shift-2> to test out configuration options before adding to rules.

4.4 No Style

Applications can be run with style disabled via the Guild menu File/Run-NoStyle.

4.5 XML

Applications can be saved as XML via the Guild menu File/Save-As-XML.

---

5. Tabset

Tabset is a notetab widget that includes the following features:

- Tear-off any number of tab-panes.
- Tab slant: left, right, both, or none.
- Tab side: top, bottom, left, or right.
- Rotate tab text labels.
- Drop shadow text support.
- Background image tiling.
- Secondary (right-side) tab image eg. a close button.
- Widget side-images for both left and right sides.
- Tabs use symbolic names to simplify programming.

Here are some screenshots:

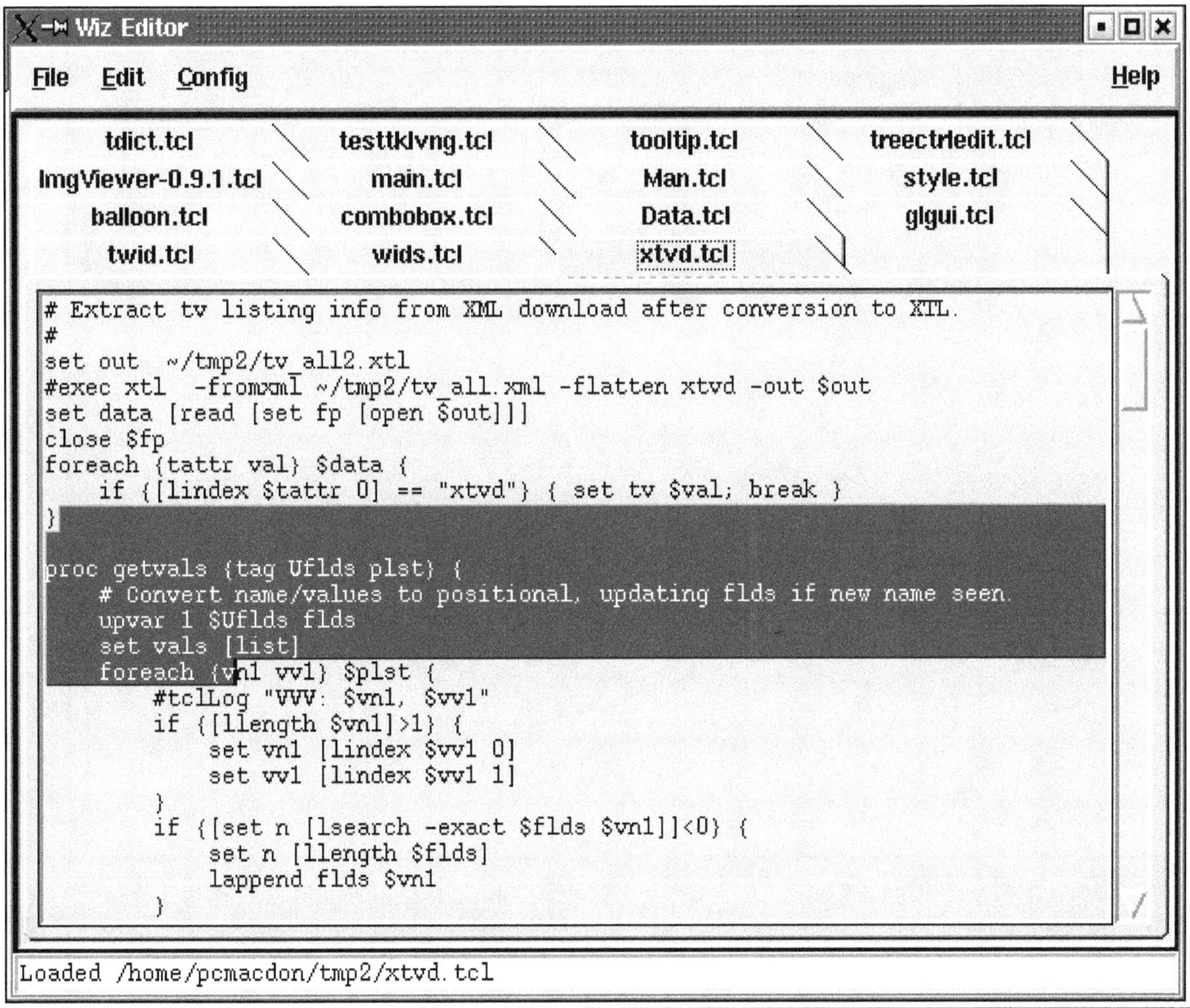
Wiz Editor
File
Edit
Config
Help
tdict.tcl
testtklvng.tcl
tooltip.tcl
treectrledit.tcl
ImgViewer-0.9.1.tcl
main.tcl
Man.tcl
style.tcl
balloon.tcl
combobox.tcl
Data.tcl
glgui.tcl
twid.tcl
wids.tcl
xtvd.tcl
Extract tv listing info from XML download after conversion to XTL.
#
set out ~/tmp2/tv_all2.xtl
#exec xtl -fromxml ~/tmp2/tv_all.xml -flatten xtvd -out $out
set data [read [set fp [open $out]]]
close $fp
foreach {tattr val} $data {
if {[lindex $tattr 0] == "xtvd"} { set tv $val; break }
}
proc getvals {tag Uflds plst} {
# Convert name/values to positional, updating flds if new name seen.
upvar 1 $Uflds flds
set vals [list]
foreach {vn1 vv1} $plst {
#tclLog "VVV: $vn1, $vv1"
if {[llength $vn1]>1} {
set vn1 [lindex $vv1 0]
set vv1 [lindex $vv1 1]
}
if {[set n [lsearch -exact $flds $vn1]]<0} {
set n [llength $flds]
lappend flds $vn1
}
Loaded /home/pcmacdon/tmp2/xtvd.tcl

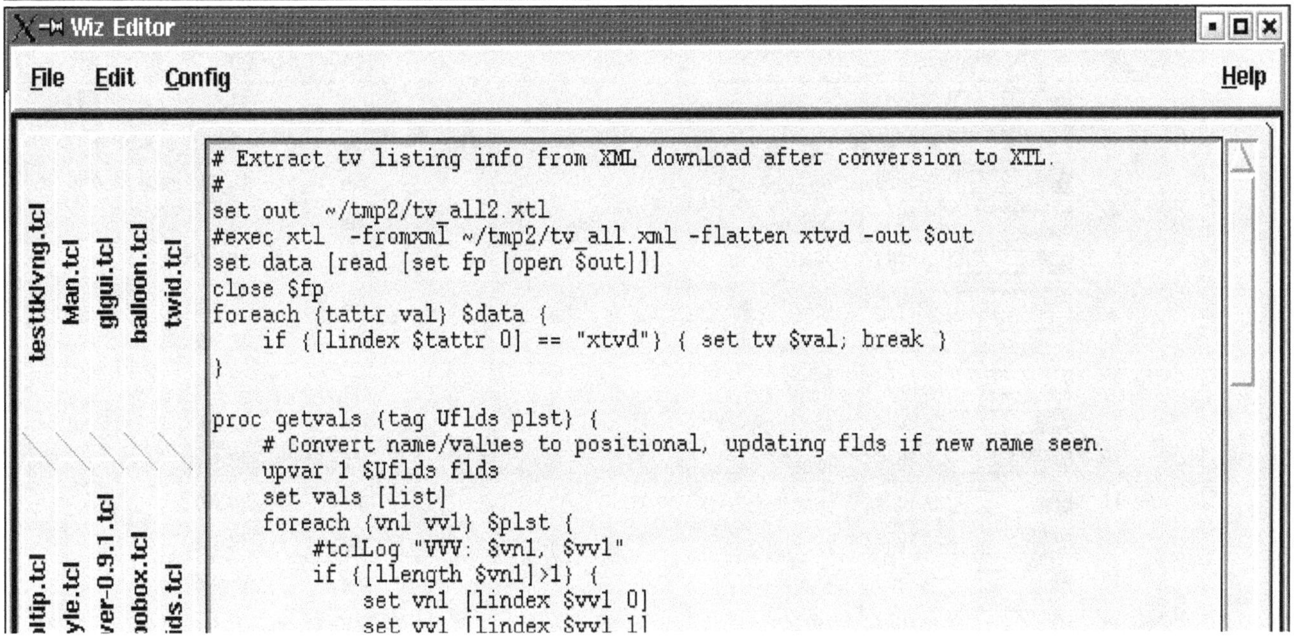
Wiz Editor
File
Edit
Config
Help
testtklvng.tcl
Man.tcl
glgui.tcl
balloon.tcl
twid.tcl
Extract tv listing info from XML download after conversion to XTL.
#
set out ~/tmp2/tv_all2.xtl
#exec xtl -fromxml ~/tmp2/tv_all.xml -flatten xtvd -out $out
set data [read [set fp [open $out]]]
close $fp
foreach {tattr val} $data {
if {[lindex $tattr 0] == "xtvd"} { set tv $val; break }
}
proc getvals {tag Uflds plst} {
# Convert name/values to positional, updating flds if new name seen.
upvar 1 $Uflds flds
set vals [list]
foreach {vn1 vv1} $plst {
#tclLog "VVV: $vn1, $vv1"
if {[llength $vn1]>1} {
set vn1 [lindex $vv1 0]

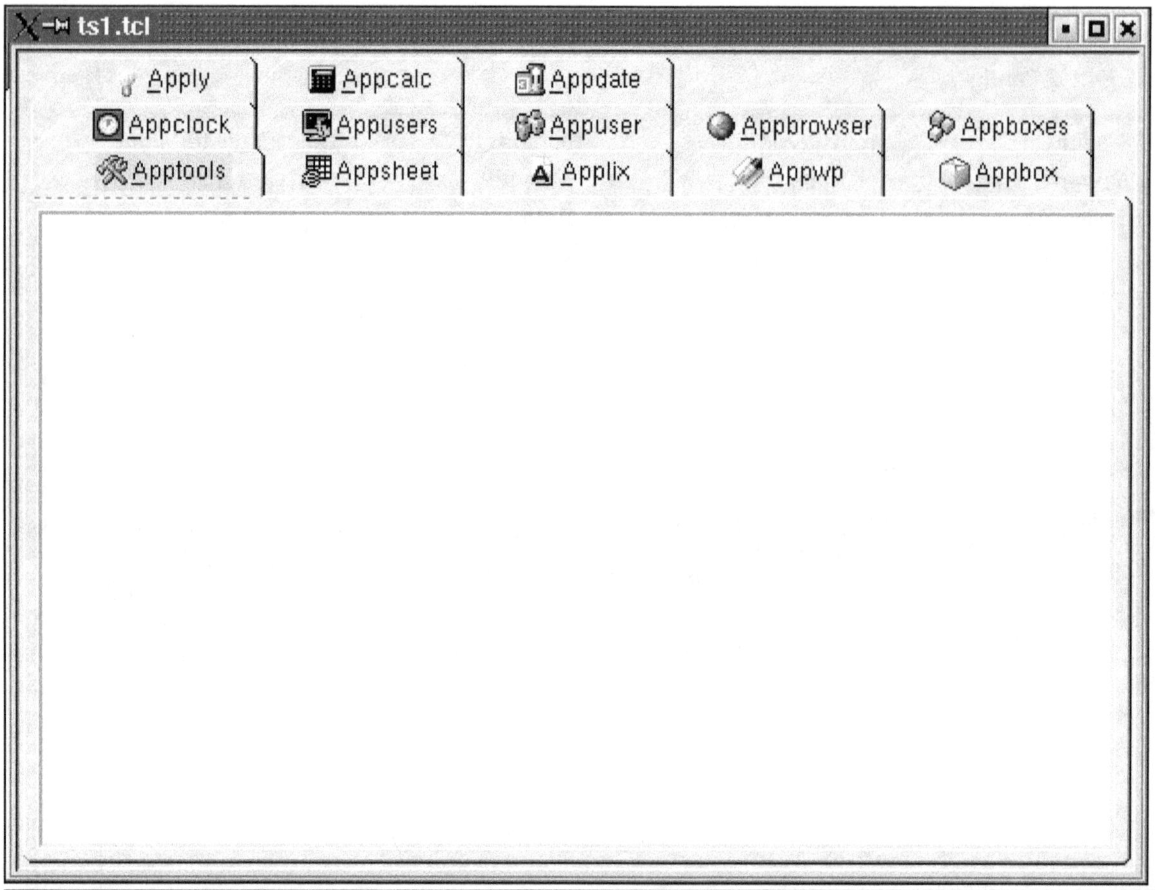
ts1.tcl
Apply
Appcalc
Appdate
Appclock
Appusers
Appuser
Appbrowser
Appboxes
Apptools
Appsheet
Applix
Appwp
Appbox

bltdemo
Appclock
Appusers
Appuser
Appbrowser
Appboxes
Apply
Table
Code
Appsheet
Applix
Appwp
Appbox
Status
File
Type
Size
Host
Active
Win
1 554.00 bzip2recover file 11,528 local 1
2 1848.00 catchsegv file 3,357 local 1
3 1450.00 gencat file 13,944 local 1
4 278.00 getconf file 13,032
5 826.00 getent file 15,144
6 1035.00 glibcbug file 7,492
7 125.00 iconv file 46,908
8 235.00 ldd file 4,786
9 908.00 lddlibc4 file 3,704
10 1576.00 locale file 25,164
11 1064.00 localedef file 294,732
12 1282.00 rpcgen file 72,808
13 625.00 sprof file 16,456
14 703.00 file 6,913

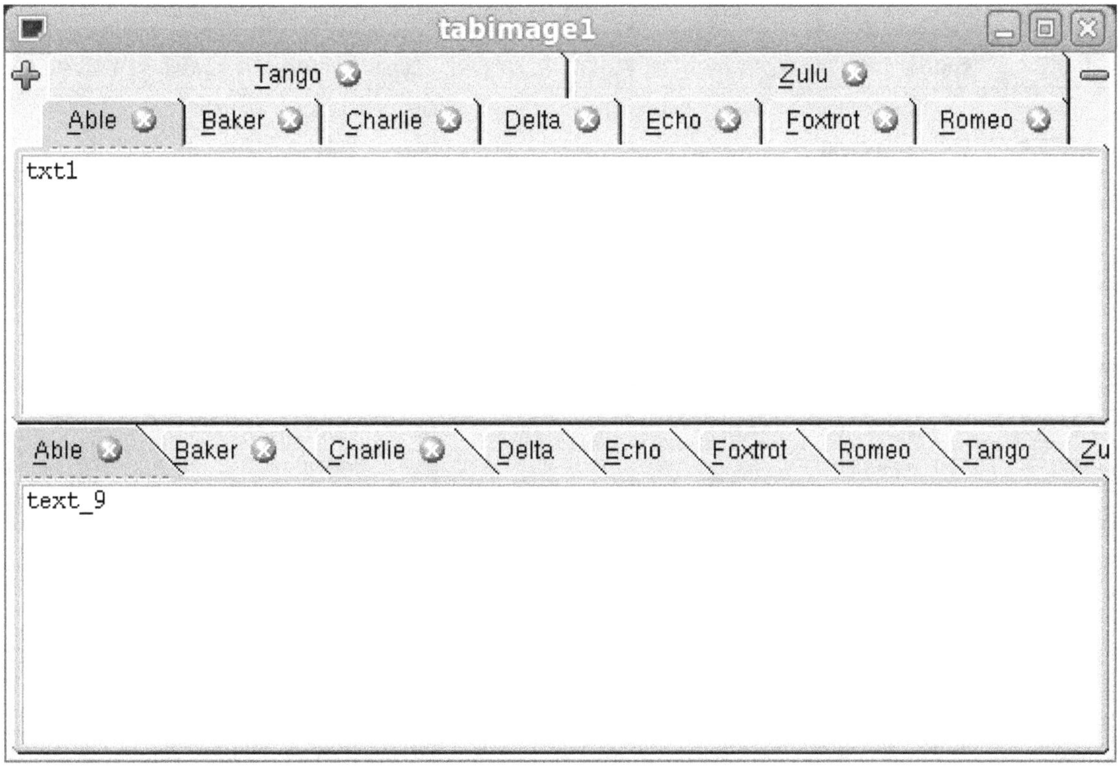

6. TreeView

TreeView is a full featured hierarchical table/**tree** widget that can handle 10s of thousands of rows.

Here is an example that displays a list of files:

```
pack [treeview .t]
foreach i [glob *] {
    .t insert end [list $i]
}
```

Note we use [list] because by default TreeView insert treats a key as a list.

Here is a TreeView screen shot:

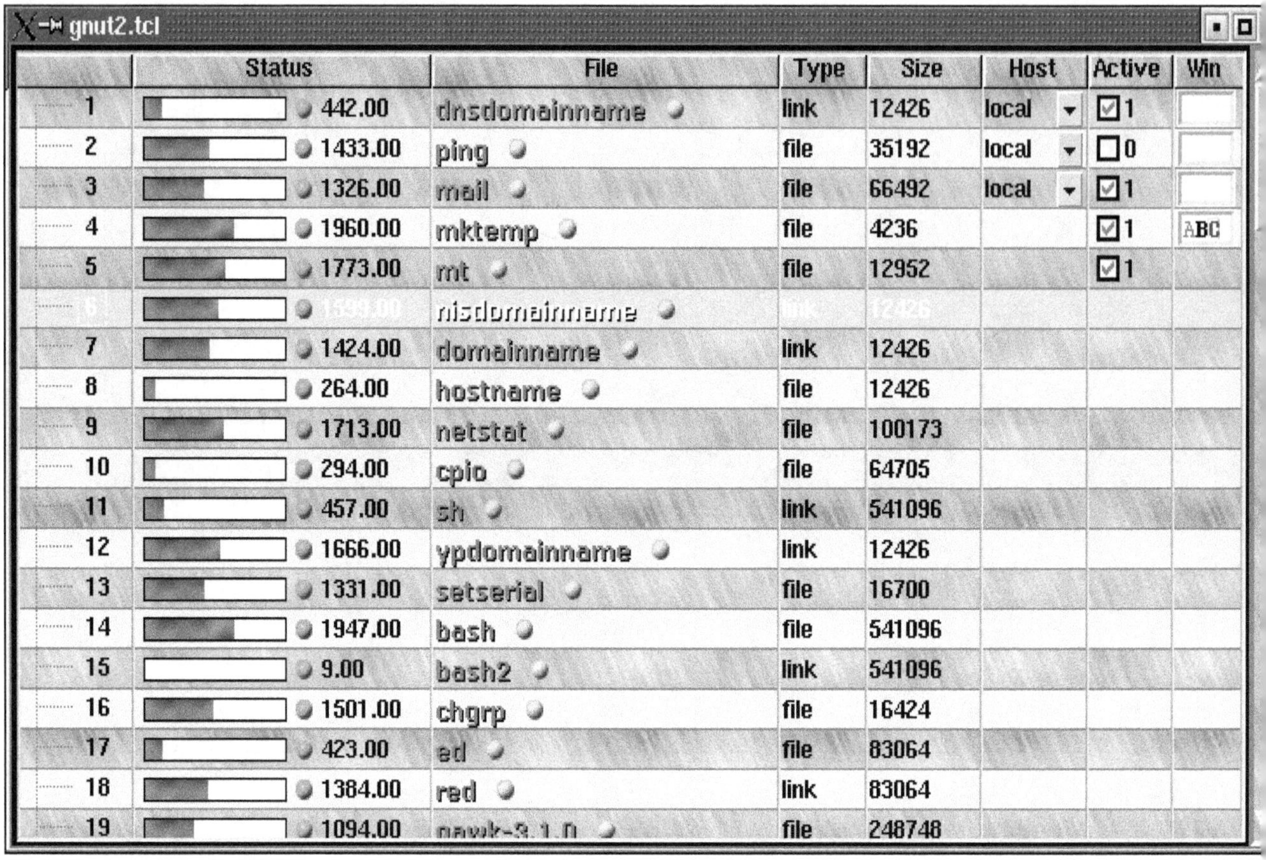

6.1 Features

Here is a list of TreeView features:

- Auto-sizing column widths and row heights.
- Hide/move columns or nodes.
- Sortable by columns or sub-trees.
- External data storage (in a **blt::tree**).
- Multiple TreeViews can share all a tree.
- Easy to use dynamic loading (for sub-trees).
- Support for multiple style types, including:
    - textbox: text cell with optional images.
    - checkbox: a boolean value.
    - combobox: a multi-choice value.
    - barbox: numeric value with progress bar.
    - windowbox: arbitrary embedded windows.
- Styles can be applied to cols, rows and/or cells
- The -altstyle option for alternating rows (bgcolor, etc).
- The -levelstyles option for per-level styles.
- Background image-tile: widget, columns, and cell-styles.
- Drop shadow text.
- Powerful builtin cell editing.

- Dual mode display: flat and tree.

6.2 Data Addressing

TreeView provides methods for updating data elements. It also supports accessing dict sub-elements using arraynotation:

```
set t .t
pack [treeview $t] -fill both -expand y
$t column insert end X Y
$t insert end A -data {X 1 Y 2}
$t insert end B -data {X 3 Y "a 1 b 2"}

$t entry incr 0->A X [$t entry get 0->B X]
$t entry set 0->A Y 3
$t entry incr 0->B Y(a) 9
```

6.3 Data Trees

TreeView data is stored externally within a tree. This also supports creating a data tree command which is attached to TreeView, eg.

```
*tree new t = {
    = Age Salary
    Managers {
        = Age Salary Title
        Tina 29 10000 President
        Tom  28 8000 VP
    }
    Staff {
        # Inherit the titles of parent ie. "Age Salary".
        Mary 10 6000
        Sam  10 6000
    }
}
pack [treeview .t -tree $t -width 600 -height 600] -fill both -expand y
eval .t col insert end [lsort [$t keys nonroot]]
.t open all
puts [$t incr 0->Managers->Tina Age]
```

See **Tree** for more details.

6.4 Changing the Key Delimiter

TreeViews insert expects a list key unless overriden with an explicit delimiter character. For example, the following displays files in a tree down to 2 directory levels:

```
pack [treeview .t -autocreate 1 -separator /] -fill both -expand y
```

```
foreach i [glob */*] {
    .t insert end $i
}
.t open [.t find -name CVS -istree]; # Open all CVS dirs.
```

6.5 Demand Loading

Data can be demand loaded into a treeview tree as it becomes visible or scrolls into view, eg.

```
pack [treeview .t] -fill both -expand y
set t [tree create]
foreach i {A B C} {
  .t col insert end $i -fillcmd [list FillMe $t $i]
}

proc FillMe {t col id} {
  return $col$id
}

$t populate 10000
.t conf -tree $t
```

One use for this is to load the rowids for an **sqlite** database table, and then loading data rows on demand.

6.6 Automatics Styles

TreeView makes it easy to apply a style to given depth levels automatically. For example, the following applies lev1 to all toplevel nodes, and lev2 to all nodes of depth 2.

```
.t style create textbox lev1 -bg LightBlue
.t style create textbox lev2 -bg LightGreen
.t conf -levelstyles {lev1 lev2}
```

Alternating row colors is another common effect used in tables. However, for trees the style has to be reapplied everytime a subtree of odd length is opened or closed. The following code snipet shows how TreeView does automatically in TreeView:

```
.t style create textbox alt -bg LightBlue
.t conf -altstyle alt
```

6.7 TreeView vs TTK

For basic usage, Blt TreeView provides a programming model that is similar to Ttk Treeview. However, TreeView provides more comprehensive autosizing support.

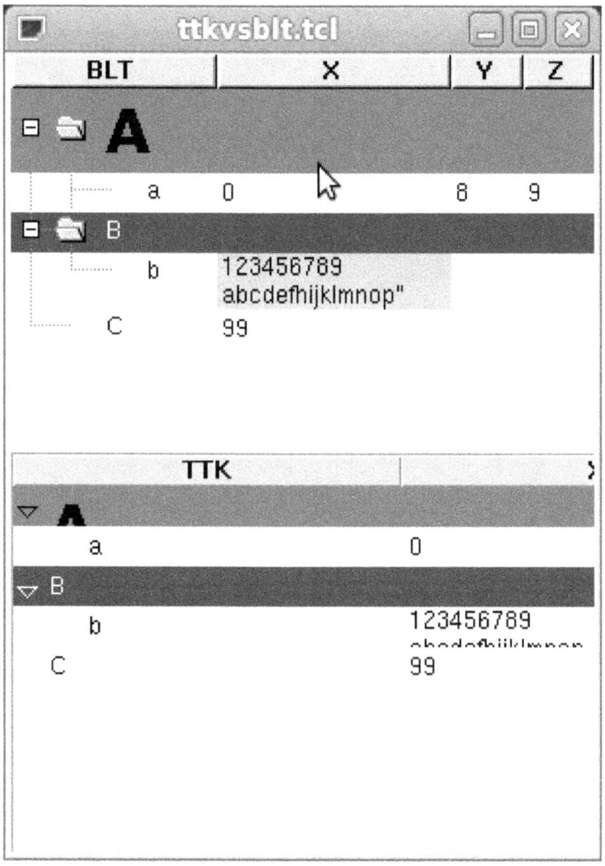

Here is the code:

```
proc TtkTree {t} {
  pack [Treeview new $t] -fill both -expand y
  Treeview conf $t -columns "X Y Z"
  foreach i {X Y Z} { Treeview heading $t $i -text $i }
  Treeview insert $t {} end -id A -text A -tags A -open 1
  Treeview insert $t A end -id a -text a -tags Aa -values {0 8 9}
  Treeview insert $t {} end -id B -text B -tags B -open 1
  Treeview insert $t B end -id b -text b -values [list "123456789\nabcdefhijklmnop"]
  Treeview insert $t {} end -id C -text C -values 99
  Treeview tag conf $t A -font "Verdana -30 bold" -background red
  Treeview tag conf $t B -background Blue -foreground White
  Treeview heading $t #0 -text TTK
}

proc BltTree {t} {
  pack [TreeView new $t] -fill both -expand y
  foreach i {X Y Z} { TreeView column insert $t end $i }
  TreeView insert $t end A -isopen 1 -font "Verdana -30 bold" -bg red
```

```
    TreeView insert $t end "A a" -data "X 0 Y 8 Z 9"
    TreeView insert $t end B -style B -isopen 1
    TreeView insert $t end "B b" -styles "X xb" -data [list X
"123456789\nabcdefhijklmnop"]
    TreeView insert $t end C -data {X 99}
    TreeView style conf $t B -bg Blue -fg white
    TreeView style conf $t xb -bg pink
    TreeView column conf $t #0 -title BLT
}

wm geom . 300x400
eval BltTree .s
eval TtkTree .t
```

7. Shaped Buttons

blt::tile:: includes a collection of widgets (button checkbutton radiobutton label) that extend Tk to add shape support. The main use for this is shaped buttons, however, any widget can have a shaped frame by packing it into a label.

blt::tile widgets support the following options (in addition to the standard Tk ones):

Option	Description
-innerbg	The background color inside of the shape.
-innertile	The tile image for inside of the shape.
-activetile	The tile image when state is active.
-disabledtile	The tile image when state is disabled.
-shape	The button shape, one of: rounded, tube or oval.
-radius	For rounded buttons, the radius of the corner curves.
-splinesteps	Steps to use in smoothing (same as the canvas polygon).
-outline	Color of shape outline (same as the canvas polygon).
-linewidth	Width of the outline (same as canvas polygon *-width*).
-shadow	Drop shadow support for text
-winshadow	Drop shadow support for shape
-rotate	Support for rotating text in degrees, eg. 90, 180.
-checksize	Specify the size of check/radio button indicator.
-icons	Give a list of 0, 2 or 3 images to use for the indicators.
-bdimage	A border image that resizes to fit the widget
-bdhalo	The number of pixels to preserve in -bdimage

Here is the shapedbutton.tcl example that defines a large number of shaped buttons, all packed in a single toplevel shaped label:

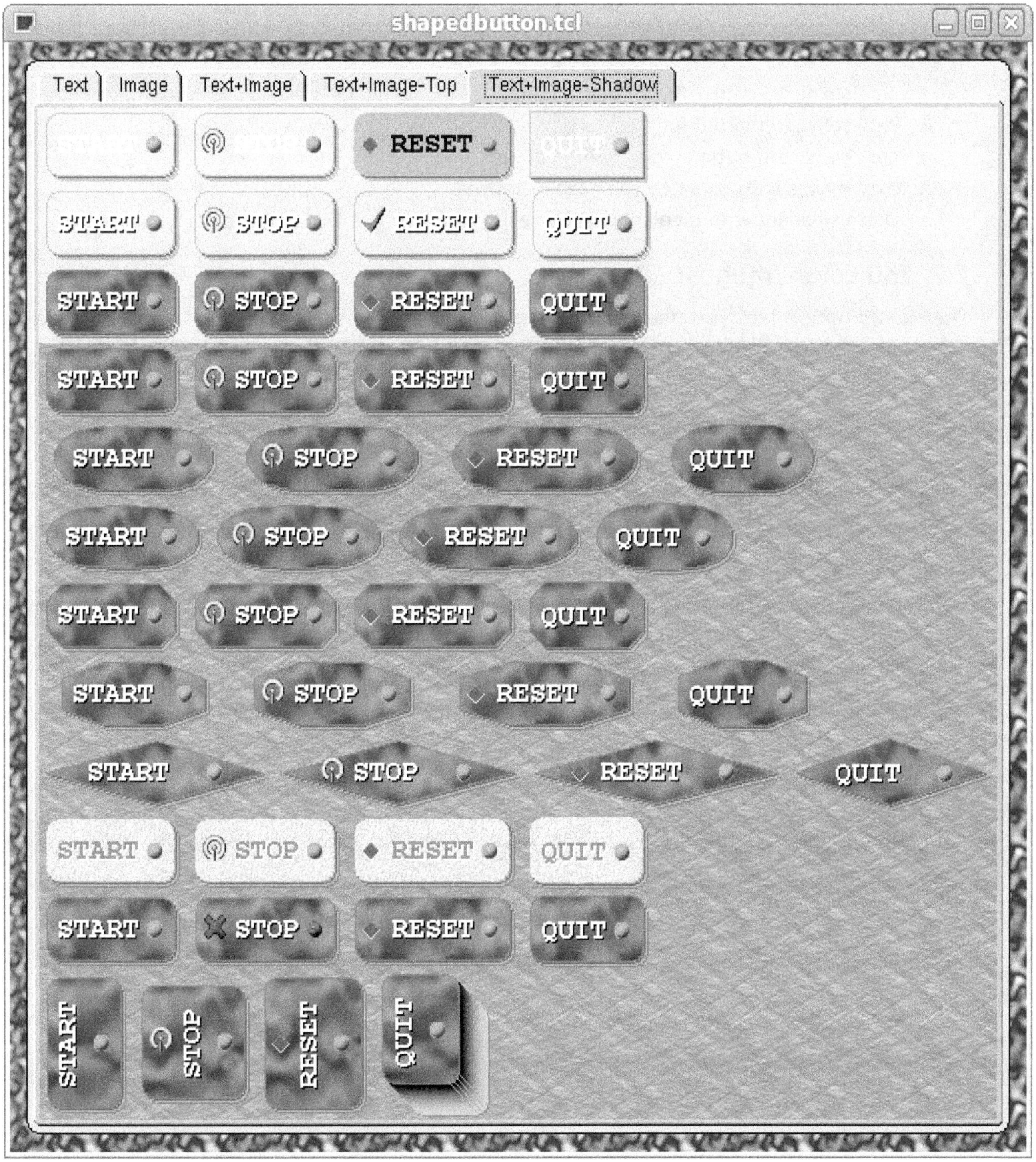

The above can be run using: wize / Gui/Shapedbutton.

7.1 Shape selection: -shape

The -shape option supports shaped buttons/labels. Three shapes are available: rounded, tube, and oval. In addition, you can:

- set -splinesteps to 1 for geometric shapes
- set -splinesteps to 0 for a square.
- set the button outline color with -outline
- use -radius with rounded to sharpen corners.
- Use -winshadow to give shapes 3D relief.

7.2 Indicator Images: -icons

The -icons option lets you use a single statement to override the default indicators used for check and radio buttons. It takes 3 image values: normal, selected, and tristate. Indicators can be globally overriden with:

```
option add *Checkbutton.icons [list $imgnormal $imgcheck $imgtristate]
```

This is easier than setting the 5 options -image, -selectimage, -tristateimage, -indicatoron and -compound. It also leaves -image available for the user.

7.3 Window Shadow: -winshadow

The -winshadow option adds a drop shadow to a button/label. It takes 3 arguments that describe a color gradient:color1 color2 width. The shapedbutton.tcl screenshot above demonstrates the results.

7.4 Border Image: -bdimage

A border image is an image that is dynamically expanded/resized (with borders preserved) to fit the current size of the widget. The image simply provides decoration for the outside of the widget rectangle. Normally 16 pixels of the border are preserved, but -bdhalo can change this. (Note -bdimage is incompatible with -shape.)

Following is an example with a bunch of buttons using -bdimage:

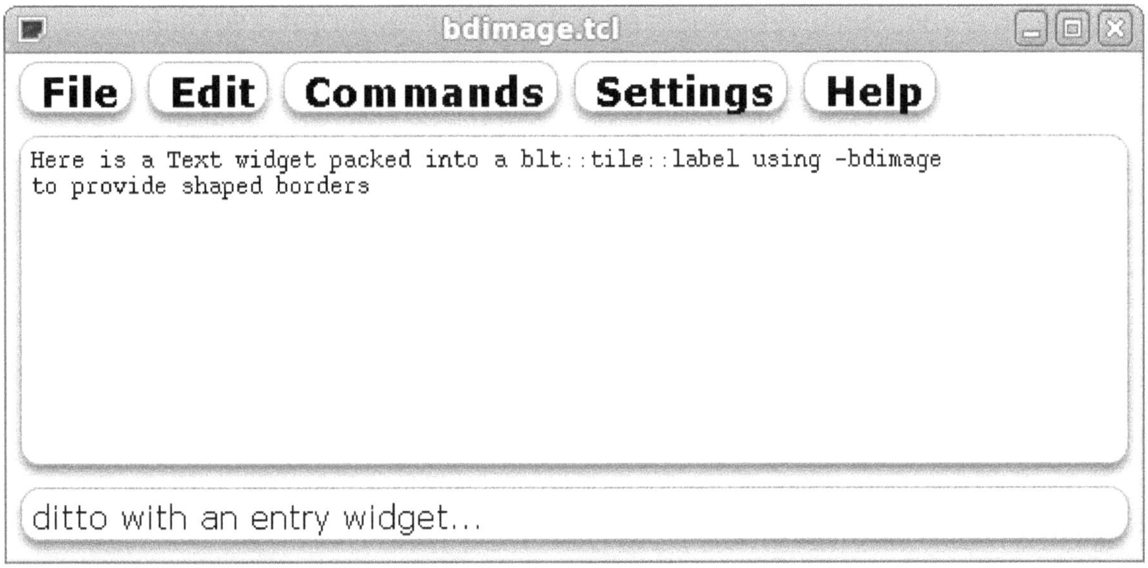

And here is the code:

```
#!/usr/bin/env wize

set bdimg [image create photo -data {
        R0lGODlhQABAAPcAAHx+fMTCxKSipOTi5JSSlNTS1LSytPTy9IyKjMzKzKyq
        rOzq7JyanNza3Ly6vPz6/ISChMTGxKSmpOTm5JSWlNTW1LS2tPT29IyOjMzO
        zKyurOzu7JyenNze3Ly+vPz+/OkAKOUA5IEAEnwAAACuQACUAAFBAAB+AFYd
        QAC0AABBAAB+AIjMAuEEABINAAAAAHMgAQAAAAAAAAAAAKjSxOIEJBIIpQAA
        sRgBMO4AAJAAAHwCAHAAAAUAAJEAAHwAAP+eEP8CZ/8Aif8AAG0BDAUAAJEA
        AHwAAIXYAOfxAIESAHwAAABAMQAbMBZGMAAAIEggJQMAIAAAAAAAfqgaXESI
        5BdBEgB+AGgALGEAABYAAAAAAACsNwAEAAAMLwAAAH61MQBIAABCM8B+AAAU
        AAAAAAAApQAAsf8Brv8AlP8AQf8Afv8AzP8A1P8AQf8AfgAArAAABAAADAAA
        AACQDADjAAASAAAAAACAAADVABZBAAB+ALjMwOIEhxINUAAAANIgAOYAAIEA
        AHwAAGjSAGEEABYIAAAAAEoBB+MAAIEAAHwCACABAJsAAFAAAAAAAGjJAGGL
        AAFBFgB+AGmIAAAQAABHAAB+APQoAOE/ABIAAAAAAADQAADjAAASAAAAAPiF
        APcrABKDAAB8ABgAGO4AAJAAqXwAAHAAAAUAAJEAAHwAAP8AAP8AAP8AAP8A
        AG0pIwW3AJGSAHx8AEocI/QAAICpAHwAAAA0SABk6xaDEgB8AAD//wD//wD/
        /wD//2gAAGEAABYAAAAAAAC0/AHj5AASEgAAAAA01gBkWACDTAB8AFf43PT3
        5IASEnwAAOAYd+PuMBKQTwB8AGgAEGG35RaSEgB8AOj/NOL/ZBL/gwD/fMkc
        q4sA5UGpEn4AAIg02xBk/0eD/358fx/4iADk5QASEgAAAALnHABkAACDqQB8
        AMyINARkZA2DgwB8fBABHL0AAEUAqQAAAIAxKOMAPxIwAAAAAIScAOPxABIS
        AAAAAIIAnQwA/0IAR3cAACwAAAAAQABAAAAI/wA/CBxIsKDBgwgTKlzIsKFD
        gxceNnxAsaLFixgzUrzAsWPFCw8kDgy5EeQDkBxPolypsmXKlx1hXnS48UEH
        CwooMCDAgIJOCjx99gz6k+jQnkWR9lRgYYDJkAk/DlAgIMICkVgHLoggQIPT
        ighVJqBQIKvZghkoZDgA8uDJAwk4bDhLd+ABBmvbjnzbgMKBuoA/bKDQgC1F
        gW8XKMgQOHABBQsMI76wIIOExo0FZIhM8sKGCQYCYA4cwcCEDSYPLOgg4Oro
        uhMEdOB84cCAChReB2ZQYcGGkxsGFGCgGzCFCh1QH5jQIW3xugwSzD4QvIIH
        4s/PUgiQYcCG4BkC5P/ObpaBhwreq18nb3Z79+8Dwo9nL9I8evjWsdOX6D59
```

```
    fPH71Xeef/kFyB93/sln4EP2Ebjegg31B5+CEDLUIH4PVqiQhOABqKFCF6qn
    34cHcfjffCQaFOJtGaZYkIkUuljQigXK+CKCE3po40A0trgjjDru+EGPI/6I
    Y4co7kikkAMBmaSNSzL5gZNSDjkghkXaaGIBHjwpY4gThJeljFt2WSWYMQpZ
    5pguUnClehS4tuMEDARQgH8FBMBBBExGwIGdAxywXAUBKHCZkAIoEEAFp33W
    QGl47ZgBAwZEwKigE1SQgAUCUDCXiwtQIIAFCTQwgaCrZeCABAzIleIGHDD/
    oIAHGUznmXABGMABT4xpmBYBHGgAKGq1ZbppThgAG8EEAW61KwYMSOBAApdy
    pNp/BkhAAQLcEqCTt+ACJW645I5rLrgEeOsTBtwiQIEElRZg61sTNBBethSw
    CwEA/Pbr778ABywwABBAgAAG7xpAq6mGUUTdAPZ6YIACsRKAAbvtZqzxxhxn
    jDG3ybbKFHf36ZVYpuE5oIGhHMTqcqswvyxzzDS/HDMHEiiggQMLDxCZXh8k
    BnEBCQTggAUGGKCB0ktr0PTTTEfttNRQT22ABR4EkEABDXgnGUEn31ZABglE
    EEAAWaeN9tpqt832221HEEECW6M3wc+Hga3SBgtMODBABw00UEEBgxdO+OGG
    J4744oZzXUEDHQxwN7F5G7QRdXxPoPkAnHfu+eeghw665n1vIKhJBQUEADs=
}]

namespace import -force ::blt::tile::*
option add *highlightThickness 0
option add *Label.borderWidth 4
option add *Label.bdImage $bdimg
font conf TkDefaultFont -family Verdana -size 15 -weight bold
set pad 5

pack [frame .f -bg white] -fill x
foreach m {File Edit Commands Settings Help } {
    pack  [button .f.b$m -bdimage $bdimg -text $m] -side left
}

pack [label .l2] -fill x -side bottom
pack [label .l1] -fill both -expand y

text .l1.t -height 12 -bd 0
pack .l1.t -padx $pad -pady $pad -fill both -expand y

entry .l2.e -bd 0
pack .l2.e -padx $pad -pady $pad -fill x

.l1.t insert end "Here is a Text widget packed into a blt::tile::label "
.l1.t insert end "using -bdimage\nto provide shaped borders"
.l2.e insert end "ditto with an entry widget..."
```

7.5 Shaped in Gui

The use of shape widgets can be enabled in **Gui** by using -blt, either in options or attributes.

```
{options - -blt 1} {}

{style} {
  Toplevel {
```

```
    @defgradients {
        bspl { SkyBlue SteelBlue -width 60 -height 10 -type split -rotate 90 }
        spl! { SteelBlue SkyBlue -width 33 -height 10 -type split -rotate 90 }
    }
   }
   Button { -font "Courier -18 bold" }
  .txtfr { -shape rounded -innerbg White -outline SteelBlue -linewidth 4}
  .txtwin { -bd 0 -highlightth 0 }
  @bspl { -bdimage ^bspl -bdhalo -1 }
  @spl  { -shape rounded -innertile ^spl! -outline Blue}
}
{Toplevel +} {
   {Frame + -subpos l -subattr {-gid spl}} {
     Button File Button Edit Button Options Button Quit
   }
   {Frame + -subpos l -subattr {-gid bspl}} {
     Button File Button Edit Button Options Button Quit
   }
   {Frame + -blt 1 -id txtfr} {
     {Text + -id txtwin} {}
   }
}
```

In the above, Button implicitly uses blt, while Frame requires -blt to override the tk::frame with blt::label. Here is the screenshot:

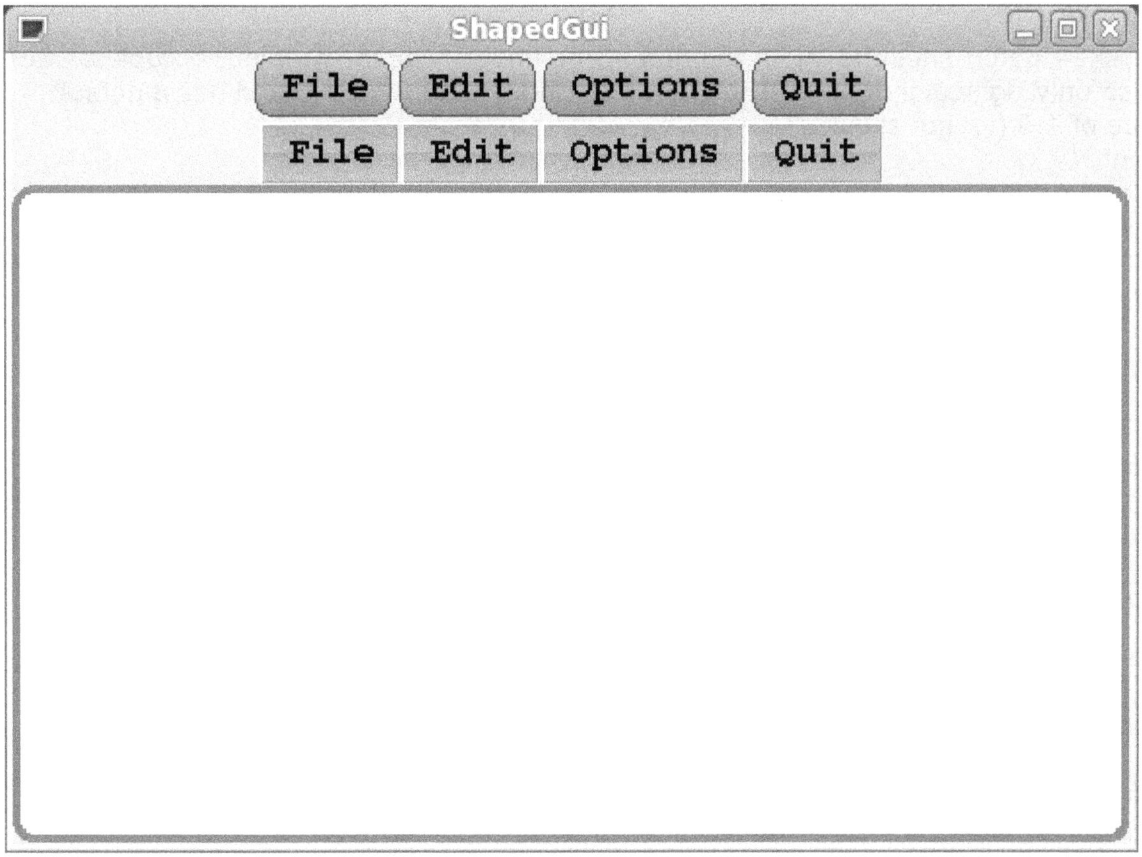

8. Gradients

Gradient images are widely used within applications and web pages to enhance appearance. Wize has built-in capabilities to generate on-the-fly, complex gradient images. This feature (provided via the Blt sub-command **winop image gradient**) is particularly useful when used with **Gui** @defgradients.

8.1 Options

The general form is:

winop image gradient image leftcolor rightcolor ?options...?

where options are:

-type halfsine|sine|linear|rectangular|radial|blank
Set the type of gradient. The default is sine.

-skew N
The skew determines the initial fraction of the image that the gradient occupies, after which only rightcolor is used. The skew must be > 0 and <= 1.0 and has a default value of 1.0 (ie. not skewed).
-slant N
Make the gradient slant where a value of 1.0 slants at 45 degrees. The value must be between -100.0 and 100.0.
-curve N
Curve the gradient by passing the Y position to a function (see -func) scaled with the given value. The value must be between -100.0 and 100.0 (typically 1.0).
-func X
Function to use with -curve. The default value is sin. The value must be one of: sin cos tan sinh cosh tanh asin acos atan log log10 exp sqrt rand circle.
-rand N
Add small random purturbations to gradient to avoid striation lines. The value must be between 0.0 and 0.1.

8.2 User Interface

There is a **user interface** for exploring the options of gradients:

wize / Gui/Gradient

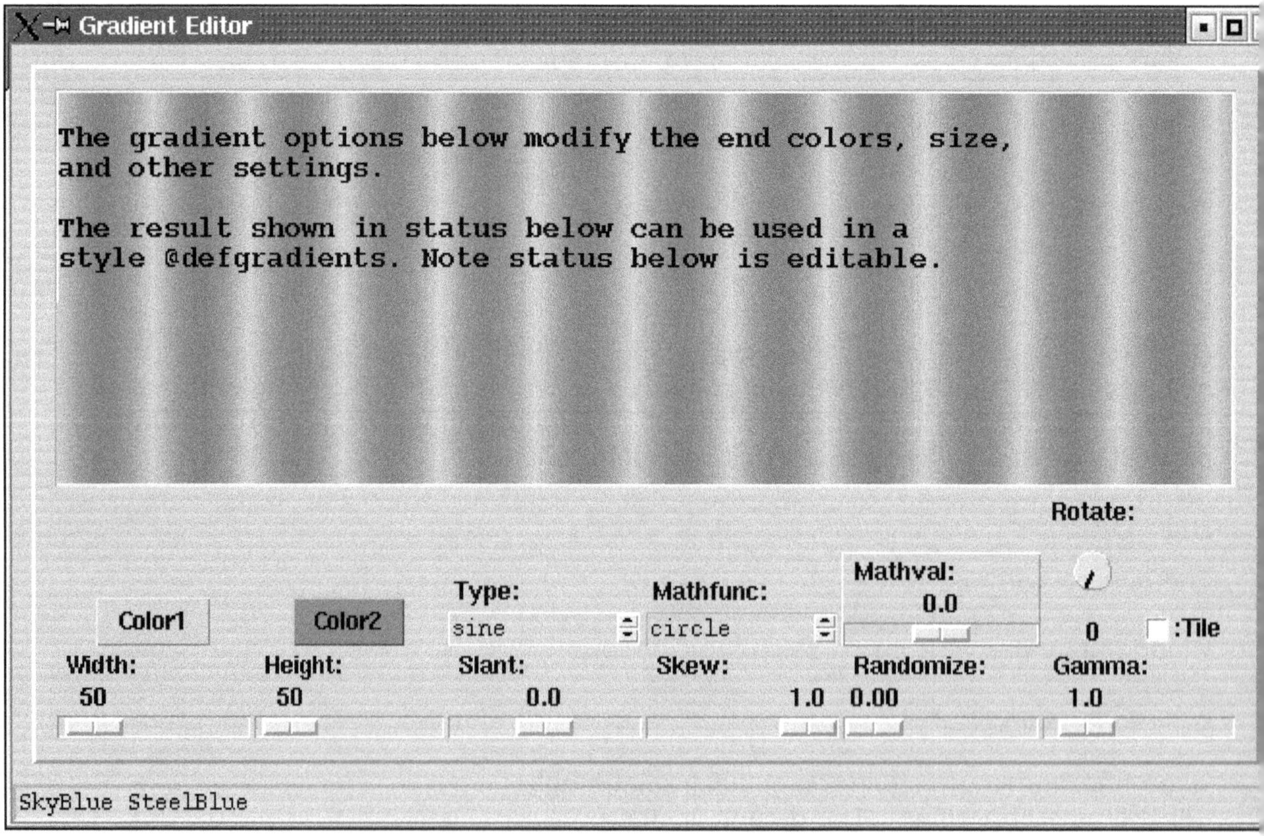

8.3 Gradients in Styles

The easiest way to use gradient is with the **Gui Styles** @defgradients macro.

Note that @defgradients support options like -rotate, -tile and -gamma.

Here is a simple gui application using gradient styles.

```
# "gtest.gui"
style {
    Toplevel {
        @defgradients {
            mybg {LightBlue White}
            butbg! {Green Yellow -rotate 90}
        }
        *tile ^mybg
    }
    Button { -tile ^butbg! }
}
{Toplevel +} {
    {Button} Quit
    {Button} Save
    {Text - -pos *} {}
    {Entry - -pos _} {}
}
```

When run, this looks like:

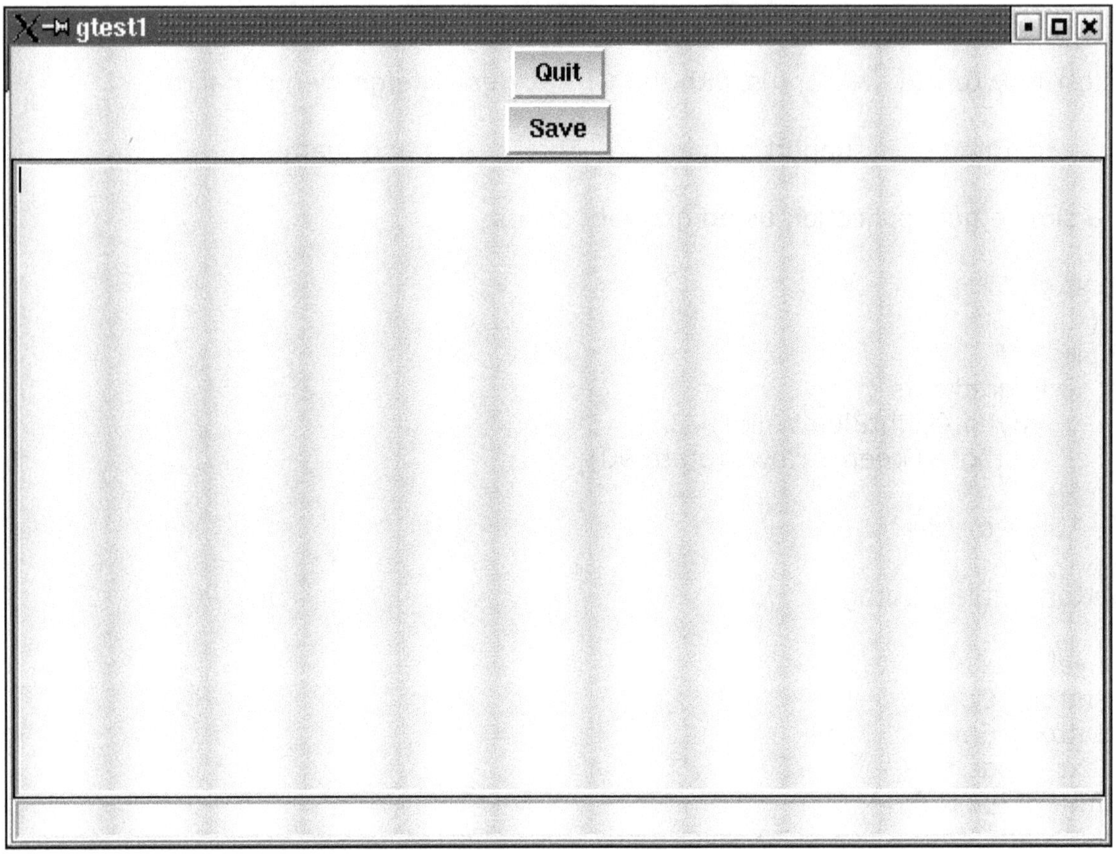

Note tiled image names containing a "!" will use a tile origin from the current window, rather than the toplevel.

Documentation is available in the gradient sub-command of the **Winop manpage**.

8.4 More Examples

Here are a few gradient examples:

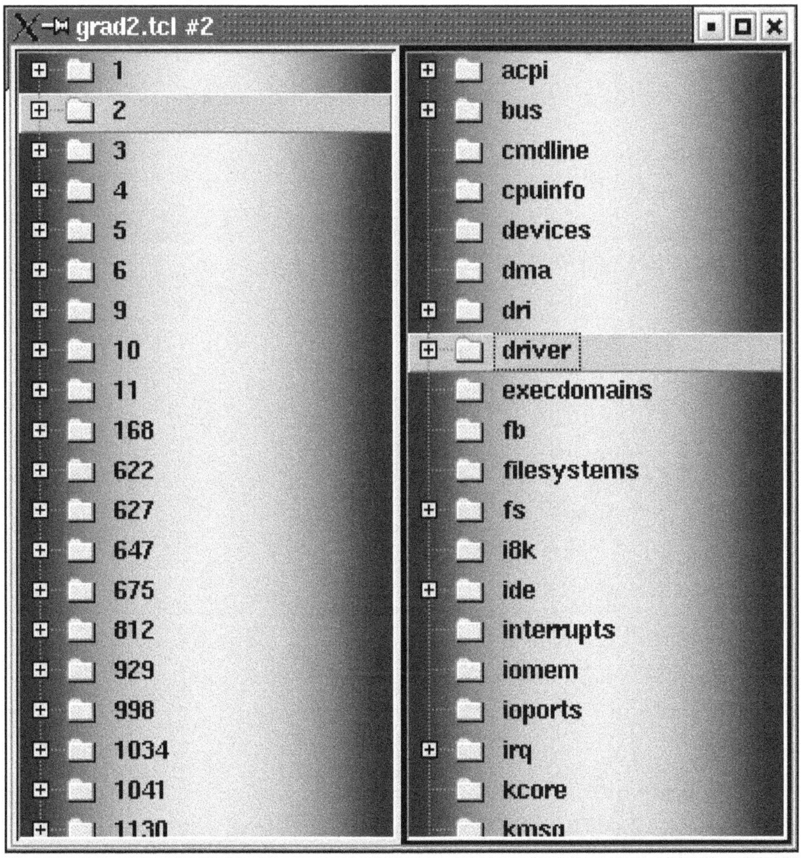
grad2.tcl #2
1
2
3
4
5
6
9
10
11
168
622
627
647
675
812
929
998
1034
1041
acpi
bus
cmdline
cpuinfo
devices
dma
dri
driver
execdomains
fb
filesystems
fs
i8k
ide
interrupts
iomem
ioports
irq
kcore

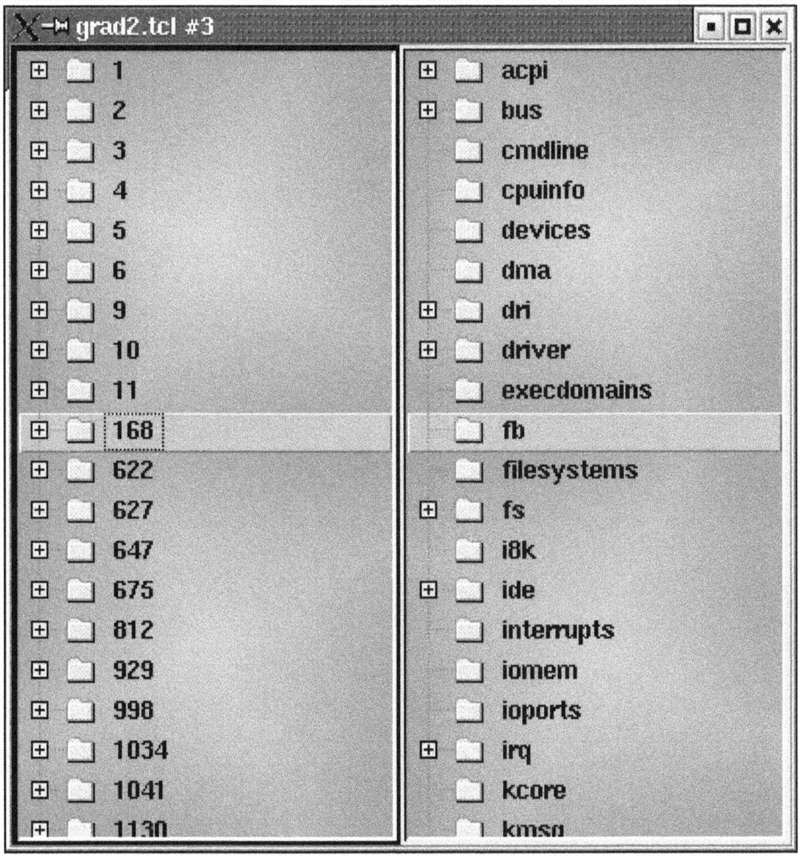
grad2.tcl #3
1
2
3
4
5
6
9
10
11
168
622
627
647
675
812
929
998
1034
1041
acpi
bus
cmdline
cpuinfo
devices
dma
dri
driver
execdomains
fb
filesystems
fs
i8k
ide
interrupts
iomem
ioports
irq
kcore

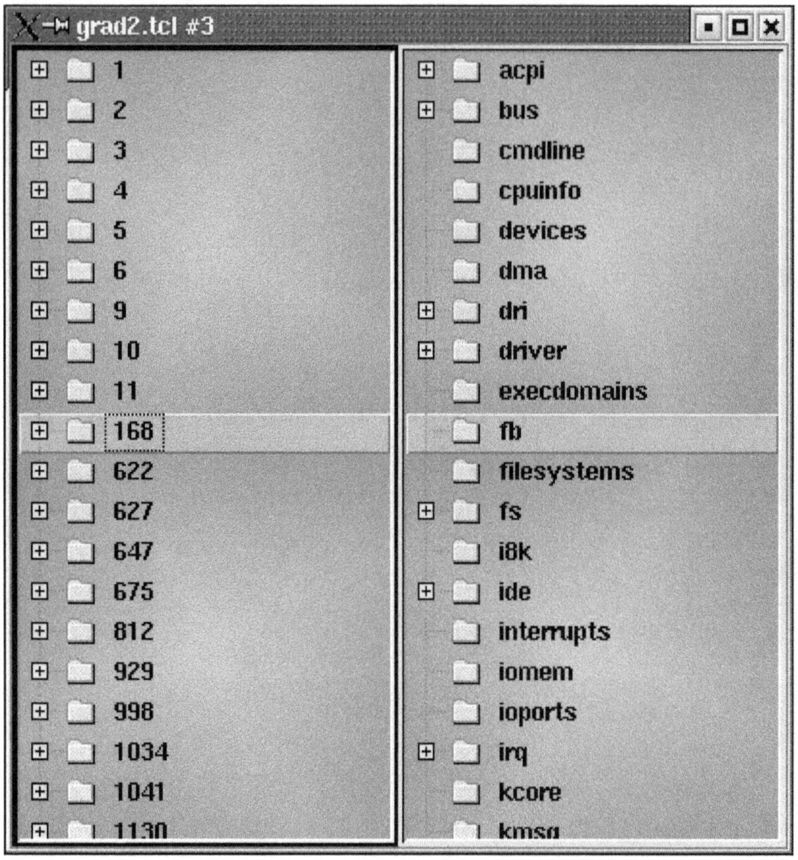
grad2.tcl #3
1
2
3
4
5
6
9
10
11
168
622
627
647
675
812
929
998
1034
1041
acpi
bus
cmdline
cpuinfo
devices
dma
dri
driver
execdomains
fb
filesystems
fs
i8k
ide
interrupts
iomem
ioports
irq
kcore

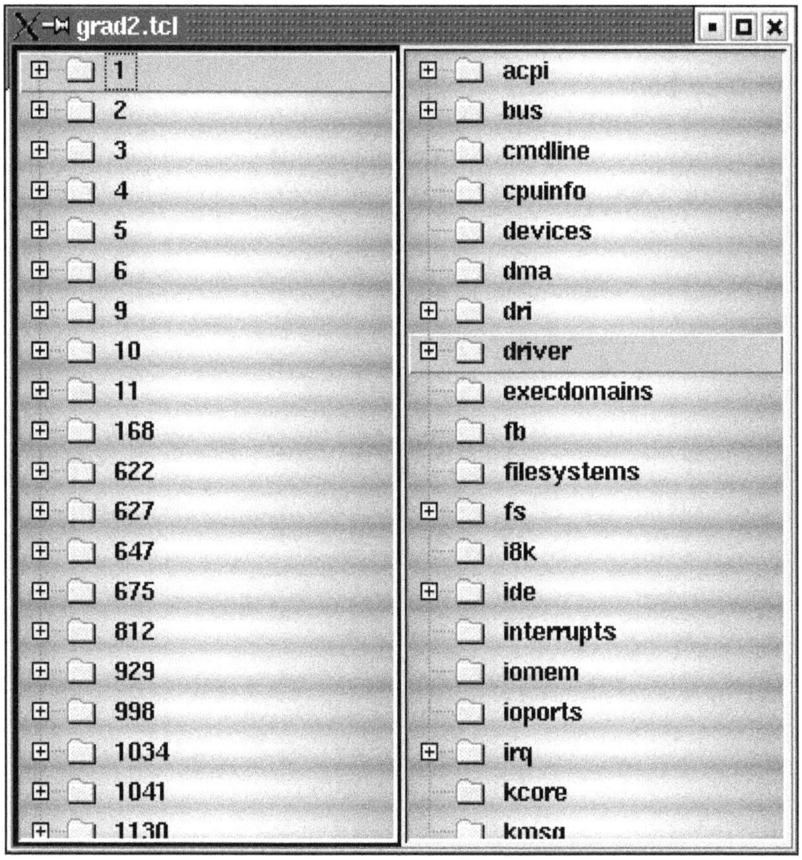

The following script can be used to generate the above images.

```
#!/usr/bin/env wize
# grad2.tcl:  demonstrates gradient tiled background generation, eg:
#
#   wize grad2.tcl -g sine -s DarkBlue -e LightBlue
#   wize grad2.tcl -g rectangular -s Orange -e  LightSlateGray
#   wize grad2.tcl -h 20

array set p { -h 200 -w 200 -s DarkGreen -e White -g radial}
array set p $argv
set img [image create photo -width $p(-w) -height $p(-h)]
winop image gradient $img $p(-s) $p(-e) -type $p(-g)

switch -- $p(-g) {
    sine - radial {}
    default {
       set img4 [image create photo]
       winop image mirror $img $img4 tile
       set img $img4
    }
```

```
}

# Create a couple of widgets with tiled background.
option add *font [eval font create [font actual {Helvetica -12 bold}]]
pack [treeview .t -tile $img -scrolltile 1] -fill both -expand y -side left
pack [treeview .t2 -tile $img] -fill both -expand y -side left
if {![file isdirectory [set dir /proc]]} { set dir "" }
foreach i [lsort -dictionary [glob -nocomplain $dir/*]] {
  set it [file tail $i]
  set isdir [file isdirectory $i]
  if {[string is integer $it]} {
      .t insert end $it -forcetree $isdir
  } else {
      .t2 insert end $it -forcetree $isdir
  }
}
foreach tt {.t .t2} {
  $tt conf -selectbackground GoldenRod
  $tt conf -nofocusselectbackground GoldenRod
  $tt conf -selectrelief raised
}
```

9. Tree

The **Blt** extension provides Tcl with a complex **tree data** structure, eg.

```
set t [tree create]
foreach i {Able Baker Charlie} { $t insert 0 -label $i }
$t set 0->Able X 1 Y 2
$t incr 0->Able X
```

9.1 Dict/Array Keys

Keys in a tree may store a dict that is accessed using an array-like notation, eg.

```
$t insert 0 -label Harry -data {X 1 Y "a 1 b 2"}
$t incr 0->Harry Y(a)
```

9.2 Static Tree.

Preloaded data trees are quite simple to define with the wize *tree command. Each line represents one row of data with the first token being the key. Subtrees are defined if the last element contains newlines. Titles fields are specified with a leading equals =. Here is an example:

```
*tree new t = {
    = Age Salary
    Managers {
        Tina 29 10000
        Tom  28 8000
    }
    Staff {
        Mary 10 6000
        Sam  10 6000
    }
  }
```

Trees are useful because of their ease of update and access:

```
*tree new t = {
    Vendors {
        = Id Status Products
        NA {
            Oracle 888001 active
            MS     888002 active
        }
        SA {
            Pemex 888008 disabled
            Snapon {
                = Class Items
                pipes {single double twin}
                tools {spanners sockets wrenches}
                wire  { 10 12 14 16 18 }
            }
        }
        Europe {
            Finetix 888009 active { pipes {single twin} wire  { 10 12 14 16 18 } }
        }
    }
}

pack [treeview .t -tree $t -width 600 -height 600] -fill both -expand y
eval .t col insert end [lsort [$t keys nonroot]]
.t open all

puts [$t get 0->Vendors->NA->Oracle]
puts [$t incr 0->Vendors->NA->Oracle Id 0.5]
puts [$t find -top 0->Vendors -name 888* -glob -key Id]
```

9.3 Flat Tree Example

The following loads a table of data into a tree, then updates it. (See also **Tables**)

```
variable Users {
     tom  { Name "Tom Brown"  Sex M Age 19  Class {4 5} Rate {A 1 B 2}}
```

```
    mary { Name "Mary Brown" Sex F Age 16  Class {5}   Rate {A 2}}
    sam  { Name "Sam Spade"  Sex M Age 19  Class {3 4} Rate {B 3}}
}

# Load it.
set t [tree create]
foreach {l d} $Users {
   $t insert end -label $l -data $d  -tags $l
}

# Update it.
$t update   tom       Sex F   Name "Tomi Brown" Age 21
$t append   sam       Name " Jr"
$t lappend  sam       Class 5
$t incr     mary      Age
$t update   tom       Rate(A) 2
$t set      tom       Sax F
$t set      sam       Rate(C) 0
$t incr     0->mary   Age;   # Address via label instead of tag.

# Display it.
pack [treeview .t -tree $t] -fill both -expand y
eval .t column insert end [$t keys all]
```

Note: nodes can be addressed using the form 0->LABEL. Tags can also be used to simplify indexing.

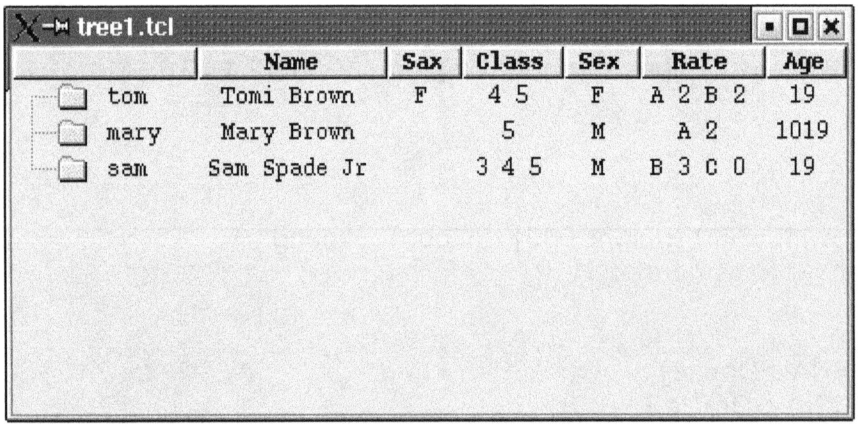

9.4 Nested Tree Example

The following example loads data into a nested tree. (See **Trees**)

```
variable Info {
    system {
```

```
        sol  { OS Linux Version 3.4 }
        bing { OS Win   Version 7 }
        gui  { OS Mac   Version 8 }
    }
    network {
        intra { Address 192.168.1  Netmask 255.255.255.0 }
        dmz   { Address 192.168.10 Netmask 255.255.255.0 }
        wan   { Address 0.0.0.0    Netmask 0.0.0.0 Class {A 1 B 4}}
    }
    admin {
        sully    { Name "Sully Van Damme"  Level 3 }
        maverick { Name "Maverick Gump"    Level 1 }
    }
}

# Load it.
set s [tree create]
foreach {n vals} $Info {
    set ind [$s insert end -label $n -tags .$n]
    foreach {l d} $vals {
        $s insert $ind -label $l -data $d -tags .$n.$l
    }
}

# Do queries.
$s update  .network.dmz  Address 192.168.11
$s update  .network.wan  Class(A) 2

set old [$s get  .system.bing]
$s update  .system.bing  OS Linux Version 3.4
eval $s set .system.bing  $old; # ROLLBACK!

$s insert  .admin -label linus -data { Name "Linus Torvalds" Level 9 }
$s delete  .admin.sully


pack [treeview .s -tree $s -width 600] -fill both -expand y
eval .s column insert end [$s keys all]
.s open all
```

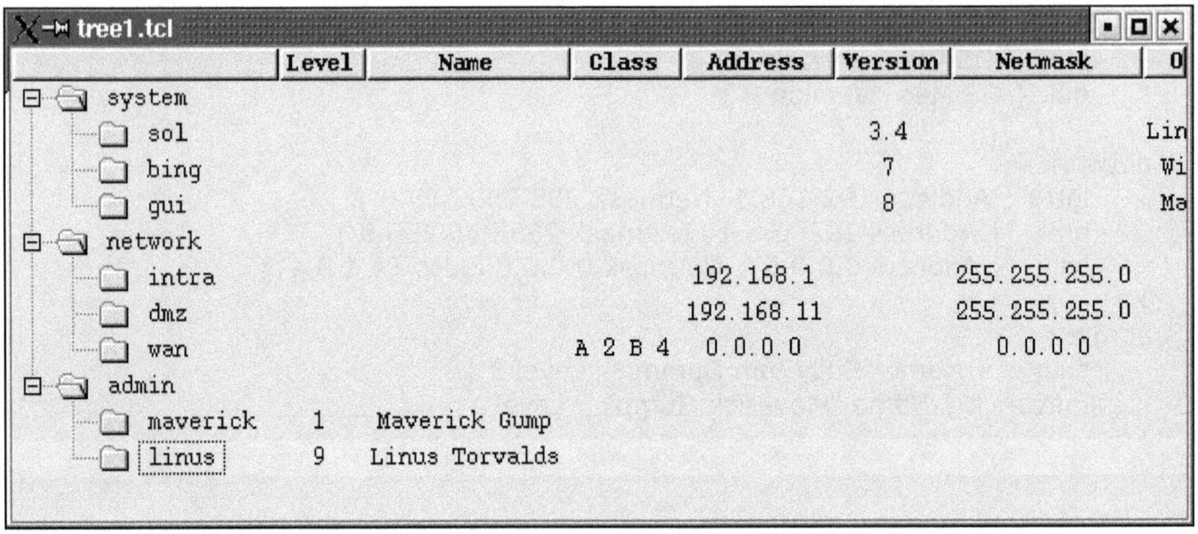

9.5 Label & Tags

Nodes can be referenced using the label relative to the root, eg:

```
$s update   0->system->bing   OS Linux Version 3.4
```

However, label indexing has several limitations.

If a duplicate labels exists in the same parent the first match is quietly used. And care must be used to avoid labels with spaces, leading integers, or the names of builtins like nextnode, or firstchild (unless quoted).

Another way is to use the index command, which suppors label path lookups, eg:

```
$s update [$s index {system bing}]  OS Linux
```

Using tags however is simpler, and when used with a **tag trace** avoids duplicates.

9.6 Enums

A tree can be used as a simple enum by simply setting keys in node 0.

```
set t [tree create]
$t set 0   apple 1 orange 2 banana 3
puts [$t get 0]        ; # "apple 1 orange 2 banana 3"
puts [$t names 0]      ; # "apple orange banana"
puts [$t values 0]     ; # "1 2 3"
puts [$t get 0 apple] ; # "1"
```

Multiple enums are also easily defined:

```
set t [tree create]
$t set 0  fruit { apple 1 orange 2 banana 3 }
$t set 0  veggy { pea 1 bean 2 cabbage 3 }

puts [$t get 0 fruit(apple)] ;  # "1"
puts [$t get 0 veggy(bean)]  ;  # "2"
```

Alternatively, create each enum in its own node:

```
set t [tree create]
$t insert end -tags fruit -data { apple 1 orange 2 banana 3 }
$t insert end -tags veggy -data { pea 1 bean 2 cabbage 3 }

puts [$t get fruit apple] ;  # "1"
puts [$t get veggy bean]  ;  # "2"
```

If using > 21 keys per node, see **9.13 Key Hashing**.

9.7 With

Tree supports the with statement for accessing key data via an array. On entry it copies key values into an array variable, and on completion copies them back out. Eg:

```
$t with s .system.sol {
      $t with b .system.bing {
            set s(OS)      $b(OS)
            set s(Version) $b(Version)
      }
}
```

See **TreeWith** for more details.

9.8 Traces

Tree supports setting traces on nodes or notifiers on the tree. See **TreeTrace** for details.

9.9 Performance

Performance is generally quite good.

9.10 Tree Iterators

The following **tree** commands iterate over a tag:

Name	Description
appendi	Append strings to key value.
incri	Increment a key value.

keys	Return keys for one or more nodes.
lappendi	Append list element to key value.
modify	Change data value for existing key.
set	Set/create data value for key.
sum	Sum values for a key field
vecdump	Dump values to a vector
vecload	Load values from a vector
with	Assign keys value to an array and eval

9.11 Code Validation

wize supports **validation** of tree commands thus enabling static checking of tree code. To use this requires writing code using the tree object as data rather than as command. Thus the first example would be rewritten as:

```
tree op update  $t tom Sex F Name "Tomi Brown" Age 19
tree op append  $t sam     Name " Jr"
tree op lappend $t sam     Class 5
tree op incr    $t mary    Age
tree op update  $t tom     Rate(A) 2
tree op set     $t tom     Sax F
tree op set     $t sam     Rate(C) 0
tree op incr    $t 0->mary Age
```

The most important use is probably for with, eg.

```
tree op with $t .system.bing b {
      set s(OS) LX
      set a b c
}
```

to detect scripting errors.

9.12 Data Validation

See **Struct** for one approach to data validation.

9.13 Key Hashing

For nodes with 21 or fewer keys, tree remembers the order of key creation. Nodes with more than 21 keys will automatically change over to hash-table based key storage. One side-affect of this is that it alters the order of key iteration, which can change the results from get/names/values. That's because list-based storage preserves the order in which keys are added, whereas a hash-based storage has an undetermined order.
This can be overcome by creating the tree with a large -keyhash size (eg. 1000000).

For example, the following sets keys from a list and avoids being hashed:

```
set t [tree create -keyhash [llength $lst]]
set n -1
foreach i $lst {
   $t set 0   $i [incr n]
}
puts [$t names 0 ; # outputs the original $lst.
```

Note that adding just one more key will cause the above to switch to hashing and thus scramble the lst order.

10. Ted - The Editor

Ted is a tabbed editor written using **Gui**. It provides several key functions, the most important of which is **completion**for Tcl and Tk commands and Tk subcommands. For example, we can type the following:

```
TreeView e
```

and in the status line note there are two matching subcommands: entry and edit. By adding an n the editor shows the matching entry which typing <Tab> will complete.
If we then type:

```
TreeView entry conf $w $id -
```

and hit <Control-space>, we get list of all the known options.
This can greatly simplify the job of writing Tk code. It virtually eliminates the need to memorize hundreds of subcommands or their thousands of options.

Despite this power, Ted is a fairly simple application. It derives much of it's functionality by hooking into the Tcl implementation of Gui.

11. Tdb - A GDB Frontend

Tdb is a Gui frontend for GDB written in **Wize** and **Gui**. It provide a compact but powerful interface that exposes most of GDBs features using MI. Unlike other such frontends, Tdb does not use a C parser to decode MI because it maps MI output directly to a Tcl list. This fact allows Tdb to be developed and distributed in pure script form.

11.1 Screenshot

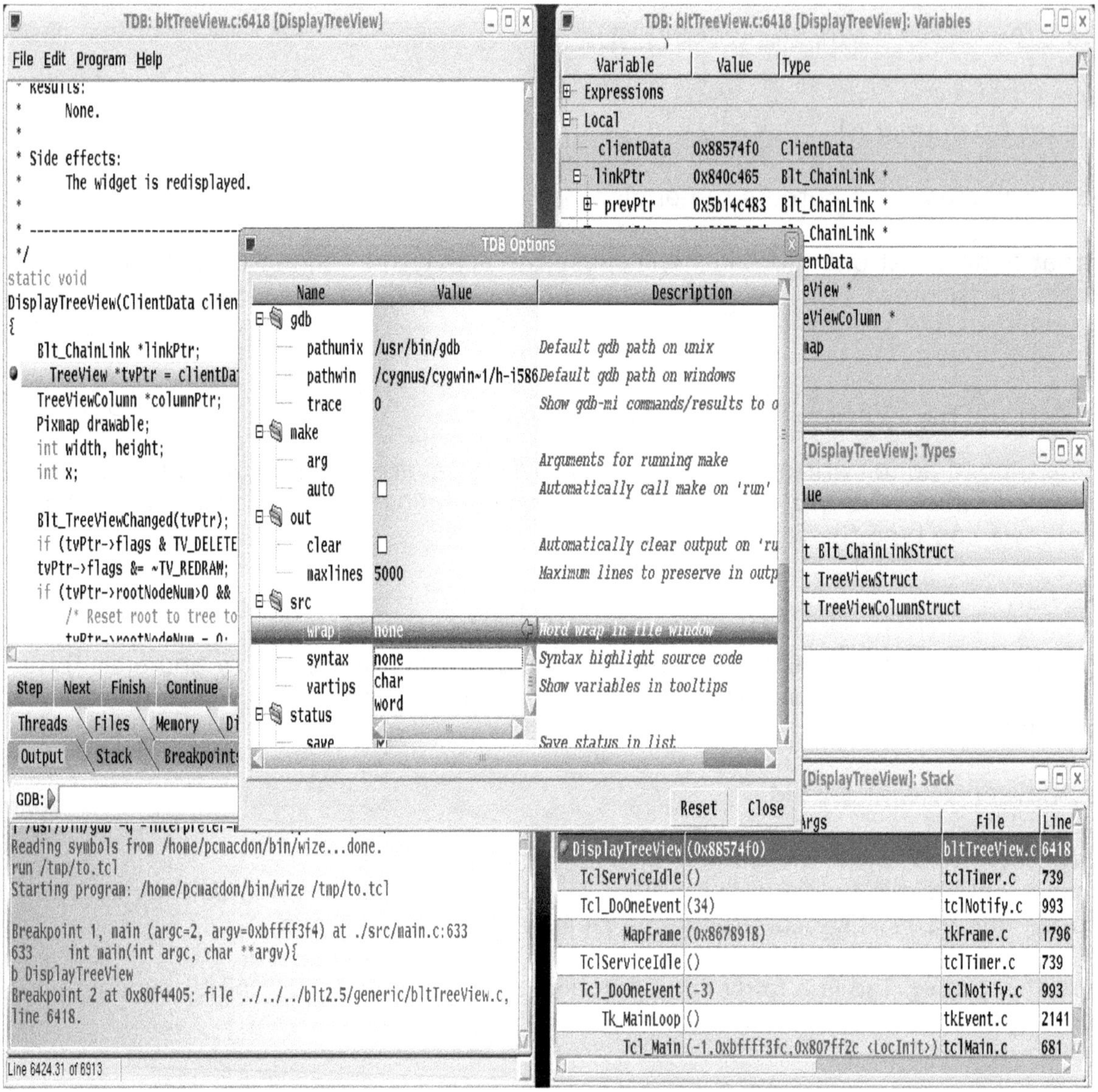

11.2 Features

Tdb provides the following features:

- A Stack browser.
- A Variable tree inspector.
- A Types tree inspector.

- Files and Functions tree with searches.
- Memory, Registers, Threads and Disassembly.
- A GDB help tree browser with searches.
- A GDB options tree browse and modify.
- Direct access to the GDB interface.

Tdb is fast, and provides most navigation just by double-clicking.

- Double clicking in the Stack tab will return to that point of execution.
- Double clicking in the Variable tab will go to the declaration.
- Double clicking in the Types tab will go to the type definition, etc.

The implementation source is about 5K lines of which 4K lines are validated Tcl code, and 600 lines are GUI specification. Of the latter, the layout and style code are about 50/50 or about 300 lines each.

The total size of tdb.zip is about 35K.

11.3 Running Tdb

Tdb can be executed thus:

```
wize tdb.zip myprog arg ....
# or
wize / Apps/Tdb myprog arg ...
```

12. Ledger

Ledger is **Gui** based personal finance application featuring:

- Fast and easy use with auto-completions.
- Reconciliation and report dialogs.
- Import/export QIF transactions/accounts.
- Uses double-entry accounting.
- Handles 10's of thousands of transactions with ease.
- Stores data as plain UTF8 text.
- Supports RCS and CVS for backup-on-save.
- Near zero dependancies (implemented in a single .tcl file).

Here are some screenshots:

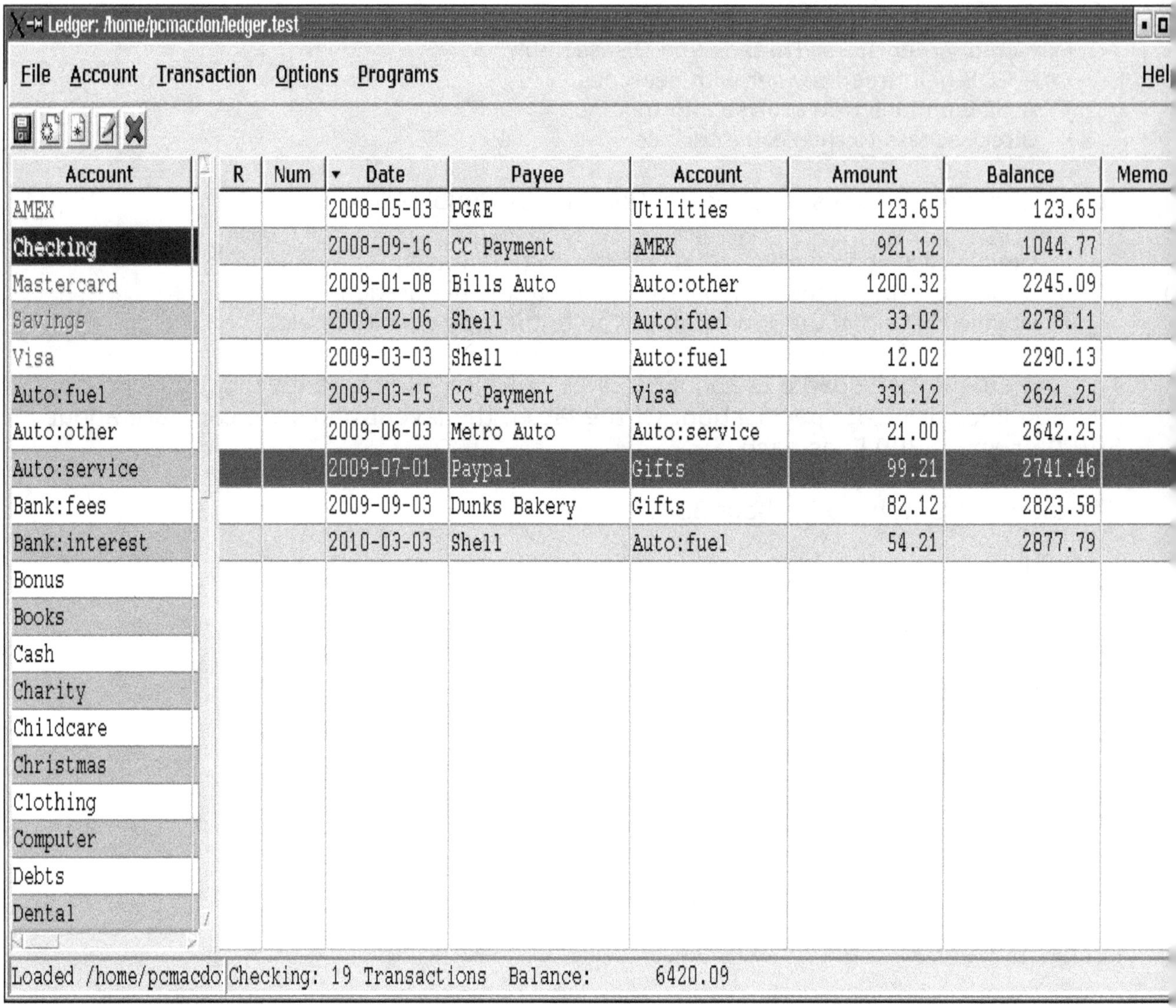
Ledger: /home/pcmacdon/ledger.test
File Account Transaction Options Programs Hel
Account
AMEX
Checking
Mastercard
Savings
Visa
Auto:fuel
Auto:other
Auto:service
Bank:fees
Bank:interest
Bonus
Books
Cash
Charity
Childcare
Christmas
Clothing
Computer
Debts
Dental
R Num Date Payee Account Amount Balance Memo
2008-05-03 PG&E Utilities 123.65 123.65
2008-09-16 CC Payment AMEX 921.12 1044.77
2009-01-08 Bills Auto Auto:other 1200.32 2245.09
2009-02-06 Shell Auto:fuel 33.02 2278.11
2009-03-03 Shell Auto:fuel 12.02 2290.13
2009-03-15 CC Payment Visa 331.12 2621.25
2009-06-03 Metro Auto Auto:service 21.00 2642.25
2009-07-01 Paypal Gifts 99.21 2741.46
2009-09-03 Dunks Bakery Gifts 82.12 2823.58
2010-03-03 Shell Auto:fuel 54.21 2877.79
Loaded /home/pcmacdo Checking: 19 Transactions Balance: 6420.09

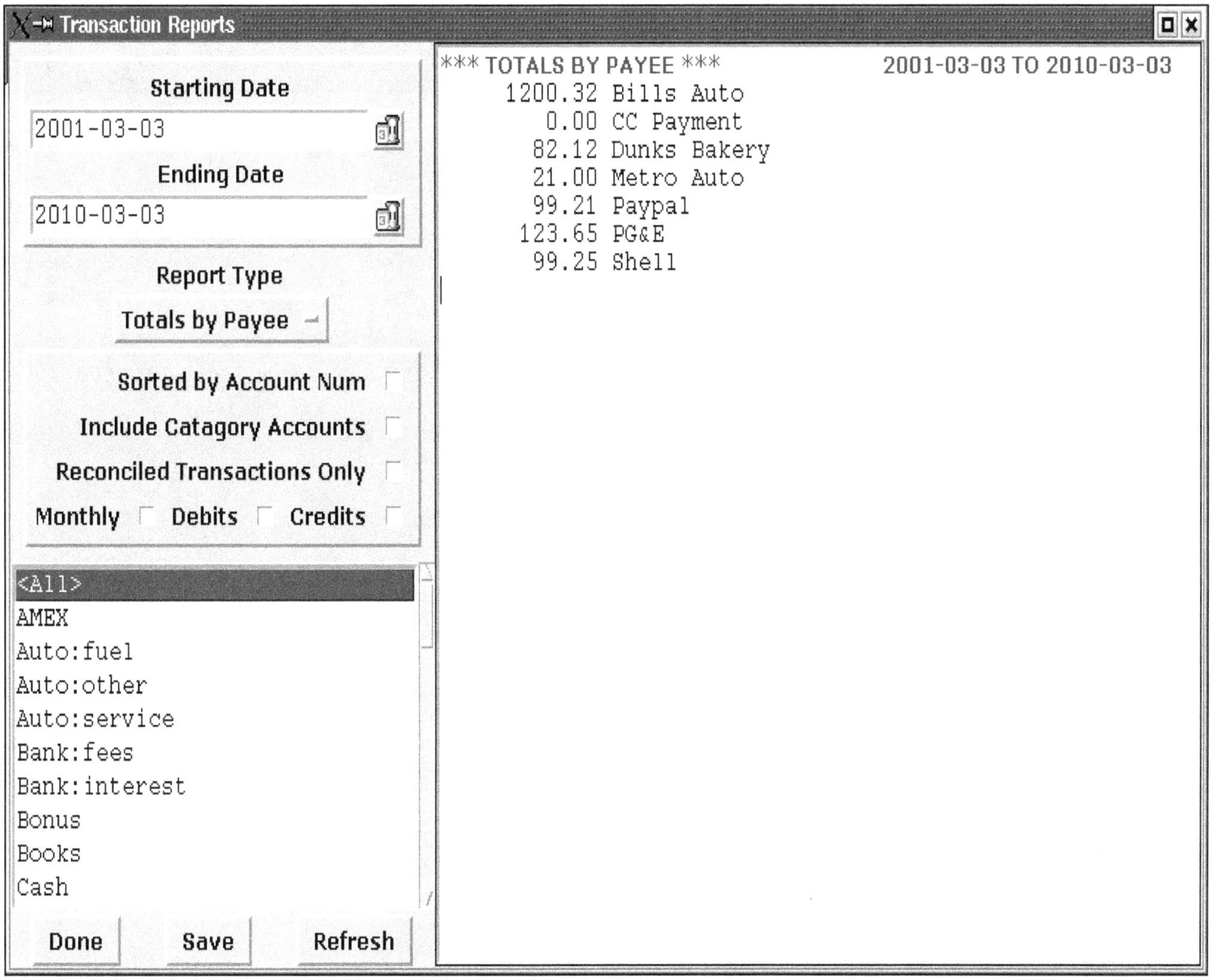
Transaction Reports
Starting Date
2001-03-03
Ending Date
2010-03-03
Report Type
Totals by Payee
Sorted by Account Num
Include Catagory Accounts
Reconciled Transactions Only
Monthly
Debits
Credits
<All>
AMEX
Auto:fuel
Auto:other
Auto:service
Bank:fees
Bank:interest
Bonus
Books
Cash
Done
Save
Refresh
*** TOTALS BY PAYEE ***
2001-03-03 TO 2010-03-03
1200.32 Bills Auto
0.00 CC Payment
82.12 Dunks Bakery
21.00 Metro Auto
99.21 Paypal
123.65 PG&E
99.25 Shell

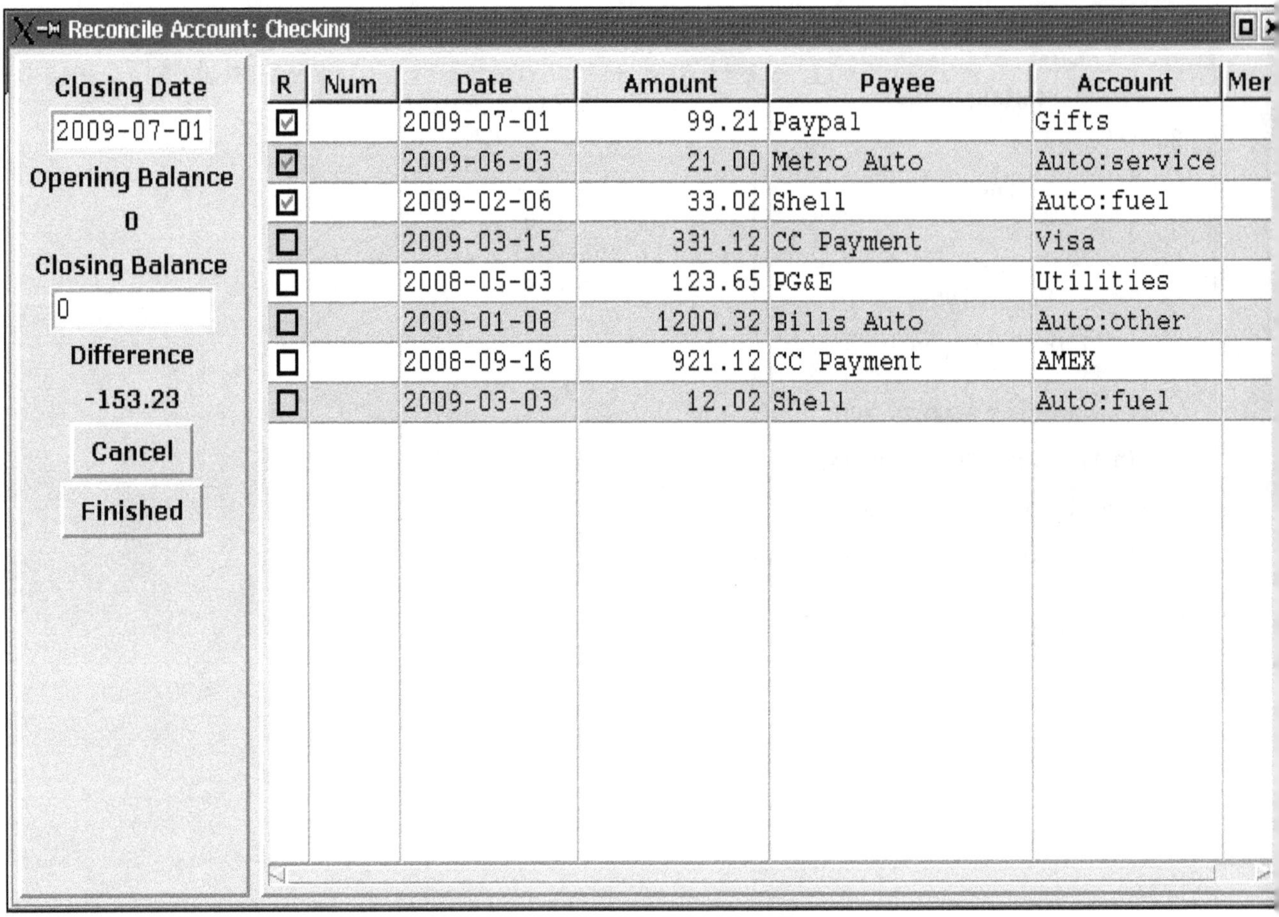

12.1 Running It

Ledger requires **Wize** and is run like so:

```
wize ledger.tcl
```

or the builtin version can be run with:

```
wize / Gui/Ledger
```

12.2 Data Storage

Since Ledger uses **Tree** saving and restoring data simply uses the sub-commands dump and restore.

12.3 Multiple Books

Multiple sets of accounts can be managed using:

```
wize / Gui/Ledger -dir ~/work
```

If -dir is not given it defaults to ~/ledger.

12.4 Exploring/Debugging

As with all Wize applications, you can use <Control-Alt-Shift-2> to **explore** it. Select aclist_1 from the "Vars" menu to examine the accounts data, or xaction_1 to examine transaction data. Or use Introspect to examine the entire program state.

12.5 Un-implemented Features

- Scheduled transactions.
- Budgets and investments.
- Multiple currencies.
- Charts, graphs, etc.
- Bank download/sync.

---

13. Top

Top is a GUI interface to the Unix text based system monitoring facility top. Its purpose is to exercise some key features of Wize, including:

- demonstrate the ease of using **Gui**.
- repeatedly insert/delete data from a TreeView widget.
- make extensive use of **Styles**.

Top can be invoked with:

```
wize / Gui/Top
```

Top has 3 main tabs, plus optional per-PID monitors.

Here are some screenshots:

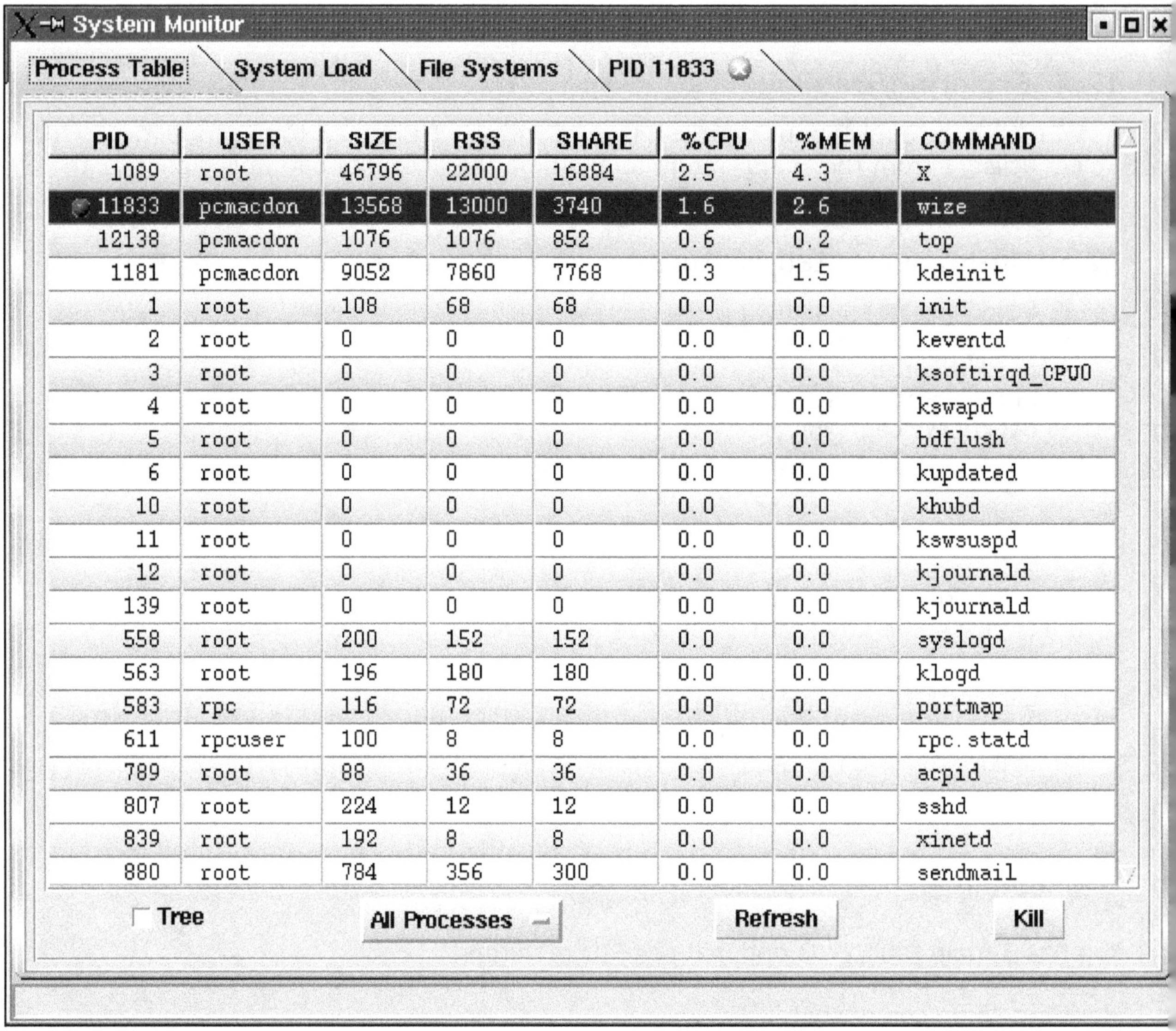

PID	USER	SIZE	RSS	SHARE	%CPU	%MEM	COMMAND
1089	root	46796	22000	16884	2.5	4.3	X
11833	pcmacdon	13568	13000	3740	1.6	2.6	wize
12138	pcmacdon	1076	1076	852	0.6	0.2	top
1181	pcmacdon	9052	7860	7768	0.3	1.5	kdeinit
1	root	108	68	68	0.0	0.0	init
2	root	0	0	0	0.0	0.0	keventd
3	root	0	0	0	0.0	0.0	ksoftirqd_CPU0
4	root	0	0	0	0.0	0.0	kswapd
5	root	0	0	0	0.0	0.0	bdflush
6	root	0	0	0	0.0	0.0	kupdated
10	root	0	0	0	0.0	0.0	khubd
11	root	0	0	0	0.0	0.0	kswsuspd
12	root	0	0	0	0.0	0.0	kjournald
139	root	0	0	0	0.0	0.0	kjournald
558	root	200	152	152	0.0	0.0	syslogd
563	root	196	180	180	0.0	0.0	klogd
583	rpc	116	72	72	0.0	0.0	portmap
611	rpcuser	100	8	8	0.0	0.0	rpc.statd
789	root	88	36	36	0.0	0.0	acpid
807	root	224	12	12	0.0	0.0	sshd
839	root	192	8	8	0.0	0.0	xinetd
880	root	784	356	300	0.0	0.0	sendmail

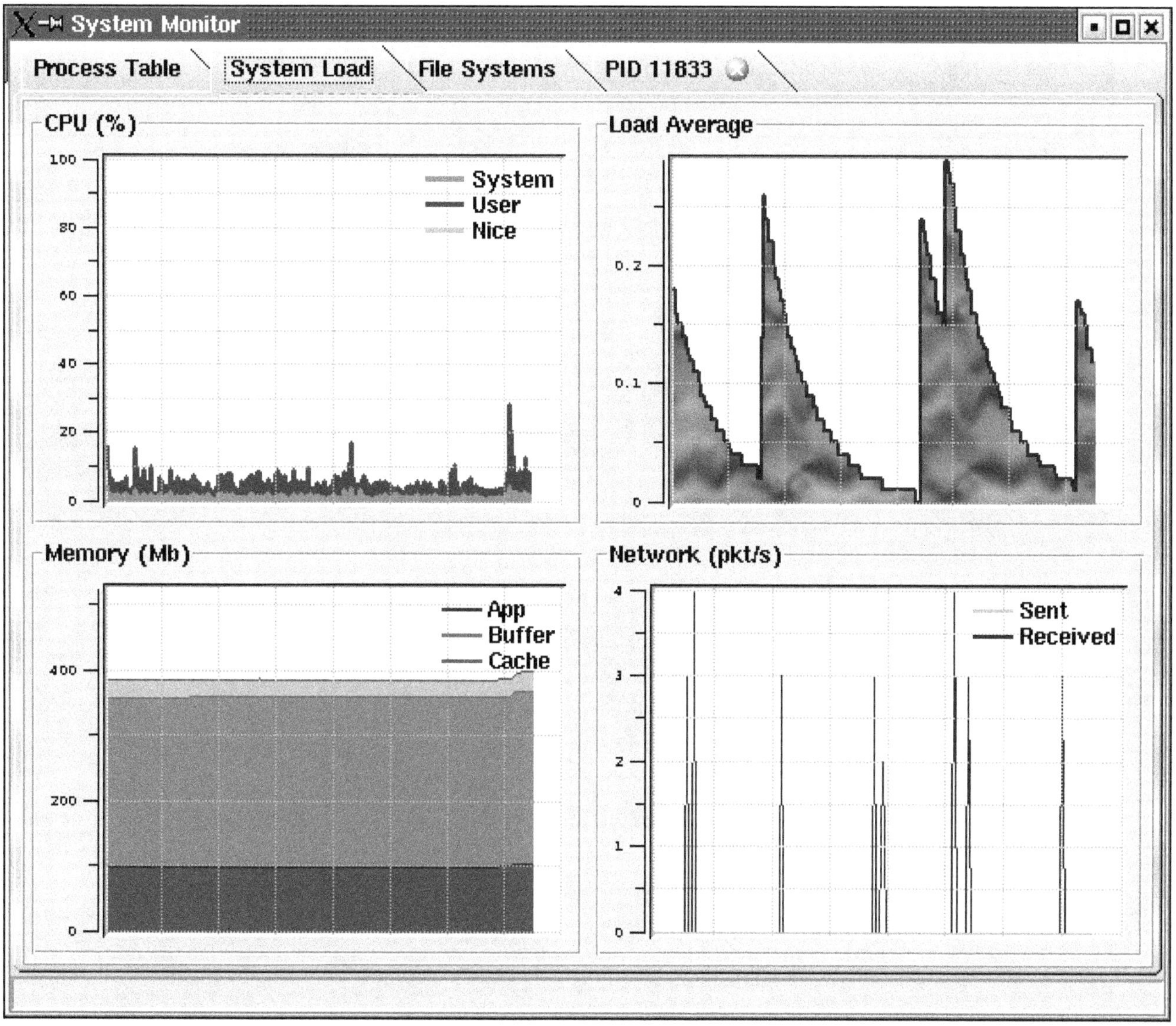
System Monitor
Process Table
System Load
File Systems
PID 11833
CPU (%)
100
80
60
40
20
0
System
User
Nice
Load Average
0.2
0.1
0
Memory (Mb)
400
200
0
App
Buffer
Cache
Network (pkt/s)
4
3
2
1
0
Sent
Received

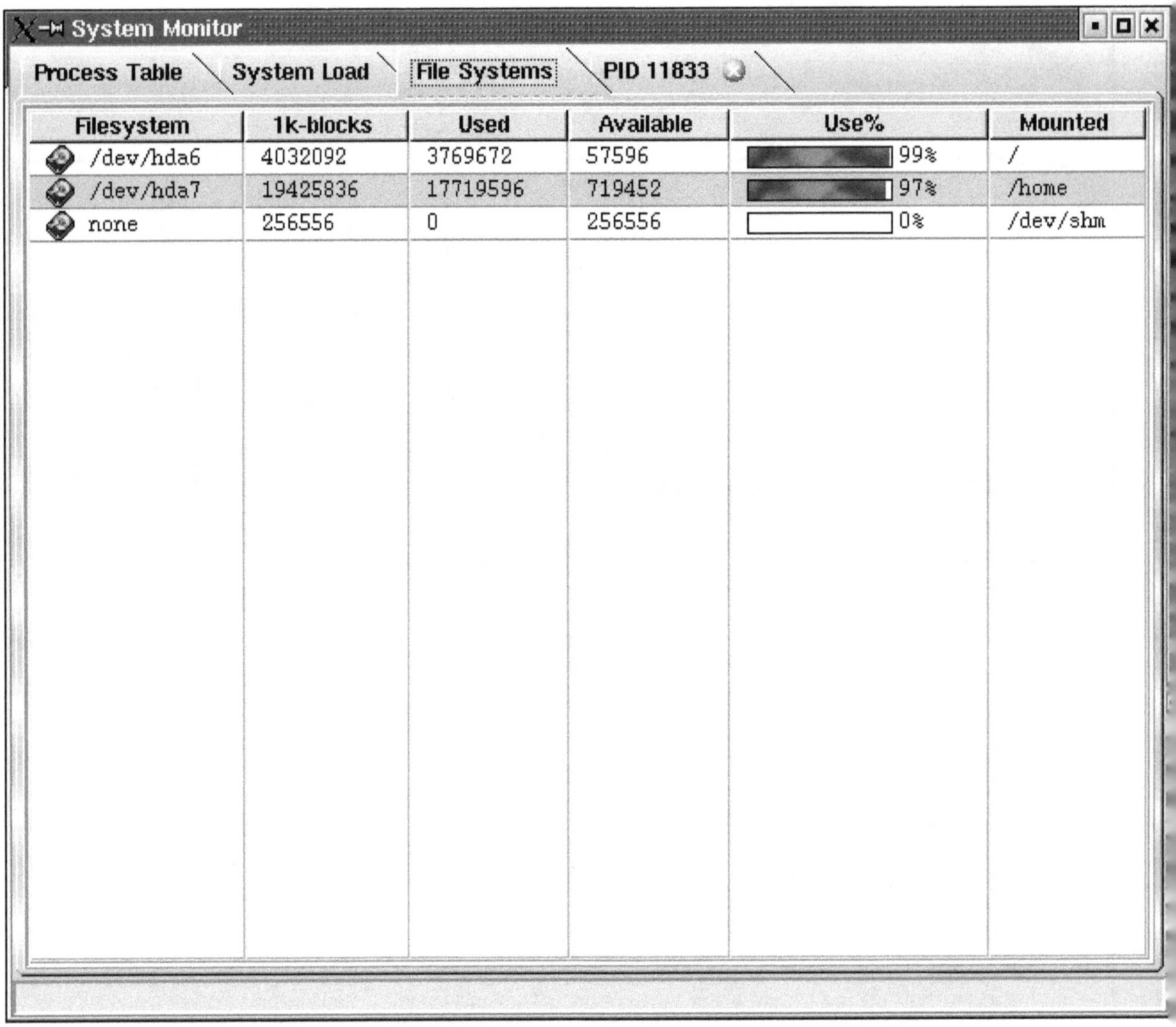
System Monitor
Process Table
System Load
File Systems
PID 11833
Filesystem
1k-blocks
Used
Available
Use%
Mounted
/dev/hda6
4032092
3769672
57596
99%
/
/dev/hda7
19425836
17719596
719452
97%
/home
none
256556
0
256556
0%
/dev/shm

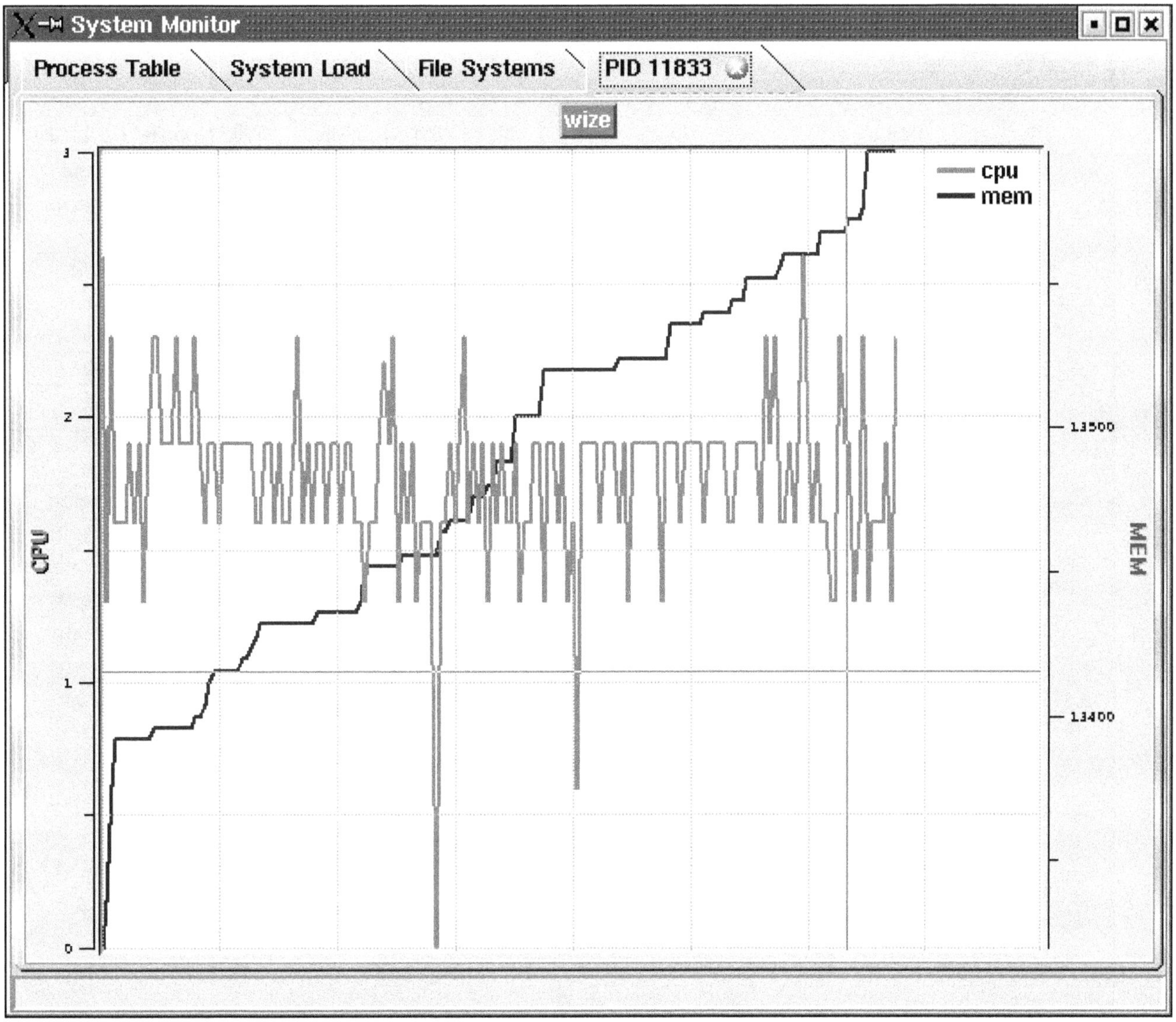

13.1 Process Table

Displays a list of all processes running on the system.

There are options for displaying only a subset of processes, as well as changing the display mode to tree.

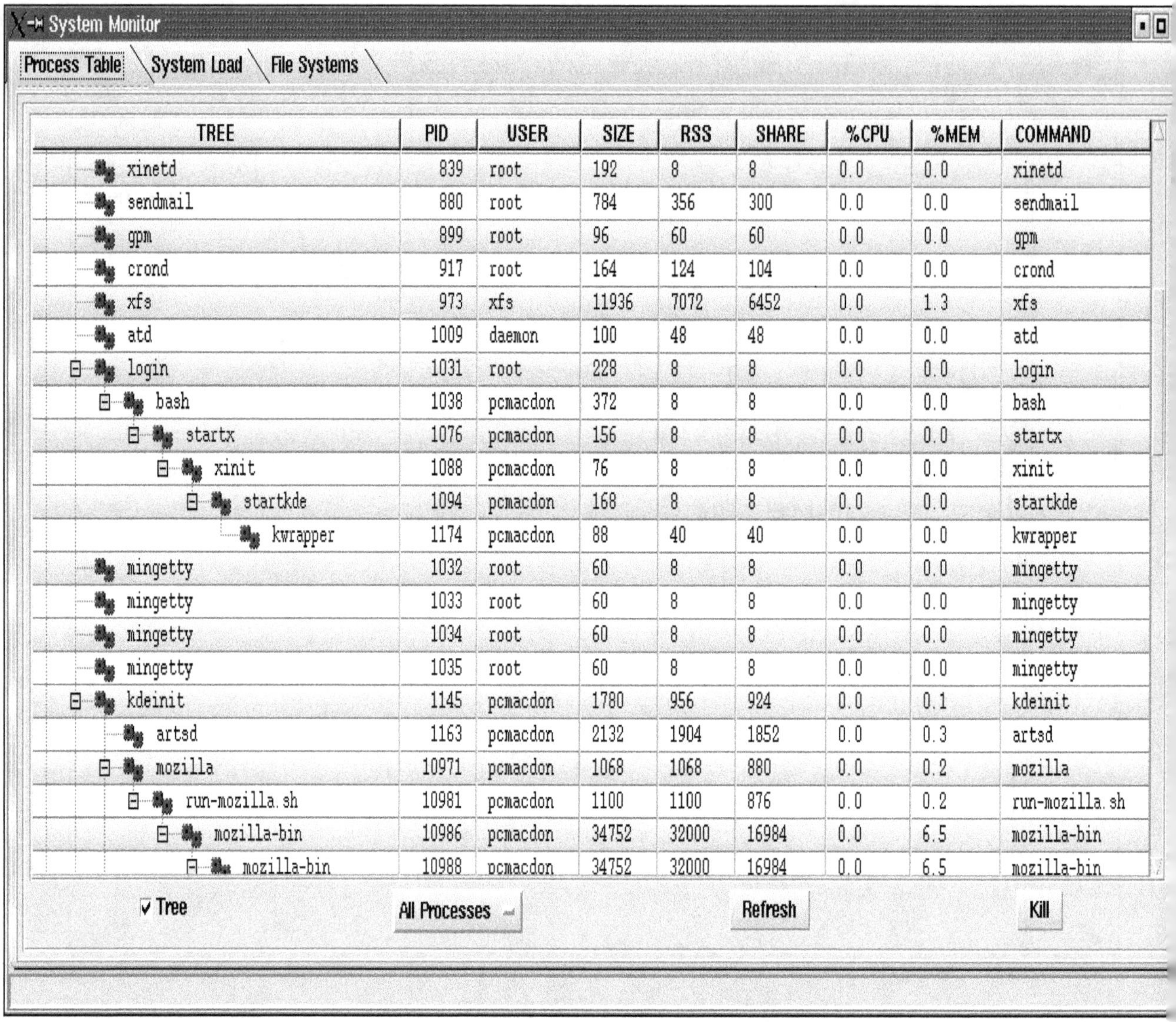

Using right-click gives a menu that allows monitoring specific PIDs, Renicing a process or sending signals to a process. It can also show or hide columns.

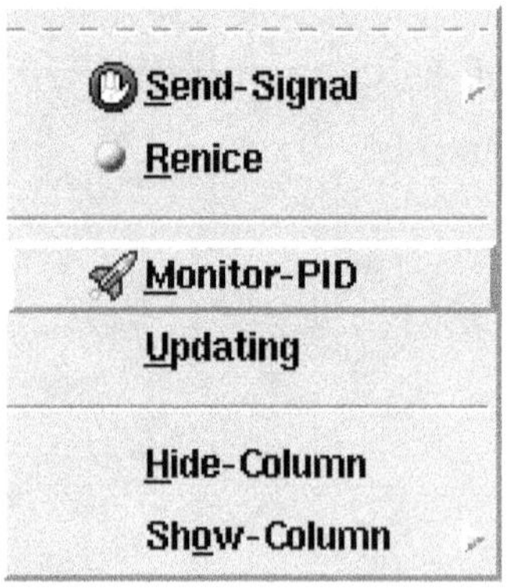

13.2 System Load

Displays 4 graphs:

- CPU% - cumultive CPU used by running processes.
- Memory - cumultive Memory used by processes.
- Load Average - the average load factor.
- Network - network activity

13.3 File Systems

This displays usage by file system.

13.4 PID Monitor

PID Monitor collects and graphs information about a single process. To close the tab, left click on the red cross.

---

14. Gsqlite

Gsqlite is a user interface for **Sqlite**. It is modeled somewhat after Sqlite Studio, but it's main purpose is to demonstrate how **Gui** can enable single file applications.

You can run Gsqlite from **Wize**, eg:

```
wize / Mod/Gsqlite mydata.db
```

There is currently no documentation other than a few screenshots:

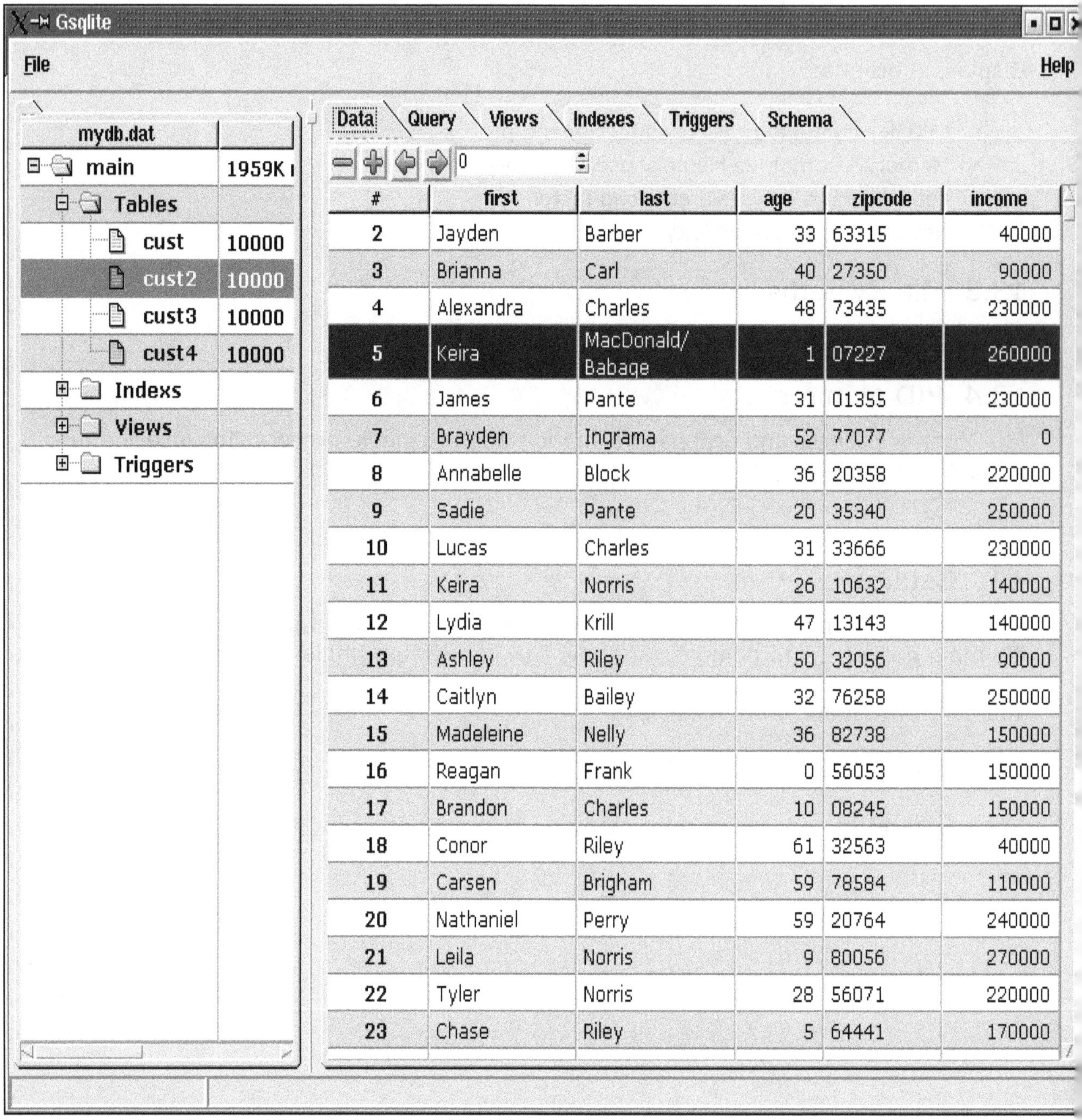
Gsqlite
File
Help
mydb.dat
main 1959K
Tables
cust 10000
cust2 10000
cust3 10000
cust4 10000
Indexs
Views
Triggers
Data
Query
Views
Indexes
Triggers
Schema
0
first last age zipcode income
2 Jayden Barber 33 63315 40000
3 Brianna Carl 40 27350 90000
4 Alexandra Charles 48 73435 230000
5 Keira MacDonald/ Babage 1 07227 260000
6 James Pante 31 01355 230000
7 Brayden Ingrama 52 77077 0
8 Annabelle Block 36 20358 220000
9 Sadie Pante 20 35340 250000
10 Lucas Charles 31 33666 230000
11 Keira Norris 26 10632 140000
12 Lydia Krill 47 13143 140000
13 Ashley Riley 50 32056 90000
14 Caitlyn Bailey 32 76258 250000
15 Madeleine Nelly 36 82738 150000
16 Reagan Frank 0 56053 150000
17 Brandon Charles 10 08245 150000
18 Conor Riley 61 32563 40000
19 Carsen Brigham 59 78584 110000
20 Nathaniel Perry 59 20764 240000
21 Leila Norris 9 80056 270000
22 Tyler Norris 28 56071 220000
23 Chase Riley 5 64441 170000

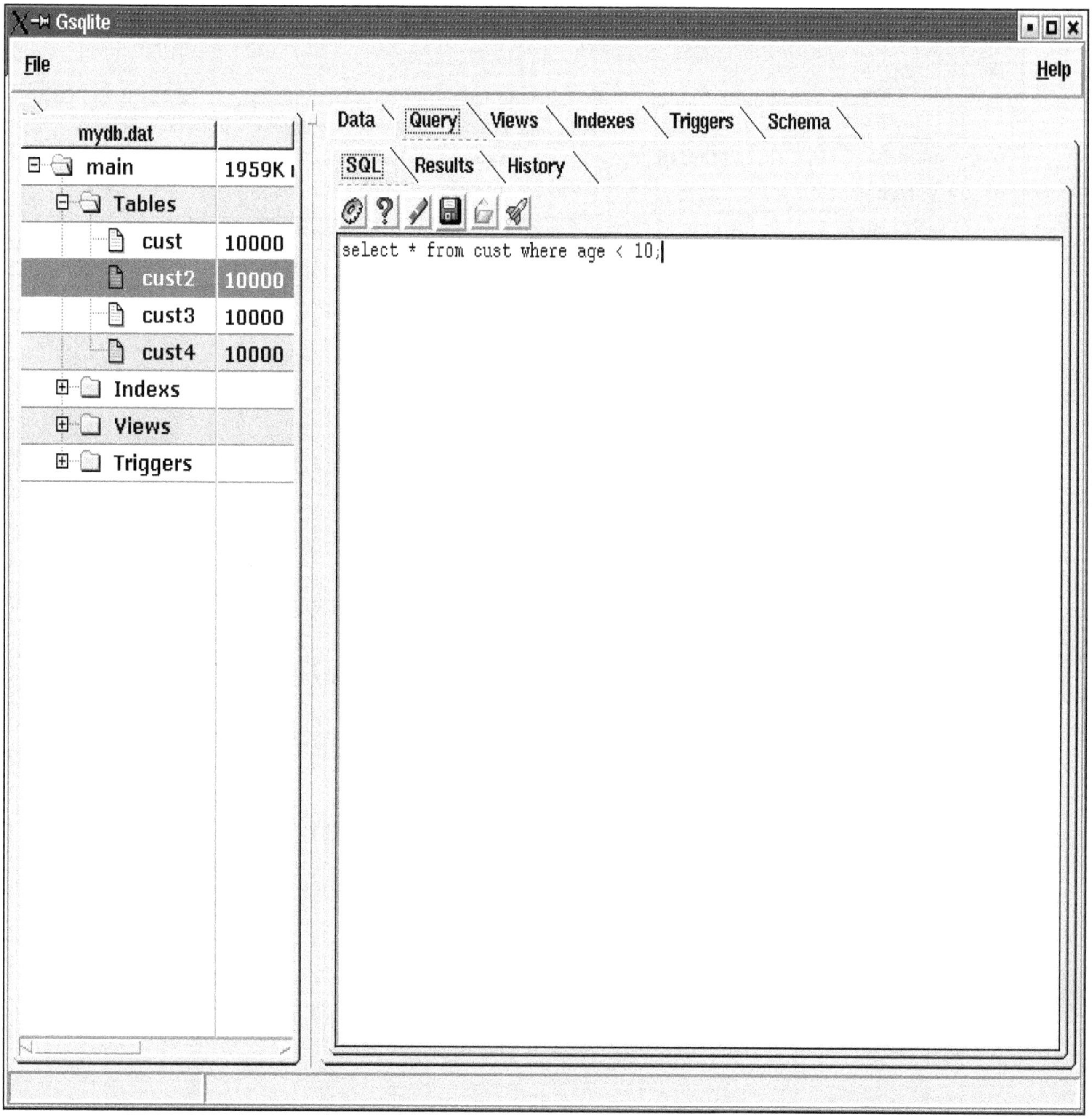
Gsqlite
File
Help
mydb.dat
main
1959K
Tables
cust
10000
cust2
10000
cust3
10000
cust4
10000
Indexs
Views
Triggers
Data
Query
Views
Indexes
Triggers
Schema
SQL
Results
History
select * from cust where age < 10;

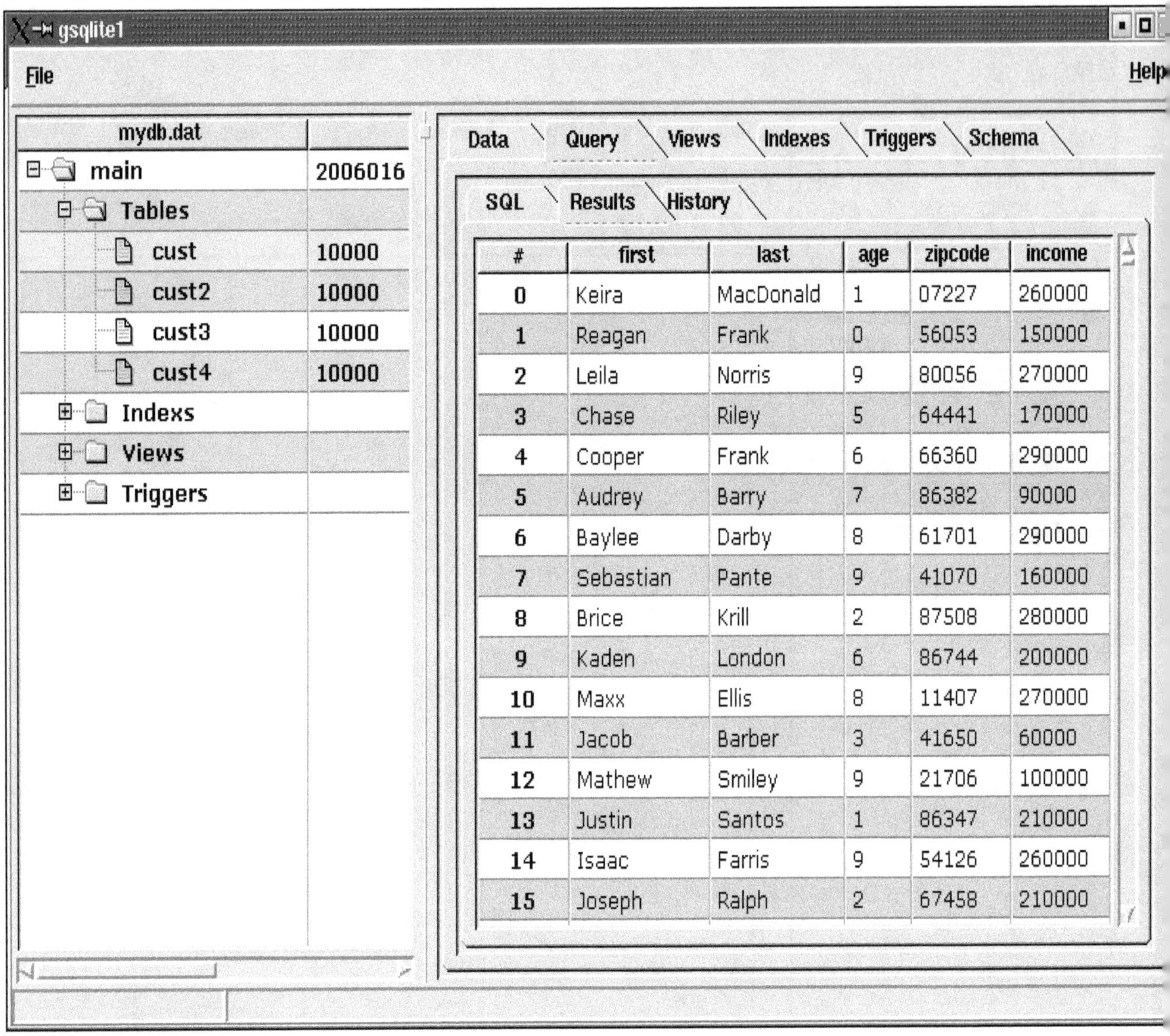
gsqlite1
File
Help
mydb.dat
main 2006016
Tables
cust 10000
cust2 10000
cust3 10000
cust4 10000
Indexs
Views
Triggers
Data
Query
Views
Indexes
Triggers
Schema
SQL
Results
History
first last age zipcode income
0 Keira MacDonald 1 07227 260000
1 Reagan Frank 0 56053 150000
2 Leila Norris 9 80056 270000
3 Chase Riley 5 64441 170000
4 Cooper Frank 6 66360 290000
5 Audrey Barry 7 86382 90000
6 Baylee Darby 8 61701 290000
7 Sebastian Pante 9 41070 160000
8 Brice Krill 2 87508 280000
9 Kaden London 6 86744 200000
10 Maxx Ellis 8 11407 270000
11 Jacob Barber 3 41650 60000
12 Mathew Smiley 9 21706 100000
13 Justin Santos 1 86347 210000
14 Isaac Farris 9 54126 260000
15 Joseph Ralph 2 67458 210000

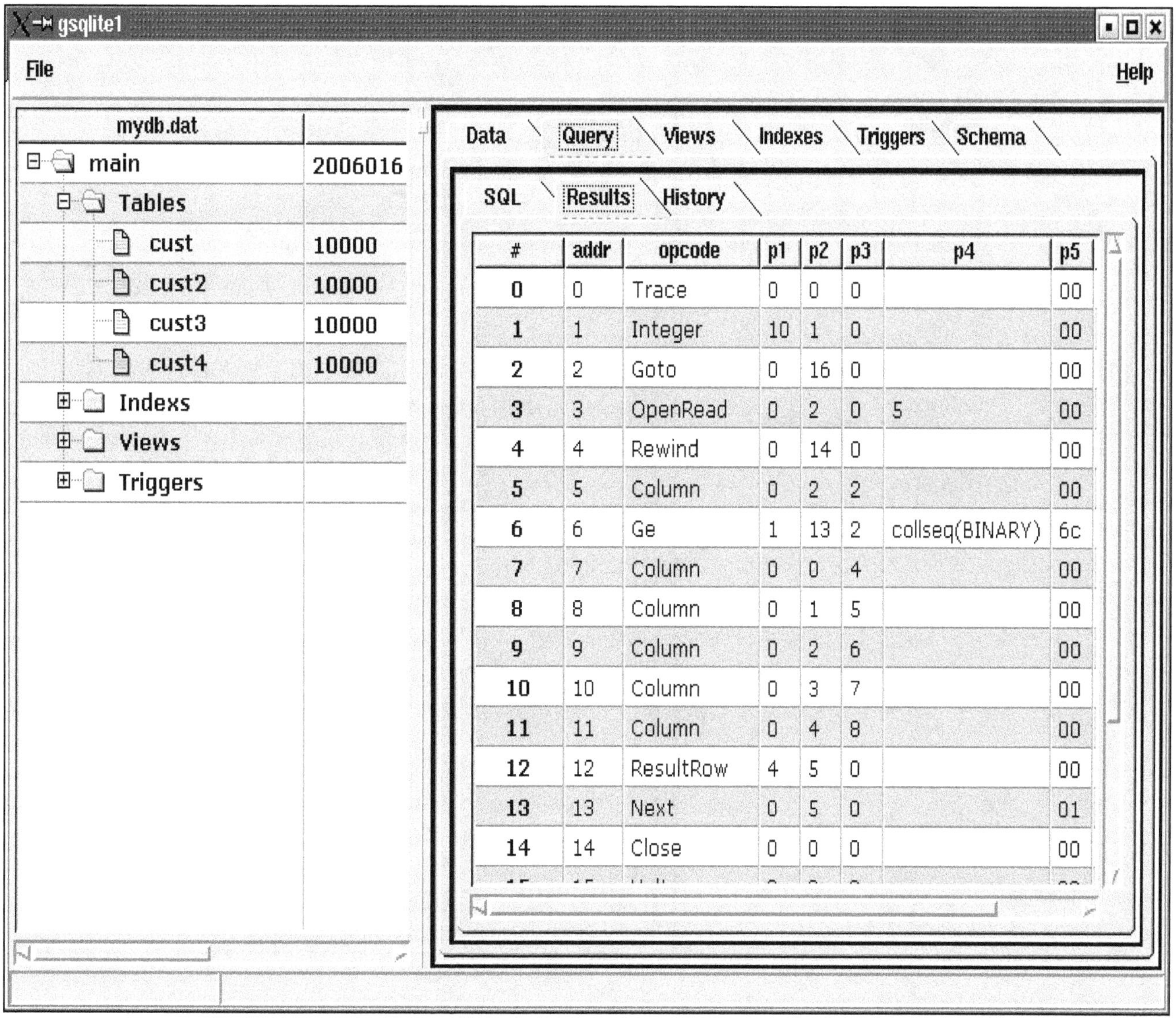
gsqlite1
File
Help
mydb.dat
main 2006016
Tables
cust 10000
cust2 10000
cust3 10000
cust4 10000
Indexs
Views
Triggers
Data
Query
Views
Indexes
Triggers
Schema
SQL
Results
History
addr opcode p1 p2 p3 p4 p5
0 0 Trace 0 0 0 00
1 1 Integer 10 1 0 00
2 2 Goto 0 16 0 00
3 3 OpenRead 0 2 0 5 00
4 4 Rewind 0 14 0 00
5 5 Column 0 2 2 00
6 6 Ge 1 13 2 collseq(BINARY) 6c
7 7 Column 0 0 4 00
8 8 Column 0 1 5 00
9 9 Column 0 2 6 00
10 10 Column 0 3 7 00
11 11 Column 0 4 8 00
12 12 ResultRow 4 5 0 00
13 13 Next 0 5 0 01
14 14 Close 0 0 0 00

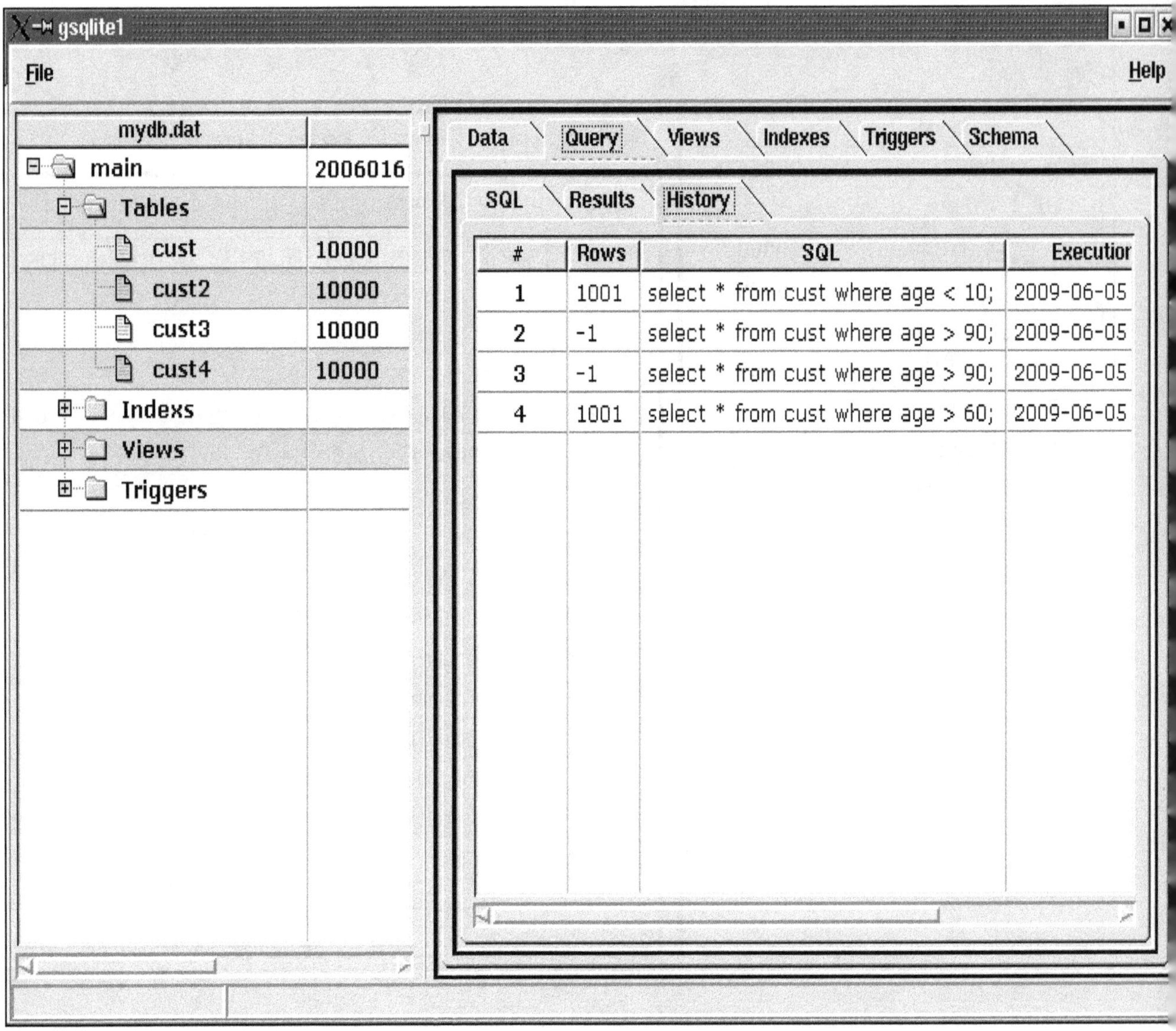

14.1 Sqlite Server

Gsqlite can run **SOS** in sqlite server mode. This is launched from the File menu.

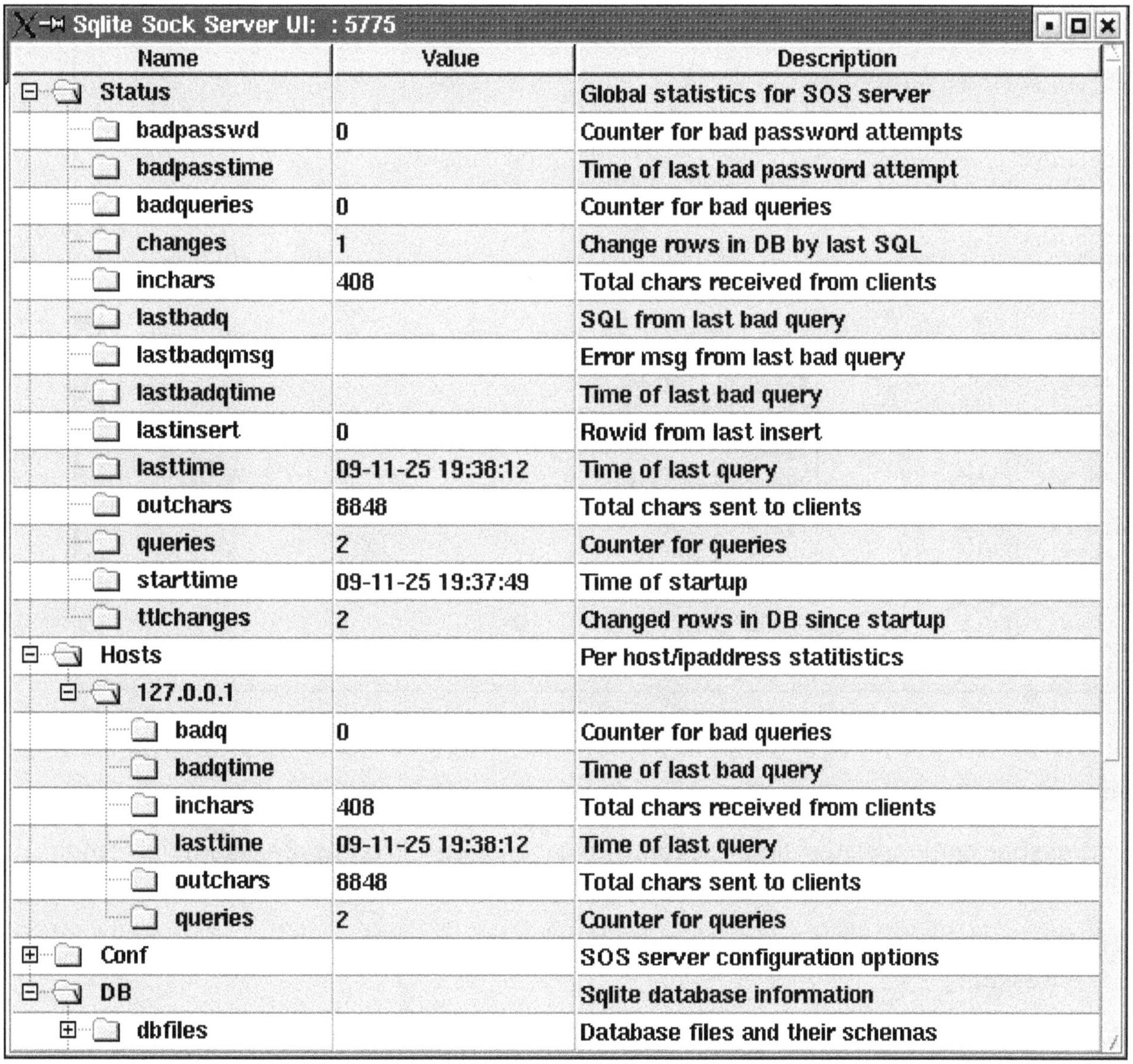

Sqlite Sock Server UI: :5775

Name	Value	Description
Status		Global statistics for SOS server
badpasswd	0	Counter for bad password attempts
badpasstime		Time of last bad password attempt
badqueries	0	Counter for bad queries
changes	1	Change rows in DB by last SQL
inchars	408	Total chars received from clients
lastbadq		SQL from last bad query
lastbadqmsg		Error msg from last bad query
lastbadqtime		Time of last bad query
lastinsert	0	Rowid from last insert
lasttime	09-11-25 19:38:12	Time of last query
outchars	8848	Total chars sent to clients
queries	2	Counter for queries
starttime	09-11-25 19:37:49	Time of startup
ttlchanges	2	Changed rows in DB since startup
Hosts		Per host/ipaddress statitistics
127.0.0.1		
badq	0	Counter for bad queries
badqtime		Time of last bad query
inchars	408	Total chars received from clients
lasttime	09-11-25 19:38:12	Time of last query
outchars	8848	Total chars sent to clients
queries	2	Counter for queries
Conf		SOS server configuration options
DB		Sqlite database information
dbfiles		Database files and their schemas

14.2 Sqlite Client

Gsqlite can run **SOS** in sqlite client mode. This is launched from the File menu.

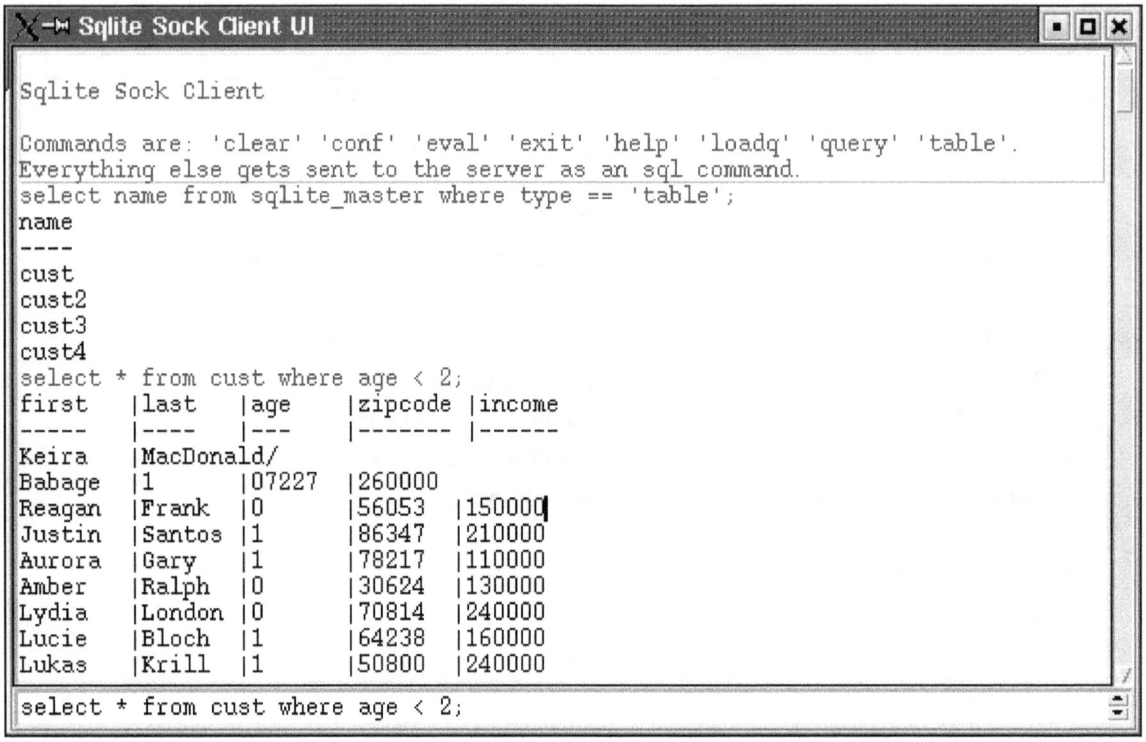

15. ProgressBar

ProgressBar demonstrates simple extension tags in **Gui**. ProgressBar is implemented using a canvas, either via an attribute to Canvas, or the ProgressBar tag, eg.

```
{Canvas - -pos _ -progressbar 1} {}
{ProgressBar} {}
```

Note that this is much easier than defining a mega-widget as it does not require a defining programmer methods such as configure, cget, etc.

15.1 Example

In this example we use Gui to define some progress bars, where:

- The left hand bar races up and down.
- The left hand bar tile image pulses.
- Mouse over the blue dot turns it red.
- Clicking the dot pauses/resumes.

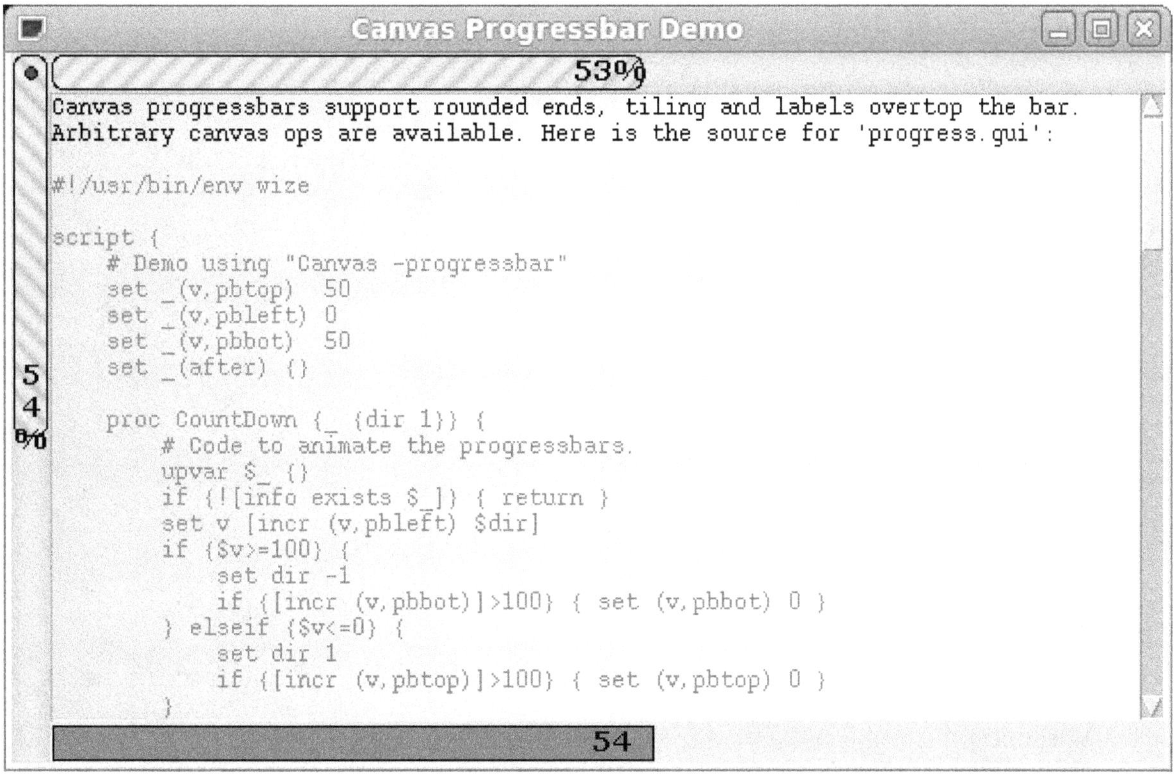

15.2 Demo Source

Here is the source for the demo. See the gui/extattrs.tcl source for the implementation.

Canvas progressbars support rounded ends, tiling and labels overtop the bar.
Arbitrary canvas ops are available. Here is the source for 'progress.gui':

```
#!/usr/bin/env wize

script {
    # Demo using "Canvas -progressbar"
    set _(v,pbtop)  50
    set _(v,pbleft) 0
    set _(v,pbbot)  50
    set _(after) {}

    proc CountDown {_ {dir 1}} {
        # Code to animate the progressbars.
        upvar $_ {}
        if {![info exists $_]} { return }
        set v [incr (v,pbleft) $dir]
        if {$v>=100} {
            set dir -1
            if {[incr (v,pbbot)]>100} { set (v,pbbot) 0 }
```

```
        } elseif {$v<=0} {
            set dir 1
            if {[incr (v,pbtop)]>100} { set (v,pbtop) 0 }
        }
        set (after) [after 30 [list [namespace current]::CountDown $_ $dir]]
    }

    proc StartStop {_} {
        # Start/stop countdown.
        upvar $_ {}
        if {$(after) != {}} {
            after cancel $(after)
            set (after) {}
            return
        }
        CountDown $_
    }

    proc Main {_} {
        # Program entry point.
        upvar $_ {}
        variable pd
        Text insert $(w,text_1) end "Canvas progressbars support rounded ends, tiling
and labels overtop the bar.\n"
        Text insert $(w,text_1) end "Arbitrary canvas ops are available. Here is the
source for 'progress.gui':\n\n"
        Text insert $(w,text_1) end $pd(gui) code
        set c $(w,pbleft)
        # Create a round button to reset start/stop.
        Canvas create oval $c {7 7 13 13} -fill Blue -width 1 -outline Black -tags o
        $c bind o <Enter> "$c itemconf 3 -fill red; $c conf -cursor hand2"
        $c bind o <Leave> "$c itemconf 3 -fill blue; $c conf -cursor {}"
        $c bind o <1> "$_ StartStop"
        CountDown $_
    }

    proc Cleanup {_} {
        # Program cleanup.
        upvar $_ {}
        *catch {after cancel $(after)}
        exit; # Exit cause this is just a demo.
    }

}

style {
    # "Style overrides for -progressbar attrs: creates image tiles, rounded, etc"
```

```
    Toplevel {
        @defgradients {
            slan  {#daa520 #ffd700 -width 13 -height 13 -slant 1.0}
            slanp {#daa520 #ffd700 -width 13 -height 13 -slant 1.0 -rotate 90}
            chal1 {#bebebe #d3d3d3 -width 20 -height 15 -rotate 90}
            chal2 {#bebebe #d3d3d3 -width 20 -height 15}
            tbg { Khaki #ffffff -width 1000 -height 6 -gamma .5}
        }
        @deffonts {
            bfnt {Verdana -14 bold}
        }

        @imgpulse { slanp }
        *highlightThickness 0
    }
    Text { -tile ^tbg -padx 0 -pady 0 @tags {code {-foreground SteelBlue} } }
    .pbtop {
        -tile ^chal1
        @@ { -progressbar {-bartile ^slan  -font ^bfnt -round 1 -suffix %}}
    }
    .pbleft {
        -tile ^chal2
        @@ { -progressbar {-bartile ^slanp -font ^bfnt -round 1 -suffix % -vertical
1 }}
    }
}

{Toplevel + -title "Canvas Progressbar Demo"} {
    {Canvas - -id pbleft -pos |l -progressbar {-vertical 1}} {}
    {Frame + -pos *l} {
        {Canvas - -id pbtop -pos _ -progressbar 1} {}
        {Text - -pos * -scroll *} {}
        {ProgressBar - -id pbbot -font ^bfnt -pos _} {}
    }
}
```

---

16. Running Wize

Wize offer a lot of flexibility for packaging and running application scripts, eg.

```
wize            ; # Run interactive shell (then type: console show)
wize file.tcl   ; # Run a script
wize file.gui   ; # Run gui script
wize file.zip   ; # Mount zip file and run main.tcl/.gui
wize file.zip:  ; # Mount zip file and browse for script.
```

```
wize file.zip:x.tcl    ; # Mount zip file and run x.tcl
wize file.so           ; # Load dll, then mount and run main.tcl
wize file.so:          ; # Load dll, mount, and browse,
```

Wize treats any .zip/.so file as a **wizapp**. ie. it looks for main.tcl in the top directory (or single subdirectory). Alternatively, a .tcl or .gui file of the same prefix as the .zip file will be used. If found, it is executed.

To browse instead, just append a colon.

16.1 Relayed Links to Wize

A wize executable can use a file link to run a .zip file indirectly. For example, suppose you've developed a Tcl application in the subdirectory foo (and it contains a foo/main.tcl). And assume that wize is located in ~/bin. You can create a new foo command using:

```
zip -r ~/bin/foo.zip foo/
ln -s ~/bin/wize ~/bin/foo
```

See **Admin** if you don't have zip on your system, or can't use ln (eg. on Windows).

16.2 Command-line Eval

Tcl can be evaluated from the command-line via:

```
wize /zvfs/wiz/eval.tcl 'pack [button .b -text Hello-World]'
```

Wize can also for run applications via http, eg:

```
wize http://pdqi.com/w/Download/hangman.zip
```

Note, this will download hangman.zip to the curent directory and then runs it.

---

17. Wize Admin

Wize comes with a builtin administrative interface invocable from the command-line via:

```
wize /
```

Here is a screenshot:

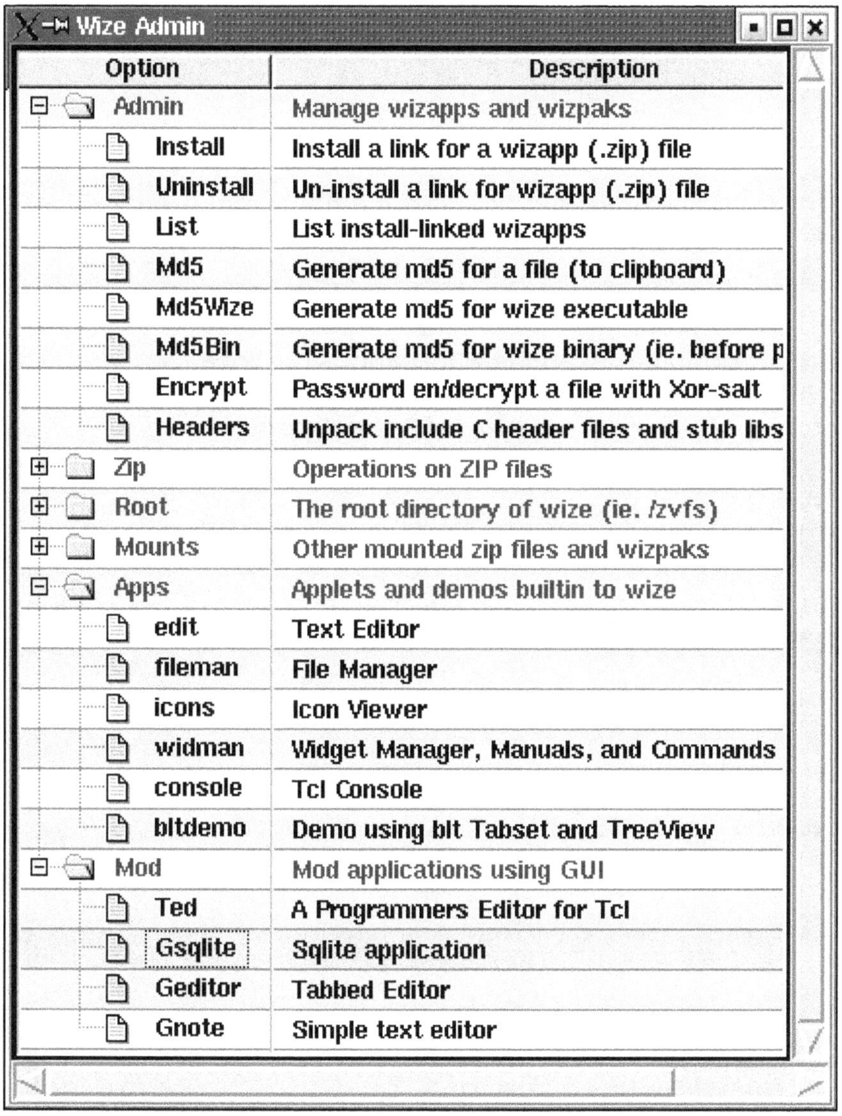

The admin interface gives access to many of the features and applications within Wize, further described below.
You can also run many Admin commands directly from the command-line, eg:

```
wize / Zip/Unzip foo.zip dstdir/
```

17.1 Admin

The Admin entry gives access to commands for installing, listing and verifying wize components.

17.2 Zip

The Zip entry gives access to commands for managing .zip files.

17.3 Root

The Root entry displays the wize builtin filesystem.

17.4 Mounts

Mounts shows all mounted wizpaks, as well as any .zip files manually mounted via Zip/ Mount.

17.5 Apps

The Apps entry contains a number of builtin example applications for Wize that you can run and examine. Source for these can be browsed from "wize /" or from CVS:
http://wize.cvs.sourceforge.net/viewvc/wize/wize2/Mod/wiz

Edit is a very simple editor. eg.

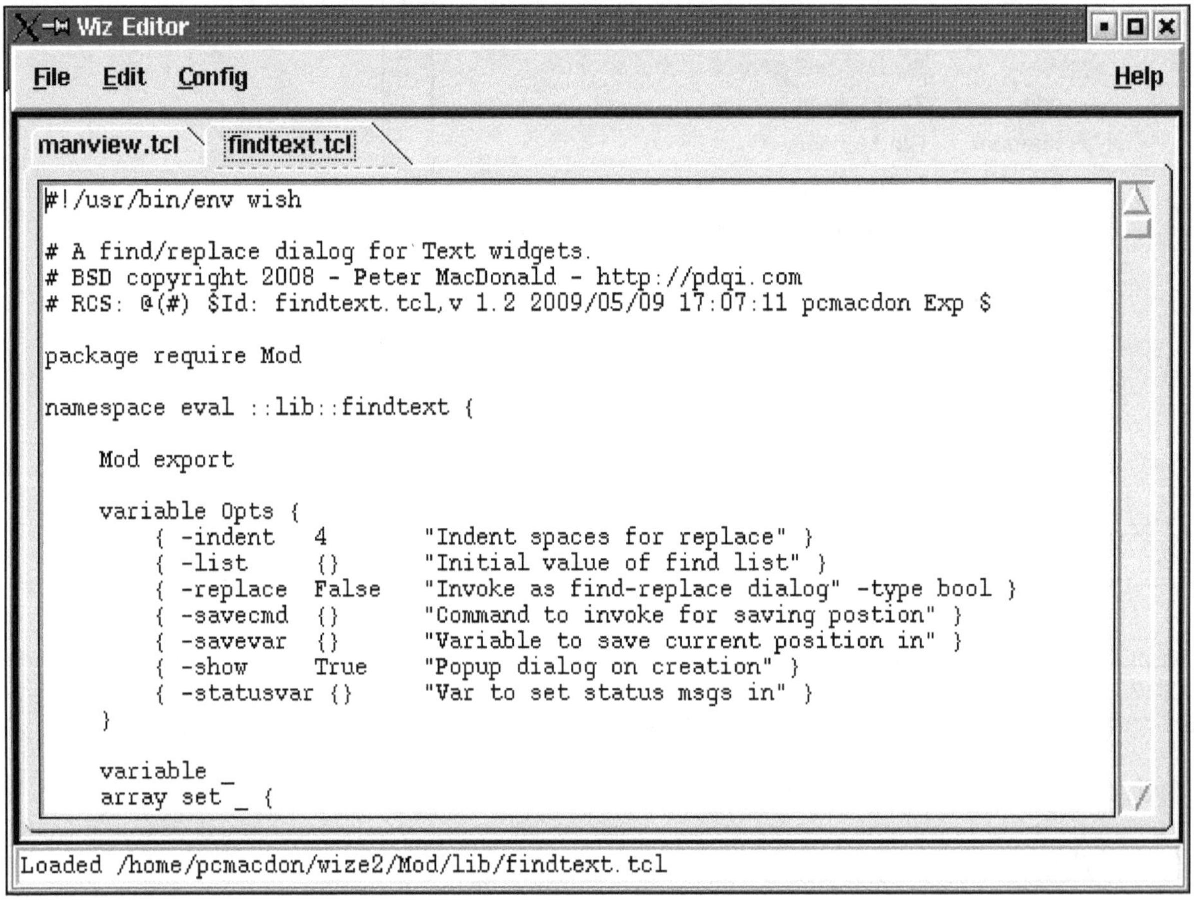

Icons is an icon/image browser. eg.

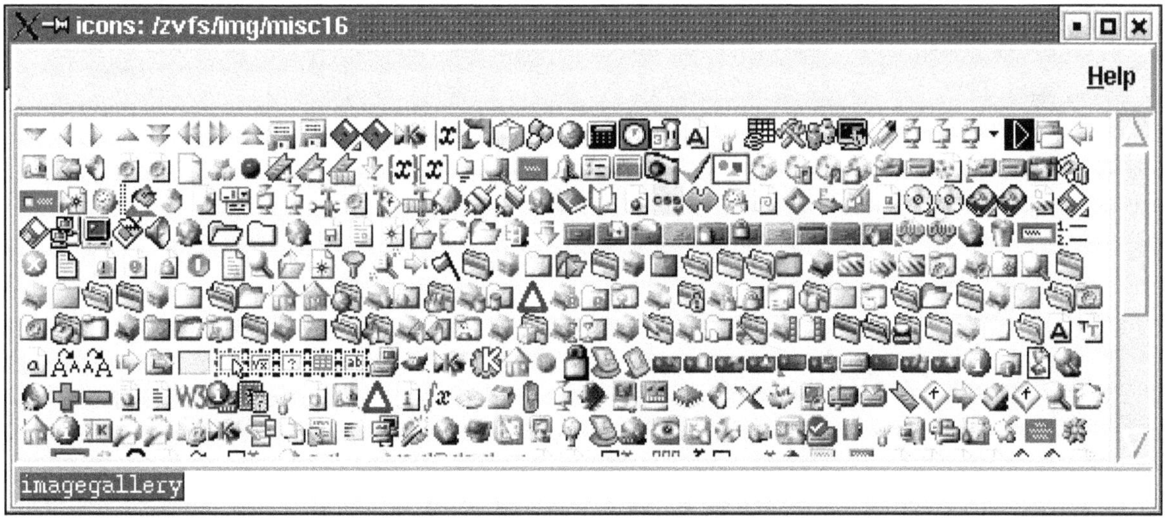

Fileman is simple file manager. eg.

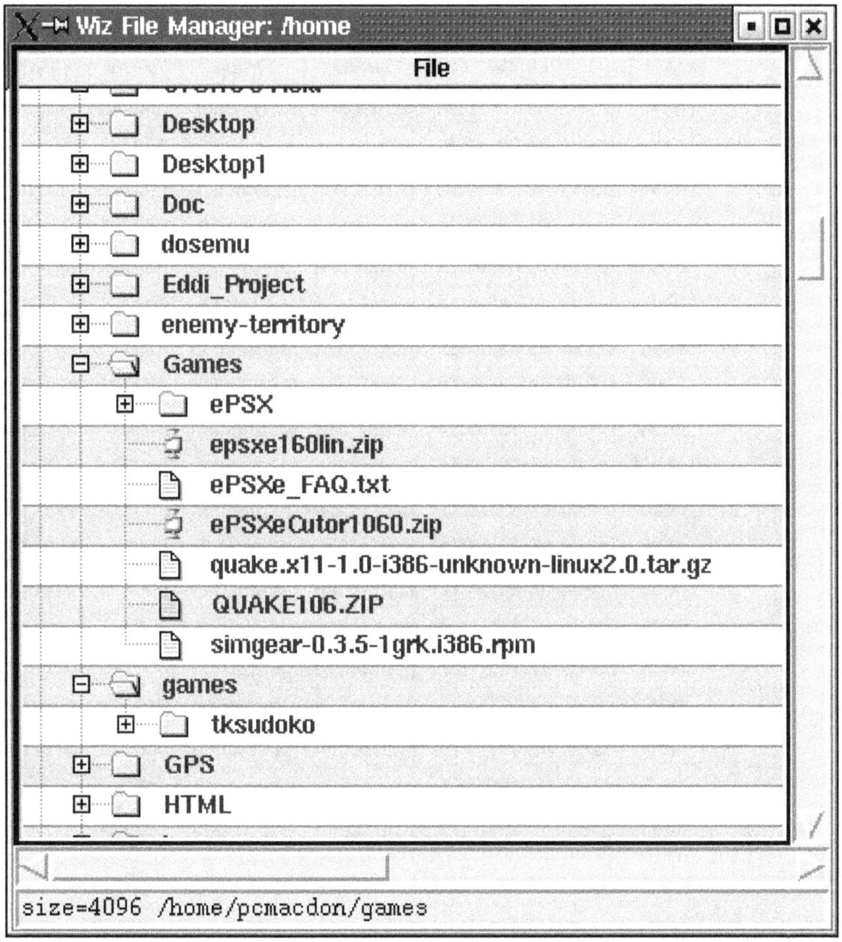
Wiz File Manager: /home
File
Desktop
Desktop1
Doc
dosemu
Eddi_Project
enemy-territory
Games
ePSX
epsxe160lin.zip
ePSXe_FAQ.txt
ePSXeCutor1060.zip
quake.x11-1.0-i386-unknown-linux2.0.tar.gz
QUAKE106.ZIP
simgear-0.3.5-1grk.i386.rpm
games
tksudoko
GPS
HTML
size=4096 /home/pcmacdon/games

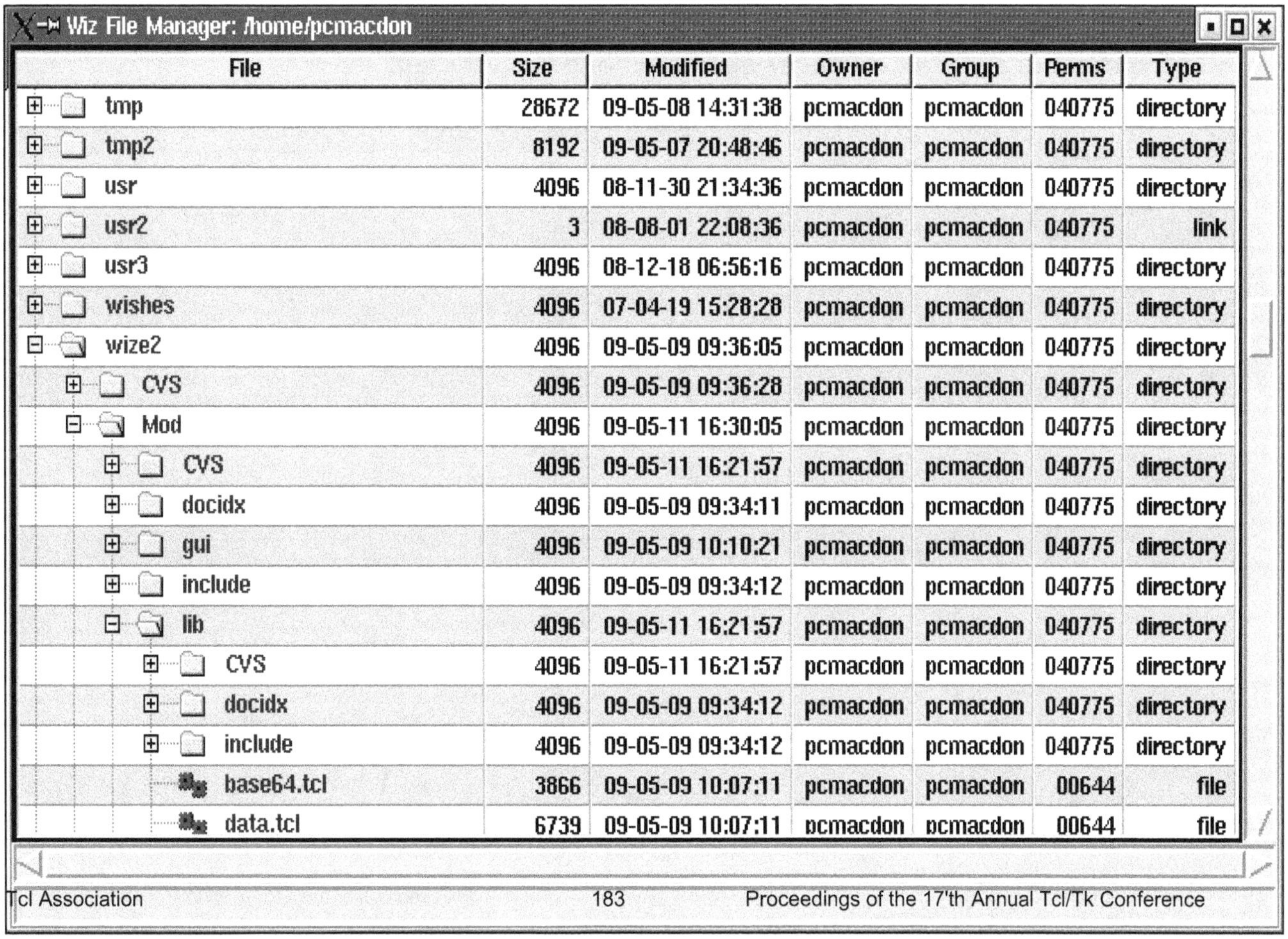
Wiz File Manager: /home/pcmacdon
File Size Modified Owner Group Perms Type
tmp 28672 09-05-08 14:31:38 pcmacdon pcmacdon 040775 directory
tmp2 8192 09-05-07 20:48:46 pcmacdon pcmacdon 040775 directory
usr 4096 08-11-30 21:34:36 pcmacdon pcmacdon 040775 directory
usr2 3 08-08-01 22:08:36 pcmacdon pcmacdon 040775 link
usr3 4096 08-12-18 06:56:16 pcmacdon pcmacdon 040775 directory
wishes 4096 07-04-19 15:28:28 pcmacdon pcmacdon 040775 directory
wize2 4096 09-05-09 09:36:05 pcmacdon pcmacdon 040775 directory
CVS 4096 09-05-09 09:36:28 pcmacdon pcmacdon 040775 directory
Mod 4096 09-05-11 16:30:05 pcmacdon pcmacdon 040775 directory
CVS 4096 09-05-11 16:21:57 pcmacdon pcmacdon 040775 directory
docidx 4096 09-05-09 09:34:11 pcmacdon pcmacdon 040775 directory
gui 4096 09-05-09 10:10:21 pcmacdon pcmacdon 040775 directory
include 4096 09-05-09 09:34:12 pcmacdon pcmacdon 040775 directory
lib 4096 09-05-11 16:21:57 pcmacdon pcmacdon 040775 directory
CVS 4096 09-05-11 16:21:57 pcmacdon pcmacdon 040775 directory
docidx 4096 09-05-09 09:34:12 pcmacdon pcmacdon 040775 directory
include 4096 09-05-09 09:34:12 pcmacdon pcmacdon 040775 directory
base64.tcl 3866 09-05-09 10:07:11 pcmacdon pcmacdon 00644 file
data.tcl 6739 09-05-09 10:07:11 pcmacdon pcmacdon 00644 file

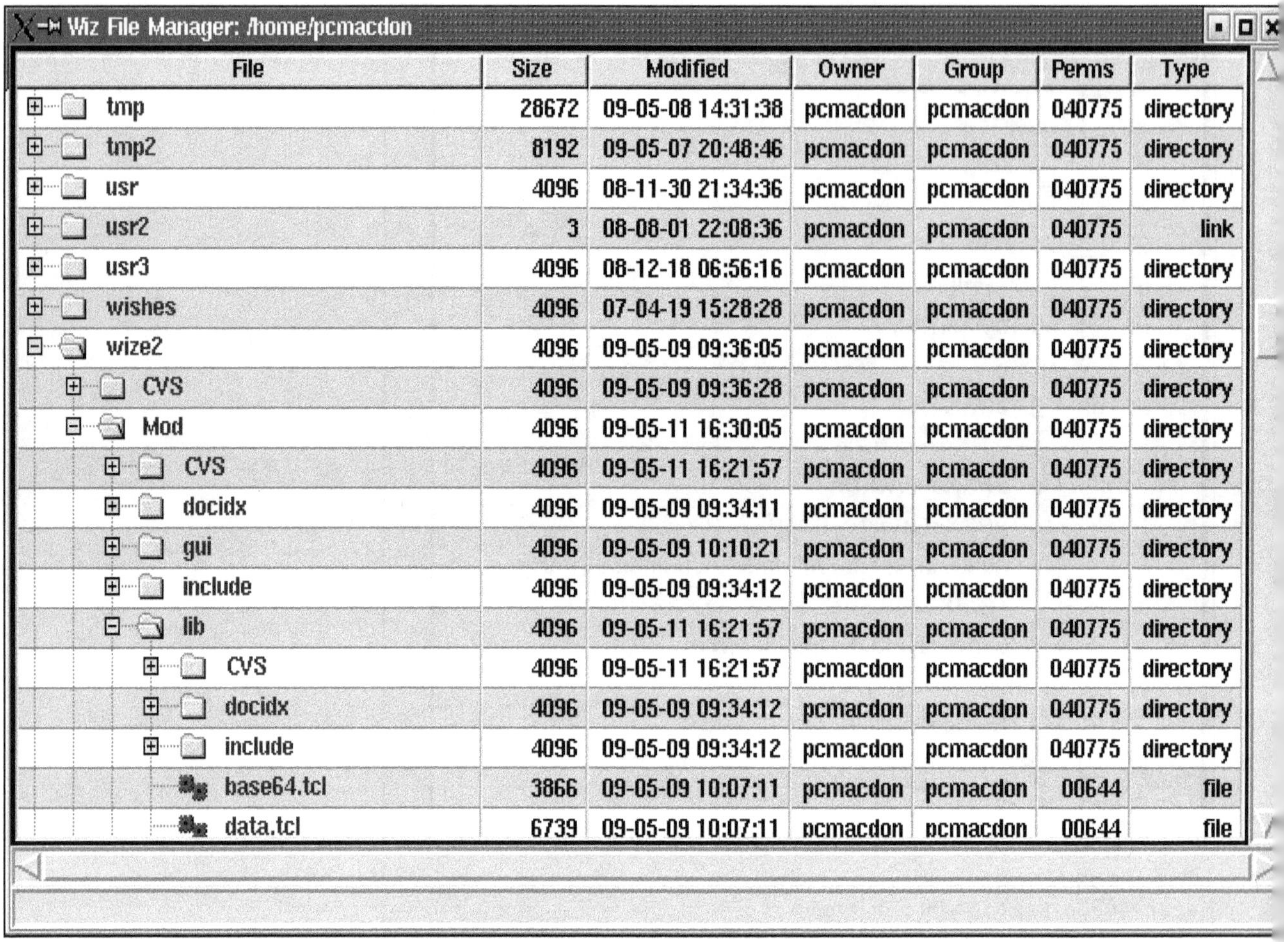
Wiz File Manager: /home/pcmacdon

File	Size	Modified	Owner	Group	Perms	Type
tmp	28672	09-05-08 14:31:38	pcmacdon	pcmacdon	040775	directory
tmp2	8192	09-05-07 20:48:46	pcmacdon	pcmacdon	040775	directory
usr	4096	08-11-30 21:34:36	pcmacdon	pcmacdon	040775	directory
usr2	3	08-08-01 22:08:36	pcmacdon	pcmacdon	040775	link
usr3	4096	08-12-18 06:56:16	pcmacdon	pcmacdon	040775	directory
wishes	4096	07-04-19 15:28:28	pcmacdon	pcmacdon	040775	directory
wize2	4096	09-05-09 09:36:05	pcmacdon	pcmacdon	040775	directory
CVS	4096	09-05-09 09:36:28	pcmacdon	pcmacdon	040775	directory
Mod	4096	09-05-11 16:30:05	pcmacdon	pcmacdon	040775	directory
CVS	4096	09-05-11 16:21:57	pcmacdon	pcmacdon	040775	directory
docidx	4096	09-05-09 09:34:11	pcmacdon	pcmacdon	040775	directory
gui	4096	09-05-09 10:10:21	pcmacdon	pcmacdon	040775	directory
include	4096	09-05-09 09:34:12	pcmacdon	pcmacdon	040775	directory
lib	4096	09-05-11 16:21:57	pcmacdon	pcmacdon	040775	directory
CVS	4096	09-05-11 16:21:57	pcmacdon	pcmacdon	040775	directory
docidx	4096	09-05-09 09:34:12	pcmacdon	pcmacdon	040775	directory
include	4096	09-05-09 09:34:12	pcmacdon	pcmacdon	040775	directory
base64.tcl	3866	09-05-09 10:07:11	pcmacdon	pcmacdon	00644	file
data.tcl	6739	09-05-09 10:07:11	pcmacdon	pcmacdon	00644	file

Introspect is a widget manager and command browser. eg.

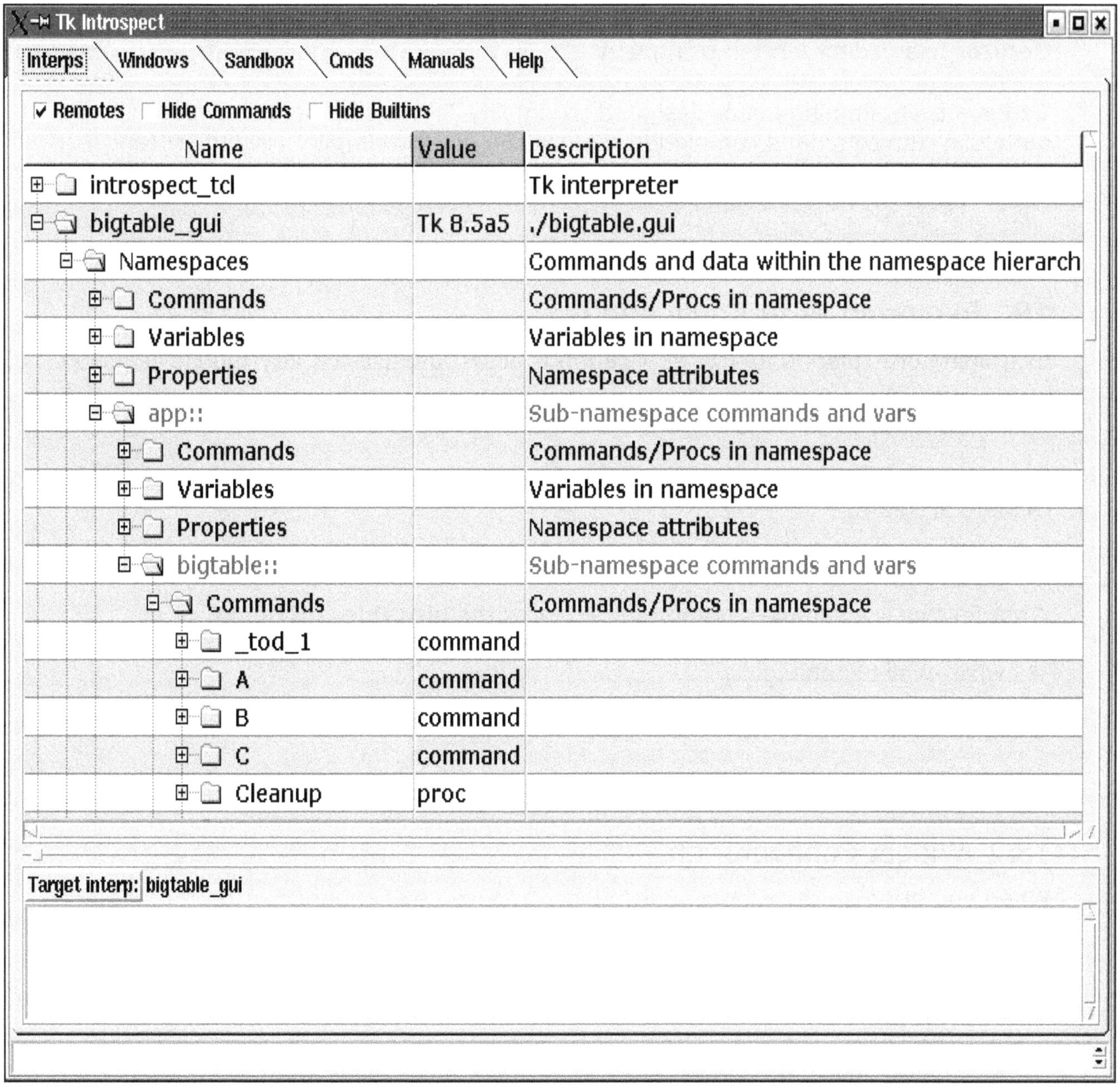

Console invokes the Tk console. Works even on Unix.

17.6 Gui (or Mod)

Mod is a package used when writing complex and sophisticated Tk applications.
The Admin entry Gui contains a number of example applications that use Gui from the Mod package (included in wizmod.zip), these include:

Gsqlite is an Sqlite client written using **Gui**

Geditor is an editor written using **Gui**

Ted is a programming editor designed to simplify Tcl development in Wize. In particular, the command completion feature can greatly simplify writing Tcl (and Tk), particularly for those who might not know the language that well.
(Note: ted is in wizapp.zip and is not part of wizmod.zip)

---

18. Exploring Wize Applications

Examining or exploring a Wize application is easy. Just use the key/mouse sequence:

```
<Control-Alt-Shift-2>
```

This opens the window config-editor, allowing you to explore various aspects of the running program.

18.1 A Sample Session

What follows is a sample session that explores the **bigtable.gui** demo.

```
% wize -Wall bigtable.gui
```

or use:

```
% wize -Wall / Gui/Bigtable
```

18.2 Widget Configuration

When you bring up the window editor using mouse/key sequence <Control-Alt-Shift-2>, [Tk::editwin] is invoked:

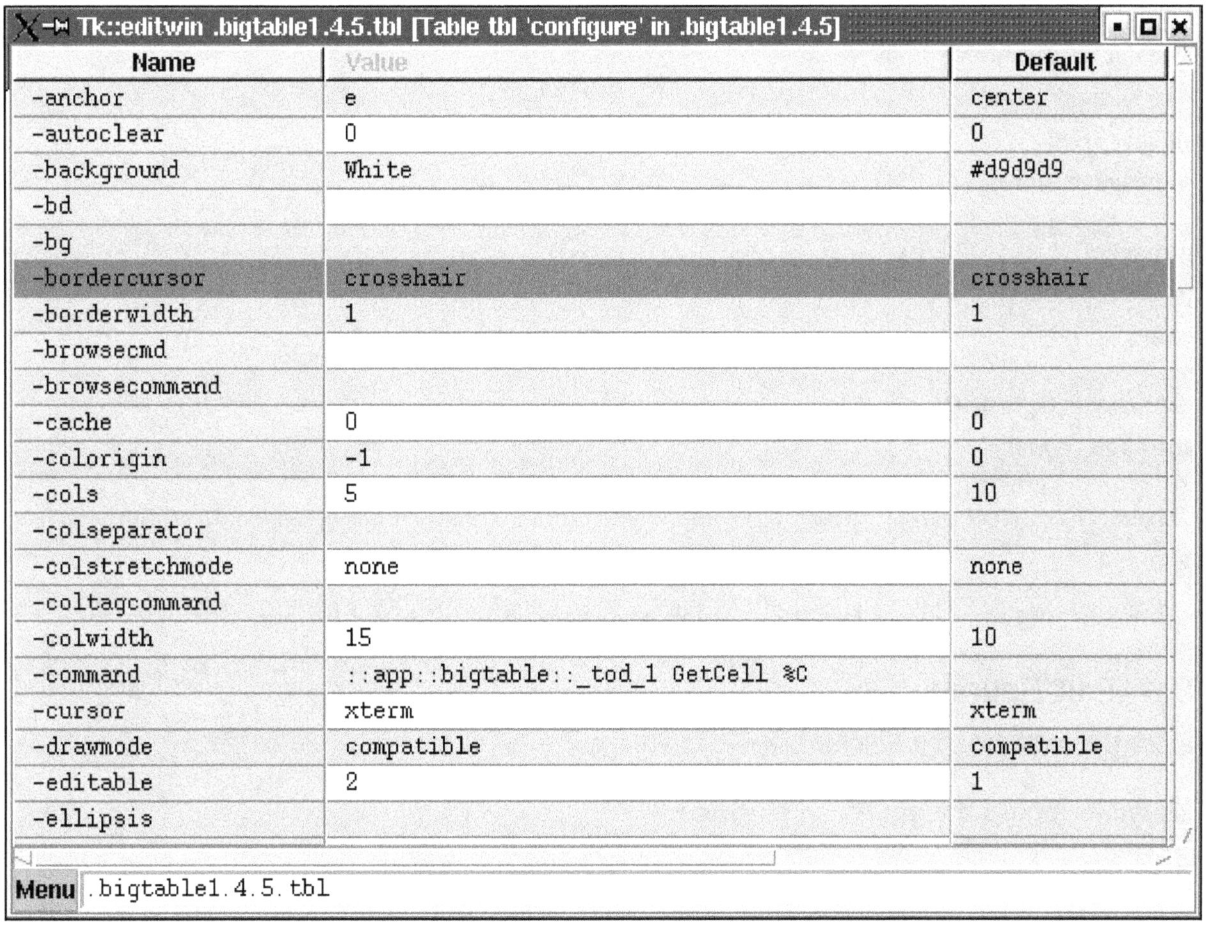

Tk::editwin .bigtable1.4.5.tbl [Table tbl 'configure' in .bigtable1.4.5]

Name	Value	Default
-anchor	e	center
-autoclear	0	0
-background	White	#d9d9d9
-bd		
-bg		
-bordercursor	crosshair	crosshair
-borderwidth	1	1
-browsecmd		
-browsecommand		
-cache	0	0
-colorigin	-1	0
-cols	5	10
-colseparator		
-colstretchmode	none	none
-coltagcommand		
-colwidth	15	10
-command	::app::bigtable::_tod_1 GetCell %C	
-cursor	xterm	xterm
-drawmode	compatible	compatible
-editable	2	1
-ellipsis		

Menu .bigtable1.4.5.tbl

You can then double-click on the Value column to edit widget values.
You may also try the following:

- open the **console** from the Menu.
- in the console, type set t, space, then paste with <Control-v>.

Now try some commands in the console, eg: $t conf -bd 4. (Note, this works because the widget is selected upon open)

18.3 The Menu

Hit <F10> or click on Menu in [Tk::editwin] to bring up the menu:

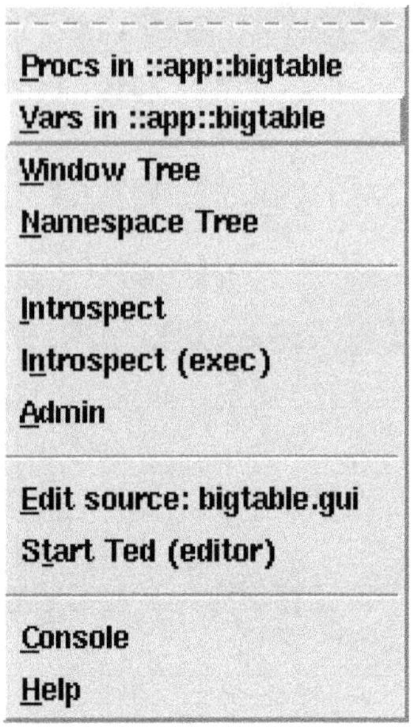

This menu has numerous facilities which are discussed in detail below.

18.4 Edit Source

Select the menu entry Edit Source: bigtable.gui.

This will bring up the source in **Geditor**.

18.5 Procs

The Procs menu entry will invoke [Tk::editproc] to allow you to edit code dynamically, right in the running program.

From the menu, select 'Procs in ::app::bigtable:

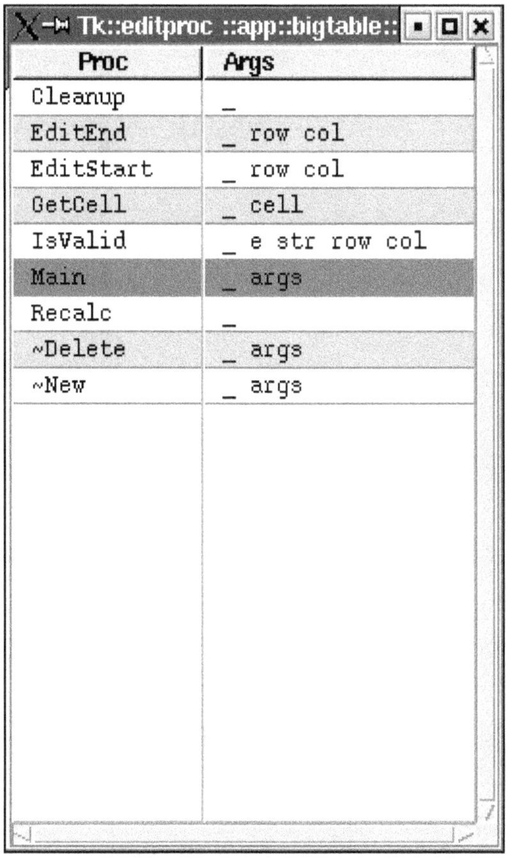

Then select EditStart and hit Enter (or double click):

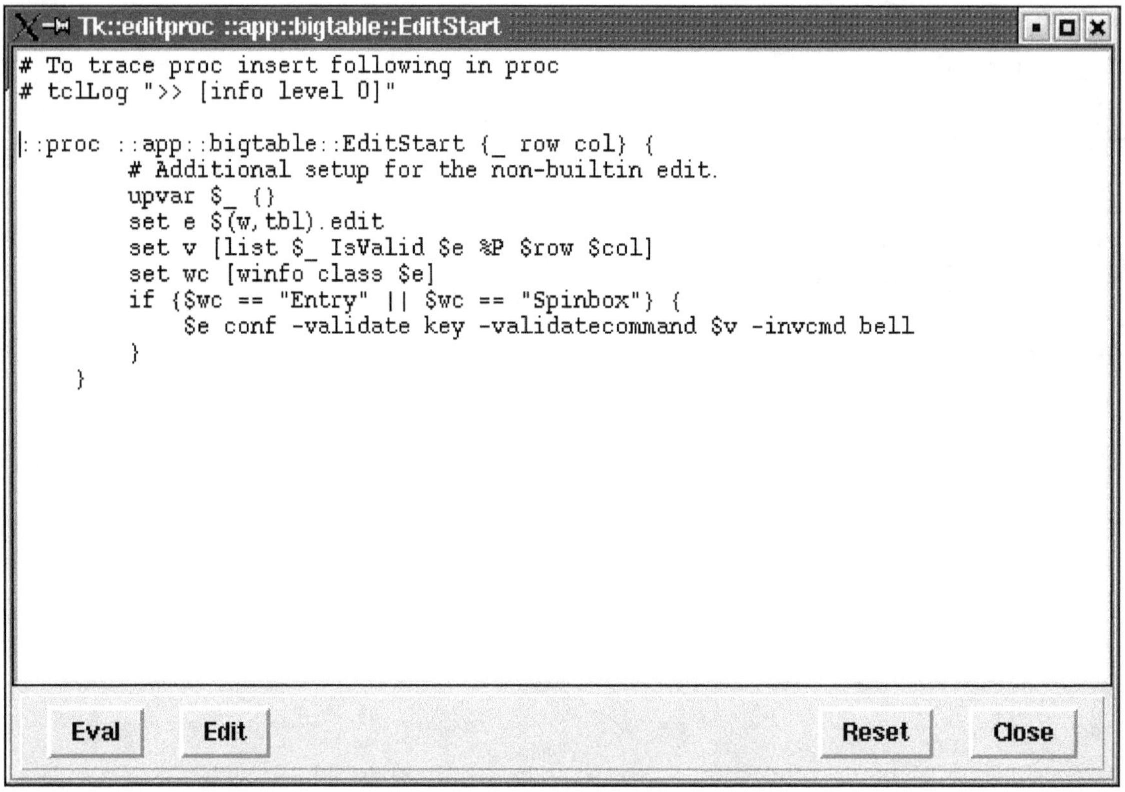


```
# To trace proc insert following in proc
# tclLog ">> [info level 0]"

::proc ::app::bigtable::EditStart {_ row col} {
        # Additional setup for the non-builtin edit.
        upvar $_ {}
        set e $(w,tbl).edit
        set v [list $_ IsValid $e %P $row $col]
        set wc [winfo class $e]
        if {$wc == "Entry" || $wc == "Spinbox"} {
            $e conf -validate key -validatecommand $v -invcmd bell
        }
    }
```

Insert a line of code in the proc, eg. puts "Editing: $row" and click Eval.
Now go back to bigtable and edit a cell by double clicking. Note how your output appears in the xterm.
Alternatively, you can open the console window and use putc.

18.6 Variables

The Vars menu entry invokes [Tk::editvar] letting you examine and change variables in the running program.

When you select 'Vars in ::app::bigtable you will see:

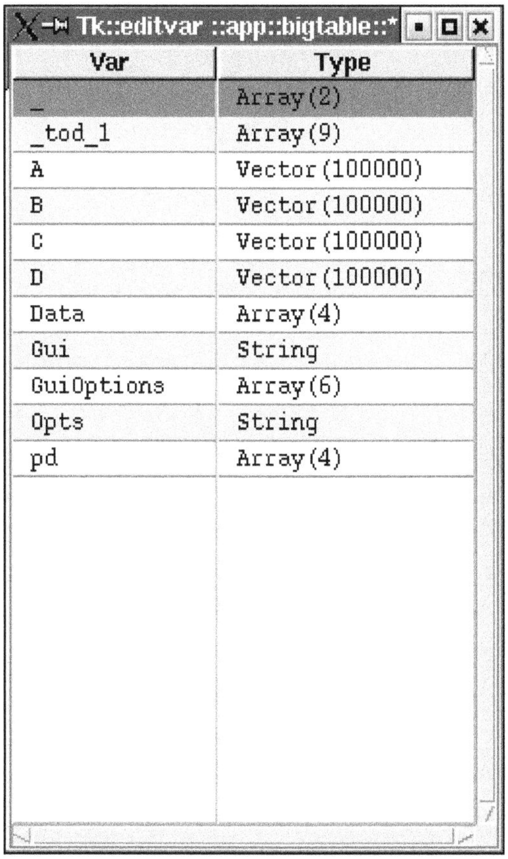

Then select _tod_1 and hit Enter:

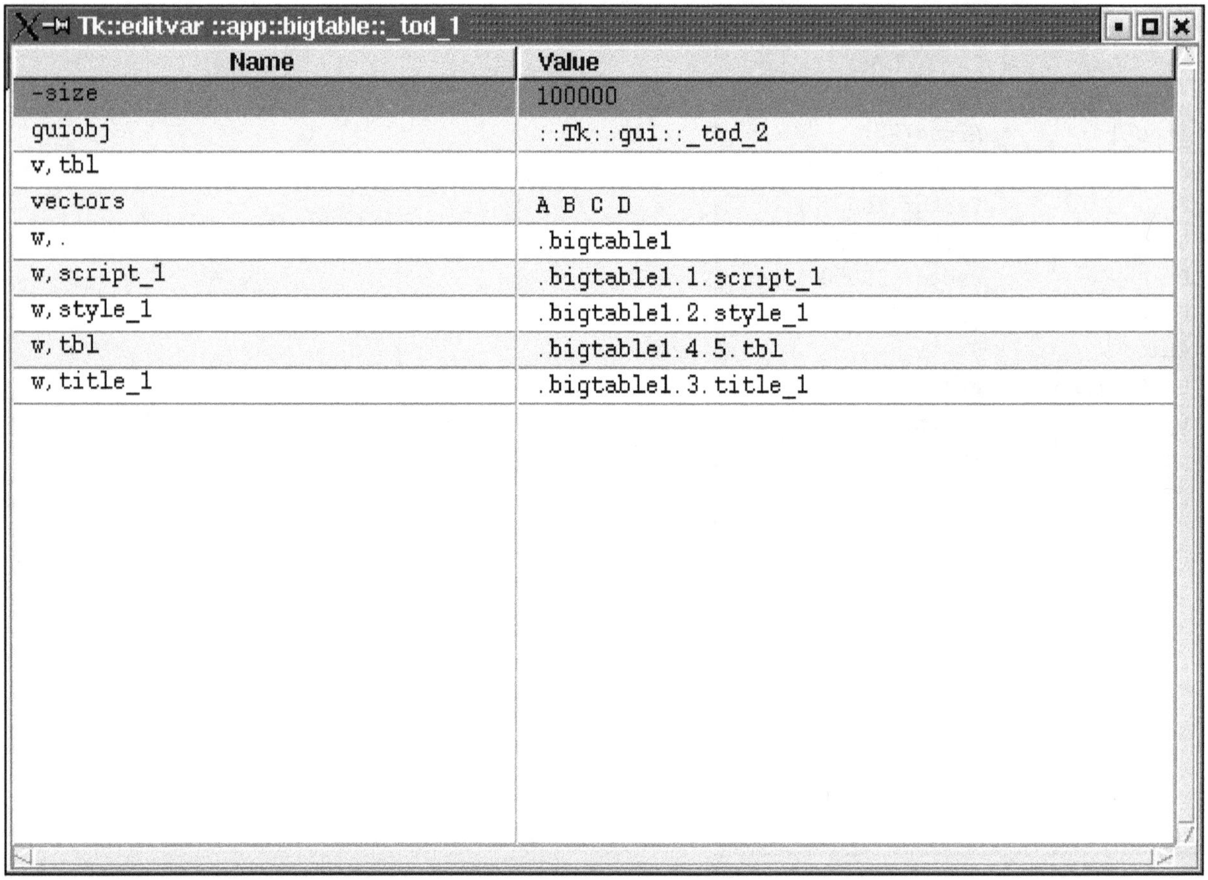

Double click or hit enter to change any variable.

18.7 Window Tree

Selecting Window Tree from the Menu will invoke:
  Tk::editwin .*

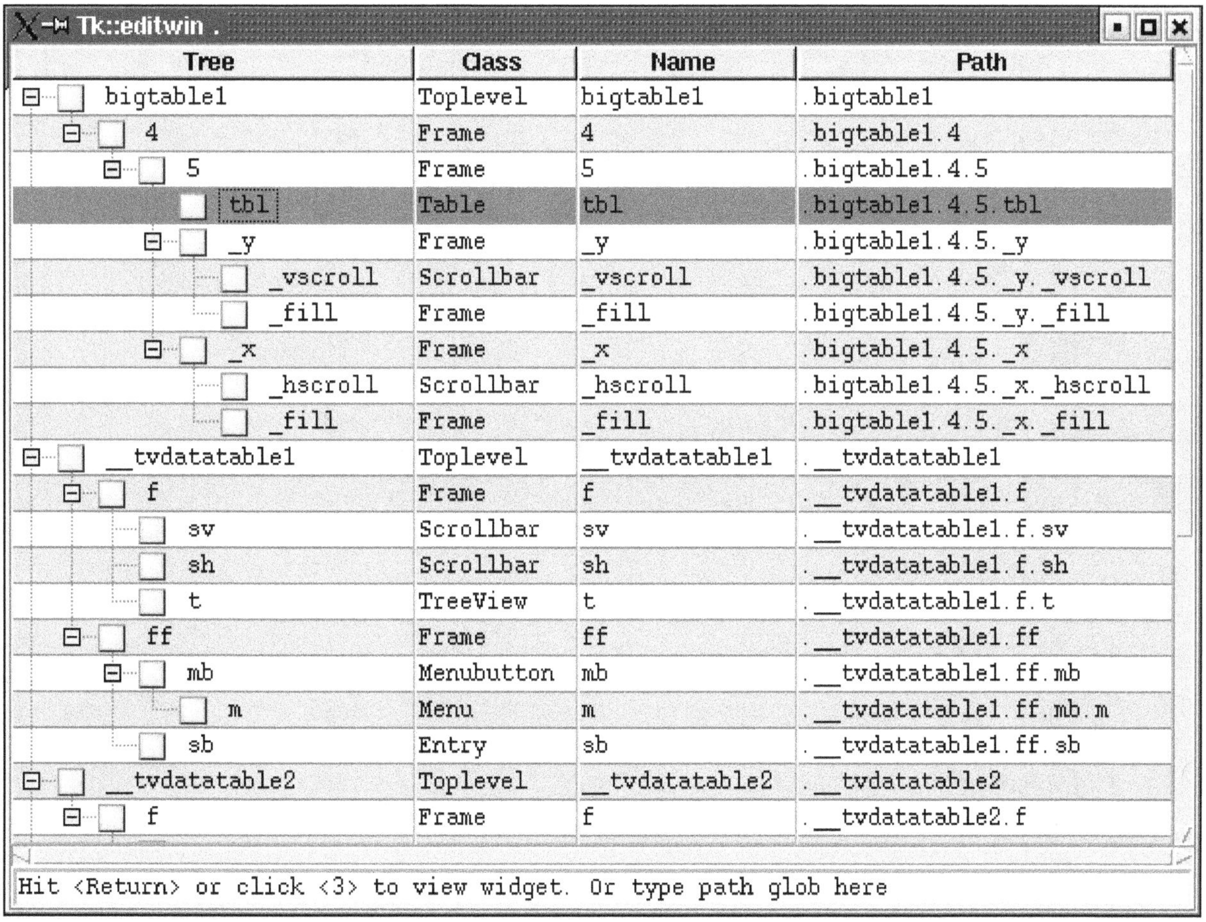

The current window will be selected. You can then select a different window and hit enter to edit it.

18.8 Namespace Tree

Selecting Namespace Tree from the Menu will invoke [Tk::editns ::*] letting you browse the namespace tree, eg:

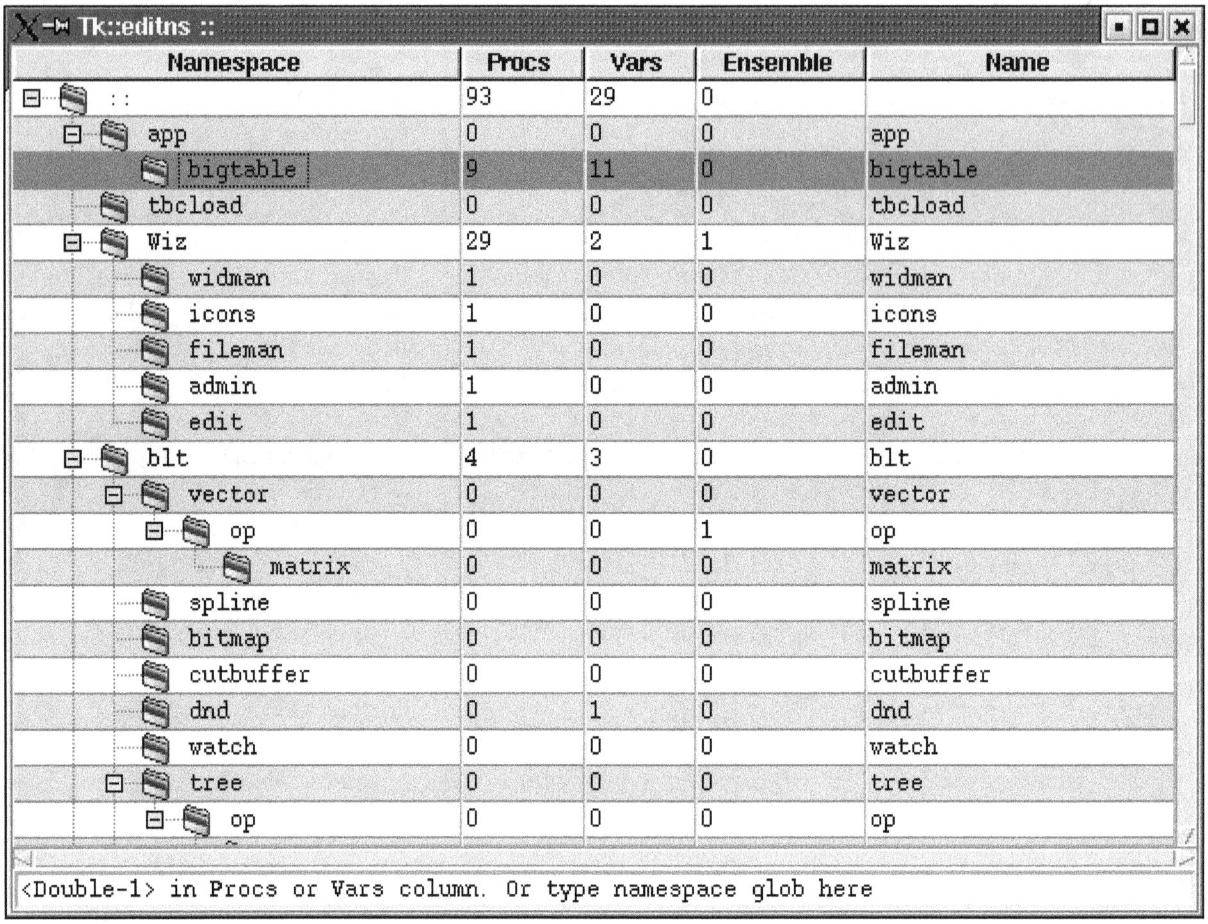

By default the current namespace is selected. You can then double-click on the Procs column to edit procs, or the Varscolumn to edit variables (in that namespace).

18.9 Introspect

Introspect is a graphical application for examining and modifying the program state of Tk applications.

The default is ot start introspect inside the application process you are debugging. The exec option however starts introspect as an external process.

18.10 Edit

Edit invokes the editor on the runtime file. See Start Ted.

18.11 Start Ted

Ted is a programming editor with builtin command completion for Tcl/Tk.
If ted is running when you invoke Edit, then the file will be edited in Ted. Otherwise, the builtin editor will be used.

18.12 Admin

Admin is the administrative interface into Wize.

18.13 The Status Line

Arguments can be appended to the path in the **editwin** status line to be evaluated, eg:

- add space, style names and hit enter.
- change above to style conf alt and hit enter.

Note, if the last or second last argument matches pattern *conf then 'Tk::editwin'' is invoked to edit widget items.
Otherwise, the results are displayed in a popup.

18.14 Console

A console can be opened from the editwin menu or by typing the key sequence <Control-Alt-Shift-space>, eg:

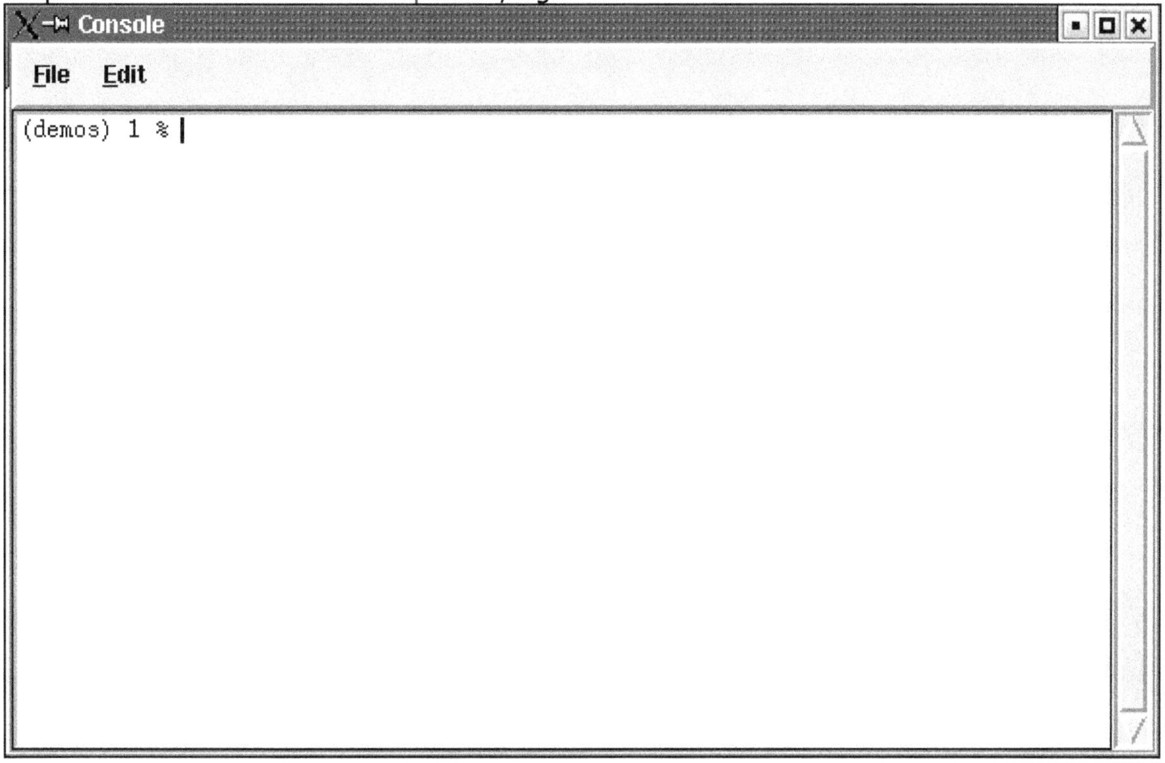

Any Tcl command can be typed into the console. However, the following are most useful:

- **Tk::find** - search for window by name or class.
- **Tk::editproc** - edit running procs
- **Tk::editvar** - visual variable editor
- **Tk::editwin** - visual widget editor/browser

* **Tk::editns** - visual namespace browser.

19. Introspect

Introspect is a graphical application for examining and modifying the application state of other programs viasend/dde. It can be invoked in an application via <Control-Alt-Shift-2> or run directly using:

```
wize /zvfs/wiz/introspect.tcl
```

Introspect uses a TreeView to display resources such as Procs, Vars, Widgets, Fonts, etc. It contains a Sandbox environment to let you experiment with widgets/elements, the command/option hierarcy of all builtin commands, and access to all online documention.
Here are screenshots of the Introspect tabs:

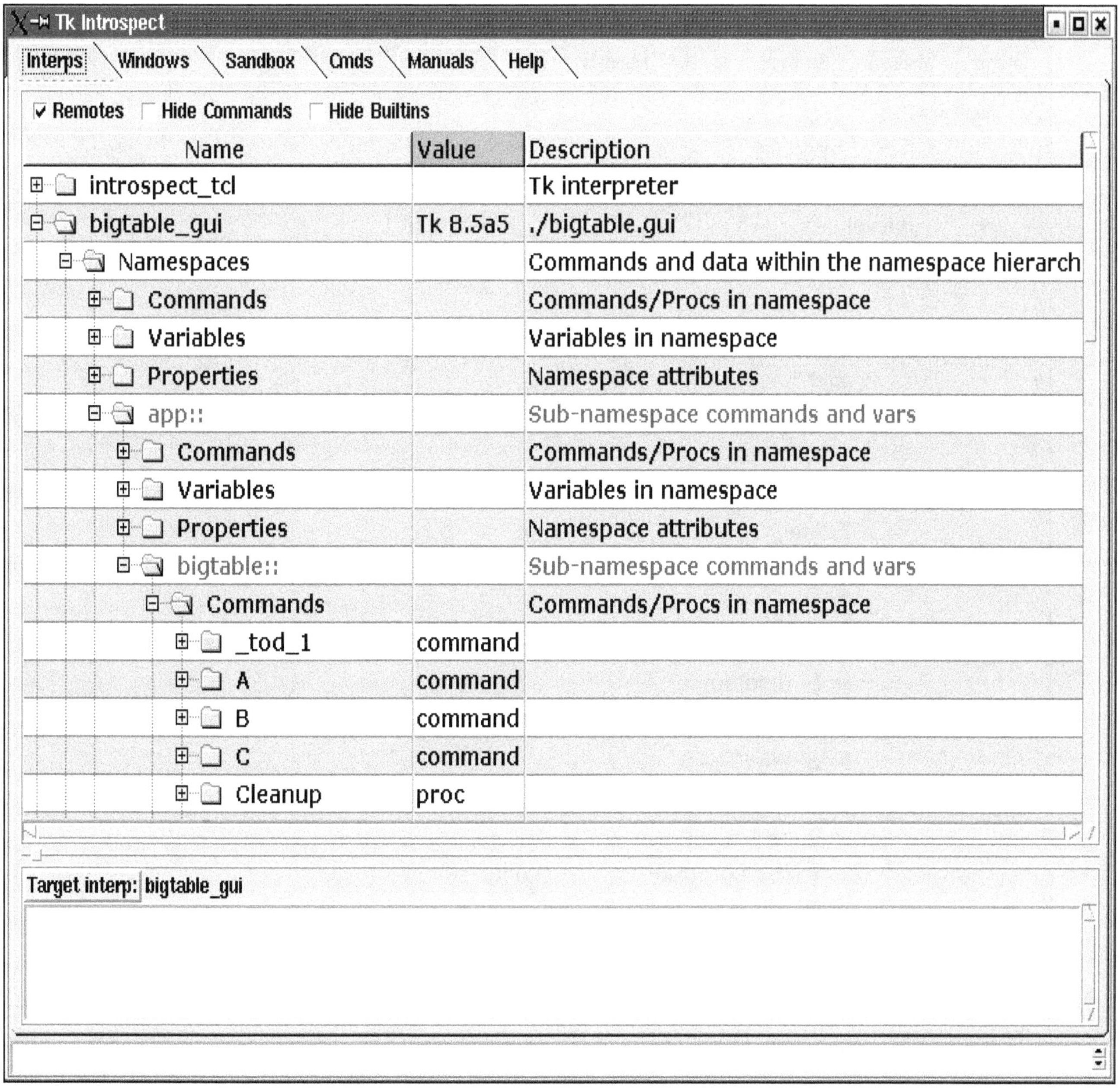
Tk Introspect
Interps
Windows
Sandbox
Cmds
Manuals
Help
Remotes
Hide Commands
Hide Builtins
Name
Value
Description
introspect_tcl
Tk interpreter
bigtable_gui
Tk 8.5a5
./bigtable.gui
Namespaces
Commands and data within the namespace hierarch
Commands
Commands/Procs in namespace
Variables
Variables in namespace
Properties
Namespace attributes
app::
Sub-namespace commands and vars
Commands
Commands/Procs in namespace
Variables
Variables in namespace
Properties
Namespace attributes
bigtable::
Sub-namespace commands and vars
Commands
Commands/Procs in namespace
_tod_1
command
A
command
B
command
C
command
Cleanup
proc
Target interp: bigtable_gui

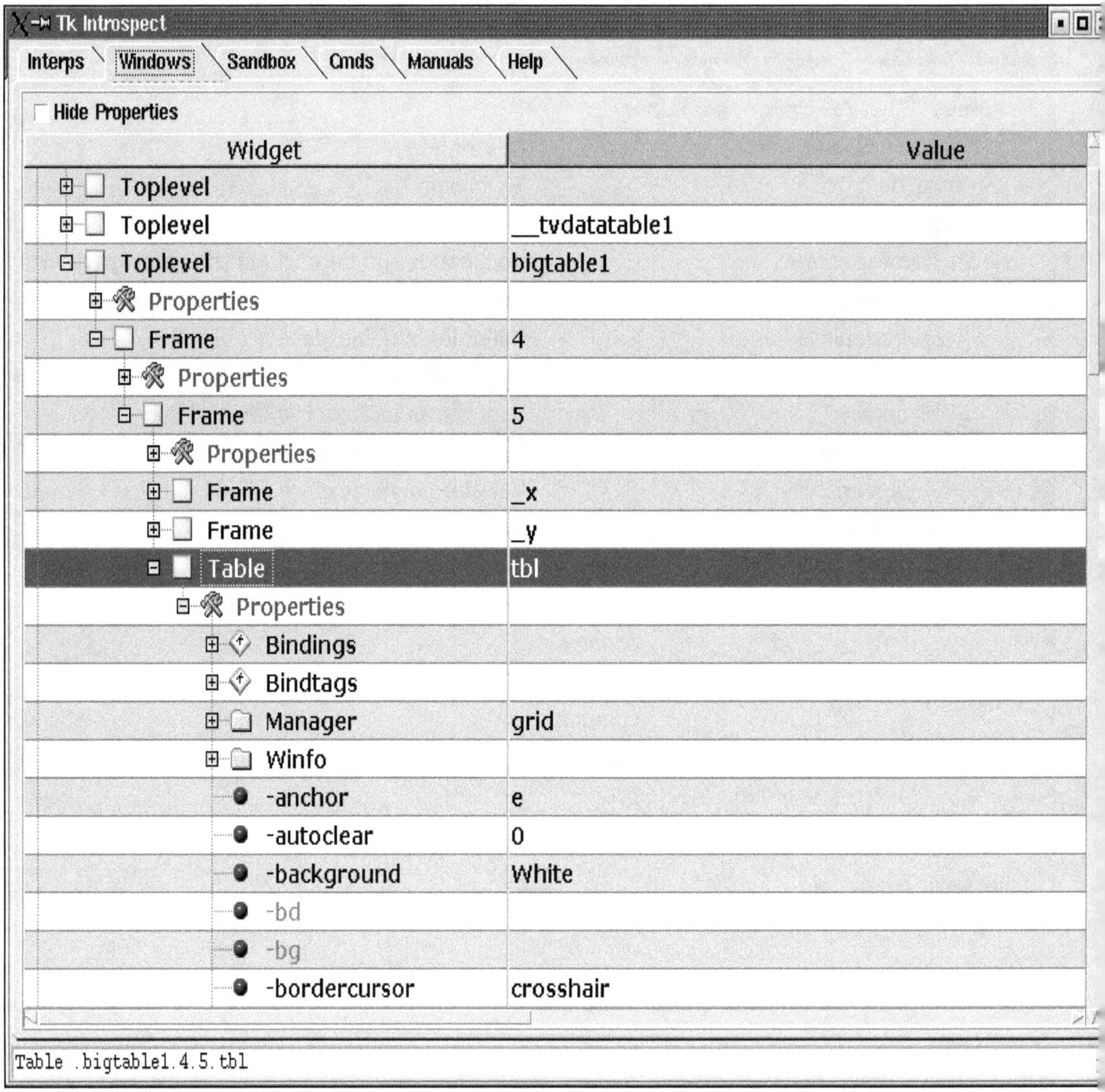
Tk Introspect
Interps
Windows
Sandbox
Cmds
Manuals
Help
Hide Properties
Widget
Value
Toplevel
Toplevel
__tvdatatable1
Toplevel
bigtable1
Properties
Frame
4
Properties
Frame
5
Properties
Frame
_x
Frame
_y
Table
tbl
Properties
Bindings
Bindtags
Manager
grid
Winfo
-anchor
e
-autoclear
0
-background
White
-bd
-bg
-bordercursor
crosshair
Table .bigtable1.4.5.tbl

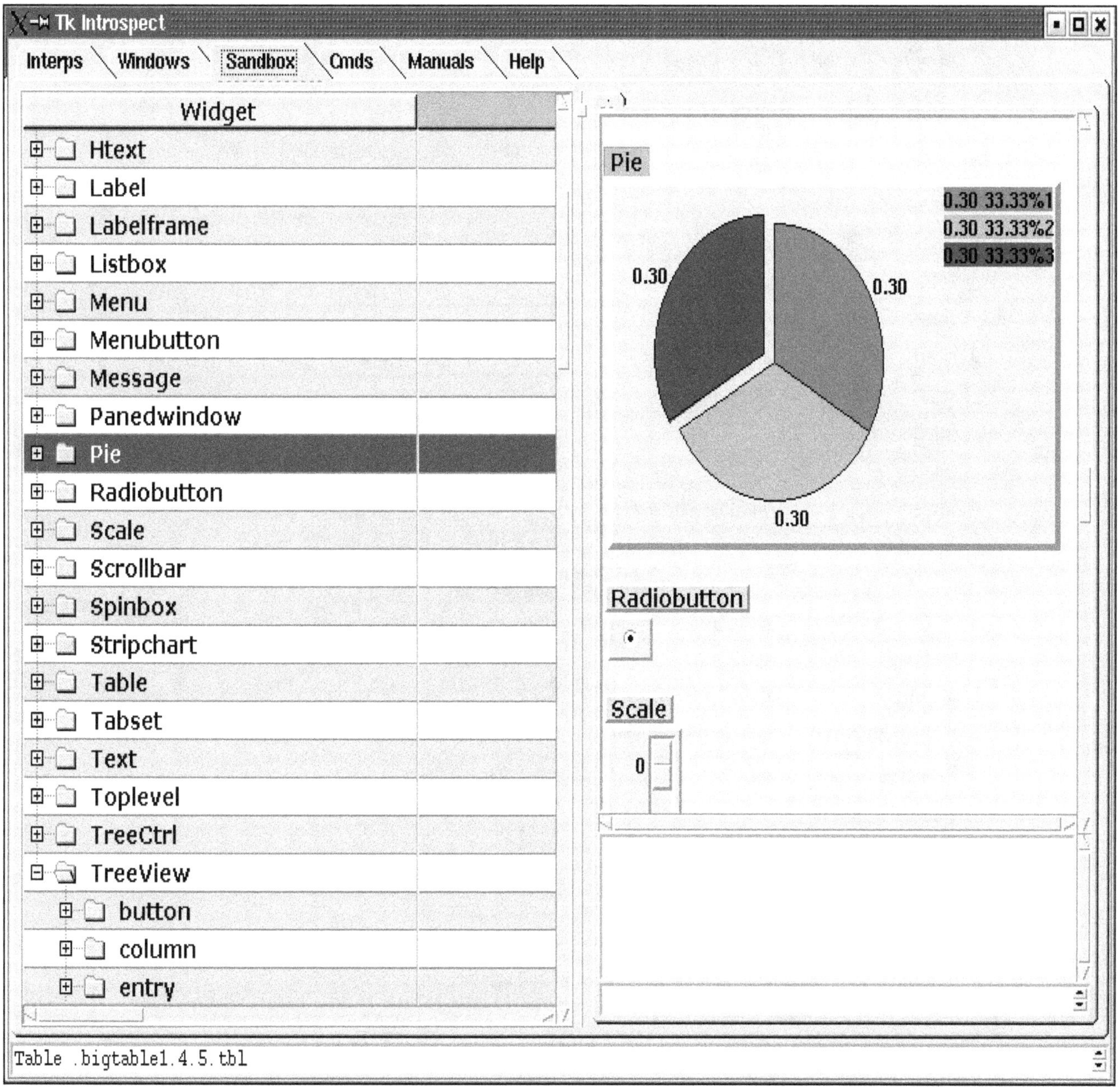
Tk Introspect
Interps
Windows
Sandbox
Cmds
Manuals
Help
Widget
Htext
Label
Labelframe
Listbox
Menu
Menubutton
Message
Panedwindow
Pie
Radiobutton
Scale
Scrollbar
Spinbox
Stripchart
Table
Tabset
Text
Toplevel
TreeCtrl
TreeView
button
column
entry
Pie
0.30 33.33%1
0.30 33.33%2
0.30 33.33%3
0.30
0.30
0.30
Radiobutton
Scale
0
Table .bigtable1.4.5.tbl

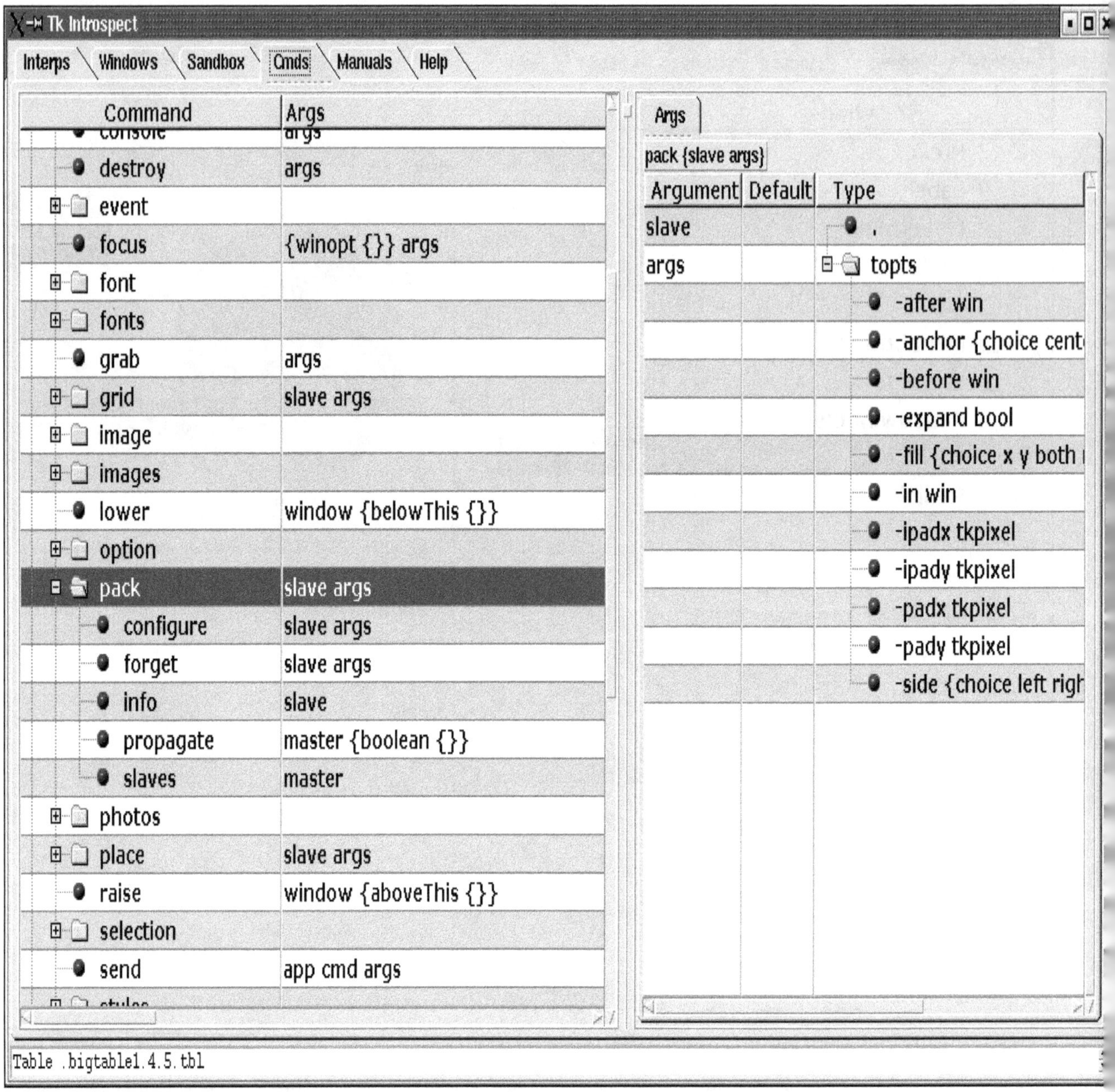
Tk Introspect
Interps
Windows
Sandbox
Cmds
Manuals
Help
Command
Args
destroy args
event
focus {winopt {}} args
font
fonts
grab args
grid slave args
image
images
lower window {belowThis {}}
option
pack slave args
configure slave args
forget slave args
info slave
propagate master {boolean {}}
slaves master
photos
place slave args
raise window {aboveThis {}}
selection
send app cmd args
Args
pack {slave args}
Argument
Default
Type
slave
args
topts
-after win
-before win
-expand bool
-in win
-ipadx tkpixel
-ipady tkpixel
-padx tkpixel
-pady tkpixel
Table .bigtable1.4.5.tbl

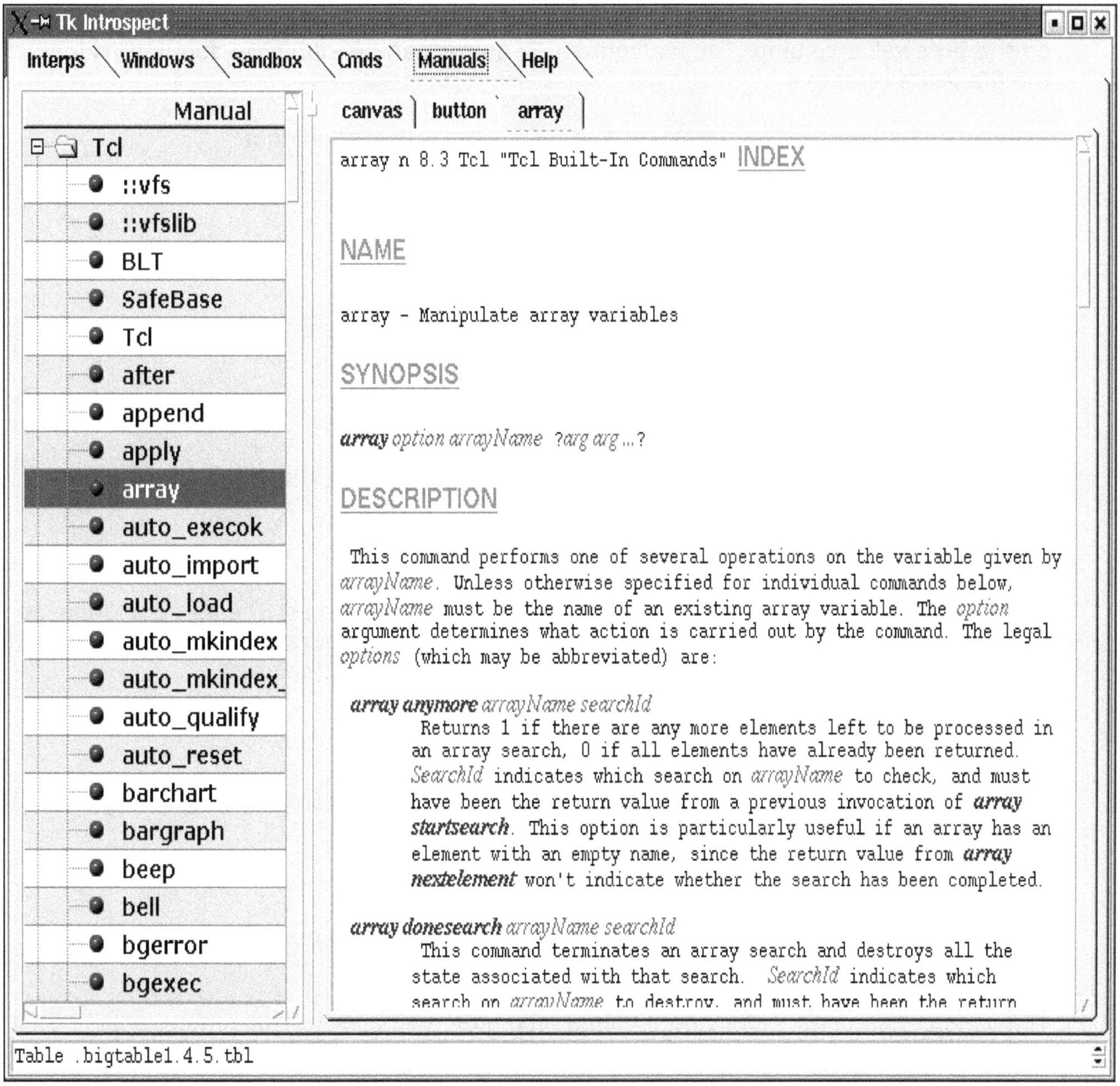

19.1 Interps

Interps uses a TreeView to display all non-windows resources. This includes namespaces (both commands and variables), fonts, images and events. These are all indexed by interp name, one for each Tk program running under the window managers display.

Variables can have their value changed by double clicking on the Value column.

Command procs can be dynamically edited in the running program by double clicking on the proc value column. The file containing a proc can be edited by double clicking on the file value column.

Usually, a sub-tree can be refreshed just by closing and reopening it.
There are several checkboxes that control viewing:

Remotes

Check to show all remote interps.

Hide Commands

Hide all non-proc commands.

Hide Builtins

Hide all commands, procs or vars that are considered builtin. These mostly affect only the :: namespace.

19.2 Windows

Windows uses a TreeView to display all widget window resources. These are all indexed by interp name, one for each Tk program running under the window managers display.
Option values can be changed by double clicking on the Value column.
The following checkbox option is available.

Hide Properties

Check to display only the window tree hierarchy, without the properties (bindings, winfo and options).

19.3 Sandbox

The Sandbox environment contains one of every Tk widgets available in Wize as well as one of each type of item (for widgets supporting items).

The widgets/items may be examined and changed dynamically. This provides instantaneous access to real working widgets and items and their options.

19.4 Cmds

The command/option hierarcy for all builtin commands in Wize. Many commands in Tcl take sub-commands and even sub-sub-commands each of which may take various arguments and options. This allows you to view the signatures for each command.

Double clicking on any command gives a detailed breakdown of that commands arguments in the right hand pane. Some commands have detailed type information included For and example, checkout Tcl/fconfigure.

These are broken down into 5 groups:

- Widgets - The widget commands.
- Tcl - The Tcl commands.
- Tk - The Tk commands
- Blt - The BLT specific extension commands.
- Misc - Reserved for future use.

19.5 Manuals

Finally, it provides access to all online documention, both for the Tcl/Tk commands and for Tcl's C-programming API.

Double clicking on any man page will display the manual in a new tab. Right click on any tab to close it. Or use <Control-s> to search the page.

Click on the INDEX link at top to go to the table of contents, where you can click on more links. Use <Alt-left> to return from a link.

---

20. Development

The devel macro commands are used to simplify debugging when **warnings** are enabled. If warnings are disabled, these all return the empty string and do nothing. Moreover, the commands can become Tcl noops by calling **Mod ndebug**: A noop has zero runtime overhead.

Here's an example:

```
proc Foo {n m} {
    .Trace
    .Assert {$n>0 && $n<1000} 1
    if {[.Debug] != {}} {
        CheckRange $m $n
    }
    .Debug {
        if {$n < $m} { .Break BadN1 }
    }
    .Warn "Begin processing"
    return $n.0
}
```

Note that all commands start with period + capital letter.

Below are the supported commands.

20.1 .Assert expr ?warnonly?

Evaluate the expression expr. The expression should use curley braces to avoid a double eval. If warnonly==1 then calls .Warn instead of causing an error. If warnonly>1 the output contains detailed stack info (ie. to help debugging).

```
.Assert {$n>0}
.Assert {$n>1} 1
.Assert {$n<-1} 2
```

20.2 .Break ?str?

Invoke **Tcl inspect**, eg.

```
.Break stop1
```

20.3 .Debug ?script?

If called with no argument it returns the current debug level. Otherwise evaluate the script and issue a warning only if an error occurs.

Usage:

```
if {[.Debug]!=""} {
    if {$m==$n} { error "equal error" }
}
.Debug {
    if {$n<$m} { error "range error" }
}
```

WARNING: Do not do the following as it can result in a runtime error:

```
if {[.Debug]} { #... }
```

20.4 .Error str ?subst?

Kick an error. If subst is true, evaluate str first.

The following are roughly equivalent:

```
.Error {bad call: $n} 1
if {[.Debug] != {}} { error "bad call: $n" }
```

20.5 .Trace ?-num cnt? ?-fmt bool? ?-prefix str?

Dump the call-stack info from the current proc. The default is to dump only the current proc, with no formatting or prefix. Using a cnt of -1 will dump the whole call-stack.

If -fmt is true, show a in name=value form

```
proc Foo {n} {
    .Trace -num -1 -fmt 1
}
```

20.6 .Warn str ?subst?

Log a warning message using tclLog. If subst is true, evaluate str first.

```
.Warn "Something bad happened"
.Warn {Range error: $m>$n} 1
```

21. Debugging Programs

In Tcl, debugging has traditionally been limited to using puts or tclLog statements in the code. Herein we discuss some other alternatives.

21.1 Validating Programs

Wize provides static code checking with:

```
wize -Wall prog.tcl
```

This statically checks Tcl procs for **validation**
Even if a program passes validation, there can still be errors. Here are a few debugging utilities.

21.2 .Break

You can inspect variables within a running proc vy inserting a **.Break XXX** statement. When this gets executed, the**TclInspect** console is invoked allowing the user to view/modify variables, procs or edit the file. The XXX label is optional and is only used in locating code with multiple .Breaks.

For example:

```
# File "foo.tcl"
package require Mod

proc Foo {n} {
    incr n
    .Break 1
    set n [expr {$n*2.3}]
    .Break 2
    return $n
}
```

```
puts [Foo 1]
exit 0
```

Run this with:

```
wize -Wall foo.tcl
```

This will invoke **TclInspect** where you can examine and change variables.

21.3 Error Trap

Sometimes it's desirable to debug a proc that is causing a traceback. Tracebacks are useful for showing that an error occurred, but unfortunately the current state information is lost by the time the stack unwinds.

With Mod an application can trap errors using ::env(TCL_TRAP). This invokes **TclInspect** right at the error, much like .Break, eg.

```
wize  -Wlevel=all,trap=1 bad.tcl
```

21.4 Tracing Proc Calls

You can trace all commands by calling **bltdebug**.

Wize supports tracing of all proc calls using:

```
wize -Wproccalls=3 prog.tcl
```

---

22. Backtrace

Decoding a Tcl error traceback can be very tedious. This is particularly true in larger applications involving hundreds of lines of backtrace and dozens of stack levels. Therefore **Mod** provides a facility that automatically decodes stack tracebacks, presenting them in one-level-per-line format. Th can also optionally stop the program right at an error, before the stack unwinds in a traceback. (note: this facility is for handling runtime errors, and presumes program files have already sourced without error.)

Mod handles background errors by unwinding the stack backtrace into a one per line listing which can then be used to navigate through source code involved in an error. Here a couple of screenshots. The first is a **real-error screenshot**and the other the **install demo-error screenshot**. Clicking on any given level, a Mini-EDitor (Med) will popup displaying the file/line of error. Med provides only rudimentary capabilities, however, it does support save and so allows immediate editing and fixing of problems.

One issue with debugging Tcl is that it normally does not collect file or line information associated with procs. Mod allows forcing this collection by adding the following to the top of your program (or setting it from command-line).

```
set ::env(TCL_WARN) all
```

When not using TCL_WARN or Wize -Wall, Mod instead falls back to show just the proc definition.

The backtrace window should look like:

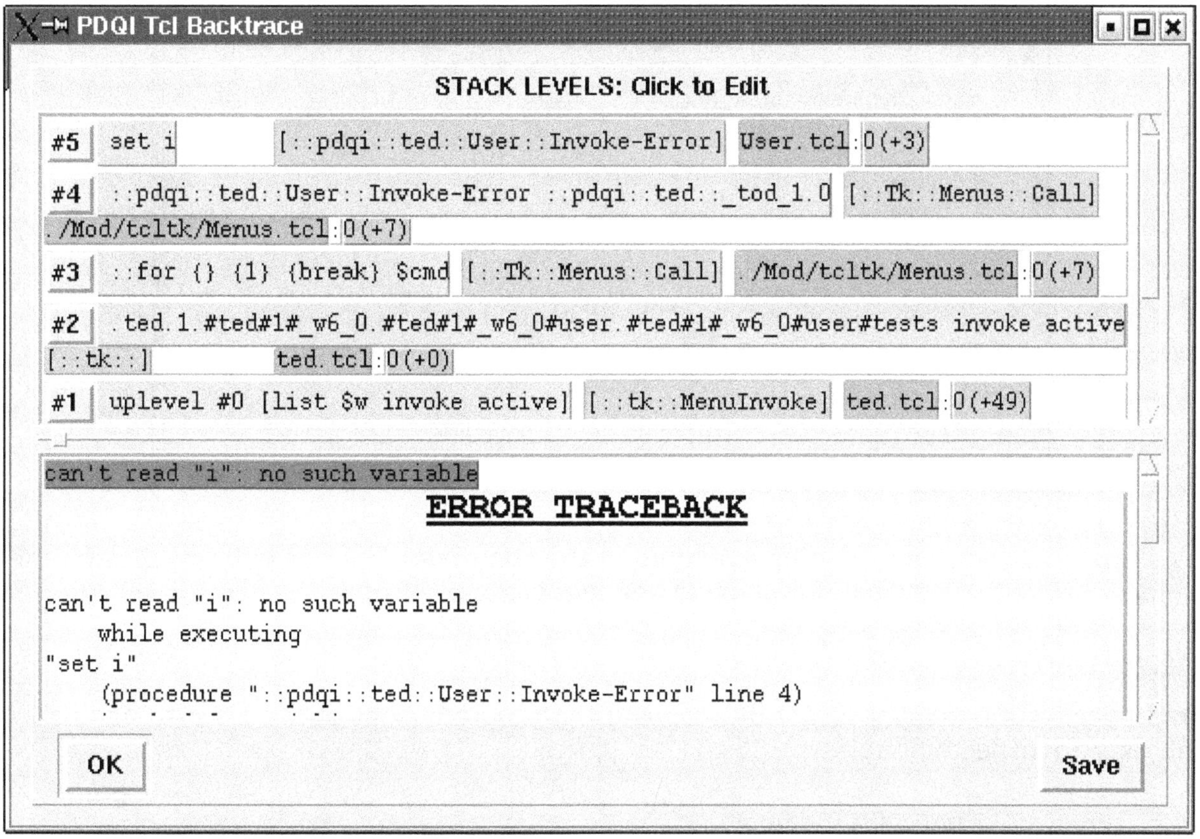

Clicking on any line should open a Mini-Editor window (see below).

22.1 Pausing A Program

It is sometimes desirable to pause a running program right inside a proc, to allow inspection of the runtime variables. This can be achieved using the .Break directive while running a program while running with -Wall.

Here is an example:.

```
proc Invoke-Stop {_} {
    # Demo of pausing a program for inspection.
    set j 1
    .Break first
    incr j
    .Break second
}
```

If run with checking on, this should open a window something like:

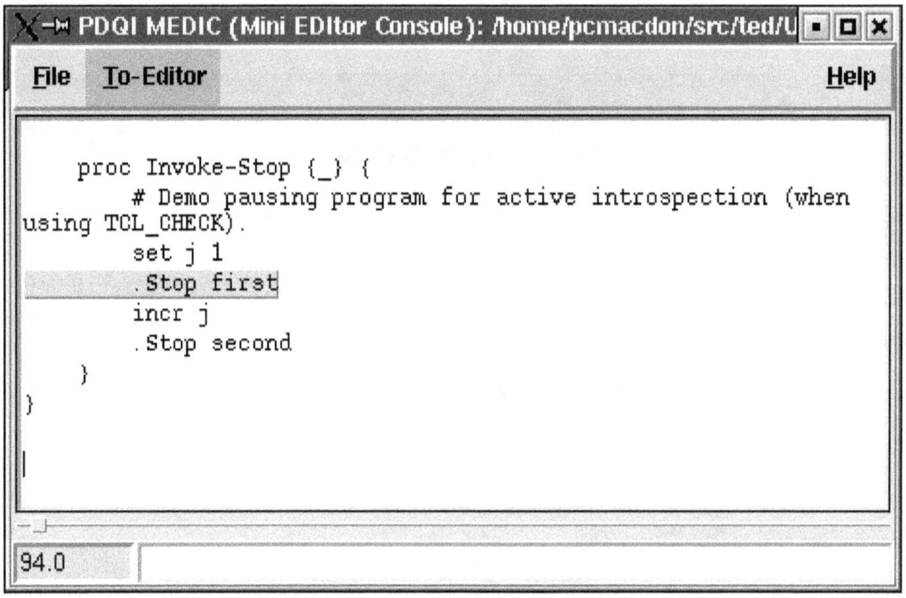

As shown, Tcl commands can be executed in the command input at bottom. Closing the window will resume execution, pausing again at the next .Break.

22.2 Trap

Trap deals with uncaught errors by stopping the program right at the error to enable the user to inspect variables.

To enable it run the program like so:

```
wize -Wlevel=all,trap=1 script.tcl
```

or put the following at the top of the main script

```
set ::env(TCL_WARN) "level=all,trap=1"
package require Mod
```

Trap stops a program-event right at the point of error, to allow introspection of the running program. Commands can then be run within a procs error context, prior to the unwinding of the stack.

Another way to use trap is selecting the trap option from Teds Run-Tcl.

WARNING: Do not always use the trap option as it exercises obscure areas of Tcl and can intermittently crash.

23. Util Macros

The **Util** macros are a collection of frequently used code. These all start with a star character *. Following are some of the more commonly used ones.

23.1 *catch

Eval with catch, displaying any errors as a warning. The warning message also contains the namespace (and proc if possible) of the offending call. When not running with wize -Wall, errors are silently ignored.

```
*catch { CallFunc 1 "X" }

# Equivalent to ...

if {[catch { CallFunc 1 "X" } erc]} {
   .Warn "Catch: $erc"
}
```

23.2 *value

Returns the value of a variable if it exists, otherwise returns the default, or if no default is given, an empty string, eg.

```
set n [*value ::MyNs::Arr(Really_Long_Value) 0]

# Equivalent to ...

if {[info exists ::MyNs::Arr(Really_Long_Value)]} {
    set n $::MyNs::Arr(Really_Long_Value)
} else {
    set n 0
}
```

23.3 *bvalue

Return the value for an element from a binary (name/value pair) list. If available, the dict command is used, otherwise falls back to a list search.

```
set LookupTable {able 1 baker 2 charlie 3}

set val [*bvalue $LookupTable baker 0]

# Equivalent to ...

if {[dict exists $LookupTable baker]} {
   set val [dict get $LookupTable baker]
} else {
   set val 0
}
```

23.4 *fread/*fwrite

Read or write a file. Additional options are passed to fconfigure:

```
set dat [*fread file1.dat]
*fwrite file2.dat $dat -translation binary

# Equivalent to ...

set fp [open file1.dat]
set dat [read $fp]
close $fp

set fp [open file2.dat w+]
fconfigure $fp -translation binary
if {[catch { puts -nonewline $fp $dat } erc]} {
   close $fp
   error $erc
}
close $fp
```

THE CTHULHU BUILD SYSTEM

Using Tcl to build C To Build Tcl Applications

Sean Woods
Test and Evaluation Solutions, LLC
for the
17th Annual Tcl/Tk Developer's Conference

THE CTHULHU BUILD SYSTEM

Using Tcl to build C To Build Tcl Applications

Sean Woods
Test and Evaluation Solutions, LLC
for the
17th Annual Tcl/Tk Developer's Conference

Introduction

This paper describes the *C and Tcl Hashtable Underpinnings for Language High-level Understanding*, or CTHULHU. CTHULHU is a series of tools to build C extensions for Tcl, from Tcl. It's focus is on computing problems that require Tcl to have access to complex data structures that are themselves manipulated by existing C code. These tools were originally developed to support the Test and Evaluation Solution's Integrated Recovery Model, but would be applicable to any problem in which Tcl needs to interact with C data structures in real-time.

CTHULHU Concepts

Overall Structure

Lets assume for a moment that we are developing a Tcl interface to a C application. This application has several different species of objects, each with their own data structure. Each object type is stored in a separate hashtable. We also provide an ensemble to manage both the hashtable and the data structures within.

CTHULHU builds on the venerable Tcl Extension Architecture (TEA). It uses a series of flat-file databases and scripts to generate C source files and headers. The scripting language used, of course, is Tcl.

The process begins with the developer writing up what he or she would like the data structures to look like. This description will serve double-duty as the meta-information that Tcl applications will later use to generate graphical interfaces for.

Containers

Let's call this master index and ensemble of methods a "container" for lack of a better term. In our hypothetical example, let's have a container that handles doorways. Well, since I'm out of creative ideas, let's just call the doors portals, and lift the example right from the kinds of problems that CTHULU was designed to solve.

```
% portal setting p1 open
1
% portal setting p1 jammed 2
```

Example: Using a container

When our program is running, we can use the **portal** command to generate our list of portals, as well as change their state throughout the simulation.

Methods

Containers all require a common set of core functions. Create a structure instance. Link it to another structure. Reset the table. Return a list of the id's in the table. Read and write to individual fields within a single structure.

In a perfect world, these core functions behave consistently across all of your containers, and your Tcl/Tk app can play on the similarities. Perhaps even glean meta information enough to build screen elements.

Some of these functions are pretty copy and paste-able. For instance, a function to spit out the IDs usually differs only in the name of the variables used. There are other functions that require a custom parser for every structure. Reading and writing individual fields of a record, for instance.

A great example of that later is the **setting** method. Setting takes in the id of a record, a field, and optionally a value. If the value is not given, the current value is returned. If the value is given, the data structure is updated with the new value for that field.

Wouldn't you know that "simple" function **setting** is one of the hairiest and most complex I have to implement? Every time I add a field, I have to drop it into 5 or 6 places in C. (And that is just for one method, mind you.)

There is also the headache of ensuring the user doesn't try to put a floating point value into a boolean field. Not to mention handling when a user tries to stuff in a value for a field that doesn't exist. Over time I was seeing a pattern emerge, a template that was being stamped out one module at a time. Being the lazy programmer I decided to stop implementing it piecemeal and write a general case automated procedure.

State Structures

Portals are very simple creatures, of course. They have a finite number of states: open, closed, opening or closing. Doors can also be damaged in two different ways:

1. Jammed open, meaning they are open and cannot be closed
2. Jammed closed: meaning they are closed and cannot be opened

So if I want to inquire about the state of a door we can use the setting method of the container.

The process begins with the user describing the structure. CTHULHU use a simple dict, with all of the information that both C and the resulting Tcl application will need captured in one place. The description for portal is to the right.

```
cstructDefine Portal {
  key id
  delta 1
  prefix p
  comment {Each portal is an ,,,
  static {
    Roid id;               /* Num...
    Entity *pType;
    Portal *delta;
    Compartment *pFrom;   /* Com...
    Compartment *pTo;     /* Com...
    Crew *holding;        /* Cre...
    Portal *airlock;      /* Poi...
  }
  fields {
    flooding {
      storage real
      desc {% of the door cover...
    }
    toid {
      storage Roid
      desc {Compartment To}
    }
    fromid {
      storage Roid
      desc {Compartment From}
    }
    jammed {
      storage u4
      values {
        0 normal {Door is normal}
        1 jam-close {Door is jamm...
        2 jam-open  {Door is jamm...
      }
    }
    reserved {
      storage bool
      desc {Door is being held clo...
    }
    open {
      storage u4
      values {
        0 normal {Door is closed}
        1 open    {Door is open}
        2 opening {Crew is opening...
        3 closing {Crew is closing...
      }
      desc {Current open status of...
    }
  }
}
```

Example: a dict describing the portal structure

The *static* field stores a block of C code. This is a great place to stuff pointers, variables you'd like hidden from the user, etc. The *fields* field is itself a dict, with an entry for each public variable that the developer wishes Tcl to be able to directly interact with. This dict also captures comments, enumerated values, and provides hints about storage requirements to C.

The data structure our cstructDefine statement produces is on the right. Major features:

1. #define statements for each enumerated field value
2. Sub-byte fields are stored in bitfields
3. The fields that are accessible to Tcl are marked public_XXXX. This makes them easier to spot while coding.
4. The flags in the toplevel of the definition trigger other fields to be automatically added. For instance set "location 1" flag added the *deckid, x, y,* and *zoff* fields.

```
/* Define the Portal Structure */
#define PORTAL_JAMMED_NORMAL 0 /* Door...
#define PORTAL_JAMMED_JAM_OPEN 2 /* Do...
#define PORTAL_OPEN_NORMAL 0 /* Door i...
#define PORTAL_OPEN_OPEN 1 /* Door is ...
#define PORTAL_OPEN_OPENING 2 /* Crew ...
#define PORTAL_OPEN_CLOSING 3 /* Crew ...
struct Portal {
   /* Place holder for ID */
   Tcl_Obj *idString;
   /* Begin hard-coded structure */

   Roid id;             /* Numeric ID ...
   Entity *pType;
   Portal *delta;

   Compartment *pFrom;  /* Compartment ...
   Compartment *pTo;    /* Compartment ...
   Crew *holding;       /* Crewmember  ...
   Portal *airlock;     /* Pointer to i...

   float public_flooding; /* flooding e...
   Roid public_fromid; /* fromid eoc */
   Roid public_toid; /* toid eoc */
   /*Begin bitmap*/
   unsigned int public_jammed    :4; /*...
   unsigned int public_open    :4; /* o...
   unsigned int public_reserved    :1; ...
};
```

Example: The C implementation of the portal structure

Data Interface

Of course, simply generating a data structure is not particularly useful in of itself. So CTHULHU has another few tricks up it's sleeve. In particular, as suite of tools to handle the interchange of data between Tcl and C.

Because it is machine generated, every field is given it's own handler to manage the unique constraints of each field. For instance, CTHULHU knows that a boolean field should use Tcl_GetBooleanFromObj, and fall back to Tcl_GetDoubleFromObj if the user was uncouth enough to put a decimal point in to represent 1.0 or 0.0. Because the machine is doing all the brute force programming, we can afford to be fancy because we only have to debug the prototype. Our work will be carried over and repeated N times for N different fields.

Properties, Entity and SimTypes

You may have noticed the pointer to a structure called **Entity** in the Portal structure. Entity is a container CTHULHU provides as a place to store properties. If you have a ship full of doors, many will be similar. Some can be opened faster than others. Some are taller, some are wider, but generally, there is usually more than one of each type of door in a model.

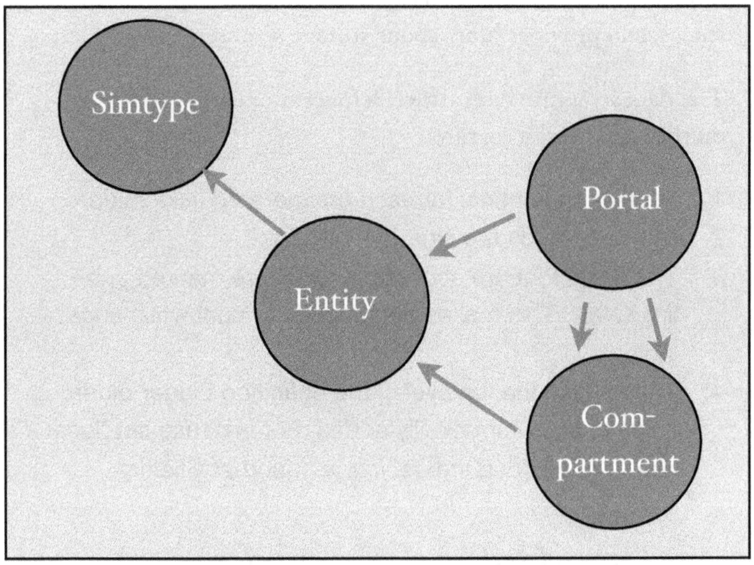

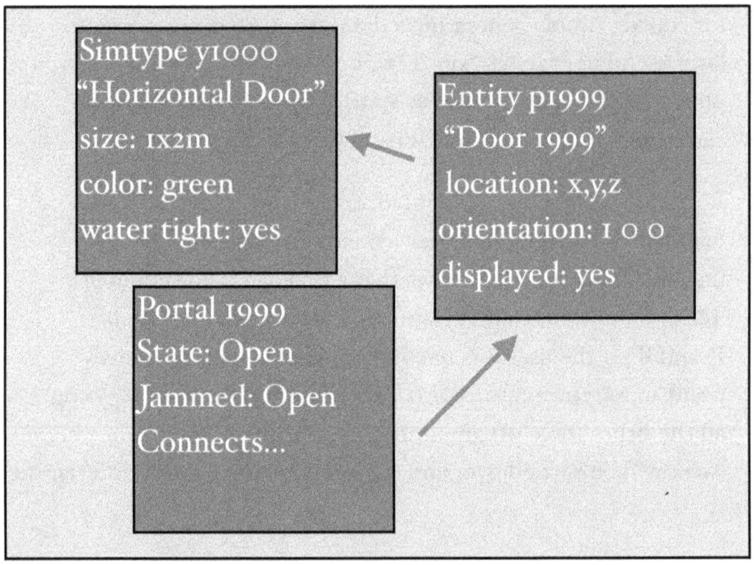

The SimType system allows you to store those properties once for all of the nodes that share it. Because we are making such efficient use of space by eliminating copies, there's very little need to break the properties up into C structures. So, we don't bother. Both SimType and Entity use a single Tcl_Obj that is formatted as a dict.

It is also handy to store information about a node that isn't part of the state C needs to access occasionally if at all. So it's nice to store that sort of information separately, with C being able to access on demand. In other cases, this is information that is needed for a Tcl representation, with no impact on the model running in C. Rather than write 1,000,001 handlers for all of the different data types, I decided to write the **Entity** data structure to handle this ephemeral data, and have all the other structures link to it.

Ok... I think I need to break out a graphic to explain what is going on. On the right you can see a chart of which data structure is pointing to which. **Portal** contains 5 links. One to an entry in **Entity**, two links to **Compartment**, one to another Portal, and the fifth to a structure called **Crew**. We won't explore crew or compartment for now.

The only link CTHULHU is concerned with is the link to Entity. When portal looks for a property, it looks to Entity. Every entry in the portal container has a corresponding entry in the Entity container.

If a property hasn't been specified for a particular entity, our search routing will route next to the Entity entry's SimType.

In our C model, let's assume the simulation itself doesn't care about things like object_size. We just need to know if the door is open, and if it can be opened or closed.

When we draw the portal on the screen, though, we do have to be concerned about size, location and direction. Our GUI can also suppress the display of the portal.

On the right you can see a sample conversation between a user at a console, the simtype, entity, and portal containers.

Delta

CTHULHU was designed with discrete time simulations in mind. One handy thing to know is what changed during the timestep. The pointer to a type of Portal called **delta** is a copy of this data structure from the last time step.

The current timestep is copied into the delta during the call to **cstruct_advance_all. cstruct_advance_all** is called after data logging has taken place, but before the next timestep kicks off. We can get away with copying the entire state of every node in the system, of course, because we represent it in such a compact form.

```
# See our portal with no type
% portal get p1
  open 1 jammed 2 fromid 100 \
  toid 101 flooding 1.0
# Create a type and stuff it with
# properties
% simtype create 1000
% simtype put 1000 {
  fullname {20" portal}
  object_size {1000 100 2000 mm}
}
# Set our portal to that new typeid
% portal typeid 1000
% portal get p1
  open 1 jammed 2 fromid 100 \
  toid 101 flooding 1.0 \
  fullname {20" portal} \
  object_size {1000 100 2000 mm}
# We also have a representation in
# entity. It stores properties,
# but has it's own state
% entity get p1
  visible 1 hidden 0 ...(etc)...
  fullname {20" portal} \
  object_size {1000 100 2000 mm}
% portal create p2
% portal typeid p2 1000
# If we add a property to portal,
# it's actually stored in entity
% portal put p2 \
   {dclocator 01-400-4}
% portal get p2
  open 0 jammed 0 fromid 0 \
  toid 0 flooding 0.0 \
  fullname {20" portal} \
  object_size {1000 100 2000 mm} \
  dc_locator 01-400-4
% entity get p2
  visible 1 hidden 0 ...(etc)...
  fullname {20" portal} \
  object_size {1000 100 2000 mm} \
  dc_locator 01-400-4
# If we add a property to entity,
# portal immediately sees it
% entity put p2 {open_time 10}
% portal get p2 open_time
  10
```

Example: Entities and Types in action

Programming CTHULHU

CTHULHU is intended to provide utility to C code. It's not a complete extension in of itself. It depends on external C code to maintain the hash tables the nodes are in, for instance. It assumes something else is doing the high-level integration of the ensemble. It's a tool with one job, and I'd like to think it does the job well: take care of the mundane exchange of data between Tcl and C.

The basic process is:

1. Document your structures in the cStructureDefine markup language, one file per structure, in the cstruct/ path in your source directory.
2. Call cstructBuild.tcl to generate your C source files: cstruct.c and cstruct.h
3. Include ctruct.c and cstruct.h in your build process
4. Include the cstruct definition files in your Tcl application

Modifications to TEA

The standard distribution of CTHULHU uses a modified version of the Tcl Extension Architecture. Certain paths have a special meaning, and some scripts have been incorporated into the makefiles.

build/

To make it easier to spot C files that are auto-generated, all of the products of the build process are placed in the build/ directory. It's designed so you can safely throw away that one path and start the build process from scratch.

conf/

The conf path is designed to store Tcl files that contain databases that will be incorporated into C and published to the resulting Tcl program as well. These files are sourced at various times during the build process, and Each instance of the cStructDefine command encountered during this pass is turned into a new data structure.

scripts/

Contains the Tcl scripts used by the modified Tea to auto-generate sources and/or chunks of the build system.

Other modifications

CTHULHU uses scripts to auto-generate the makefile lines needed to produce a .o file in the build directory for every C file it encounters in the generic/ directory. It also wraps those resulting .o files into a library automatically. This requires a custom Makefile, If you have additional makefile requirements, place them in static.mk Other than that, to build your extension is simply "./configure" and "make install"

CTHULHU Structure Descriptions

The markup language for CTHULHU is based on dicts. Each field is a signal for the meta-compiler. Here are the major fields implemented:

---

keytype

Tells CTHULU what kind of key type the container uses. If the keytype is int CTHULU will auto-generate a *StructName*_**Identify** and *StructName*_**TypeId** function. Otherwise those functions will need to be provided by the developer.

---

hashtype

Tells CTHULU what type of hash table the container uses to indexing nodes. The only supported hashtype at the moment is **tcl**.

---

dictstore

Used to differentiate between containers like **Entity** that store dict information, and others who link to entity for that function.

---

prefix

A one letter prefix that is used to build the node's ID in the Entity container. For instance, portal 199 is simply 199 in the portal container. But in entity it is p199, to differentiate it from, say e199 or v199.

---

key

Identifies the static field in the data structure that represents the node's identity.

---

name

A human readable name for the container

---

location

True or false. When true, add fields and methods to track and manipulate the location of the node within the model.

---

static

Block of code that is added, verbatim to the top of the data structure

---

static_bitfield

Block of code that is added after the bitfield fields in the data structure. Usually other sub-byte flags.

delta

True or False. When true, this structure tracks a delta

alloc_free

When non-empty, a block of C code to replace the standard *StructName*_Generic_Alloc and *StructName*_Generic_Free functions.

comment

Human readable comment

fields

A dict containing the definitions for the public fields of the structure.

Field names CTHULHU interacts with are all mapped to lower case, and all prepended with **public_**. If you see **public_foo**, the user in Tcl methods will address the field as **foo**.

CTHULHU Field Descriptions

The markup language for CTHULHU fields are also based on dicts. CTHULHU builds the structure based on the content of the following fields: (other fields are ignored, and assumed to be important to your app.)

storage

Tells CTHULHU how to represent the field in C. CTHULHU understands the values in the table on the right. Fields with a storage other than those understood by CTHULHU are treated as short integer.

Type	C Type	Tcl Type
Bitmask	Tcl_WideInt	wide integer
bool	unsigned int :1	boolean
blob	*stored as a property	
char	char	integer
double	double	double
float	float	double
matrix	*stored as a property	
real	float	double
Roid	unsigned int	integer
script	*stored as a property	
string	*stored as a property	
text	*stored as a property	
u1	unsigned int :1	boolean
u2	unsigned int :2	integer
u3	unsigned int :3	integer
u4	unsigned int :4	integer
u8	unsigned char	integer
u16	unsigned short	integer
u32	unsigned int	wide int
u64	Tcl_WideInt	wide integer

CTHULHU Storage Types

values

Values are mapped as a series of triplets: literal, code, description. A define statement for every literal/code mapping is created for the programmer's convenience.

Calls of the CTHULHU

The following are functions that interact with entities, simtypes, and properties. They can be used on any CTHULHU generated structure.

SimType_GetReal

```
double SimType_GetReal(Entity *pType, const char *field);
```

Searches for a property named **field** and returns the value as a double precision floating point.

SimType_GetInt

```
int SimType_GetInt(Entity *pType, const char *field);
```

Searches for a property named **field** and returns the value as an integer.

SimType_GetWideInt

```
Tcl_WideInt SimType_GetWideInt(Entity *pType, const char *field);
```

Searches for a property named **field** and returns the value as a wide integer.

SimType_GetTclObj

```
Tcl_Obj *SimType_GetTclObj(Entity *pType, const char *field);
```

Searches for a property named **field** and returns the value as a Tcl_Obj structure.

SimType_SetInt

```
void SimType_SetInt(Entity *pType, const char *field, int value);
```

Inserts or modifies a property named **field**, using the int value.

SimType_SetReal

```
void SimType_SetInt(Entity *pType, const char *field, double value);
```

Inserts or modifies a property named **field**, using the double value.

SimType_SetWideInt

```
void SimType_SetInt(Entity *pType, const char *field, Tcl_WideInt value);
```

Inserts or modifies a property named **field**, using the wide int value.

SimType_SetFromObj

```
int SimType_SetFromObj(Tcl_Interp *interp,Entity *pType, Tcl_Obj *field,
    Tcl_Obj *value);
```

Inserts or modifies a property named **field**, using the Tcl_Obj **value**. Returns TCL_OK on success, or TCL_ERROR otherwise.

SimType_GetFromObj

```
Tcl_Obj *SimType_SetFromObj(Tcl_Interp *interp,Entity *pType, Tcl_Obj *field);
```

Retrieves a property named **field**. Returns NULL if the field was not found.

SimType_GetAll

```
Tcl_Obj *SimType_GetAll(Tcl_Interp *interp,SimType *p,Tcl_Obj *local);
```

Combines all of the properties from the dict stored in *SimType* with the properties in *local* and returns them as a single dict.

Structure Functions of CTHULHU

CTHULHU defines a series of functions that govern the interactions on the C level of containers.

---

*StructName*ById

```
StructName *StructName ById( Roid id, int createflag);
```

Returns a structure given an integer ID, or NULL of the ID does not exist. If the createflag is true, generate a new structure if ID does not exist. **Roid** is typedef set aside for Record IDs. By default it's defined as a 32 bit *unsigned int*.

`StructName`ByID is provided by the developer.

---

*StructName*_Generic_Alloc

```
void StructName_Generic_Alloc(StructName *pNode);
```

A function external to CTHULHU that allocates the and initializes the structure. For structures with a key-type of int, CTHULHU provides a generic version.

---

*StructName*_Generic_Free

```
void StructName_Generic_Free(StructName *pNode);
```

A function external to CTHULHU that frees any memory allocated within the structure.

For structures with a keytype of int, CTHULHU provides a generic version.

---

*StructName*_ApplySettings

```
void StructName_Apply_Settings(StructName *pNode);
```

Called after a setting has been changed by the Tcl interface to CTHULHU, allowing the C code a chance to be notified and or alter other fields in response.

The CTHULHU Build System

*StructName*_Identify

`Tcl_Obj *StructName_Identify(StructName *pNode);`

Returns a Tcl object that represents the identity of this node, and is capable of being read back in by *StructName*_**FromTclObj**. If the container's **keytype** is int, this function is generated by CTHULU.

*StructName*_TypeId

`Tcl_Obj *StructName_TypeId(StructName *pNode);`

Returns a Tcl object that represents the identity of this node's type. Or zero if this structure has no type.

If the container's **keytype** is int, this function is generated by CTHULU.

*StructName*_FromTclObj

`int StructName_FromTclObj(Tcl_Interp*, Tcl_Obj*, StructName **pNode);`

Converts the ID of a node given in a Tcl object to a pointer to a structure. Return TCL_OK on success, or TCL_ERROR otherwise.

*StructName*_ToDict

`int StructName_FromTclObj(Tcl_Interp*, Tcl_Obj*,StructName **pNode);`

Converts the ID of a node given in a Tcl object to a pointer to a structure. Return TCL_OK on success, or TCL_ERROR otherwise.

*StructName*_SetType

`void StructName_SetType(StructName *p,SimType *pType);`

Associates an CTHULHU node with a type given by the a pointer of **SimType**.

*StructName*_GetType

`SimType *StructName_GetType(StructName *p);`

Returns either a the pointer to the **SimType** structure that contains properties for this node, or NULL if no type has been associated with it.

*StructName*_DictPut

`void StructName_DictPut(StructName *p,Tcl_Obj *field,Tcl_Obj *value);`

*StructName*_DictGet

```
Tcl_Obj *StructName_DictGet(StructName *p,Tcl_Obj *field);
```

---

*StructName*_**ValueOffset**

```
int StructName_ValueOffset(Tcl_Interp *interp, Tcl_Obj *pObj, int *pIndex, int
*pType);
```

---

*StructName*_**FromTclObj**

```
int StructName_FromTclObj(Tcl_Interp *interp, Tcl_Obj *nodeid, StructName **pNode);
```

Using the information about a node given in the Tcl_Obj **nodeid**, map the pointer **pNode** to the data structure that represents it. If the node does not exist, **pNode** will be null. If a problem was encountered converting **nodeid** to a useable form, the function will return **TCL_ERROR**. Otherwise, it will return **TCL_OK**.

---

*StructName*_**ToDict**

```
Tcl_Obj *StructName_ToDict(Tcl_Interp *interp, StructName *p);
```

Converts `StructName` to a dict that is capable of being exported to Tcl.

---

*StructName*_**nodeeval**

```
int StructName_nodeeval(Tcl_Interp*, StructName*, Tcl_Obj *body);
```

Loads the fields and values from `StructName` to the local interpreter, evaluates the block of code given in **body** and returns the standard Tcl reply codes: **TCL_OK, TCL_CONTINUE, TCL_BREAK,** or **TCL_ERROR**. On replies other the **TCL_ERROR**, changes made to the variables derived from `Struct-Name` are saved back to the structure.

Tcl Commands Provided by CTHULHU

In addition to routines intended to be used by C, CTHULHU also adds ready-made Tcl commands. To include them into the interpreter, one simply needs to add them with your desired name using **Tcl_CreateObjCommand**.

---

*StructName*_**method_count**

`Arguments: (none)`

Returns a headcount of all of the nodes in the container

---

*StructName*_**method_exists**

`Arguments: nodeid`

Returns true if *nodeid* was found in the container, false otherwise.

---

*StructName*_**method_for**

Arguments: keyvar ?valvar? body

Operates like a foreach loop, with the ID of the node stored in the keyvar, and optionally, a dict representation of the node stored in valvar.

Example:

```
%structname% for nodeid nodeinfo { puts [list $nodeid $nodeinfo] }
```

---

*StructName*_method_foreach

Arguments: body

The ID number of the node is loaded into the interpreter as the local variable "id." All fields are loaded into the local interpreter as variables of the same name. Any modifications to those variables will write the changes back to the data structure.

Example:

```
%structname% foreach { set hidden 1 }
```

---

*StructName*_method_list

Arguments: (none)

Returns a list of all of the nodes in the container

---

*StructName*_method_nodedelta

Arguments: nodeid ?field?

Returns a list of parameters that have changed since the last instance of "changes." Optionally, return a true or falseif a specific field has changed.

---

*StructName*_method_nodeget

Arguments: nodeid ?field?

If *field* is given, return the value for *field*. If *field* is not in the data structure, the system searches for a value in the following order:

1. In the local dict of the node
2. In the dict of the node's type
3. Null

If *field* is not given, return a key/value list containing all of the values:

1. Published from the data structure
2. Written into the local dict of the node
3. Written into the dict of the node's type

---

*StructName*_method_nodeput

`Arguments: nodeid {field value ?field value? ...}`

Writes values to node. If a *field* matches a field in the data structure, the data structure is updated. Fields that do not match a field in the data structure are written to a local dict.

---

*StructName*_method_nodewith

`Arguments: nodeid body`

Operates in a similar manner to *dict with*. The state and properties of the node are fed into the interpreter as local variables. If the script modifies one or more of the variable representing state, the change is written back into the structure.

---

*StructName*_method_setting

`Arguments: nodeid field ?value?`

When value is given, update the *field* in the data structure. *field* must be on of the fields of the data structure, or an exception is returned.

When value is not given, return the value for *field*. In this case *field* is permitted to be a field in the structure, or any property that is expected to be passed from the node's type.

---

*StructName*_method_typeid

`Arguments: nodeid ?typeid?`

If typeid is given, set the type for *nodeid* to the simtype identified by *typeid*.

If *typeid* is omitted, return the id of the current type for *nodeid*, or 0 if none has been set.

Getting CTHULHU

A public release for CTHULHU is available on T&E Solution's open source site:

`http://oss.tnesolutions.net/home`

CTHULHU is released under a BSD-style license, modeled after the Tcl core.

You can contact Sean Woods for more details at yoda@etoyoc.com

Credits

Cover Art: Möbius strip, http://en.wikipedia.org/wiki/File:Möbius_strip.jpg

The Tcl Extension Architecture (TEA) is published at: http://www.tcl.tk/doc/tea/

Supporting Embedded Software Development

Doing the Heavy Lifting with Tcl/Tk

Andrew Mangogna
amangogna@modelrealization.com

17th Annual Tcl/Tk Conference
October 13-15, 2010

Copyright

© 2010, by G. Andrew Mangogna. Permission to copy and distribute this article by any means is granted by the copyright holder provided the work is distributed in its entirety and this notice appears on all copies.

Abstract

Software development on micro-controller based computing platforms is very challenging due to minimal computing resources and I/O capabilities. These micro-controller platforms are deployed widely in areas such as home automation, consumer electronics, automotive and medical devices. This paper discusses a set of software tools, implemented in Tcl / Tk, that support software code generation for small embedded micro-controller based systems. The core tool is a program called, **pycca**, which is a domain specific language for specifying data structures, data relationships and finite state machine behavior. The focus of the paper is not on the functionality of **pycca** but rather the underlying Tcl technology used to implement the tools. Although it is not possible to run a Tcl interpreter on small micro-controller based systems, Tcl is a valuable tool used to support the development and testing of this class of system. All the programs discussed are available as part of an open source project.

1. Introduction

This paper is a about a program called, **pycca**. **Pycca** is an acronym for Pass Your "C" Code Along[1]. **Pycca** is coded in Tcl and implements a domain specific language that supports generating "C" code that is useful in building software for highly embedded micro-controller based computing platforms.

The remainder of this section discusses the background and motivation behind **pycca**. **Pycca** is a supporting program for an execution architecture that is appropriate for many types of applications fielded on small computing platforms. The next section shows how **pycca** fits into the development workflow and shows a simple example.

The remainder of the paper is devoted to the internals of **pycca** highlighting the Tcl / Tk technology that is used in its implementation. Language parsing, internal data structures and semantic analysis are discussed. The use of relationally structured data is emphasized. The output from **pycca** is generated by template expansion and an example of the expansion is shown. Finally, other programs that use the parsed data that **pycca** can save are discussed. These programs provide another set of supporting functionality to help in debugging and visualizing the resulting software.

1.1. Resources

The software described in this paper is available as an open source project that is licensed in the same manner as Tcl / Tk itself[2].

1.2. An Execution Architecture for Embedded Systems

One very difficult aspect of developing software on a micro-controller is the *bare metal* aspect of running that software. There is often no operating system to protect against errant execution. Many times the computer architecture is so primitive that there is no notion of supervisory execution. It is important to keep strict control over the data and execution sequencing. To that end, a well defined execution architecture which controls all the essential aspects of program execution needs to be in place. The idea is to factor away from the application into a common code base all the policy decisions about how data is handled and how execution is sequenced.

One can view the execution architecture as a different model of computation that has a higher level of abstraction. Rather than the traditional view of sequential lines of code where control is transferred explicitly, the computation model is more along the lines seen in a conventional GUI program. An event loop, which is not generally seen by the programmer, handles the control sequencing as events are generated. Events are used to cause transitions in finite state machines. This is different from the usual event loop that simply maps events to a callback function. State machines can generate events to other state machines and one very powerful aspect of the execution model derives from the sequencing of interactions of what are usually small state machines.

Such an execution architecture is generally applicable to a range of application subject matters and is only dependent upon the demands the applications make on the computing environment rather than the details of the application semantics. This is an important distinction. The

---

[1] Rest assured that despite a name beginning with *py*, Python is not involved.

[2] http://tcl-cm3.sourceforge.net
Although this project is described as a set of tools for the ARM® Cortex-M3®, the scope is substantially larger than a single processor platform.

execution environment tailored for small systems is not universally suitable as it will scale to the computational requirements of the system only within certain bounds. However, it is not dependent upon the particular subject matter of any application.

1.3. STSA

We describe here a Single Threaded Software Architecture (STSA). As the name implies there is only a single thread of execution, although interrupts are allowed to preempt that single thread. This execution architecture encompasses all the policy decisions on how data is managed and how execution is sequenced.

Although the small memory footprint of micro-controller based platforms means the quantity of data in these types of systems is small, the data can be of a rather complex organization. For many of these applications, no system heap is used and all data is managed from fixed, worst case sized pools. Safety critical systems in particular avoid a global system pool since they tend to be long running[3] and the concern is that the heap will fragment over time and the system may not be able to allocate a critical data structure. Individual memory pools also offer easier allocation and management but, because the worst case allocation must be accommodated, sometimes do not give the most efficient memory usage.

The STSA also manages the the sequencing of execution. Although conventional multi-tasking operating environments are sometimes available, they do incur additional unwelcome overhead of context switching and frequently negatively affect interrupt service latencies. The usual requirements for small system applications can also be met by having a means of terminating a computation and then resuming that computation in response to some other happening. This can be done using finite state machines techniques that do not require keeping a virtual CPU context and switching between multiple contexts. Many applications for small systems function perfectly well using a single threaded, event driven approach to execution sequencing. This model of execution is analogous to the Tcl event loop with two significant differences.

- The STSA dispatches events to Moore type state machines.[4] By contrast, the Tcl event loop binds arbitrary Tcl scripts to the event. STSA has a much tighter set of rules for how execution is sequenced and supports the execution semantics of Executable UML.[5]
- The STSA binds the events to application functionality at link time whereas Tcl, naturally enough, accomplishes this binding at run time. STSA accomplishes the binding by being completely data driven, requiring a set of data structures be provided by the application. This has two advantages that are significant in small systems. First, it eliminates a large fraction of initialization code. For long running systems initialization code is run only once yet still occupies valuable memory space. Second, the paths through the state space of the code are fixed giving much tighter control over the system execution. Indeed, the entire state space of the application is determined before run time. This is considered a substantial benefit since tight control is more desirable than run-time flexibility for these types of systems.

---

[3] An example of a long running system is one that is battery powered, begins to run when the battery is installed and continues to do so until the battery fails to provide enough energy.

[4] http://en.wikipedia.org/wiki/Moore_machine

[5] http://en.wikipedia.org/wiki/Executable_UML

See also:

Mellor, Stephen J. and Marc J. Balcer, *Executable UML: a foundation for model-driven architecture*, Addison-Wesley, 2002, ISBN 0-201-74804-5

and

Raistrick, Chris, Paul Francis, John Wright, Colin Carter and Ian Wilkie, *Model Driven Architecture with Executable UML*, Cambridge University Press, 2004, ISBN 0-521-53771-1

The arguments usually used for event driven versus thread based programming in Tcl apply to the small system context as well. Preemptive multi-tasking with shared state in a small system carries with it the same difficulties that it does in larger systems, namely, the extreme, if not impossible, difficulty of insuring that there is no critical section violation of the shared state information. Such violations create small timing based windows where errors can occur and such errors are very difficult to reproduce and therefore correct. Event driven, single threaded execution models eliminate many of these potential errors *by design*. Of course, not all applications have computational demands that can be easily satisfied by and event driven approach. If the worst case computation time for a particular thread of control is longer than the response latency time required of the application, then some way to defer the long running computation must be devised. But most often the applications running on small embedded targets are usually completely driven by responses to happenings in the environment in which they reside and the computation of those responses is well within the overall response latency time requirements of the system. This is especially true given that interrupts can be used to handle most of the hard real time response requirements.

An application is bound to the STSA execution environment at link time and STSA is completely data driven. Applications supply instances of a well defined data structure (as an initialized "C" variable) as part of the interface to STSA and that data structure contains all the information STSA needs to manage data memory and execution sequencing. This arrangement has several advantages such as the tight and early binding of application functionality and the fact that most of the data required by STSA is constant and therefore can be placed in read-only memory which is often more available than RAM. The disadvantage is that the data that must be supplied to STSA is tedious to specify and arrange into "C" variables. For example, part of the data required by STSA is the state transition matrix for the state machines. In the case of the Moore type machines that are supported by STSA, the transition matrix is usually implemented as a two dimensional array indexed by a state number and event number with each entry containing the new state for the transition. Although very convenient and efficient for the implementation, it is tedious and error prone to manually encode states and events into sequential integers that are suitable for use as indices into the transition matrix. This is especially the case in the face of changes in the state machine graph that inevitably occur during development.

Pycca was written specifically to help this problem. **Pycca** accepts declarations of data structures and data relationships and of state machines and other procedural operations. All algorithmic actions are specified in "C" which is wrapped as a function and ordered in the output to match the "C" compiler's needs, but is otherwise passed through unchanged. What **pycca** generates from the specification data are the data structures required by STSA to bind together the state transitions with the passed through "C" code producing a single code file and a single header file. Hence the name, **pycca**, an acronym for Pass Your "C" Code Along.

1.4. STSA Concepts

Below we list the *concepts* behind STSA. This will define terms that are further discussed below. It is beyond the scope of this paper to cover each of these concepts in detail, but it is sufficient to say that **pycca** allows each concept to be specified to the STSA.

(1) Software is organized into Domains. Domains represent a coherent subject matter. Domains interface to each other by a set of Domain Operations. All other aspects of a domain are not visible outside of the domain.

(2) Domains consist of a set of Classes. Classes, in turn, consist of attributes. Classes hold the data of a Domain. The set of Classes of the Domain represents the time invariant aspect of the Domain semantics as they are encoded into data.

(3) Classes may have relationships between them that model the subject matter associations that class instances have.

(4) A Class may be instantiated an arbitrary number of times. Each Instance of a Class has the same data and behavior.

(5) An Instance may be created in one of three ways.
(a) An initial instance. Initial instances come into existence, conceptually, when the system is started.
(b) Synchronous creation. One instance may request another instance to be created as part of its behavior.
(c) Asynchronous creation. One Instance may request that a Creation Event be posted, that when dispatched will result in an Class Instance being created.

(6) A Class may define Class Operations. Class Operations are common processing associated to a particular Class.

(7) A Class may define Instance Operations. Instance Operations are common processing defined by a Class and implicitly associated with a particular Instance of the Class. Instance Operations perform the same operations on all Instances of the Class.

(8) A Class may define a State Model. The state model is a Moore state machine. Every Instance of such a Class has its own implicit state variable and Instances change state independently.

(9) Each state of the State Model may contain an Action. The Action of a state may execute arbitrary processing.

(10) An Instance transitions from its current state to another state (possibly the same as the current state) as a result of receiving an Event. Events may carry additional parameters and these values are available to the Action that is executing when the transition occurs.

(11) Instances may send Events to other Instances including themselves. Any Event sent by an Instance to itself is received before any Event sent by a different Instance. Events are not lost and the order of Events sent by an Instance to a particular receiving Instance is preserved. However, the sender of an Event does not know when the Event is actually dispatched.

(12) Instances may request that an Event be sent after some delay. No more than one Delayed Event of a given type may be outstanding between a given source Instance and a given target Instance (where source and target may be the same Instance). This has same effect as sending the Event, except that STSA manages the timing. Delayed events may be canceled and it is possible to inquire as to the amount of delay remaining for a particular delayed event.

(13) For one particular type of relationship, a Class (the super-type) may be completely partitioned into disjoint sub-Classes (the subtypes). In this case the super-type Class may define state machine events that are re-mapped at run-time into a corresponding Event of the subtype to which the super-type is currently related. Such an event is called a Polymorphic Event.

(14) An Instance of a Class may be deleted in one of two ways:
(a) Synchronous deletion One instance may request that another instance is deleted.
(b) Asynchronous deletion A state of a State Model may be designated as a Final state. Instances entering such a state are deleted automatically at the end of the execution of the final state Action.

2. Pycca

Pycca is a domain specific language. The domain of interest here is specifying data structures, relationships between data and lifecycles of processing modeled as Moore type finite state machines. The semantics are those implemented by STSA as described above. **Pycca** can be thought of as a partial code generator for STSA based applications. In truth, **pycca** generates no code other than trivial instrumentation and functions wrappers. The hard work of expressing computation is accomplished in "C" with the "C" code being passed through to a compiler. Consequently, **pycca** is very much a declarative language since it understands nothing about the "C" code that is passed along. This outlook goes well with focus of **pycca** generated data structures required by STSA.

2.1. Example

For the purposes of this paper, we will use a simple running example. This example is about controlling a very simple automatic washing machine. Undoubtedly real washing machines are not controlled in the manner implied by this example and any reader who knows how washing machines actually are controlled would probably be horrified by this example. It is not the purpose here to build a real washing machine control system. The purpose here is to choose a subject matter that most people will know something about and avoid a long explanation of the subject matter itself.

With that caveat, the figure below shows the class diagram of our washing machine.

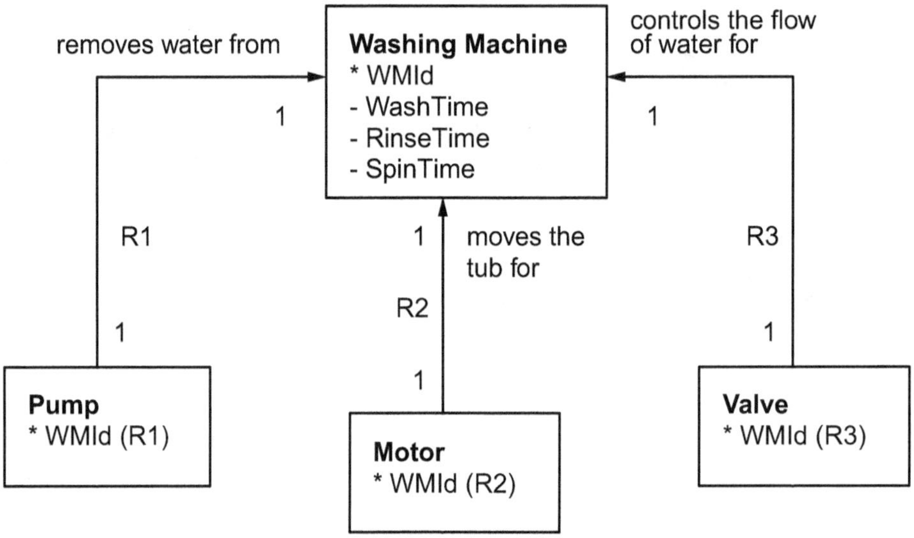

Figure 1. Washing Machine Class Diagram

The details of the graphical notation are explained below. For now, it is sufficient to view this as a picture of a relational schema and a set of referential integrity constraints.

One particular class in the diagram also exhibits interesting life-cycle behavior which is modeled as a state machine. That figure is shown below.

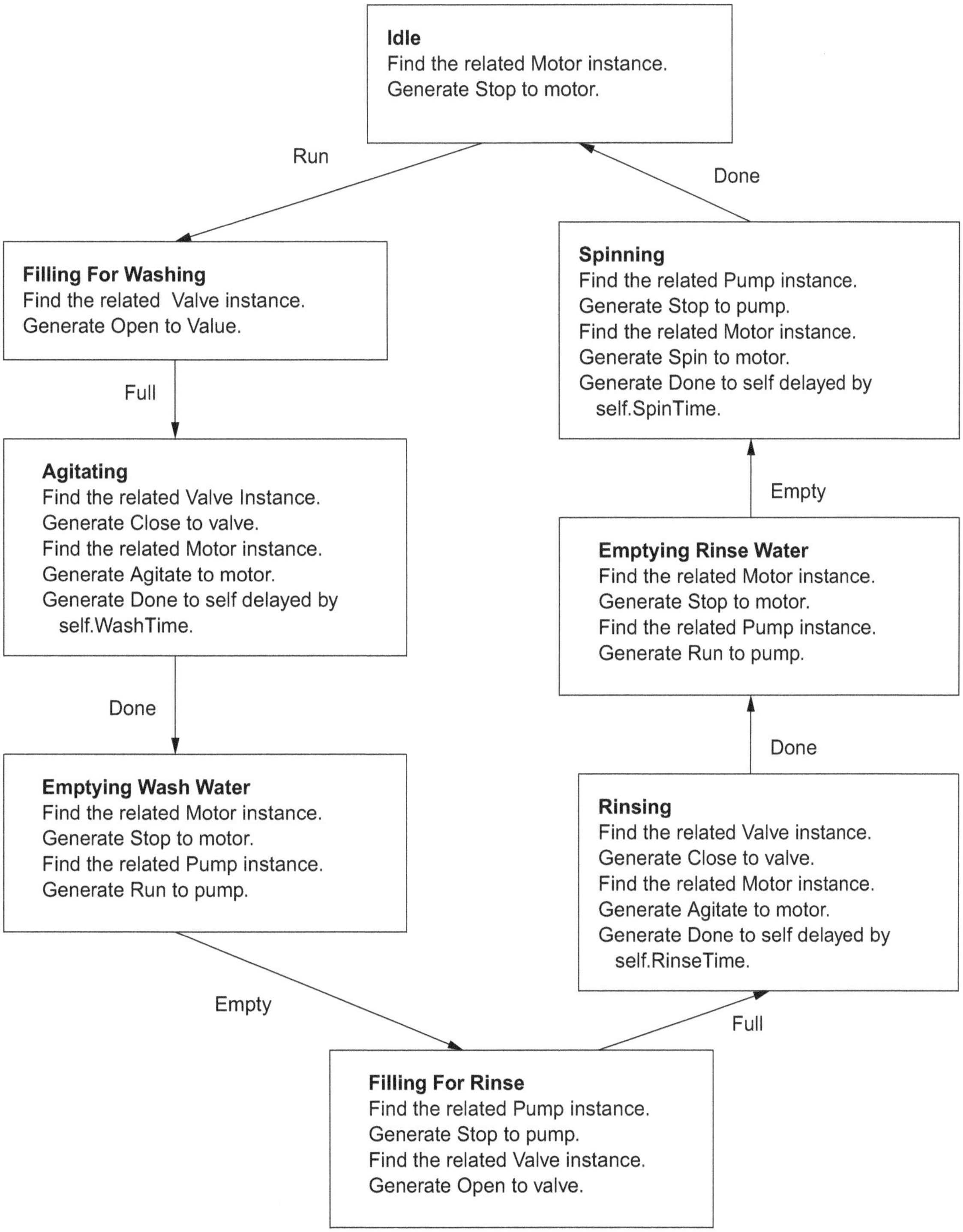

Figure 2. State Model for Washing Machine Class

In this diagram, each rectangle is a state and transitions between states are represented by a directed line segment labeled with the name of the event that causes the transition. This state machine is in the Moore formulation of state models which means that the action of the state is performed when the state is entered. So, when in machine is in the **Idle** state, receiving the **Run** event will cause a transition to the **Filling For Washing** state and will perform the logic contained in the rectangle of that state.

2.2. Example Pycca Source

As is usually the case, even small, simple examples often end up needing more source code than is convenient to include in a paper of this type. So we will include only part of the **pycca** source for the example. Here we show the Washing Machine class definition. This should be sufficient for you to get the general idea.

```
class WashingMachine
    attribute (unsigned WashTime) default {10}
    attribute (unsigned RinseTime) default {10}
    attribute (unsigned SpinTime) default {10}
    reference R1 -> Pump
    reference R2 -> Motor
    reference R3 -> Valve

    machine
        state Idle() {
        //# Find the related Motor instance.
        //# Generate Stop to motor.

            PYCCA_generate(Stop, Motor, self->R2, self) ;
        }
        transition Idle - Run -> FillingForWashing

        state FillingForWashing() {
        //# Find the related Valve instance.
        //# Generate Open to Value.

            PYCCA_generate(Open, Valve, self->R3, self) ;
        }
        transition FillingForWashing - Full -> Agitating

        state Agitating () {
        //# Find the related Valve Instance.
        //# Generate Close to valve.
        //# Find the related Motor instance.
        //# Generate Agitate to motor.
        //# Generate Done to self delayed by self.WashTime.

            PYCCA_generate(Close, Valve, self->R3, self) ;
            PYCCA_generate(Agitate, Motor, self->R2, self) ;
            PYCCA_generateDelayedToSelf(Done, self->WashTime) ;
        }
        transition Agitating - Done -> EmptyingWashWater

        state EmptyingWashWater () {
        //# Find the related Motor instance.
        //# Generate Stop to motor.
        //# Find the related Pump instance.
        //# Generate Run to pump.

            PYCCA_generate(Stop, Motor, self->R2, self) ;
            PYCCA_generate(Run, Pump, self->R1, self) ;
        }
        transition EmptyingWashWater - Empty -> FillingForRinse

        state FillingForRinse() {
        //# Find the related Pump instance.
        //# Generate Stop to pump.
        //# Find the related Valve instance.
```

```
        //# Generate Open to valve.

            PYCCA_generate(Stop, Pump, self->R1, self) ;
            PYCCA_generate(Open, Valve, self->R3, self) ;
        }
        transition FillingForRinse - Full -> Rinsing

        state Rinsing() {
        //# Find the related Valve instance.
        //# Generate Close to valve.
        //# Find the related Motor instance.
        //# Generate Agitate to motor.
        //# Generate Done to self delayed by self.RinseTime.

            PYCCA_generate(Close, Valve, self->R3, self) ;
            PYCCA_generate(Agitate, Motor, self->R2, self) ;
            PYCCA_generateDelayedToSelf(Done, self->RinseTime) ;
        }
        transition Rinsing - Done -> EmptyingRinseWater

        state EmptyingRinseWater() {
        //# Find the related Motor instance.
        //# Generate Stop to motor.
        //# Find the related Pump instance.
        //# Generate Run to pump.

            PYCCA_generate(Stop, Motor, self->R2, self) ;
            PYCCA_generate(Run, Pump, self->R1, self) ;
        }
        transition EmptyingRinseWater - Empty -> Spinning

        state Spinning() {
        //# Find the related Pump instance.
        //# Generate Stop to pump.
        //# Find the related Motor instance.
        //# Generate Spin to motor.
        //# Generate Done to self delayed by self.SpinTime.

            PYCCA_generate(Stop, Pump, self->R1, self) ;
            PYCCA_generate(Spin, Motor, self->R2, self) ;
            PYCCA_generateDelayedToSelf(Done, self->SpinTime) ;
        }
        transition Spinning - Done -> Idle
    end
end
```

Figure 3. Pycca Source for Washing Machine Class

Compare the source text above to the graphic of Figure 1 and the state graph of Figure 2. There are three attributes of the Washing Machine class, corresponding to the times that are used in controlling the cycle. There are three references to the Pump, Motor and Valve classes. The full text of the source has definitions for those classes. The state machine definition includes definitions for each state and the transitions between states.

It is worth noting that there is no order dependency in **pycca**. Classes may be defined in any order. State machine definitions are also order independent in the sense that you may define all the states or all the transitions and in any order. The style of the example is to define states and follow them by their outbound transitions, but that is strictly a coding convention and not a requirement of **pycca** syntax. Note that there is no separate definition of the events, they are gleaned from the **transition** statements. The body of the state definitions is "C" language code. In the above example it consist entirely of macros that are used to generate events. **Pycca** inserts a set of "C" pre-processor macros into the output that are very useful for hiding the naming conventions and interfacing with the STSA execution architecture. Indeed the "C" code for a **pycca** state machine is often very stylized since the macros provide the interface to a large part of the ordinary processing that state actions perform. Clearly, this particular example is dominated by state behavior, but other types of applications would have more of what would be considered normal "C" statements.

2.3. Pycca Workflow

The figure below shows the general workflow when using **pycca**.

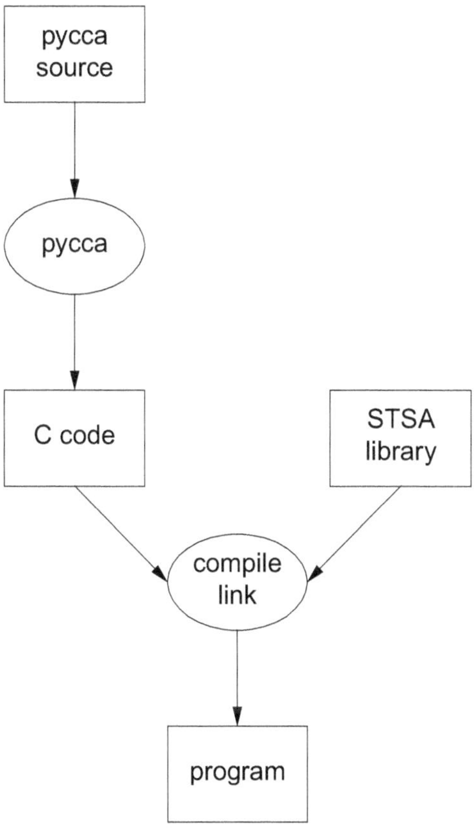

Figure 4. Building a Program with pycca

Pycca source is processed by **pycca** to produce a single "C" language code file and a single "C" header file. **Pycca** can process several source files together as if they were one file. The "C" output must be compiled and linked against the STSA library. Of course, other code files may be linked into the program and the program may have many **pycca** generated files. **Pycca** is able to insert line numbers into the generated code file that references the original source or to leave out those numbers if they should confuse your debugger.

In general, the difficulties of working with **pycca** come more from the translation of the design ideas into source. From there on, the workflow is quite traditional.

3. Pycca Internals

Up to now, there has been a lot of background and not much Tcl. However, **pycca** is implemented in Tcl. Now we will consider the design of the internals of **pycca** and attempt to highlight the Tcl technology that was used.

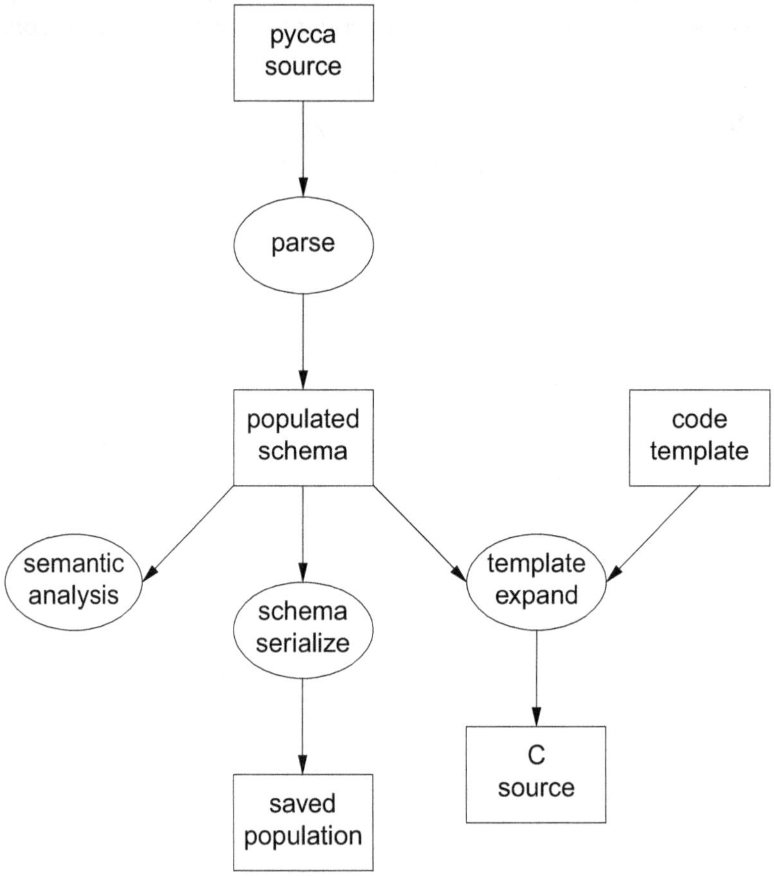

Figure 5. Pycca Internal Data Flow

Figure 5 above shows a high level view of the design of the internals of **pycca**. The **pycca** source is first parsed. The parsed components are stored in a normalized relational schema. Like most language processing programs, after the syntax is verified, it is necessary to do some semantic analysis to insure that the language statements are meaningful. Unlike most computer languages, **pycca** is not expression oriented. Rather the **pycca** language itself is declarative in nature. Algorithmic computation is left to "C" code statements that are passed along to a compiler. This means that the generation of output is amenable to using template expansion techniques. **Pycca** expands a template by querying the data from the populated schema to produce the desired "C" code file. Optionally, **pycca** can save the populated schema by serializing it. We will find that useful later.

In the following sections we will examine the details of each of these steps, again looking at the Tcl technology used to implement them. What we will see is that **pycca** looks very much like a traditional database application and less like a language compiler than might initially be recognized.

3.1. Parsing Techniques

There are many options in Tcl for parsing domain specific languages. The usual advice to those with less experience in Tcl is use the Tcl parser itself to parse a language. Being a command language with a very simple syntax, Tcl is well suited to apply to domain specific languages. The language syntax can be defined in terms of Tcl commands with parameters that pass the required information. It is relatively easy to support a hierarchy of definitions by evaluating a script body in a namespace that exposes a limited set of commands suitable to the context. However, exposing some Tcl syntax is unavoidable with this approach and that may not be acceptable in all circumstances.

In the case of **pycca** it was decided that a more conventional syntax would be better for the target audience. **Fickle** and **tackle** are Tcl analogs to the venerable lex / yacc (or flex / bison) lexical analyzer and parser generators. They use an input file syntax that very close to that of lex and yacc and generate a lexical analyzer or parser in Tcl code. Unfortunately, the generated parser is not as robust as one might desire. Detection of language grammar issues is very limited. A number of small problems with the **tackle** code itself were found. In the end, the generated parser is sufficient for the purposes, but a future version of **pycca** will probably return to using Tcl syntax and the Tcl parser.

3.2. Parsing Results

In conventional language processing programs, as language statements are recognized the parsed components are used to build symbol tables and syntax trees. This is especially true of languages that are generating code for statements and expressions. Since the usual infix notation provides a convenient way to specify a tree in a linear fashion, grammar reductions are usually used to construct an expression as a syntax tree that is much easier to manipulate programmatically.

However, the **pycca** language is not used for code generation, *per se*. As we discussed above, what **pycca** does is to pass along "C" code, somewhat repackaged and reorganized, and to generate data structures that are used as the interface to the execution architecture. Symbol tables and syntax trees do not help in this type of processing. Rather, what **pycca** does is to populate a normalized relational schema. This relational schema constitutes a *meta-model* of the domain for which **pycca** is the domain specific language.

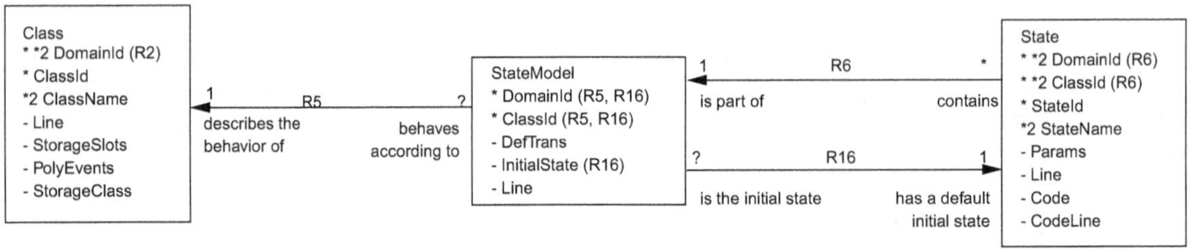

Figure 6. Part of the pycca Meta-model

Figure 6 above shows a graphical representation of very small part of the relational schema that constitutes the **pycca** meta-model. This is only a small part of the schema that we will use for an example and the full schema graphic is available with the project source. In this graphic, rectangles represent relation variables with their attributes given in a list. Attributes that begin with an asterisk (*) are identifiers. If there are multiple identifiers, the asterisk is followed by a number, *e.g.* *2. An identifier may consists of several attributes and a given attribute may be part of multiple identifiers. All relation variables have at least one identifier and all tuples of the relation must be unique in the values of all identifiers. Thus relation variables hold sets. Attributes that have a leading hyphen (-) are descriptive attributes that define a variable in the predicate that the relation variable intends to model.

Arrows in the diagram indicate a relationship between the relation variables. Relationships are implemented via referential attributes and constraints on the values of those referential attributes, *i.e.* attributes in one relation variable whose values must match the values of attributes in another relation variable. The direction of the relationship is from the referring attributes to the referred-to attributes. Relationships are given a moniker, *e.g.* **R16**, and attributes that are used to implement that relationship have a parenthesized list of relationship monikers following their name. Relationships are functions or partial functions between the participating relation variable sets. The cardinality of the relationship is also given by a single character that is mnemonic of the use of that character in regular expression notation. So, **1** means exactly one, **?** means at most one, **+** means one or more and * means zero or more. The relationship is traditionally annotated with the semantic meaning of the set mapping implied by the relationship function.

The graphic describes a relational schema that in turn describes a set of logical predicates that we insist be true. Using the **State** class as an example, we can make the following statements:

- A **State** is identified by the Domain in which it resides (DomainId), the Class to which it belongs (ClassId) and an arbitrary number (StateId).
- A **State** is also identified by the Domain in which it resides (DomainId), the Class to which it belongs (ClassId) and its name (StateName).
- A **State** is characterized by a set of parameters (Params), the number of the line in the pycca file on which the State definition begins (Line), a body of "C" code (Code) and the line on which the state code first appears (CodeLine).

Considering the relationship, R16, we can say:

- A **StateModel** *has **exactly one** default initial* **State**.
- A **State** *is the default initial state for **at most one*** **StateModel**.

All of these statements define rules that must be true for the domain for which **pycca** is the domain specific language. The actual number of rules is quite large. The **pycca** domain is a bit abstract since it is involved with defining classes and state models, but does have a well defined set of semantics and there is a well defined set of rules that is captured by the relational schema.

3.3. Storing the Parsing Results

As we stated above, the parsing results of **pycca** are not stored in the conventional manner of symbol tables and syntax trees. Rather, it is stored as set of relation variables. There are many ways in Tcl to store relational information. One obvious choice is to use a Database Management System (DBMS). Most DBMS are programmed in some dialect of SQL and with careful SQL programming the relational qualities of the meta-model may be preserved.

Another alternative is to use **TclRAL**. TclRAL is a "C" based Tcl extension that provides a complete relational algebra. It does this by extending the internal type system of Tcl to define the new types of *Tuple* and *Relation* and adds a new shadow variable system specifically to hold relation values. TclRAL is analogous to a data base system that only has in-memory tables and is programmed in Tcl rather than SQL. It is convenient to use TclRAL as we do not have to deal with other languages like SQL, there is no *impedance mismatch* between the query language and the programming language as they are both Tcl, it interacts well with other Tcl constructs such as the existing Tcl data types, interpreters, threads and starpacks and the amount of data that **pycca** handles easily fits within program memory.

Here we present the commands to create the relation variables that correspond to the graphic above (here we assume that `::ral::*` has been imported into the namespace).

```
relvar create Class {
    DomainId int
    ClassId int
    ClassName string
    Line int
    StorageSlots int
    PolyEvents list
    StorageClass string
} {DomainId ClassId} {DomainId ClassName}

relvar create StateModel {
    DomainId int
    ClassId int
    DefTrans string
    InitialState string
    Line int
} {DomainId ClassId}

relvar association R5\
    StateModel {DomainId ClassId} ?\
    Class {DomainId ClassId} 1

relvar create State {
    DomainId int
    ClassId int
    StateId int
    StateName string
    Params list
    Line int
    Code string
    CodeLine int
} {DomainId ClassId StateId} {DomainId ClassId StateName}

relvar association R6\
    State {DomainId ClassId} *\
    StateModel {DomainId ClassId} 1

relvar association R16\
    StateModel {DomainId ClassId InitialState} ?\
    State {DomainId ClassId StateName} 1
```

Figure 7. Pycca Meta-model Expressed in TclRAL

Figure 7 shows the translation of the above graphic into TclRAL. The close correspondence between the graphics and the TclRAL script is by design. The `relvar create` command creates a relation variable that can hold a relation value of the type given by the heading. The heading consists of both attribute names and data types, the data type names being any valid Tcl data type. The identifiers of the relvar are given as additional arguments that are lists of attribute names that constitute each identifier.

It may seem unusual to have to specify type information in a language like Tcl. This is actually a data validation constraint. TclRAL will insist that any value stored in an attribute be able to be coerced into the type of that attribute. This avoids any problems in future usage of the attribute. Since `string` is the universal Tcl type, any attribute declared as a string type will accept any value.

The code segment below is taken from the `tackle` source of the **pycca** parser and shows the action taken when a state is defined and when an initial state is declared.

```
machineProp
    :   STATE NAME varList CODE {
            newState [dict get $2 value] $3 [dict get $1 line]\
                [dict get $4 value] [dict get $4 line]
        }
    |   INITIAL STATE NAME {
            setInitialState [dict get $3 value]
        }
    •••
    ;
```

Figure 8. Grammar Reduction for a State

As we can see from above, when a state declaration is recognized then the procedure `newState` is invoked. That procedure is shown below.

```
proc ::newState {name params line code codeline} {
    catchDuplicate {
        relvar insert State [list\
            DomainId $::DomainId\
            ClassId $::ClassId\
            StateName $name\
            Params $params\
            Line $line\
            Code $code\
            CodeLine $codeline\
        ]
    } $name
}
```

Figure 9. Relvar Population when a State is Recognized

The `newState` procedure simply performs an insert into the State relvar (the `catchDuplicate` procedure is a control structure that emits a friendlier error message should the state already be defined).

Similarly, defining an initial state results in updating the appropriate attribute in the StateModel relvar as shown below.

```
proc ::setInitialState {state} {
    relvar updateone StateModel sm\
            [list DomainId $::DomainId ClassId $::ClassId] {
        tuple update $sm InitialState $state
    }
}
```

Figure 10. Relvar Population when an Initial State is Specified

In this procedure the global variables `::DomainId` and `::ClassId` are set by other grammar reductions to provide a context for statements that are organized hierarchically in a particular domain or class. The body of the procedure simply updates the InitialState attribute of a single StateModel tuple.

The above is intended to illustrate the point of how **pycca** stores the results of parsing by populating a relational schema. Viewed another way, the **pycca** language is then simply a more convenient textual representation for the schema population. The schema could have been populated, like any other relational schema, by directly providing tuples to be inserted into the relation variables. Although applicable to any schema, such population methods require knowledge of the relation variables in the schema and such generic ways of populating the schema are devoid of the semantics of the problem that the domain specific language is intended to help.

As we shall see, populating a relational schema provides a very powerful method of manipulating and querying the data. We now begin to exploit that property of well organized data.

3.4. Semantic Analysis

Every computer language allows many statements that are syntactically correct but otherwise meaningless. In this section we examine how **pycca** evaluates its input to determine if all the language statements can be given a precise meaning.

3.5. Semantics Enforced by Referential Integrity

As we saw above, **pycca** uses a relational schema to store the parsed data. That schema has many integrity constraints associated with it. Previously we had looked at one of those constraints that defined the relationship between a StateModel and a State that was specified to be the default initial state. For R16 we said that:

- A **StateModel** *has **exactly one** default initial* **State**.
- A **State** *is the default initial state for **at most one*** **StateModel**.

So at the end of populating the schema, R16 will insure that somewhere along the way exactly one state was specified to be the default initial state and that the state is part of the StateModel being specified. TclRAL will enforce the association constraint that was defined as R16 to insure that the data entry is performed correctly.

That's really rather nice. For no extra coding, we used referential integrity constraints to enforce the semantics of our underlying meta-model. This is one of the reasons integrity constraints are so important. Other than specifying the constraint to TclRAL, we have no other coding to do and the **system** (*i.e.* TclRAL) will insure that state of the stored data always satisfies the constraint.

This naturally brings up the question of whether or not all the semantic analysis can be accomplished this way. That is an open question. Certainly, **pycca** does not accomplish all the semantic analysis by using relvar constraints. The underlying meta-model used by **pycca** is not that sophisticated containing only 18 relvar constraints. There is a certain trade-off between the complexity of the data model (and consequently the amount of the semantics that are encoded in the referential integrity constraints) and the simplicity of doing some semantic analysis in code. **Pycca** uses both techniques as we will see below. Also there seem to be some problem semantics that are difficult or impossible to compose entirely into data constraints. In particular, constraining a directed graph to be acyclic may be impossible to do with referential integrity constraints alone.[6]

3.6. Semantics Enforced by Schema Query

In addition to referential integrity constraints, **pycca** also verifies 18 different semantic aspects of the source by querying the schema and examining the results. Here we look at one example, the declaration of isolated states. It is possible to declare a State in a StateModel that has no inbound state transition and no outbound state transitions. Such a state cannot be reached and therefore any code that is associated with that state will never be executed. This is the state machine equivalent of *dead code*. **Pycca** considers it an error to declare an isolated state in a state machine.

```
# Find isolated states, i.e. states that have no outgoing or
# incoming transitions
set noIns [relation semiminus $::Transition $::State\
        -using {DomainId DomainId ClassId ClassId NewState StateName}]
set noOuts [relation semiminus $::NormalTrans $::State\
        -using {DomainId DomainId ClassId ClassId StateName StateName}]
set isoStates [relation intersect $noIns $noOuts]
relation foreach isolated $isoStates {
    relation assign $isolated Line StateName
    reporterror "state has no incoming or outgoing transitions"\
        $Line $StateName
}
```

Figure 11. Finding Isolated States

The query in Figure 11 above shows how isolated states are detected. The strategy is to find all the states that have no incoming transitions and all the states that have no outgoing transitions. Then simple set intersection of those two relations then gives the set of isolated states for which an error needs to be reported.

Finding the set of states without any incoming transitions is done with the *semiminus* operation. Semiminus gives, roughly speaking, the set of tuples in one relation that are *not* related to those in another relation. In the above example, we find those tuples of State that are *not* related to a Transition using the NewState attribute. The NewState attribute gives the destination of a transition, so those States whose StateName values are not associated with the NewState attribute have no incoming transitions. Similar reasoning holds for the semiminus operation with respect to the NormalTrans relvar where the StateName attribute holds the source state of a transition. Once those two sets are determined, it is then just a simple matter of taking the intersection and iterating through the tuples to report the errors.

What is most noticeable about the above code sequence is the lack of any looping construct. Relational algebraic operation always apply the the entire set represented by the relation value. The only loop is that implied by the `relation foreach` command which is used to access the

[6] Private communications from Paul Higham for whom this is a favorite problem.

individual attributes for error reporting. It is common in the relational realm only to use tuple iteration at the end of the computation where it is necessary to interface to other non-relational constructs.

3.7. Template Expansion

Since the primary purpose of **pycca** is to pass along "C" code as opposed to actually compiling a source language to a target language, it does not use the usual language processing strategy of building syntax trees and flow graphs. The bulk of the work is building data structures, encapsulating code fragments and then emitting "C" code and header files. Since "C" source code requires substantial type annotation and "C" compilers insist upon a certain ordering in the code, **pycca** uses template expansion as a means of generating its output. The **textutil::expander** package in **tcllib** is well suited to this purpose. Using the expander is simple enough. You define a template, generate an instance of the expander and request the expander to do its job. Embedded in the template are Tcl scripts that are extracted and executed with the result being inserted into the generated text.

The example below is the template that **pycca** uses to emit its code file. We have instantiated the expander as:

```
textutil::expander ex
ex setbrackets %< >%
```

The default of square brackets ([]) for enclosing the embedded Tcl script is not convenient for "C" code. Below is the template string for the generated "C" code file. It is generated by invoking:

```
ex expand $code_body
```

```
set code_body {
%<domain_name>%
%<instrument_define>%
%<emit_auxiliary Impl Prolog>%

#ifdef INSTRUMENT
#   ifndef INSTR_FUNC
#       define INSTR_FUNC(s) printf("%s: %s %d0, s, __FILE__, __LINE__)
#   endif /* INSTR_FUNC */
#endif /* INSTRUMENT */

%<state_defines>%
%<event_defines>%
%<subcode_defines>%
%<inst_name_defines>%
%<class_struct_decl>%
%<class_struct_define>%
%<event_param_struct>%

%<operation_decl>%
%<ctor_decl>%
%<dtor_decl>%
%<action_decl>%
%<domain_op_decl false>%
%<initial_inst_ctor_decl>%
%<storage_decl>%

%<iab_define>%
%<odb_define>%
%<pdb_define>%
%<class_define>%

%<multi_refs>%
%<inst_define>%
%<operation_define>%
%<ctor_define>%
%<dtor_define>%
%<action_define>%
%<domain_op_define>%
%<initial_inst_ctor_define>%

%<emit_auxiliary Impl Epilog>%
}
```

Figure 12. Pycca Code Template

Each command between the %< and >% brackets is a query on the relational schema that was populated during the parsing phase.

As an example, we will consider part of what happens to the code of a state action. Each action is turned into a function by wrapping a signature around the code. These functions are file static in scope and, since the order of reference is not known, it is necessary to place forward declarations to them into the code. This is accomplished by the `action_decl` command.

Before we examine the query for the action declarations, we need some preliminaries. We'd like to emit the declarations on a class by class basis, so it is useful to be able to have a relation value that relates the name of a class to all of its state machine information. The `getStatesByClass` command does this.

```
proc ::getStatesByClass {} {
    return [pipe {
        relation semijoin $::currentDomain $::State\
                -using {DomainId DomainId} |
        relation group ~ States StateId StateName Params Line Code CodeLine |
        relation join ~ $::Class -using {DomainId DomainId ClassId ClassId} |
        relation project ~ ClassName States
    }]
}
```

Lets examine this query. First the `pipe` command is a control structure that allows you to write a nested set of commands in a sequential fashion. It has nothing to do with relational algebra *per se*, although it is particularly useful in that context. In the above example, `pipe` allows us to write the four commands of the query is a clearer order. Commands are separated by a vertical bar (|) and the result of the previous command is substituted for the tilde (~) character argument in the subsequent command. `Pipe` is supplied as part of the **ralutil** package.

There are four steps in this query.

(1) Find all the states in the current domain. The **relation semijoin** operation returns a relation that has the same heading as the State relvar with those tuples that are related to the current domain. The `::currentDomain` variable is an ordinary Tcl variable that is global in scope and assigned a relation value by other processing. The heading of the State relation is:

DomainId	ClassId	StateId	StateName	Params	Line	Code	CodeLine
int	int	int	string	list	int	string	int

The result of this operation is the set of all states in the current domain.

(2) The **relation group** operation creates a relation valued attribute from attributes in the original relation. In this case we are grouping all the attributes that pertain to the states of a class into a single attribute. The result will have a new attribute named **States** that is a relation valued attribute[7]. The resulting heading is:

DomainId	ClassId	States					
int	int	StateId	StateName	Params	Line	Code	CodeLine
		int	string	list	int	string	int

(3) The **relation join** operation is used to relate the ClassId attribute to is corresponding name. In this case we are interested in the name of the class rather than its numeric identifier that is used internally.

(4) Finally, the **relation project** operation gives us only the attributes that we are interested in, namely the ClassName and its corresponding set of states. Note that the States

[7] Readers steeped in SQL will find relation valued attributes unusual, but they have many legitimate uses as well as a host of abusive uses.

attribute is a relation itself and contains the complete set of states that correspond to ClassName. The heading of the result relation is:

ClassName	States					
string	**StateId**	**StateName**	**Params**	**Line**	**Code**	**CodeLine**
	int	string	list	int	string	int

With the preliminaries out of the way, we proceed to the `action_decl` command that generates a set of forward function declarations.

```
proc ::action_decl {} {
    append result [comment "Forward Declarations of State Action Functions"]
    relation foreach state [getStatesByClass] -ascending ClassName {
        relation assign $state
        relation foreach stateinfo $States -ascending StateName {
            relation assign $stateinfo
            append result [emit_action_signature $ClassName $StateName] " ;\n"
        }
    }

    return $result
}

proc ::emit_action_signature {className stateName} {
    append result\
        "static void ${className}_${stateName}\("\
        "void *const s_, "\
        "void *const p_)"
}
```

Figure 13. State Action Declaration Query

It is a relatively simple matter to use the **relation foreach** command to iterate through each class and then to iterate through each state generating a static "C" function declaration. The **relation assign** command takes a singleton relation value and creates a Tcl variable for each attribute with the variable named the same as the attribute. for each attribute that has the same name as the attribute.

The result of template expansion query for our running example is:

```
/*
 * Forward Declarations of State Action Functions
 */
static void Motor_Agitating(void *const s_, void *const p_) ;
static void Motor_Off(void *const s_, void *const p_) ;
static void Motor_Spinning(void *const s_, void *const p_) ;
static void Pump_Off(void *const s_, void *const p_) ;
static void Pump_Running(void *const s_, void *const p_) ;
static void Valve_Closed(void *const s_, void *const p_) ;
static void Valve_Open(void *const s_, void *const p_) ;
static void WashingMachine_Agitating(void *const s_, void *const p_) ;
static void WashingMachine_EmptyingRinseWater(void *const s_, void *const p_) ;
static void WashingMachine_EmptyingWashWater(void *const s_, void *const p_) ;
static void WashingMachine_FillingForRinse(void *const s_, void *const p_) ;
static void WashingMachine_FillingForWashing(void *const s_, void *const p_) ;
static void WashingMachine_Idle(void *const s_, void *const p_) ;
static void WashingMachine_Rinsing(void *const s_, void *const p_) ;
static void WashingMachine_Spinning(void *const s_, void *const p_) ;
```

Figure 14. State Action Declaration Example Results

So the strategy here is to use the code template to specify the order in which fragments will be presented to the "C" compiler. Those fragments are generated by expanding the template which in turn invokes a series of commands that are queries on the schema population that was built up during the parsing phase. The query commands build up a *report* that is inserted into the result of the template expansion. Here it happens to be that the generated report is "C" code.

4. Friends of Pycca

It is often difficult to determine precisely what functionality a program or suite of programs will need when first starting out. That was certainly the case with **pycca**. The original idea for **pycca** was simply to ease to burden of constructing the data structures needed by the STSA. It is easy to convince yourself that a fixed set of implementation data structures will meet the immediate needs of the program you are constructing. However, using relational data structures provides substantially more power and flexibility. Since TclRAL can serialize a set of relvars to external storage, once parsed any given **pycca** file can be easily saved for later use. One aspect that relation data structures support is the notion of *ad hoc* query. Most programmers don't deal with *ad hoc* queries as part of a program with fixed functionality. But support of these types of queries is a powerful way to extend programs or create sets of programs that work well together, bound by a common relational data schema.

These consideration lead to several auxiliary programs for **pycca**. In the section below, we discuss three of the most useful examples of programs that use the serialized **pycca** output to provide additional support for building embedded software programs. The serialized relvars that **pycca** saves contain all the information that is in the original **pycca** source but in an already parsed and organized form. This makes writing the helper program usually a simple matter of reading in the file and performing a different set of queries to produce the needed output.

4.1. Pyccaexplore

Although **pycca** allows states and events to be specified as named entities, in truth the execution architecture works strictly off of numbers. State and event names are converted by **pycca** to integers that are ultimately used as indices into an array that holds the state transition matrix. In small embedded systems, there is no memory to hold the original string names for the states and events and **pycca** does not attempt to put those strings into the generated program. Consequently, during debugging one is often faced with trying to determine the state of a particular class instance and where it might transition under a given event. Sadly, when looking at a source level debugger the information that is available will be something to the effect of:

> Instance 0x57ae is in state 3 and is about to receive event 1 causing a transition to state 4.

This is not very helpful. What is needed is the mapping between state and event names and the numbers that **pycca** assigned to them. This is why **pyccaexplore** was written.

Pyccaexplore will read the serialized relvars saved by **pycca** and display the state transition matrix of all the classes. That display contains both the name and number of each state and event.

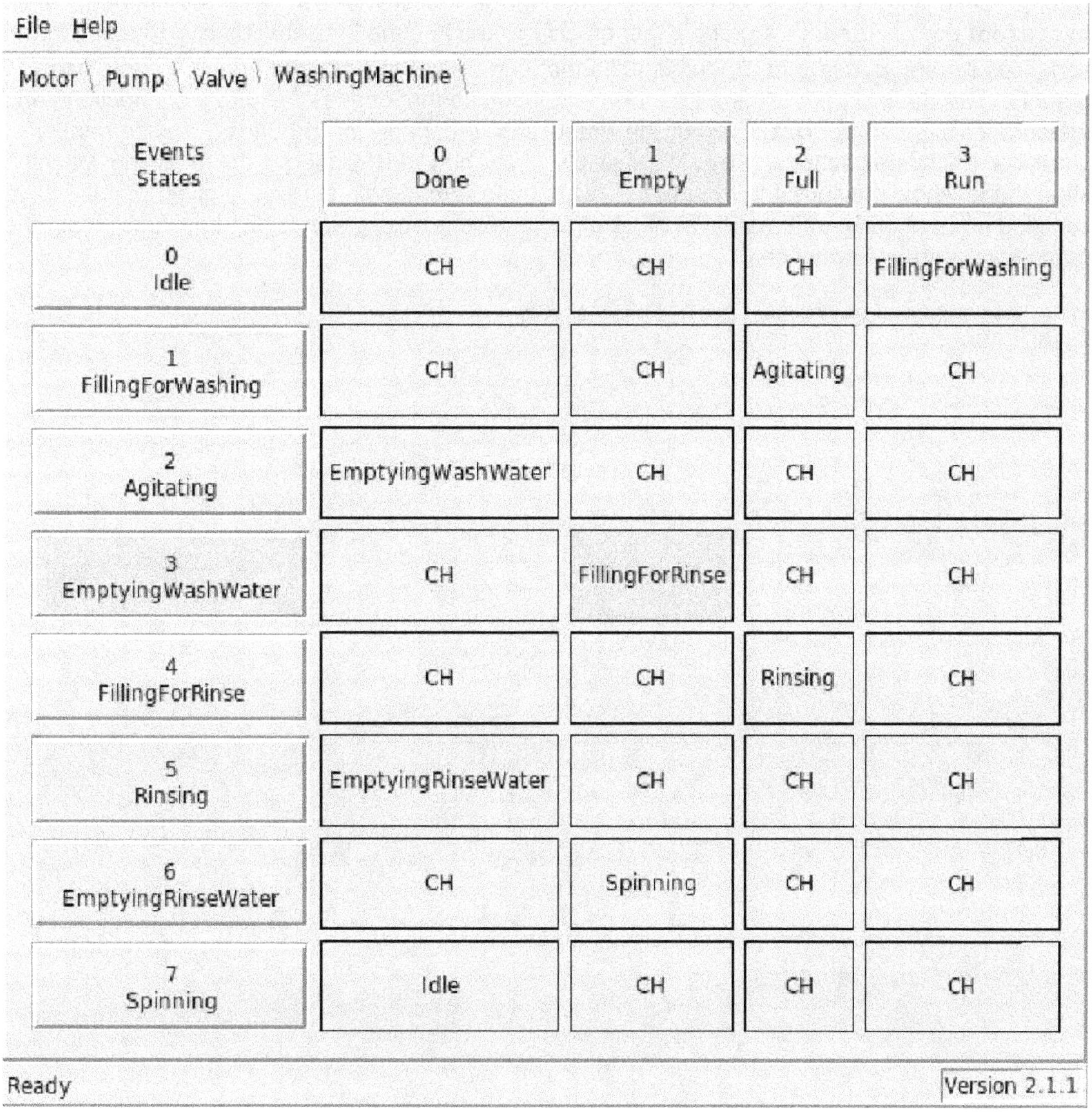

Figure 15. Screen Shot of Pyccaexplore

The figure above is a screen shot of **pyccaexplore** for the example state machine. Buttons along the left allow selection of rows that correspond to states. Buttons along the top allow selection of columns that correspond to events. When both a row and column are selected, a single cell is highlighted showing the transition that would happen when the highlighted event is received in the highlighted state. The above figure can be interpreted as indicating that when state 3 (Emptying-WashWater) receives event 1 (Empty) it transitions to the FillingForRinse state which is numbered 4.

4.2. Pycca2dot

The **pycca** source that defines a state machine is relatively easy to read and does not depend upon the ordering of state and transition declarations. But, state machines are sometimes better represented as directed graphs. Usually when designing a state machine, I do so graphically. Often, maintaining the design time graphics during the implementation does not happen. What **pycca2dot** does is produce a graphic that precisely matches the implementation. Reading in the serialized relvars, **pycca2dot** produces a file that can be fed to **dot**[8] to produce a state machine graphic. The **dot** program takes a free form text input file that defines the graph connections and appearance properties. **Dot** lays out the graph and is capable of producing a wide variety of graphical file format outputs. The figure below show how **dot** rendered the Washing Machine state model show previously in Figure 2. This is quite remarkable especially given that we have supplied no positioning information at all. **Dot** accomplishes the graph layout based solely on the graph connectivity information.

[8] www.graphviz.org

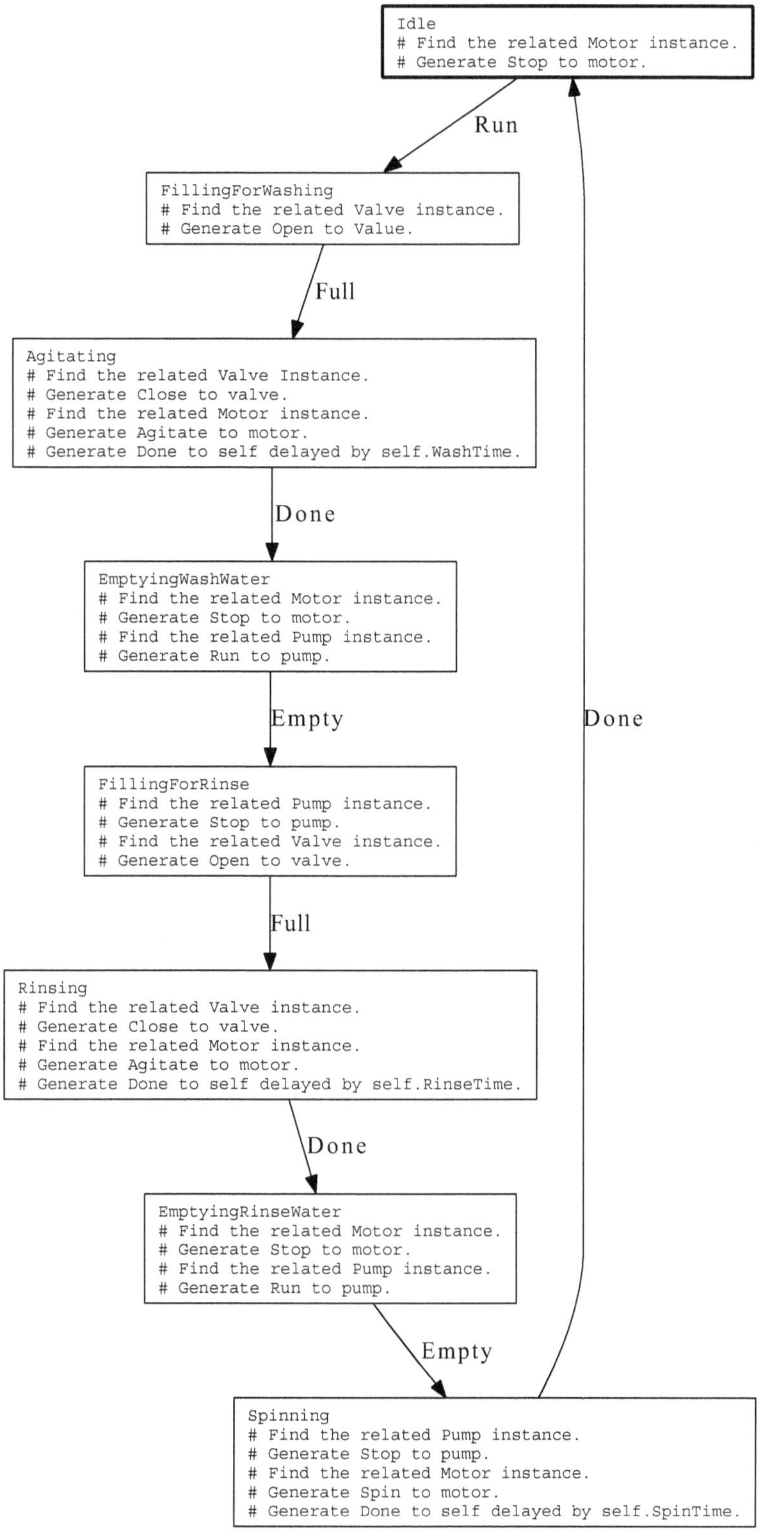

Figure 16. Washing Machine State Model from pycca2dot

4.3. Tracing State Machine Dispatch

The STSA execution architecture can be conditionally compiled to trace the dispatch of state machine events. Programs may supply a callback function that is invoked during the tracing and that function can store or transmit the trace data. However, as we have seen, there is no string information in the embedded system and all the trace data is numeric. It takes knowledge of the state and event name to number mapping as well as knowledge of the link map to translate the numerical trace information back into meaningful strings for human consumption. The **mech-trace** package reads the saved relvars from **pycca** and the ELF file of the executable and is able to translate a packet of trace information into a human readable string.

The most immediately useful consequence of this is to obtain a chronological sequence of event dispatches. This is extraordinarily useful information since the execution sequencing of the program is not easily followed just from the code alone. The STSA implements state machine call-back type of execution sequencing. So all the significant code in the program ends up packaged into functions that are called as part of dispatching an event. The invoked callback may indeed generate other events, but does not directly affect the execution sequencing as other events may already be queued. The effect is very similar to typical GUI programs where the sequencing of event dispatches is centralized and not directly visible to the programmer. So a chronological sequence of state transitions can provide enormous insight into the run-time behavior of a program.

Another benefit of obtaining trace data is related to testing. Because all the execution sequencing is centralized, the sequence of trace data can be used to compute the state transition coverage for testing purposes. In well designed state machines, the state action code is small and contains little conditional logic. Indeed deeply nested conditional logic in a state action is an indication that the analysis should be revisited to look for the possibility of several classes being confused as one or that other state information is being hidden in instance variables. The **mechtrace** package includes procedures to tally the transitions that are implied by the tracing data and then to compute the transitions that were not taken in the state machines. This gives objective evidence of the testing that has been done as well as indicates any short comings in the test case coverage, at least at a state transition level. Given that state diagrams are directed graphs, then a depth-first search of the graph can be used to compute a spanning tree the arcs which are labeled with the events necessary to visit every state in the machine. Thus much of the work of determining a set of test cases that will cover the transitions of the state machine can be computed *a priori*.

5. Conclusions

Pycca is a program that implements a domain specific language. The language that **pycca** implements is used as a helper to specify data and control structures for highly embedded micro-controller based software applications.

Yet the internals of **pycca** look more like a traditional database application. **Pycca** uses language statements to populate a normalized relational schema. The language provides a more convenient syntax that is focused on the declarative aspects of the application and hides the details of the underlying schema. The output of **pycca** is generated by query on the population and the report of that query is generated by template expansion to produce "C" code. The relational data structure provide a number of distinct advantages.

(1) The algebra of relations is independent of the headings of the relations. So there is only one set of access methods that need to be learned. It is not necessary to code *ad hoc* data structures and a set of access mechanisms for them. Especially since in practice, such access layers rarely get the attention and detailed error checking that they need.

(2) Referential integrity constraints are a powerful tool to validate the schema population and enforce the rules of the application. Integrity constraints are declarative in nature and

correspond to the semantic rules of the application. Specifying the integrity constraints is usually easier than writing code to accomplish the validation and enables a substantial part of the application semantics to be checked during the data population.

(3) There are a variety of implementation choices for relational data in Tcl that can be matched against the scale of the application. For simpler, in-memory applications TclRAL is a good choice and does not involve a separate query language. If the file storage nature of the application is more important, SQLite is good choice. It is easy to use, readily available and does not involve extensive administration, albeit the queries must be programmed in a separate language from Tcl. Finally, for large scale applications it may be advisable to use one of the server based DBMS accessed via TDBC.

(4) A relational schema serves as a convenient way to bind a suite of programs together, each performing specific tasks associated with the overall application. This makes phasing in a toolbox of programs for the application much easier to accomplish and argues against monolithic programs that try to provide all the functionality of an application. Such programs inevitably become unwieldy and hard to maintain.

None of these points is particularly new or novel. Much of the motivation of creating DBMS in the past was to reap just these benefits. What has changed is the array of choices in the implementation technology that allows even simple programs that one might never consider to be database applications to take advantage of the power of relationally structured data.

17th ANNUAL TCL/TK 2010 CONFERENCE Chicago (USA) 11-15 October

TK I

Thu October 14, 2010 14:30-16:15

TclA Publications

Porting a large scale enterprise application from *Tcl/Tk* 8.4 to 8.5 - A Case Study

Prashant Thakre, Tushar Gupta
{prashant_thakre, tushar_gupta}@mentor.com

1.0 Abstract

This paper describes the challenges involved in porting a large scale enterprise application from *Tcl/Tk* 8.4 to *Tcl/Tk* 8.5, and lists down all issues encountered during the migration. The migration to *Tcl/Tk* 8.5 required adjustments in application code, necessitated due to changes in interface, or as a result of unexpected functional behaviour. On some occasions it was required to patch the *Tcl/Tk* 8.5 distribution with fixes which are now expected to be included into standard *Tcl/Tk* release.

The case-study describes in detail various external and internal dependencies requiring resolution and covers performance related benchmarks/issues. Also, changes in various packages (core and external) resulting in regressions are discussed. The objective of the case-study is to provide other developers an in-sight into typical issues faced, and suggest solutions wherever available.

2.0 Glossary

Description of terms used in the paper:

[incr Tcl] - is an OO system for *Tcl,* and *[incr Tcl]* provides a similar object model, including multiple inheritance, and public and private classes and variables.

[incr Tk] - Megawidget framework based upon *[incr Tcl].*
Iwidgtes - is an object-oriented mega-widget set which extends *Tcl/Tk* and is based on *[incr Tcl]* and *[incr Tk].*

[mti Widgets] - Collection of mega-widget, additions and enhancements to *Iwidgets.* This megawidget requires TIP #125 *(wm toplevel)*

3.0 Motivation

The application Veloce GUI, is from the Mentor Emulation Division (MED) at Mentor Graphics Corp. The Veloce GUI is used for emulation compiles, emulation runtime control, and project management and most importantly for design debug. Typically customers use emulation for some of the largest and the most complex System-on-a-chip (SOC) designs, and the Veloce GUI is tuned to handle large design databases as well as huge waveform data. Each such set of generated debug data having information about design hierarchy; waveform and design connectivity is called a dataset. The application uses object Object-oriented programming provided by *[incr Tcl]* package, to support multiple simultaneous dataset debug, potentially belonging to different design databases.

The code base for Veloce GUI primarily consists of *Tcl/Tk* and C/C++. Veloce GUI in general uses various *Tcl/Tk* packages and required custom build of *Tk* (8.4) necessitated by usage of *[mti Widgets]* (TIP 125: Converting between *frame* and *toplevel* windows). Over time, we have observed various *Tcl/Tk* related issues in 8.4 have been fixed in 8.5. Also, since 8.5 release of *Tcl/Tk* has incorporated TIP #125 (using new subcommands *wm manage* and *wm forget*), has various new features and is actively maintained, migrating from 8.4 was a necessity.

As with any migration to a major release (8.5 in this case), it's bound to throw challenges during build, implementation and testing stage. The paper describes the changes required to build process along with changes to code base. Changes to code are result of core *Tcl/Tk* changes or due to changes in the packages like *[incr Tk]*. Also, the paper covers areas where change in behaviour of *Tcl/Tk* commands and rendering is observed as compared to 8.4 release. Performance benchmark data is also reported in a separate section.

The paper concludes by sharing the findings and by providing our recommendations on how to catch issues during early stages of migration.

4.0 Changes required

This section describes in detail various external and internal dependencies requiring resolution. Also, change in various packages (core and external) resulting in regressions are discussed.

- tk/library/button.tcl:

  Package:
  This is part of standard distribution.

  Issue:
  Application uses *check buton and radio button,* and global variable linked to the *buttons* are specified using *itcl::scope.* This caused Tcl exception at runtime.

  Solution:
  Patch the tcl distribution with available fix for bug # 87409. This fix uses *uplevel set* instead of *set* ::to work with *itcl.*

- *[list]*-Quoting of the '#' character:

  Package:
  This is part of standard distribution.

  Issue:
  Application dumps the tree contents during automated testing to check for new regressions if any. Starting with *Tcl/Tk* 8.5, name of tree nodes starting with '#' are quoted by default.

  Solution:
  Application could either modify the routine dumping the contents of the tree if possible or update the gold files.

- *[info level]*

  Package:
  This is part of standard distribution.

  Issue:
  Change in information returned by *[info level]* command. Application in question disables *cd* command for a user. However, various *tk* routines like *tk_chooseDirectory*, *tk_getOpenFile*, and *tk_getSaveFile* internally call *cd*. Until *Tcl/Tk* 8.4 application would call [*info level*] with level argument as -1 in order to verify that the caller is *tk::dialog::file*. However, this no longer returns the required information in *Tcl/Tk* 8.5.

  Solution:
  Level argument passed to *[info level]* should be -2 instead of -1.

- *[pwd]*

  Package:
  This is part of standard distribution.

  Issue:
  In *Tcl/Tk* 8.4 if a present working directory gets deleted a call to *pwd* throws exception. However, starting with *Tcl/Tk* 8.5 *pwd* returns an empty string and no longer throws exception.

  Solution:
  Add check for empty string on return value of *pwd*.

- *[tk_getOpenFile]*

  Package:
  This is part of standard distribution.

  Issue:
  In *Tcl/Tk* 8.4 multiple file and directory

selection using ctrl throws an exception.

Solution:

This has been fixed in *Tcl/Tk* 8.5. No change is required in application code.

- *[incr Tk]: 3.4*

Package:

This package is included with *[incr Tcl]* distribution.

Issue:

[incr Tk] supplies three base classes that reside in the *itk* namespace:

1. *itk::Archetype*
2. *itk::Widget*
3. *itk::Toplevel*

Application uses *[incr Tk] 3.2* with *Tcl/Tk 8.4* and *"–menu"* option is defined in base class *itk::Archetype*. However, with *[incr Tk] 3.4* this option is now defined only for toplevel windows i.e. *itk::Toplevel*.

Solution:

Widgets derived from *itk::Archetype* will no longer have *"-menu"* option defined and will require necessary changes i.e. use *itk::Toplevel* instead.

- *[TIP 125]: wm manage and wm forget*

Package:

This is part of standard distribution.

Issue:

Application allows docking and undocking of child windows. This was implemented in *Tcl/Tk* 8.4 using patch for *[wm toplevel]*.

However, this TIP was incorporated into standard distribution with new *wm* subcommands *manage* and *forget*.

Solution:

A procedure *wm_toplevel* was defined to handle all calls to *[wm toplevel]*. Following is the definition of the procedure.

```
    proc wm_toplevel {win
{bool {}}} {
       if {[llength [info level
0]] == 2} {
         return [expr {[winfo
manager $win] eq "wm"}]
        } else {
         if {$bool} {
             wm manage $win
         } else {
             wm forget $win
         }
        }
      }
```

- *BWidget: 1.9.2*

Package:

This package is part of *Tcllib* and is available at http://tcllib.sf.net/.

Issue:

Application was using *BWidget* 1.6 and many interfaces level changes have occurred since 1.6. The command *Widget::create* does the renaming of the widgets to $path:cmd and creates the proc to redirect the widget commands.

Solution:

Change usage of *BWlabel::create* to *Label::create*. Also, *BWidget* 1.9.1 release was a development snapshot from the Tile enabled version. This release has some compatibility issues and users are encouraged to upgrade to 1.9.2.

- *Incorrect gridding/packing of elements*

Package:

This is part of standard distribution.

Issue:

This relates to incorrect display in *Tcl/Tk* 8.5 as compared to 8.4. For example following would display the middle element correctly in 8.4 but not in 8.5 where button_frame contains add and remove buttons.

```
pack $left $button_frame $right -expand yes -fill both -side left =padx -pady 5
```

Solution:

Required changes to application code on case by case basis. Above mentioned code had to be replaced with

```
pack $left -expand yes -fill both -side left -padx 5 -pady 5
pack $button_frame -dise left -padx 5 -pady 5
pack $right -expand yes -fill both -side left -padx 5 -pady 5
```

- *Drag and drop*

Package:

This is part of tkdnd distribution.

Issue:

Application uses tkdnd for supporting drag and drop. Incorrect text was dropped in some cases.

Solution:

A close inspection revealed that unnecessary quoting was causing an issue i.e. "%T" instead of %T in the bind script.

- *Tk crash while trying to dock/undock a window repeatedly.*

Package:

This is part of standard distribution.

Issue:

Repeated docking and undocking of child windows would result in a *Tk* crash. On closer inspection it seemed that this was due to change in the way *"-menu"* option was configured. Most of these child windows were derived from *itk::Archetype*. Also, due to changes to *"menu"* in *[incr Tk]* 3.4, *"menu"* was configured after first undock operation. This resulted in abnormal termination during docking process.

Solution:

Configure *"menu"* option to empty during all docking operations and configure it back to correct menu during undocking.

- *Change in font size.*

Package:

This is part of standard distribution.

Issue:

Veloce GUI uses custom widget and it was observed that default font size has changed across release i.e. in *Tcl/Tk* 8.5. This was cause of many regressions in our test suites.

Solution:

Preferences were modified in the application to select a larger font to fix regression issues found during automated testing.

5.0 Performance

Moving to newer release of *Tcl/Tk* 8.5 has caused some unexpected regressions in terms of performance. In a particular computation intensive task (happens on *C/C++* side) it was observed that the performance penalty can be as high as 30%. Application is busy with the computation and does not take user inputs i.e. no change in display of the application.

Solution:

Currently we are trying to profile the application in order to narrow down the exact cause of the problem. However, the same application without any modification when linked to *Tcl/Tk* 8.4 produces much better performance results. We have tried to build the application by linking it to single threaded version of *Tcl/Tk* libraries. However, this hasn't yielded desired results.

6.0 Recommendations

1. A regression setup helps to track initial set of issues.
2. Change log of all external and internal packages required by an application can help narrow down code level changes.
3. Performance benchmarking is required for critical portion of the code.

7.0 Bibliography

1. *Tcl* wiki, http://wiki.tcl.tk
2. *[incr Widgets]* An Object Oriented Mega-Widget Set, Mark L. Ulferts, http://incrtcl.sourceforge.net/iwidgets/paper/paper.html

Augmented Reality, Google Earth and Tcl/Tk

Steve Landers and David Roseman
steve@digitalsmarties.com
dlr@eolas.com

Abstract

This paper will describe the implementation of an augmented reality simulation of a proposed wind farm, combining Google Earth (either standalone or via a browser plugin) with animated turbine models to give realistic impressions of the visual impact of a proposed offshore wind farm in Lake Michigan.

Several aspects of the simulation will be discussed, including the use of a Tcl/Tk application for the generation and layout of KML (geographic data) files, the use of Tcl CGI programs for generating dynamically sized images and data, and a Tcl/Tk program to control Google Earth.

Mention will also be made of some of the non-programming issues encountered, including visual perception issues such as Field of View and the Moon Illusion.

Background

This project was prompted by a proposal to place a 100-200 turbine wind farm near the shore in Lake Michigan. On hearing of the proposal, the question asked by local residents was "what would these things look like? ". And so a method of drawing accurate representations from arbitrary viewpoints was required.

After considering OpenGL[1] based approaches, it was decided to first investigate "off the shelf" or "consumer" solutions since one requirement was the ability to view the results on a typical desktop or notebook computer.

Google provides a couple of tools that seemed promising. Google Sketchup[2] is a drawing program that allows accurate, scaled renderings of three dimensional objects. Google Earth[3] allows 3D objects (including Google Sketchup models) to be placed in arbitrary locations. Any modeled object can be placed in any geographic location, at any orientation. Google Earth provides a "camera" which allows the rendered objects to be viewed from any location. The data may be passed to Google Earth using Keyhole Markup Language (KML) [4].

There were some desired features that Google Earth did not appear to support, especially animation and variable "focal lengths" of the camera. These would need to be implemented using work-arounds, but even so, it was decided to proceed with a Google Sketchup / Google Earth solution.

Two approaches were developed in parallel, a standalone Tcl/Tk program that controlled the Google Earth application, and a web-based version using Tcl and Javascript to control the Google Earth web browser plugin. The advantages and disadvantages of each will be discussed in this paper.

The rough sequence of development was:

- obtain and modify turbine model(s) and other models
- define turbine locations
- determine viewing parameters (location, elevation, viewing angles)
- build KML files
- define methods of passing data to Google Earth (both standalone and browser plugin version)
- validate visuals

Turbine Models

The first step in producing the wind farm simulation was to obtain suitable Google Sketchup models of approximately the same size as the proposed turbines. The Sketchup community has made available a large number of models, including wind turbines. A suitable model was downloaded, and re-scaled to the dimensions of the proposed turbines and the model was exported to a Collada Digital Asset Exchange (.dae) file [5], the format required by Google Earth.

The dimensions used were those of a 10 MW turbine being developed by Clipper Windpower [6]. The height to the top of a vertical blade is 574 feet.

Laying out the wind farm using Google maps and Tcl/Tk

The next step in producing the wind farm simulation is to produce a Google Earth model with the required number of turbines equally spaced throughout the wind farm footprint.

Ideally, the geographic coordinates of the footprint would be provided by the wind farm developers. In this case, a polygon of the footprint was printed in the local newspapers and, by inserting a copy of this into a geographic information system (GIS) program, the latitude and longitude of the polygon vertices were determined.

A Tcl/Tk program was written that accepts two inputs: the number of turbines, and a series of rhomboid polygons describing the wind farm footprint (the vertices of each polygon are specified in latitude/longitude). The program produces a Google Earth model with the required number of turbines equally spaced throughout the wind farm footprint.

To allow visual inspection of the layout by the user, the program uses the Google Maps REST API [7] (via the Tcl http [8] package) to retrieve and display a static map containing the wind farm footprint. The map is returned as a 512x512 gif image of the local area, containing the wind farm footprint as a shaded polygon. The program then places the turbines equi-spaced within the wind farm footprint. The number of pixels per kilometre is calculated using the spherical geographical distance code from the Geodesy page on the Tclers' Wiki [9]. This is used to calculate the latitude and longitude of each turbine location, and the static map (displayed in a Tk canvas) is overlaid with a dot indicating the location of the turbine.

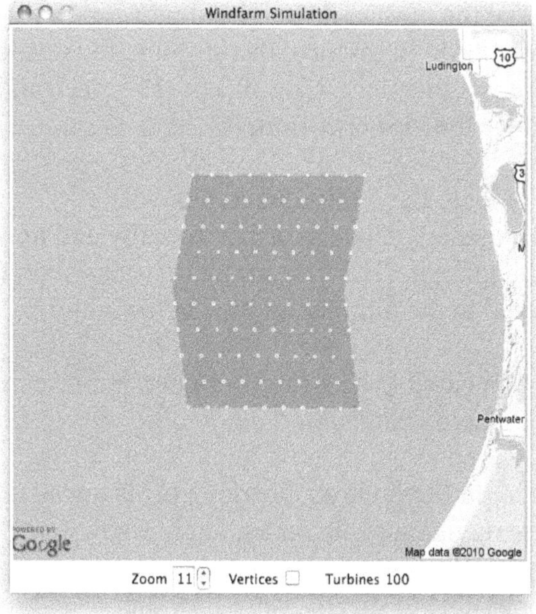

To generate the Google Earth model, the program substitutes the latitude and longitude of each turbine into an XML template, along with the bearing corresponding to the prevailing wind direction. The result is a single KML file describing the entire wind farm. To this is added the Sketchup model(s) for the turbines, and the resulting files archived as a zip (KMZ) file (the typical distribution format for a Google Earth model).

Viewing Parameters

The next step in producing the wind farm simulation was to produce Google Earth KML models for each of the desired viewpoints. Each viewing point comprises a latitude and longitude, altitude (above the ground level), heading (i.e. the direction the camera faces) and the tilt and roll of the camera. These are read from a text file, and substituted into an XML template, generating one KML file per viewing point.

This information is the simple part of the viewing parameters. The more difficult part to achieve is the Field of View.

The Field of View (FOV or Field of Vision or Angle of Vision) [10] is the angular extent of a given scene that can be viewed at a point in time. The FOV has two components, the horizontal and vertical FOV values (hFOV and vFOV respectively).

The Design Eye Point (or Design Eye Position) [11] is the position from which the user will optimally view the user interface (and therefore, achieve the most realistic visual perception of the simulation). In essence, this says the FOV value to use is a function of the size of the screen and the distance the viewer is from it.

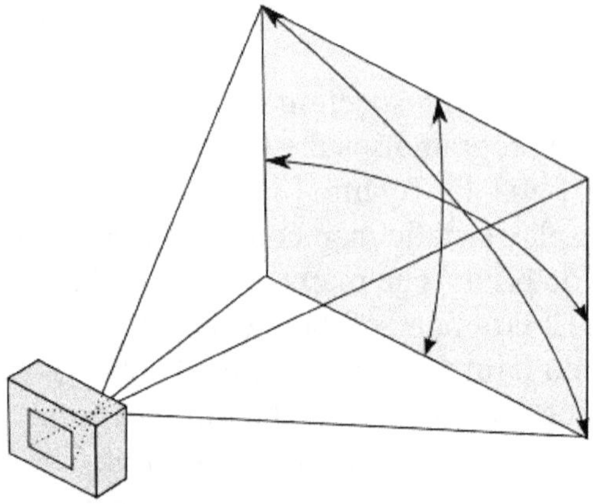

But Google Earth has a fixed FOV of approximately 60 degrees horizontally and no way of changing it. The first simulations based on this resulted in the turbines appearing too small.

This appeared to be a show-stopper, but research revealed that the FOV can be approximated using Photo Overlays.

A Google Earth Photo Overlay [12] is a way of overlaying a photo on a Google Earth scene. When specifying the photo overlay, it is possible to specify values for the horizontal and vertical fields of view. If the image is specified as a transparent png, the FOV values are applied to the underlying Google Earth scene, resulting in an approximation of the required FOV values.

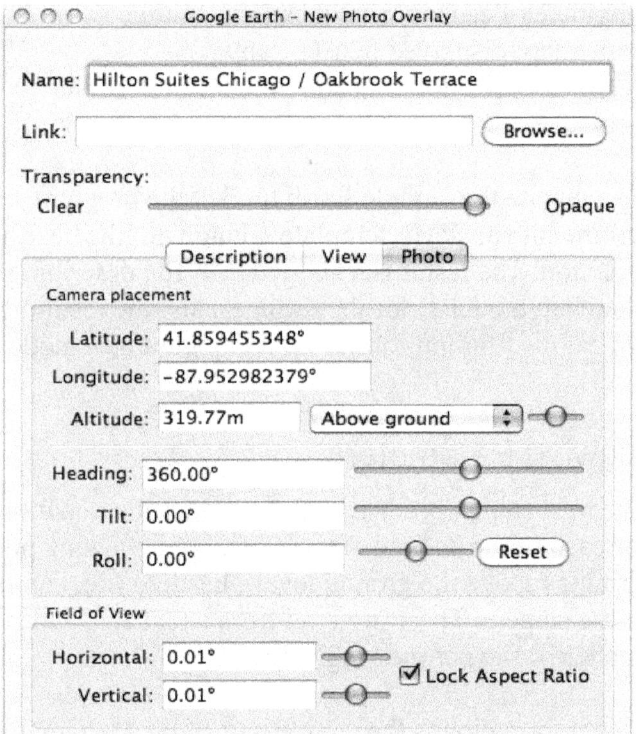

So the decision was made to derive the FOV values based on an arbitrary viewing distance of 30 inches and the current screen size. The intention is to eventually provide several viewing distances, corresponding to a notebook, desktop, group, and auditorium settings.

The formulae for calculating the FOV are:

hFOV = atan(width / distance)*180/pi

vFOV = atan(height / distance)*180/pi

These can be derived by the simulation program (either standalone or web-based) at runtime using the width and height values for the current computer's display.

So the Google Earth KML files for each viewpoint were generated containing references to the FOV values (rather than the actual values).

```
<?xml version="1.0" encoding="UTF-8"?>
<kml xmlns="http://www.opengis.net/kml/2.2"
     xmlns:gx="http://www.google.com/kml/ext/2.2"
     xmlns:kml="http://www.opengis.net/kml/2.2"
     xmlns:atom="http://www.w3.org/2005/Atom">
    <PhotoOverlay>
        <name>Ludington South Pierhead</name>
        <Camera>
            <longitude>-86.46923</longitude>
            <latitude>43.95198</latitude>
            <altitude>4</altitude>
            <heading>-146</heading>
            <tilt>85</tilt>
            <roll>0</roll>
            <altitudeMode>relativeToGround</altitudeMode>
        </Camera>
        <Icon>
            <href>http://$url/cgi-bin/transparent.png</href>
        </Icon>
        <ViewVolume>
            <leftFov>$leftFOV</leftFov>
            <rightFov>$rightFOV</rightFov>
            <bottomFov>$botFOV</bottomFov>
            <topFov>$topFOV</topFov>
            <near>0.1</near>
        </ViewVolume>
    </PhotoOverlay>
</kml>
```

These KML files are served at runtime from a Tcl CGI script [13] that accepts the width and height values as arguments (via the URL query string), generates values for leftFOV, rightFOV, botFOV and topFOV, substitutes them into a template then returns the resulting text with the correct content-type (application/vnd.google-earth.kml+xml) and Last-Modified / ETag value to avoid any caching.
At 30” viewing distance, the FOV horizontal values typically vary from 23.96° on a 13” display to 26.7° on a 27” display. By comparison, an 85mm focal length lens gives a hFOV of 23.9° and a 70mm focal length lens results in a hFOV of 28.8°.

The Tcl/Tk application to control Google Earth using COM

The stand-alone application requires Google Earth to be installed on the local computer. The application is deployed as a Starkit [14] and uses the Tcl Tcom package [15] to communicate with Google Earth.

The application GUI allows the user to locate the Google Earth executable and select options to build wind farm simulations, add comparison objects (such as the Mackinac Bridge [16] and

Statue of Liberty), define viewpoints ("camera" locations), and desired focal length (in 35 mm camera terms). Each of these actions causes a KML file to be generated, and that file is passed via Tcom to Google Earth.

The advantage of the stand-alone application is flexibility, in that a new KML file is generated for each combination of options. The disadvantage is that it only runs on Windows at this stage, and that it requires Google Earth to be installed on the local computer.

To address these issues a Google Earth plugin application was developed in parallel.

The Google Earth plugin application

The web-based browser simulation uses the Google Earth browser plugin [17] to display the wind farm simulation. The majority of the program code is Javascript running in the browser (~400 lines). This uses the Google Earth API [18] to control the plugin instance, allowing a dynamic interface to be presented to the user.

On starting, the Javascript code calculates the appropriate Field of View (FOV) values based on the size of the users screen and an arbitrary viewing distance of 30 inches.

It then displays the wind farm footprint on a Google Earth map, along with placemarkers for each of the predefined viewing points. Finally, the Google Earth display is centered over the wind farm.

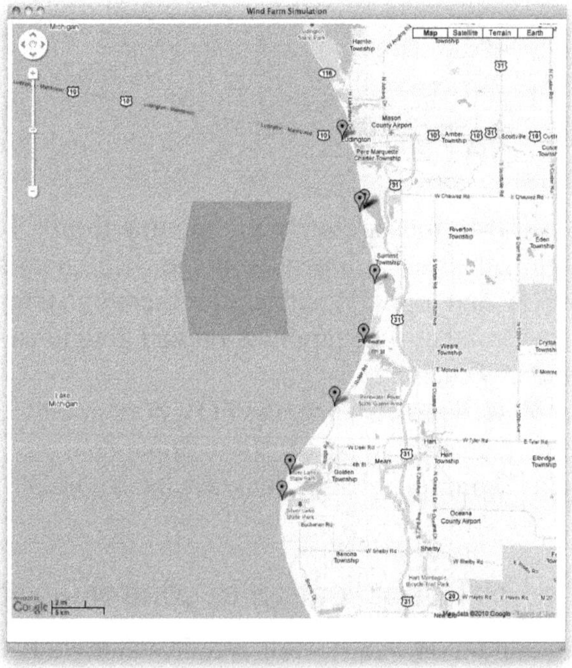

When the user selects a viewpoint, the display is changed to a Google Earth "Satellite 3D map" (a.k.a. aerial view) and the viewing point moved to the placemark. As described previously, the KML placemark corresponding to the viewpoint is extracted via a Tcl CGI script which substitutes the appropriate FOV values, and Google Earth "flies" the display to the viewing point.

The user can zoom or reposition the viewing point as usual using Google Earth features.

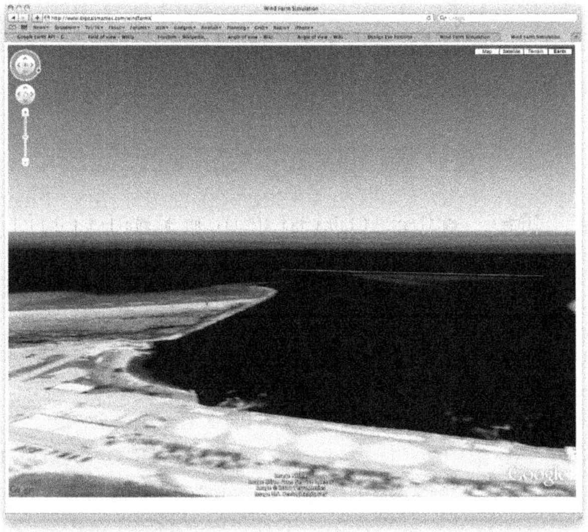

Subsequently, animation of the turbines was added. This involved two three modifications to the previously described scheme:

- multiple Sketchup models were defined, each a variant with the turbine blades at different angles
- the wind farm layout program was modified to randomly pick an initial blade position for each turbine
- the browser Javascript code was modified to update each turbine KML dynamically so that they stepped through the Sketchup models for each turbine blade position.

Validating Visuals

After incorporating Field of View support, it was observed that the turbines still didn't have the same visual impact as observed structures of a similar size.

For example, the towers on the Mackinac Bridge are 550' high, not quite as tall as the proposed turbines. From the south-west corner of the Mackinac Island the nearest tower is about 3.5 miles away, the same distance as the nearest turbines from shore. To the naked eye the towers appear to be huge, dominating the view.

The wind farm simulation was very close to how photographs of the turbines would look when taken with a normal lens (50mm in a 35mm camera). But the simulation seriously underestimated the visual impact on a human viewing the wind farm directly.

The reason for this is what is known as the Moon Illusion [19], an optical illusion in which to the naked eye the Moon appears larger near the horizon than it does when further up in the sky. This illusion also occurs with other celestial objects (e.g. the Sun looks much larger when rising or setting). It is known to be an illusion rather than an optical effect, because measurements of the angle that the full Moon subtends at an observer's eye show it remains constant as the moon rises or sinks.

The Moon Illusion has been known about since ancient times and across various cultures. No single explanation of the illusion is universally accepted, although one explanation (or is it a best guess?) arrived at after eliminating others theories is that the moon illusion is probably related to the way our brains are wired. Threats to primitive humans usually came from eye level not from overhead, therefore our brains perceiving eye level objects as bigger than overhead objects had adaptive (survival) value.

The solution used in the wind farm simulation was based on the observation that a larger focal length lens generally gives a more accurate representation of the visual perception of an object. A lens with a focal length of 85mm gives a reasonable approximation of the visual perception of the moon illusion) so the ratio of this focal length to the 50mm length was used to arrive at a scaling factor of 1.7, which results in a more typical visual perception. The scaling factor is applied within the KML for the turbines, as shown by this section of the turbine KML template:

```
<Placemark targetId="turbine$turbine">
    <name>Turbine $turbine</name>
    <Model id="turbine$turbine">
        <altitudeMode>relativeToGround</altitudeMode>
        <Location>
            <longitude>$lon</longitude>
            <latitude>$lat</latitude>
            <altitude>0</altitude>
        </Location>
        <Orientation>
            <heading>45</heading>
            <tilt>0</tilt>
            <roll>0</roll>
        </Orientation>
        <Scale>
            <x>1.7</x>
            <y>1.7</y>
            <z>1.7</z>
        </Scale>
        <Link>
            <href>windfarm.kmz/$model</href>
        </Link>
    </Model>
</Placemark>
```

This scaling factor has turned out to be a reasonable approximation for typical displays, but perhaps could be refined further by taking into account the characteristics of the current display.

An ongoing area of research is the "calibration" of the visual parameters by comparing images of the Mackinac Bridge created in Google Earth with actual photographs at varying focal lengths. At the moment the Moon Illusion correction is linear, but it is is anticipated the relationship will turn out to vary with the focal lengths.

Summary + conclusions

This project has once again demonstrated the value of Tcl/Tk as both a prototyping language, and as a glue language for combining other technologies. Further, the use of Tcl/Tk has extended to web-based technologies such as the Google Earth plugin and Google Maps.

But we knew this would be the case before we started tilting at windmills.

References

1 OpenGL - http://en.wikipedia.org/wiki/Opengl
2 Google Sketchup - http://sketchup.google.com/
3 Google Earth - http://www.google.com/earth
4 Keyhole Markup Language (KML) - http://en.wikipedia.org/wiki/Keyhole_Markup_Language
5 Digital Asset Exchange (DAE) - http://en.wikipedia.org/wiki/COLLADA
6 Clipper Windpower - http://www.clipperwind.com
7 Google Maps REST API - http://code.google.com/apis/maps/documentation/javascript/
8 The Tcl http package - http://wiki.tcl.tk/http
9 Geodesy - http://wiki.tcl.tk/geodesy
10 Field of View - http://en.wikipedia.org/wiki/Field_of_view
- http://en.wikipedia.org/wiki/Angle_of_view
11 Design Eye Position - http://en.wikipedia.org/wiki/Design_Eye_Position
12 Google Earth Photo Overlays - http://code.google.com/apis/kml/documentation/photos.html
13 Tcl CGI - http://wiki.tcl.tk/cgi
14 Starkit Deployment Technology - http://wiki.tcl.tk/starkit
15 Tcl Tcom package - http://wiki.tcl.tk/tcom
16 Mackinac Bridge - http://en.wikipedia.org/wiki/Mackinac_Bridge
17 Google Earth browser plugin - http://www.google.com/earth/explore/products/plugin.html
18 Google Earth API - http://code.google.com/apis/earth/documentation/
19 The Moon Illusion - http://en.wikipedia.org/wiki/Moon_illusion

All web references as at September 2010.

TkDND: a cross-platform drag'n'drop package

Georgios Petasis

Software and Knowledge Engineering Laboratory,
Institute of Informatics and Telecommunications,
National Centre for Scientific Research "Demokritos",
Athens, Greece
petasis@iit.demokritos.gr

Abstract

This paper is about TkDND, a Tcl/Tk extension that aims to add cross-application drag and drop support to Tk, for popular operating systems, such as Microsoft Windows, Apple OS X and GNU/Linux. Being in its second rewrite, TkDND 2.x has a stable implementation for Windows and OS X, while support for Linux and the XDND protocol is still under development.

1 Introduction

This paper is about TkDND, a cross-platform and multi-protocol Tcl/Tk extension, which aims in extending Tk with cross-application drag and drop capabilities. The term "drag and drop" refers to the action of clicking on a virtual object, and either dragging it to a different location, or onto a different virtual object. Being an important element of modern UI development, several attempts have been made in order to extend Tk with drag and drop (from now on denoted as "DnD") capabilities. Several projects are listed in the relevant Tcl Wiki page [1], which can be categorised into two main categories: approaches that target DnD within the same application, and approaches that target DnD among different applications. Implementing DnD within the context of a single application is a relatively easy task: a simple communication mechanism among virtual objects needs to be devised, which can be implemented even in Tcl. Thus, several intra-application DnD approaches are available, especially within packages that implement composite widgets or "megawidgets", such as BWidget [2]. On the other hand, supporting inter-application DnD is a more challenging task, but nevertheless a more interesting and useful task. Initial approaches in this category devised several inter-application communication schemes, which targeted other Tk applications, such as BLT [3] with its communication scheme based on Tk's "send" command. More recent approaches tried to solve an even more complex task, intra-application DnD without any restriction on the type of applications (i.e. even for non-Tk applications), by exploiting standardised DnD communication protocols available for the various operating systems. These approaches targeted mainly popular operating systems, such as Microsoft Windows. Olednd [4], developed by Gordon Chaffee, is amongst the first DnD approaches for Tk that can be characterised as complete: Olednd supported DnD with any application running on the Microsoft Windows operating system, by exploiting the platform's native DnD protocol, OLE DnD. Olednd has been the main inspiration of the extension described in this paper, TkDND, whose main motivation was to enhance the functionality offered by Olednd under Windows, and provide the same functionality under other popular operating systems, such as Gnu/Linux and Mac OS X.

TkDND is not a recent extension, as its development started in 2000. With an API for applications inspired by Olednd but targeting multiple operating systems, TkDND initially concentrated on implementing DnD for the Windows operating system using OLE DnD, and having the Olednd implementation as a guide. Once the Windows implementation was in place, implementation shifted in supporting DnD under the Linux operating system. At that time, two communication protocols were available under Linux, all of which bind with a specific widget toolkit. The older of these protocol was the Motif [5] DnD protocol, supported by Motif and LessTif [6] applications, and partially by the GTK [7] and GNOME [8] applications. The second protocol was an open standard, in early stage of development, known as XDND [9]. XDND was mainly supported by Qt [10] and KDE [11] applications.

TkDND tried to compromise the two protocols: the 1.x series of TkDND tried to implement support for the XDND for both dragging and dropping actions, and support for dropping actions under the Motif DnD protocol. All implementation for both was done from scratch, as there were no general-purpose libraries implementing these protocols beside the widget toolkits implementing them. The end result was not satisfactory, as it exhibited several problems:

- The implementation was not stable enough. The primary author of TkDND tried to tackle the problem of implementing two protocols from scratch, without having adequate knowledge of Xlib [12], led a prolonged development period and a result of low quality.
- The XDND protocol was not mature enough and was under constant revisions. TkDND was forced to support several versions of the protocol, constituting XDND support a moving target.
- Several compatibility problems arose in practice. Despite both GTK and Motif applications sharing the same protocol (Motif), it was not uncommon drops from Motif applications or Firefox [13] to always succeed, while dropping from Gnome applications to exhibit random behaviour. The situation regarding XDND was no better: not only the protocol was changing, but also support from the applications was changing with each Qt release.

In addition to all these, TkDND 1.x was an ambitious attempt, targeting support for as much types as possible, including transferring of plain text, Unicode text, files, links, images, etc. All these problems led to the decision of abandoning the 1.x series of TkDND, and start a new, novel implementation of TkDND, the 2.x series, in 2006. TkDND brought yet another API for applications, although TkDND 1.x applications are still supported through an emulation layer written in Tcl. The main implementation guideline followed by TkDND 2.x is to re-implement as few elements as possible in C/C++, and implement as much as possible in Tcl. The current public release of TkDND is 2.2, which offers support for DnD under Windows and OS X in transferring text and files, but drops Linux support. For a while, TkDND 2.x offered support for the dropping operation under the XDND protocol, but this support has ceased working with recent versions of the Qt library. Regarding this issue, a TIP [14] has been proposed to enhance the "selection" Tk command, which hopefully will solve this incompatibility. In addition, TkDND 2.x introduces support for cross-platform types, by adding an abstraction layer over them: applications can use types such as DND_Text and DND_Files, with TkDND performing the necessary mappings to types depended on the operating system. Finally, TkDND would have not been possible without the work and ideas of several contributors: Gordon Chaffee, for providing the inspiration and OLE DnD prototype, Laurent Riesterer for helping in the implementation of various parts of TkDND 1.x, and Kevin Walzer, who with Daniel A. Steffen, was the motivation power behind the Mac OS X implementation, by driving the development, contributing a large part of the OS X implementation and testing TkDND under OS X.

The rest of the paper is organised as follows: chapter two briefly describes the motivation behind the implementation of TkDND 2.x, along with an overview of how TkDND can be used by Tcl/Tk applications. Chapter three provides some details about the protocols employed under the supported operating systems, while chapter four concludes this document.

2 Design and usage

One of the main aims of TkDND 2.x re-write was simplicity, through the implementation of a large part in Tcl/Tk, instead of C, which dominated the implementation of TkDND 1.x. Doing so, eases the development overhead, but also allows the easy adaptation of TkDND to specific needs, even by the end users. For example, TkDND 1.x offered a more complex API, where the various event callbacks had to be specified/configured through the TkDND API, whereas in TkDND 2.x callbacks are implemented through Tk virtual events: not only it is easier for users, as they are already familiar with Tk events, but it is also easier for TkDND maintainers, as the management/destruction/association with Tk widgets is done by Tk.

2.1 Using TkDND

Using TkDND is quite easy. Drag and Drop operations can be separated in two categories:

- Accepting a drop (either from the same or from another application). Widgets registered to accept drops (data) are named as "Drop Targets" in TkDND terminology.
- Initiating a drag operation, allowing the transfer of data from a Tk widget to another widget (either to the same or to another application). Widgets registered to initiate drag operations are named as "Drag Sources" in TkDND terminology.

2.1.1 Drop targets

A drop target can be registered as:

```
tkdnd::drop_target register window ?type-list?
```

where type-list can be a list of cross-platform types (such as DND_Text or DND_Files), platform dependent types (such as CF_TEXT – although usage of platform dependent types is discouraged), or the type "*", interpreted by TkDND as "any type".

When a drop operation occurs over a Tk widget registered as a drop target, TkDND will deliver the following virtual events:

- <<DropEnter>>: This event is triggered when the mouse enters the window during a drop action. The purpose of this event is to change the visual state of the window, so as to notify the user whether the drop will be accepted or not. The binding script is expected to return a single value that will define the drop action. This returned action can be one of **copy**, **move**, **link**, **ask**, **private**, and **refuse_drop**. This event is not mandatory, but if it is defined, it has to return an action. In case an action is not returned, the drop is refused for this window.
- <<DropPosition>>: This event is triggered when the mouse moves inside the window during a drop action. The purpose of this event is to let window decide if it will accept the drop and the action of the drop, if a drop is going to happen at *the specific mouse coordinates*. Thus, the script binding for such an event can get the mouse coordinates and the pressed modifier buttons (such as ctrl, shift or alt), and is expected to return the drop action, which again must be one of **copy**, **move**, **link**, **ask**, **private**, and **refuse_drop**. This event is not mandatory, but if it is defined, it has

to return an action. In case an action is not returned, the drop is refused for this window.

- <<DropLeave>>: This event is triggered when the mouse leaves outside the area covered by the window, without a drop happening. The binding of such an event is expected to restore the visual state of the window to normal (i.e. the visual state the window was in before the <<DropEnter>> event was triggered). The binding for such an event is not expected to return a value.
- <<Drop>>: This event is triggered by a drop action, and it is expected to handle the dropped data and reset the visual state of the window. The binding script is expected to return a value, which will be the action that has been performed to the data, and must be one of **copy**, **move**, **link**, **ask**, **private**, and **refuse_drop**. This event is not mandatory, but if it is defined, it has to return an action. In case an action is not returned, the drop is refused for this window.
- <<Drop:*type*>>:This event is a specialisation of the generic <<Drop>> event, augmented with a type. If such a binding exists and the drop type matches *type*, this event binding will be executed, instead of the generic <<Drop>> event binding. These events allow for easy specialisation of drop bindings, according to the type of the dropped data. *type* can be either a platform independent or a platform specific type. The binding script of such an event is expected to return a value, which will be the action that has been performed to the data, and must be one of **copy**, **move**, **link**, **ask**, **private**, and **refuse_drop**. This event is not mandatory, but if it is defined, it has to return an action. In case an action is not returned, the drop is refused for this window.

2.1.2 Drag sources

A drag source can be registered as:

```
tkdnd::drag_source register window ?type-list? ?mouse-button?
```

where:

- type-list can be a list of cross-platform types (such as DND_Text or DND_Files), platform dependent types (such as CF_TEXT – although usage of platform dependent types is discouraged), or the type "*", interpreted by TkDND as "any type".
- mouse-button is the mouse button (i.e. "1", "2",. "3", etc.) that will be used in the binding for initiating a drag operation. If not specified, it defaults to "1", i.e. the left mouse button.

Once a widget is registered as a drag source, TkDND will add the proper bindings to initiate a drag operation. During the drag operation TkDND will not deliver any virtual events to the widget. The only event that will be delivered relates only to retrieving the data:

- <<DragInitCmd>>: This event is triggered when a drag action is about to start. This is a mandatory event (whose absence will cancel the dragging action), and is responsible for providing three things: the list of actions and format types supported by the drag source, and of course the data to be dropped. Thus, the binding script for such an event must return a list of three elements: the drop actions supported by the drag source (which can be any of **copy**, **move**, **link**, **ask**, and **private**), the format type list that the data can be dropped as (which can be any platform independent or platform specific type), and finally the data. A simple example of such a binding, is:

```
bind .drag_source <<DragInitCmd>> \
```

```
{list copy DND_Text {Hellow world!}}
```

- <<DragEndCmd>>: This event is triggered when the dragging action has finished (either when the drop was successful or not). Its main purpose is to process the dropped data according to the drop action returned by the drop target. Binding for such an event is not mandatory, and the binding is not expected to return a value.

3 Protocols and Operating Systems

TkDND implements support for different platforms under different operating systems. Currently, the supported protocols are OLE DnD (Windows), XDND (Linux) and Cocoa DnD (Mac OS X).

3.1 Microsoft Windows

The drag and drop under the Windows operating system is implemented through Object Linking and Embedding (OLE) [15]. The operating system provides a convenient public API for initialising OLE support in the application, registering a widget as a drop target, and performing drag operations.

3.1.1 Initialising OLE

The initialisation of OLE version 2 is very easy, through a call to OleInitialize().

3.1.2 Registering a widget as a drop target

The registration of a Tk widget as a drop target is performed through the RegisterDragDrop() function, which requires two parameters:

- The handle (HWND) of the widget.
- An object of type IDropTarget.

The IDropTarget object is used by the operating system to communicate the required events (DragEnter, DragOver, DragLeave, and Drop), to retrieve the types supported by the drop target, and to accept the dropped data. TkDND subclasses IDropTarget, in order to interface it with Tk.

3.1.3 Performing a drag operation

The operating system provides a function for performing drags from widgets, through the function DoDragDrop(), which requires four arguments:

- A data object of type IDataObject, which contains the data that will be transferred if the drop operation is successfully completed.
- A drag source object, of type IDropSource, which controls when the drop will happen, and what cursors will be used during the drag operation.
- The list of actions supported by the drag source (like copy, move, link, etc.).
- The action decided by the drop target, if the drag operation has not been cancelled.

3.1.4 Communicating events

OLE DnD supports four types of events that can occur during a drag and drop session, and most of them involve the drop target. These events are:

- DragEnter
- DragOver
- DragLeave
- Drop
- QueryContinueDrag

- GiveFeedback

All these events are communicated to the application by calling the corresponding methods on the provided by the application objects (IDropTarget and IDropSource).

3.2 Apple Mac OS X

The implementation of TkDND for the OS X operating system is written in Objective C, and uses the DnD facilities offered by the operating system for the Cocoa framework [16]. The Cocoa DnD protocol is very similar to the XDND protocol supported by GNU/Linux, as there exists great resemblance on how the two protocols operate, how the types are named, and the communication events exchange. However, there is significant difference between the two protocols: The Cocoa DnD offers a convenient API any application can use to support DnD: applications can either accept drops or initiate dragging actions without having to re-implement the protocol from scratch (as is the case for XDND). From a programmer's point of view, Cocoa DnD can be regarded as "XDND done right". Of course, TkDND took advantage of the similarities between the two toolkits, in re-using all the support code (written in Tcl, in the library section of TkDND) initially written for XDND under the Linux operating system.

3.2.1 Initialising Cocoa DnD

No specific initialisation is required.

3.2.2 Registering a widget as a drop target

The registration of a Tk widget as a drop target is performed through the registerForDraggedTypes() method of the NSView, associated to the widget. This method requires a single parameter:

- An array of the supported types of the drop target.

3.2.3 Performing a drag operation

The operating system provides a method for performing drags from widgets, through NSView, associated with the drag source widget. The data must be copied to the clipboard, prior to invoking the dragging action. In order to initiate a dragging action, the following parameters are required:

- An icon that will be used during the dragging operation.
- The location of the icon (screen coordinates) when the dragging operation is initiated. These coordinates are used to provide visual feedback of a failed dragging operation.
- The mouse event that initiated the dragging operation.
- The clipboard containing the data to be dropped.
- The NSView of the window initiating the dragging operation.
- A Boolean flag, denoting whether the icon will slide back in case the drag action fails.

Under the Cocoa DND there is no support in retrieving the action applied to the data during a successful drop action. TkDND assumes that this action is always **copy**.

3.2.4 Communicating events

Cocoa DnD supports five types of events that can occur during a drag and drop session, and most of them involve the drop target. These events are:

- draggingEntered
- draggingUpdated
- draggingExited

- prepareForDragOperation
- performDragOperation

3.3 GNU/Linux

Gnu/Linux is currently the least supported operating system by TkDND 2.x. The main obstacle of this platform is the complete absence of any public API that can be used for DnD operations, along with various compatibility issues observed among the various widget toolkits available for the platform. The dominant DnD protocol under Linux is XDND, details of which can be found at [9]. TkDND offers limited support for this protocol, by supporting only dropping actions. However, currently dropping from applications on Tk applications does not work: while the dropping operation is performed, TkDND is unable to retrieve the dropped data from the clipboard due to timestamp mismatches. Regarding this issue, a TIP [14] has been proposed to enhance the "selection" Tk command, which hopefully will solve this incompatibility.

4 Conclusions

This paper presents TkDND, a Tcl/Tk extension that aims to add cross-application drag and drop support to Tk, for popular operating systems, such as Microsoft Windows, Apple OS X and GNU/Linux. TkDND is an open source project, implementing a Tcl extension written in C, C++ and Objective C, distributed under the BSD license. The source code is hosted at the SVN repositories of SourceForge [17]. The current public release is TkDND 2.2, offering stable support for the Microsoft Windows and Apple OS X (Cocoa framework) operating systems. Support for the Linux operation system is currently missing, with stable support under Linux being a desirable, but difficult to achieve, target.

5 References

[1] Drag and Drop in Tk: http://wiki.tcl.tk/571
[2] The BWidget toolkit: http://wiki.tcl.tk/2251
[3]BLT: http://blt.sourceforge.net/
[4] Olednd: http://wiki.tcl.tk/571
[5] Motif: http://www.opengroup.org/motif/
[6] LessTif: http://lesstif.sourceforge.net/
[7] The GTK+ Project: http://www.gtk.org/
[8] GNOME: The Free Software Desktop Project: http://www.gnome.org/
[9] XDND – Drag-and-Drop Protocol for the X Window System: http://www.newplanetsoftware.com/xdnd/
[10] Qt – A cross-platform application and UI framework: http://qt.nokia.com/
[11] The KDE Community: http://www.kde.org/
[12] Xlib: http://en.wikipedia.org/wiki/Xlib
[13] Mozilla Firefox: http://www.mozilla-europe.org/
[14] TIP 370: http://www.tcl.tk/cgi-bin/tct/tip/370.html
[15] OLE – Object Linking and Embedding: http://en.wikipedia.org/wiki/Object_Linking_and_Embedding
[16] Drag and Drop Programming Topics for Cocoa: http://developer.apple.com/library/mac/#documentation/Cocoa/Conceptual/DragandDrop/DragandDrop.html
[17] TkDND at SourceForge: https://sourceforge.net/projects/tkdnd/

17th ANNUAL TCL/TK 2010 CONFERENCE Chicago (USA) 11-15 October

Mixed Bag

Thu October 14, 2010 16:15-18:00

TclA Publications

Ellogon and the challenge of threads

Georgios Petasis

Software and Knowledge Engineering Laboratory,
Institute of Informatics and Telecommunications,
National Centre for Scientific Research "Demokritos",
Athens, Greece
petasis@iit.demokritos.gr

Abstract

This paper is about the Ellogon language engineering platform, and the challenges faced in modernising it, in order to better exploit contemporary hardware. Ellogon is an open-source infrastructure, specialised in natural language processing. Following a data model that closely resembles TIPSTER, Ellogon can be used either as an autonomous application, offering a graphical user interface, or it can be embedded in a C/C++ application as a library. Ellogon has been implemented in C/C++ and Tcl/Tk: in fact Ellogon is a vanilla Tcl interpreter, with the Ellogon core loaded as a Tcl extension, and a set of Tcl/Tk scripts that implement the GUI. The core component of Ellogon, being a Tcl extension, heavily relies on Tcl objects to implement its data model, a decision made more than a decade ago, which poses difficulties into making Ellogon a multi-threaded application.

1 Introduction

In this paper we describe Ellogon [Petasis et al., 2002; 2003], a multi-lingual, cross-platform, general-purpose language engineering environment, developed in order to aid a wide range of users – from researchers in the natural language field or computational linguistics, to companies that produce and deliver language engineering systems. Being in constant development since 1998, Ellogon is a mature and well tested infrastructure, as it has been used in many Greek and European funded projects. Its facilities have been used for creating a wide range of applications, from multilingual information extraction systems to controlled language checkers and ontology-based information extraction systems.

Ellogon as a text engineering platform offers an extensive set of facilities, including tools for visualising textual/HTML/XML data and the associated linguistic information, support for lexical resources (like creating and embedding lexicons), tools for creating annotated corpora, accessing databases, comparing annotated data, or transforming linguistic information into vectors for use with various machine learning algorithms. Additionally, Ellogon offers some unique features, like the ability to freely modify annotated textual data (with Ellogon automatically applying the required transformations on the associated linguistic information), and the ability to create stand-alone applications with customised user interfaces that perform specific tasks.

Ellogon was amongst the first platforms to offer complete multi-lingual support, both in its processing core, and its GUI. The main reason behind this feature was, of course, the Unicode support offered by Tcl 8.1, which was available in a beta form when Ellogon development started, along with the decision to use Tcl objects as a basis for the data model of Ellogon. The idea for relying the data model of Ellogon on Tcl objects was a promising approach, about a decade ago, when Ellogon development was starting. The data model could be implemented by objects holding Tcl lists, indexed by Tcl Hash tables. The modularity and reference counting of Tcl objects ensured reusability, and no conversions were needed in order to expose the data model to Tcl. However, modularity and reusability comes with a small cost: each Tcl object has an overhead in the used memory, and processing a document can produce tenths of thousands of objects. But again a solution was found, based on the observation that objects tend to contain the same information: build a cache of objects, and reuse objects whenever appropriate. This approach worked well for many years, but recent hardware brings a new challenge: how can the data model meet multiple threads?

The rest of the paper is organised as follows: in chapter two, the architecture and data model of Ellogon are described, along with some implementation details. Chapter three presents the objects cache, the motivation behind this cache, the advantages the cache offers with respect to memory usage, and the issues raised by this cache in a multi-threaded environment. Finally chapter four concludes this document.

2 The Architecture and Data Model of Ellogon

2.1 Ellogon Architecture

Ellogon aims to be a versatile infrastructure that can be used either as an NLP integrated development environment (IDE), or as a library that can be embedded to foreign applications. As a result, Ellogon proposes a modular architecture with four independent subsystems (Figure 1):

- A highly efficient core developed in C, which implements an extended version of the TIPSTER data model. Its main responsibility is to manage the storage of the textual data and the associated linguistic information, and to provide a well-defined programming interface (API) that can be used in order to retrieve/modify the stored information.
- An object oriented C++ API, which increases the usability of the C core API. This object oriented API is exposed to a wide range of programming languages, including C++, Java, Tcl, Perl and Python.
- An extensive and easy to use graphical user interface (GUI). This interface can be easily tailored to the needs of the end user.
- A modular pluggable component system. All linguistic processing within the platform is performed with the help of external, loaded at run-time, components. These components can be implemented in a wide range of programming languages, including C, C++, Java, Tcl, Perl and Python.

2.2 Ellogon Data Model

Ellogon shares the same data model as the TIPSTER architecture (Figure 2). The central element for storing data in Ellogon is the Collection. A collection is a finite set of documents. An Ellogon document consists of textual data, as well as linguistic information about the textual data. This linguistic information is stored in the form of attributes and annotations.

An attribute associates a specific type of information with a typed value. An annotation, on the other hand, associates arbitrary information (in the form of attributes) with portions of the textual data. Each such portion, named span, consists of two character offsets denoting the start and the end characters of the portion, as measured from the first character of some textual data. Annotations typically consist of four elements:

- A numeric identifier. This identifier is unique for every annotation within a document, and can be used to unambiguously identify the annotation.
- A type. Annotation types are textual values that are used to classify annotations into categories.

- A set of spans, each of which denotes a range of annotated textual data.
- A set of attributes. These attributes usually encode the necessary linguistic information.

A visual representation of Ellogon's data model can be seen in Figure 2.

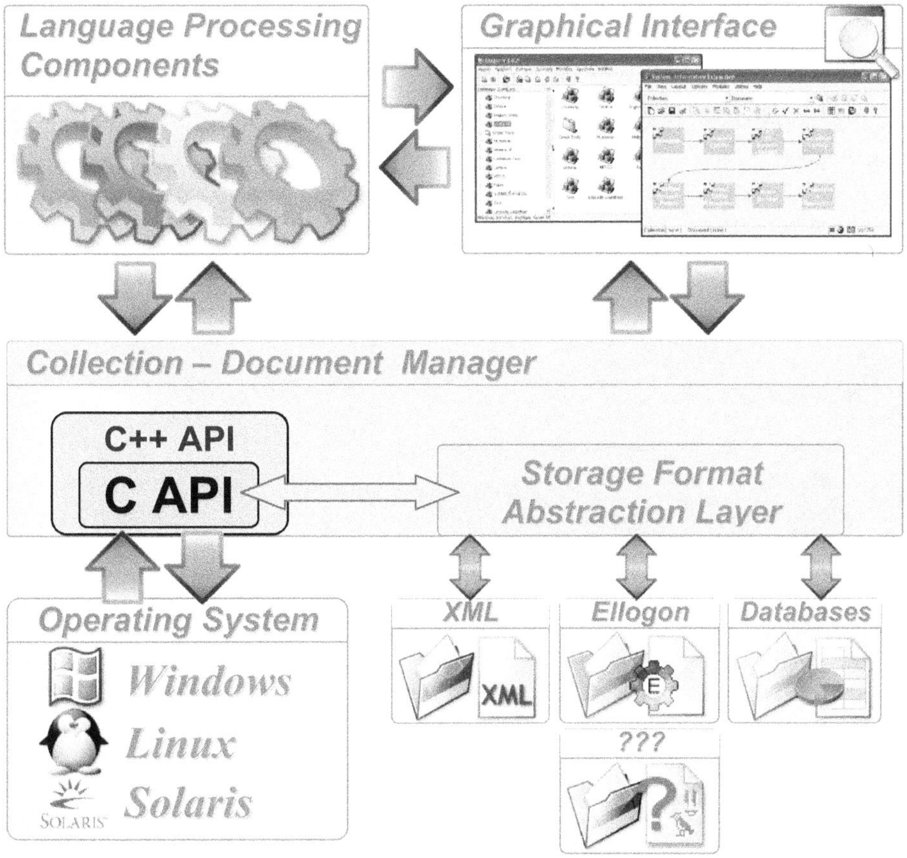

Figure 1: Ellogon Architecture.

2.3 Implementing the Data Model

The top-level object of Ellogon's data model is the collection. The collection has been implemented as a C structure, which contains a set of Tcl objects among other elements:

- A Tcl list object, containing the documents to be deleted (if any).
- A Tcl command token, holding the Tcl command that represents a collection at the Tcl level.
- A Tcl Hash table that contains the attributes of the collection. Each attribute is a Tcl list object.
- Two Tcl objects that can hold arbitrary information, such as notes and associated information.

Additionally, the collection maintains a list of documents. A document is implemented as a C structure, and has similar features to the collection, like a Tcl command token, a Tcl object holding the text of the document, and two Tcl Hash tables, storing the attributes and annotations of the document. Both attributes and annotations are implemented as Tcl objects. Each attribute is a Tcl list object, which contains three elements:

- The attribute name: the name can be an arbitrary string.

- The type of the attribute value: this can be an item from a predefined set of value types.
- The value of the attribute, which can be an arbitrary (even binary) string.

An annotation is a slightly more complex type, again represented by Tcl object of custom type. It can be roughly seen as a list of four elements:

- The annotation id: an integer, which uniquely identifies the annotation inside a document.
- The annotation type: an arbitrary string that classifies the annotation into a category.
- A list of spans: each span is a Tcl list object, holding two integers, the start/end character offsets of the text annotated by the span.
- A list of attributes: a Tcl list object, whose elements are attributes.

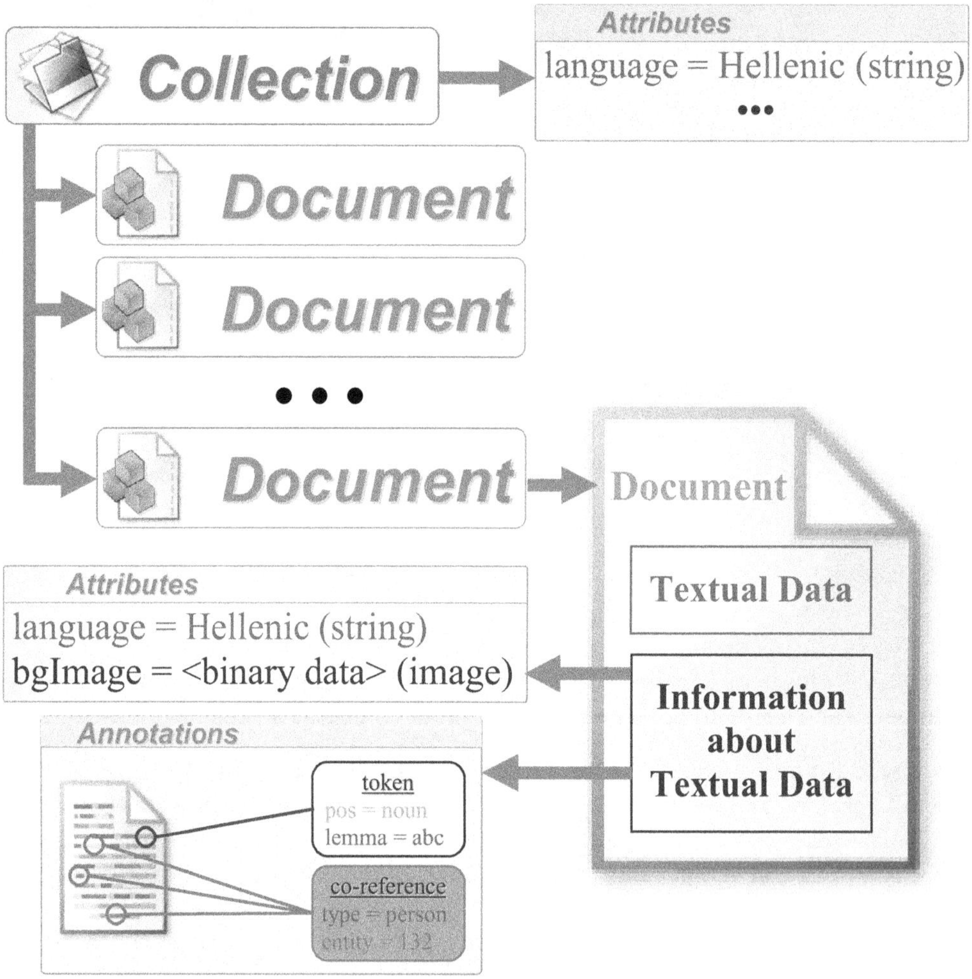

Figure 2: The Data Model of Ellogon.

3 Caching Tcl objects

Memory consumption is always an issue in Ellogon, as it directly limits the size and the number of documents that can be processed. Ellogon has chosen to implement a global memory cache for Tcl objects, containing information from all opened Collections and Documents. The motivation behind the creation of this cache was a simple observation that linguistic information tends to repeat a lot. Consider for example a part-of-speech tagger, analysing a document containing 10.000 words. Each word will be assigned an annotation of type "token" (so the annotation type "token" will be repeated 10.000 times), and each annotation will contain at least an attribute, named "pos", that will hold the part-of-speech tag of the word. Assuming that a tag set of 10 possible part-of-speech categories is used, each tag has a potential repetition in the thousands. Keeping a cache, so as not to repeat "token' and "pos" 10.000 times, but share 10.000 times two Tcl objects, makes sense. And caching and reusing larger clusters of Tcl objects makes even more sense, as the memory reduction can be drastically reduced. Memory reduction is even greater as more documents are added, and information is shared among collections. The current implementation of the object cache contains many heuristics that can cache and share a range of objects, from attribute names, annotation types or objects holding integers (i.e. used as identifiers or spans) to more complex constructs like spans or whole attributes.

3.1 Thread safety

Of course, a major concern involving a global caching mechanism, spanning the data model of a whole application, is how thread safety is ensured. Tcl objects cannot be shared across threads, constituting the approach followed so far thread unfriendly. This is an open question for the Ellogon platform, which may not have an easy answer, despite the fact that parallel processing of documents in different threads is a highly desirable feature.

The core component of Ellogon (Collection and Document Manager – CMD) that implements the data model (and the object cache) is already thread-safe:

- The global variables/objects are few, and their access is protected by mutexes.
- The object cache is global, and protected again with a mutex.
- Ellogon plug-in components use thread-specific storage for storing their "global" variables (through special pre-processor definitions for C/C++ components).

However, the fact that the core is thread safe does not mean that threads can be used: as long as a cached object is passed back to Tcl, it is no longer protected by the mutexes the core uses: Tcl will assume that the object is local to the current thread the interpreter is running on, and will modify its reference count (at least) without any restriction.

3.2 So, can Ellogon become multi-threaded?

This is a difficult question to be answered, and the motivation for this paper. A multi-threaded Ellogon must fulfil the following requirements:

- The graphical user interface must not block during component execution, suggesting that it is running on its own thread.
- Each execution chain (a set of loaded at runtime components named as "System" in Ellogon terminology) must run on its own thread.
- Since each "System" executes all components on a single document before advancing into the next document, the documents of a collection can be distributed into N threads, and can be processed in parallel. This is a highly desired feature.

However, this threading design poses some difficulties in its implementation:

- The object cache: the object cache limits memory usage both within a single document, but also across documents. In the current implementation, Tcl objects are managed by the cache, which suggests that they are created in the "main" thread of the application. In case documents are created and used on different threads, the cached Tcl objects will be accessed by different threads, an operation that is not allowed by the Tcl threading model.

- The Graphical User Interface: the GUI is not limited to instrumentation of the component execution, but offers many operations on the linguistic data produced during component execution, including a wide range of viewers for browsing this information. Since the GUI runs on a separate thread than the documents were processed, again Tcl objects will be shared by multiple threads.

The Data Model of Ellogon has been designed to rely heavily on Tcl objects, as this seemed a good idea back in 1998, for the following reasons:

- Tcl objects are reusable bits, due to the reference counting and the well defined C API for their management. Structuring the data model upon them, allows parts of the model to be cached and shared in multiple documents, as it has been implemented by the object cache.
- The GUI of the application is in Tcl/Tk, and the linguistic data does not need to be converted to Tcl objects, in order to be displayed/managed by the GUI, if it is already stored as Tcl objects.
- Despite that there is an extensive API for managing the various elements of the data model, it is far more convenient to use the Tcl commands to manipulate them, especially for plug-in components written in Tcl. For example, it is easier to get the annotations contained in an "annotation set" through "foreach", than through a "for" with a counter, which calls "tip_Nth" to get the Nth element from the annotation set.

However, nowadays computers with multiple processing CPU cores are common, and supporting multiple threads seems a natural extension. But, it is unclear if such an extension is feasible without a major re-implementation of the core component and without sacrificing the significant memory reduction offered by the object cache.

4 Conclusions

This paper describes a language engineering platform known as "Ellogon", one of the first general-purpose language engineering infrastructures to offer complete Unicode support. Being in constant usage for more than a decade, the platform has to continuously evolve in order to better exploit a constantly improving hardware, without introducing major and incompatible changes to the infrastructure. Since CPUs with multiple processing cores are becoming more affordable and thus wide spread, the introduction of multiple processing threads in the Ellogon platform is a major concern. However, it is currently unclear if multiple threads can be introduced without a significant reorganisation of the platform, a question that is the main motivation for this paper.

5 References

[Grishman, 1996]: Grishman, R. 1996. "TIPSTER Architecture Design Document Version 2.2". *Technical Report, DARPA*. Available at http://www.tipster.org

[Petasis et al., 2002]: G. Petasis, V. Karkaletsis, G. Paliouras, I. Androutsopoulos and C. D. Spyropoulos, "Ellogon: A New Text Engineering Platform". In Proceedings of the 3rd International Conference on Language Resources and Evaluation (LREC 2002), Las Palmas, Canary Islands, Spain, vol. I, pp. 72 – 78, May 2002.

[Petasis et al., 2003]: G. Petasis, V. Karkaletsis, G. Paliouras and C. D. Spyropoulos, "Using the Ellogon Natural Language Engineering Infrastructure". In Proceedings of the Workshop on Balkan Language Resources and Tools, 1st Balkan Conference in Informatics (BCI'2003), Thessaloniki, Greece, November 21, 2003.

Handling Email with a Tcl assist

Clif Flynt
Noumena Corporation,
8888 Black Pine Ln,
Whitmore Lake, MI 48189,
`http://www.noucorp.com`
`clif at noucorp dot com`

September 30, 2010

Abstract

Handling email has become a greater and greater burden on the average computer user. The user must be able to read mail safely, including examining the non-obvious fake mail. There is a need to sort valid from invalid, urgent and non-critical, or just sorting into mail from mailing lists, friends, relatives, etc.

This problem is worse for the systems administrator who also has to deal with the quantities of mail clogging the networks, filling the disks and filling the administrator mailbox with failure notices.

There are many tools to mitigate these problems, ranging from using a webmail service like Gmail, letting Microsoft solve your problems by using Outlook, or using *ix tools like procmail, etc.

All of these tools are written in compiled languages. The speed is good, but the ability to reconfigure and adapt is low.

Tools written in Tcl are as fast as the average user, and are more easily adapted to the ever-changing email environment.

1 Introduction

I've been dealing with email since the early 1980s, when the address `clif!clif` was a unique address, and `ihnp4!clif!clif` would guarantee delivery.

When a big email day was 5 messages, `mail` and `mailx` were great. As time passed, and email volume approached 20 messages a day, `elm` and `pine` were even better.

The graph in **Figure 1** shows the email server activity logged over a period of a few weeks. The black bar is the number of connections made to the server. The dark gray bar is the number that were rejected by hard-coded rules (invalid sender, invalid recipient, etc). The light gray bar is the number of valid messages sent to users.

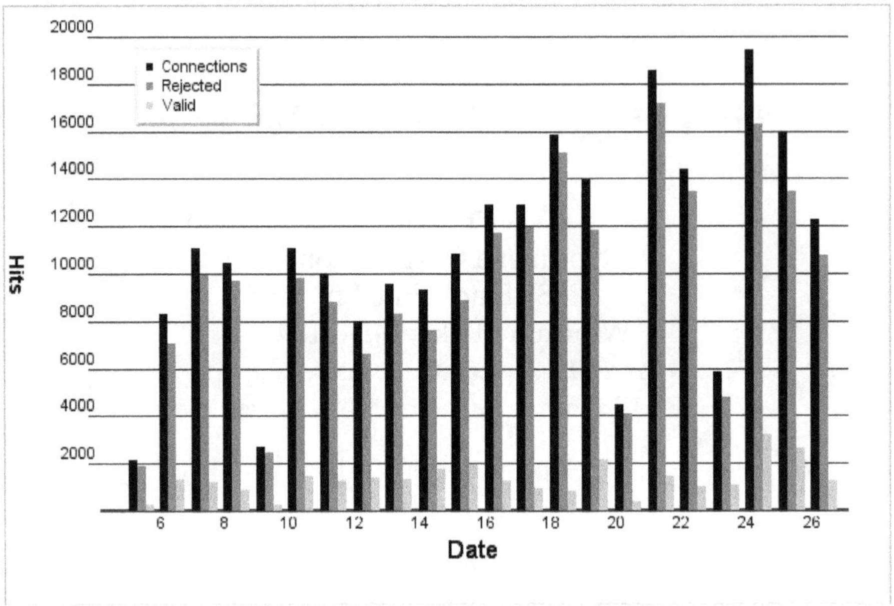

Figure 1: Connections, Rejections and Valid emails

The number of valid messages is much smaller than the number of invalid attempts, but still tops 1000 emails / day for each user on the system.

Obviously, the modern connected user needs tools allow them easy access to potentially hundreds of emails per day and to protect themselves while reading them.

My preference is to host my mail server and read mail locally on a *ix system.

This paper will discuss tools that I use to handle the volumes of mail I receive, avoid viruses, avoid spam and control the system.

2 Reading Mail

I happen to like the `mutt` mailreader for general use. It provides a simple user interface, handles MIME attachments and doesn't put too much of its own philosophy on how I read mail.

However, it does become awkward when receiving over 200 emails per day, spread across several mailing lists.

One feature of `mutt` and other text based mail readers is that they will read any file, as long as it is in the standard Unix mail format. This hook allows sorting mail into multiple mailboxes and then reading the email via mutt with a command like `mutt -f tcl_core_list`.

2.1 Trivial solutions aren't

My presorting application started life as an application for a client who needed a simple email application to accept email, parse it for simple commands like "send info" and generate canned responses. The client wanted something cheap and fast, so it was necessary to use tools I knew would work.

It seems simple to open the Unix mail file, read in the data, process it and clear the file.

This isn't quite the case.

The system may be putting new mail into the mail file while your application is emptying it for instance. Your application needs to be careful about understanding how the file locking is implemented. The existing email readers already have locking code that works.

Having been warned that the `procmail` developers went through several iterations before they got the locking right, I side-stepped the issue by using the traditional `mail` text mail reader and `expect` to read and process the mail.

The `mail` mail reader is a first generation mail reader designed for use on a printing terminal. It has single letter commands to find out how many messages exist, read a message and delete a message.

An expect script to read email looks a bit like this:

```
spawn mail
# First message resembles:
# "/var/spool/mail/clif": 10 messages 6 unread
 # Look for the : and a set of numbers.
 expect {
    -re {: *([0-9]+) } {
           set messageCount $expect_out(1,string)
        }
 }
 # Step through messages
 for {set i 1} {$i <= $messageCount} {incr i} {
   exp_send "$i\n"
   # Read message
   # Process message
 }
```

In the real world it gets a bit more complex.

- Messages get large

  The `mail` application it pure text. If a friend sends you a video, `expect` will need to read several megabytes of text. This will overflow the `expect` input buffer unless you use the `match_max` command to reset the buffer size. I'm currently using 4 million as the buffer size.

- Large messages take a long time to be read

Using `mail` as a front end means that text is flowing through stdin and stdout. Pushing a few megabytes through standard I/O can take time. The `expect` command `set timeout` will increase the length of the timeout interval. This is currently set for 500 seconds.

- Trivial parsing won't work.

  There are dozens of email systems out there. I doubt that any of them conform to the complete RFC standard. For example, an email address may be reported in several ways including:

```
From: Your Friend <friend@spamsite.com>
From: Facebook <notification+o64s0y26@facebookmail.com>
From: User Name [mailto:username@roadrunner.com]
From: Local User
From: remoteuser@att.net
```

  The parsing code needs to understand all of them, and perhaps a few more. (Note that the + format means disregard the part of the email address between + and `@` when delivering email.)

  Tcl's `regexp` command returns a 1 if it matches a pattern in the string, and a 0 if the string does not match a pattern. Assuming that an email address will not include the illegal characters you can use a `regexp` to identify the address portion from one of those strings.

```
if {[regexp {([^!^;^:^ ^\[^<]+@[^:^ ^>]*)} $string m1 addr] == 0} {
  # Must be local address
  set addr $string
}
```

2.2 Out of sorts

The main functionality needed from a mail sorting program is to sort the mail into different known bins. The mail reading program starts by parsing the headers into a (relatively) consistent format and storing the data in a Tcl array where the index is a header field.

```
% parray Parts
Parts(from)    = client@customer.com
Parts(subject) = New Project
Parts(to)      = clif@noucorp.com
```

This data structure makes it easy to write a set of rules that looks like this:

```
set Actions {
 { reply-to {
   {{[firstNsave ltsp-discuss@lists.sourceforge.net %s LTSP]} {}}
```

```
    {{[firstNsave googlegroups %s GSoC]} {}}
    {{[firstNsave -nextgen@noucorp.c %s tk-nextgen]} {}}
  }
  }
  { sender {
    {{[firstNsave ev-bounces@lists.sjsu.edu %s ev]} {}}
    {{[firstNsave tcl-webmaste %s TclWeb]} {}}
    {{[firstNsave snort-users %s snort]} {}}
    {{[firstNsave starkit %s starkit]} {}}
  }
  }
```

The rule engine steps through rules in the order they appear until one succeeds. The `firstNsave` procedure examines the provided string and if a pattern is matched, saves the message and returns a true.

This started life as a trivial application. At this point, it's become about 700 lines of Tcl code sorting on about 80 criteria. It runs fast enough to keep up with the mail stream, taking under a second to identify most messages.

If a message is not matched by any rule, it's checked to see if it's spam and if it passes that test, it's put into an `unknown` folder.

2.3 Spam, Spam, Spam, Spam

Hard rules are great for figuring out if an email came from a particular mailing list or a friend with just a few email addresses.

Hard rules don't always work for detecting spam.

One rule that does work (frequently) is to check whether or not the `To:` field of the header matches the expected user. This doesn't work for many mailing lists where the `To:` field is modified. (The Google Summer of Code `To:` field is sometimes `To: Google Summer of Code Mentors List .` Mail from mailing lists can usually be matched by checking the `Sender:` and `Reply-To:` fields. Once these have been weeded out, the test for `To:` works.

2.4 Open the pod baysean door, Hal

Given the dynamic and changing spam contents, you need a dynamic spam detection technique, not hard-coded algorithms or even sets of keywords.

The baysean statistical tests work by checking word counts in a suspect piece of mail against good mail and known spam mail. Put simply, the test mail gets a point for every word that only appears in good mail, and loses a point for every word that only appears in spam mail.

In the implementation, each word is assigned a positive value between 0 and 1 based on how often it appears in spam or good email, then the average value for the words in an email is calculated. If the value exceeds 0.7, it's very likely to be spam.

A sample of words from my dictionary looks like this:

```
purported 0.1
brownie 0.1
bytes 0.1
TANSTAAFL 0.1
listening 0.200642136694
routine 0.200838638462
automated 0.601255325782
warranties 0.601255325782
Funds 0.846210738272
funds 0.855801144836
FUNDS .9
Sexually .9
phonesex .9
```

As you can see, words that aren't commonly used by spammers get low scores. The words that are in fairly common use get medium scores, and words that appear in requests for assistance in moving large funds, or email suggesting illicit encounters are most likely to be spam.

This proves that I'm a geek, not a playboy.

Before checking an email, it needs to be cleaned a bit. Removing punctuation marks allows the code to use simple Tcl list commands and not treat a word followed by period as a different word than one not followed by a period.

This cleanup can be done with regular expressions, or the Tcl `string replace` command. Each of these techniques worked, but both were unreasonably slow.

To improve the speed, I wrote a small "C" extension to convert punctuation to spaces. This extension was compiled with `critcl`. It was a few minutes worth of work, and sped up the code greatly.

The addition of the `string map` command in more recent versions of Tcl removed the need for compiled code to clean a message before processing it.

The word definition file contains about 80,000 words. It takes a significant amount of time to read this much data. This becomes an issue when many emails arrive in a clump (for instance, when all the spam-bots owners turn on their PC's in the morning).

The solution to this issue was to make the baysean comparison application a server application which the mail sorting program calls.

The simplicity of using Tcl sockets made this a obvious solution.

The guts of the server simply opens a socket in server mode, waits for a connection and reads lines into a buffer. When an end-of-message marker is received, it processes the message and sends the score back to the client socket.

```
proc readLine {channel} {
   global Server

   set len [gets $channel line]
```

```
   # if we read 0 chars, check for EOF.  Close the
   #   channel if we've hit the end of the road.

     if {($len <= 0) & [eof $channel]} {
         close $channel
         return
     }
     # Watch for an unlikely end-of-message string
     # If it appears, process the message and clear the buffer
     # else append this line to the message being processed
     if {[string match $line "EndOfMailEndOfMail---liaMfOdnEliamFodnE"]} {
          set return [processMessage $Server(input.$channel)]
          puts $channel $return
          flush $channel
          set Server(input.$channel) ""
          return
        } else {
          append Server(input.$channel) " " $line
}
}

proc serverOpen {channel addr port} {
   global Server

   # Set up fileevent to be called when input is available

   fileevent $channel readable "readLine $channel"
   fconfigure $channel -buffering line
}


#
# Open the server for business
#
set server [socket -server serverOpen $Server(port)]
```

This reduced the lag time for sorting mail significantly.

2.5 Double, Double, Toil and Trouble

Occaissionally, my system will end up on a spam-bot's list. The first time this happened, I received over a thousand pieces of identical email each hour.

This event made it obvious that having an easily modified sorting system is a good. It was the work of a few minutes to add a new test to see if a the body of incoming email matched the md5 of previously received email and discard duplicates. The `tcllib` md5 support just worked.

Making this the first test in the sorting application reduced the system load enough that other work could be done while the system was discarding email.

2.5.1 Subtracting with logs

One trick that reduces spam-bot email is greylisting. This technique refuses email from a new sender with a "temporary mail failure" message. The greylist milter waits a given length of time (usually about 1/2 hour) before the email from a new site will be accepted.

The justification for this technique is that legitimate email processors will accept a temporary failure for an email server and will retry. The spam-bots will either give up after one attempt or the user may turn the machine off before the retry interval elapses.

When I first installed the greylist milter on my mail server it reduced the spam count to about 1/10'th the amount of spam I had been receiving.

The commonly used greylist milter provides an easy to read ASCII log that includes the name of systems that have attempted to deliver email, the time of the attempt and the recipient address (which may be `bogusName@mysite.com`).

It's simple with Tcl to read that file and look for sites that have tried multiple times to send email to many different addresses (legit and otherwise). These sites (particularly ones trying to send to invalid addresses) are probably spam bots.

It's nice to not receive spam email, but it's even nicer to not even have to process it. Most Linux and Unix systems have firewall support that allows the system to reject any connection from a host.

The Tcl `exec` command provides a simple way to add a firewall rule that will drop any future connection from a given IP address. This reduces the load on the email server (it doesn't need to process data) and potentially crashes the spam-bot.

After a couple hours the IPTables rules are removed. If a site is actually legit, but being misused (for instance, an ISP that has had a number of customer's machines become infested), email will be received from that site again (until the site goes rogue again).

3 Mr. MUA Check and see - is there some email, some email for me?

These techniques work for reducing the amount of email that gets into the system, but eventually a user would like to read the email that's been sorted, folded, spindled and mutilated.

The mail read/sort application puts the email into individual files using the in Unix Mail format based on the sort criteria. All of the files go into the same folder.

Since the only files in this folder are mailboxes, a data-driven GUI can be built to provide a simple MUA to access the mail. The GUI learns what to put on the buttons using the `glob` command, and thus does not need to be modified when a new rule (and new mailbox) is added to the read/sort application.

The main portion of a button based MUA is built from code like this.

```
proc readMail {name}  {
  global Internal

  exec rxvt -e mutt -f $Internal(holderDir)/$name

  fillGUI
}

proc fillGUI {} {
  global Internal
  eval destroy [winfo children .files]
  foreach f [lsort [glob -types f -nocomplain $Internal(holderDir)/*]] {
    set fileName [file tail $f]

    set date [clock format [file mtime $f] -format "%b %d %H:%M"]
    set displ [format "%-12s %10s" $fileName $date]

    set w [button .files.f_$fileName -text $displ -pady 2 \
      -command "readMail $fileName"]
    pack $w -side top -anchor w -expand y -fill x
  }
}
pack [frame .files]
```

3.1 A MIME is a terrible thing to waste

The `mutt` mail reader, like `pine`, `elm` and other modern text-based mail readers works for many things and supports helper applications to read various MIME formats.

A glitch is reading HTML mail. The default choice for many folks is to invoke `firefox`, `konqueror`, `opera` or some other web browser to read HTML mail.

The problem with this technique is that the spammers who send mail with HTML attachments get tricky and just checking to see if this mail is *really* from Paypal can be enough to mark your email address as a valid addresss and ensure you years of overflowing mailboxes.

This problem led me to write my own HTML viewer. I did this initially using Steve Uhler's HTML widget, and later reworked it to use D. Richard Hipp's htmlwidget.

The advantage of this widget from a security/paranois aspect is that it's absolutely stupid. It does not have any HTTP support. It can't load an image, follow a link, run Javascript or do anything that might alert the outside world that you've read the email.

What it will do is provide a highlighted version of the HTML code to make it easy to find the HREF tags and see if the `Click Here` actually goes to your bank, or to some site in Nigeria.

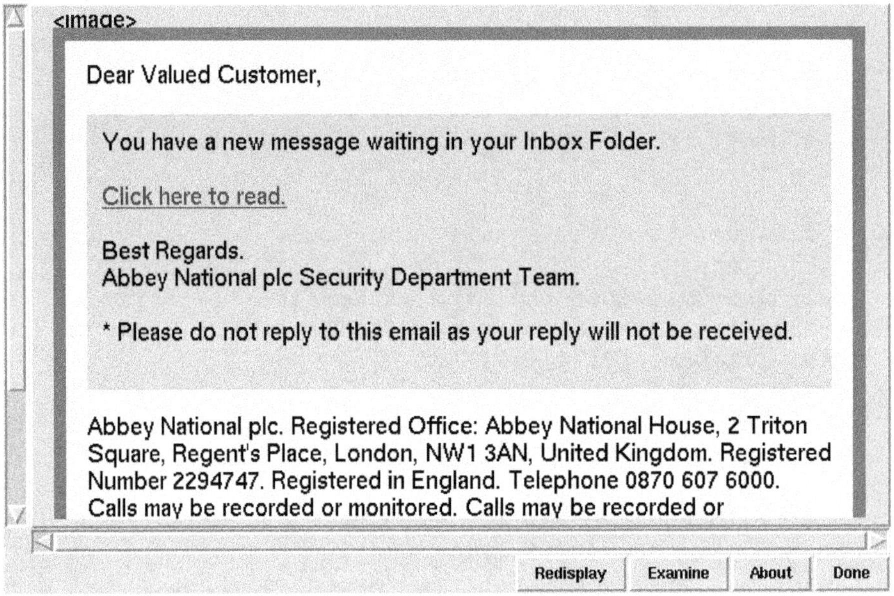

Figure 2: A phish message as viewed in an HTML reader

Figure 2 shows the `htmlview` application displaying a phish attack for a casual read. **Figure 3** shows the same message in `Examine` mode, highlighting the HREF and showing that the actual URL is `abbeynational.co.uk.0e3f0bc994.com`, not `abbeynational.co.uk`.

This application is available at `http://www.cwflynt.com/htmlview/`.

4 Getting to the root of the problem

All of these tools were fairly easy to write and made handling large amounts of email and larger amounts of spam possible.

To truly control the levels of spam, you need to catch it before it gets into your Mail User Agent. It's best if you can even drop something before it's fully sent to the mail server.

`Sendmail` and `postfix` support user written Mail Filters (milters). The `libmilter` library has hooks so that external filtering applications can connect to the Mail Transfer Agent (MTA), receive information about the email as

Figure 3: The same image with the actual URL highlighted

it arrives and send Go/No-Go messages back to the MTA as the connection evolves.

Architecturally, a `sendmail` milter is familiar to a Tcl programmer: a milter registers a callback to be invoked when an event occurs. In this case events include receiving a connection from a remote mail server, receiving envelope information, reading a field in an email header, reading the body of an email and closing a session.

Because a `sendmail` application may be receiving many messages at the same time it uses threads to control the conversations.

At this point, it looks like Tcl and Milters are made for each other.

4.1 It ain't necessarily so

Several years ago, Michael Kirkham `<mikek@muonics.com>` wrote a Tcl Milter extension.

Unfortunately, the `libmilter` has been a moving target, and his need for this extension evaporated, so it was not maintained. His extension is a good start for someone doing more work with `libmilter`, and is available at `http://www.muonics.com/FreeStuff/TclMilter/`.

I downloaded this extension, and discovered that there were some simple issues with thread locking that could be fixed by changing only a few lines of code.

Then the fun started.

4.1.1 Hanging by a Thread

One feature of the `libmilter` architecture is that when an application calls `smfi_main` to enter the libmilter loop the `smfi_main` function will not return until the application exits. After this call, all activity is done via the callbacks to new threads.

Each time a new email message arrives, a temporary thread is created and the filter callback is evaluated in that thread. The overhead in creating a new Tcl interpreter is fairly low, but initializing an interpreter - loading extensions and command files, etc can be slow.

It makes more sense for a Tcl oriented mail filter to maintain a single persistent fully initialized interpreter and only use the per-message threads to redirect control into the primary interpreter.

Each message that the `libmilter` is processing gets a unique identification value that's passed to the "C" layer, and can be passed to the Tcl layer.

For a Tcl programmer, this makes the multiple threads rather redundant. We're used to dealing with this sort of construct with an `upvar` command:

```
proc doStuff {identifier value1 value2} {
  upvar #0 State_$identifier State
  global UniversalState
  # Do what needs to be done
}
```

The `thread::send` command will let one thread send a script to another thread to be evaluated in the target thread. The value returned by evaluating that script in the target thread will be return value of the `thread::send` command.

This feature could allow a procedure running in a per-message thread to send information to be retained to the primary, persistent thread. It also allows a per-message thread pass control to a filtering procedure in the primary thread, and only return the final result to the `libmilter` code.

From a Tcl script writer's perspective, this makes more sense than writing a filter in a thread that has to initialize an interpreter, load extensions, load command files, etc for each email that arrives.

The architecture I ended up with looks like **Figure 4**.

4.1.2 If I had a hammer

This pattern works well. It has been easy to write simple milters to do white, gray and black listing.

One common spam pattern is mail that comes from outside your domain with an Envelope From field from inside the domain. This could be valid mail, if you are the size of IBM with mail servers spread around the planet. Since I

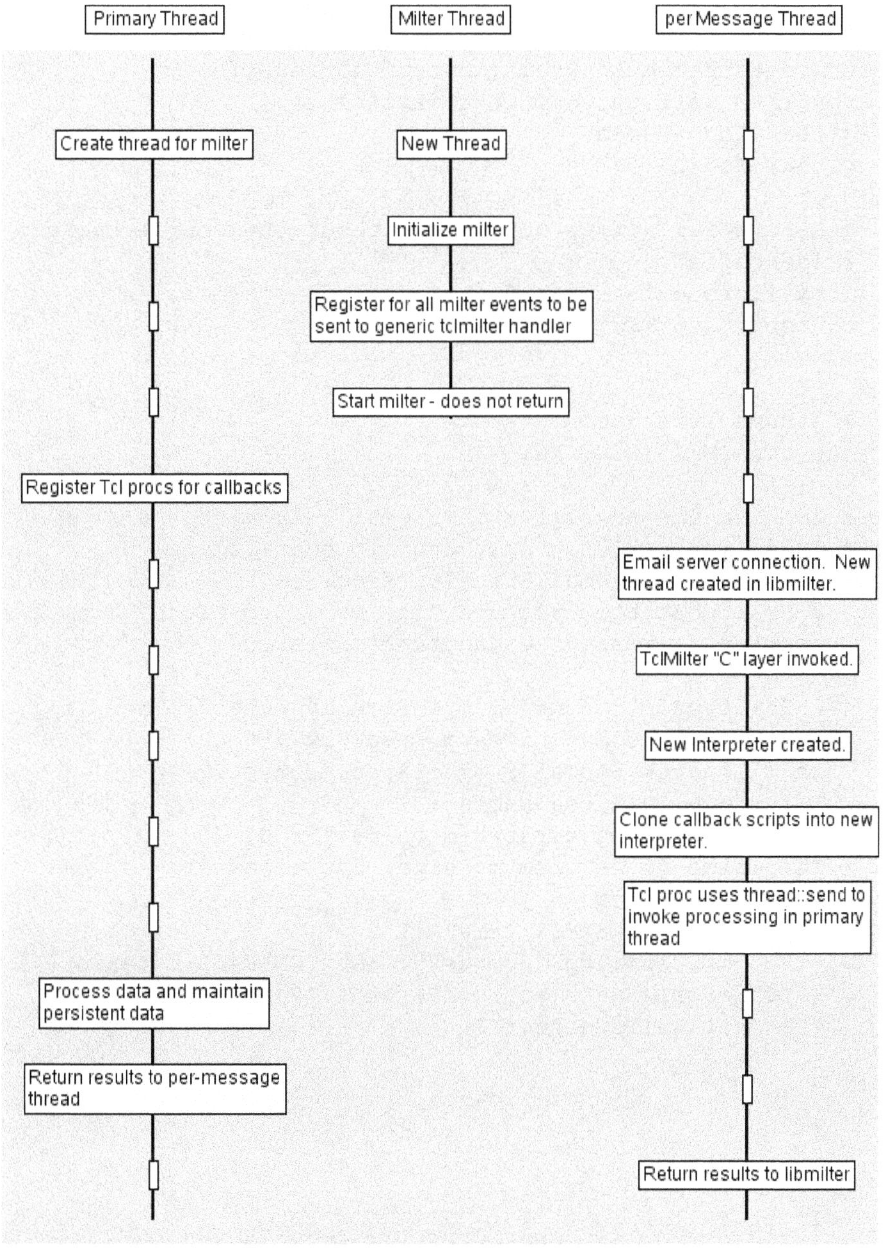

Figure 4: Multi-Thread Flow for TclMilter

only have one mail server, outside mail *never* comes from any of the domains I host.

The code to reject a forged `From:` address is fairly simple:

```
proc rejectForgedEnvFrom {context addressList } {
  upvar #0 mailState$context mailState
  global localNames
  global localIP

  # Return fail if we got here without the source being
  # identified.
  if {![info exists mailState(sourceIP)]} {
     return "SMFIS_TEMPFAIL"
  }

  # Assume it's good mail
  set rtn SMFIS_CONTINUE

  # Look at the addresses this email claims to be from.
  # This list *SHOULD* only contain one element.
  foreach address $mailState(envfrom) {
    # Split out the user and site portions of the From field
    lassign [getNameSite $address] nm site

    # If it didn't come from inside my network, see if it
    # claims to come inside my network.
    if {[lsearch $localIP $mailState(sourceIP)] < 0} {
      foreach id $localNames {
        if {[string first $id $site] >= 0} {
  # It claims to be from my site, but it isn't
  # Fail it and log it.
          set rtn SMFIS_TEMPFAIL
          milter::log "$context: Set TEMPFAIL because \
      from=$mailState(sourceIP) and ..$address.. \
      is not valid sender"
        }
      }
    }
  }

  # If it fails,
  if {$rtn eq "SMFIS_TEMPFAIL"} {
     setreply 451 4.9.8 "Invalid Sender"
  }
  return $rtn
}
```

Another annoying spammer trick is sending email to every possible user on the system - not valid users, but lists like `alpha@noucorp.com`, `baker@noucorp.com`, `gamma@noucorp.com`, etc.

These are never delivered, but the bounce messages clog the mail admin mailbox (making it impossible to actually use the mailbox) and chew up bandwidth.

A procedure similar to the `rejectForgedEnvFrom` proc removed all of that garbage from my system.

Greylisting is not so simple a task. However, the procedure uses under 150 lines of code.

4.1.3 Making Memories

The architecture seems simple and obvious and in small tests the filters worked just fine.

When I put the code into production, it wasn't so much fun.

Within an hour, the milter was using up almost 500 megabytes of RAM, and it was still growing.

Libmilter doesn't simply use threads to control email. It creates N threads at startup, and reuses them as necessary, rather than add the overhead of creating new threads. To further complicate matters, since `sendmail` may need to handle N+M threads at a time (to service N+M connections), it has facilities to handle multiple conversations per thread. Each connection is given a thread and a *context* within that thread to identify the message being processed.

The *context* construct that `libmilter` uses provides a clean just-like-new thread for each conversation, whether the thread has been used before (or is in use by another message currently) or not.

For something as simple as a pure "C" language milter, this isn't a problem.

For an interpreter like Tcl, it's a large issue. Tcl expects a thread to be created, used and to die, or to hang around and have some persistent data available.

The pthread library includes two functions to set and retrieve persistent data.

- `pthread_setspecific`

  Associates a key with a value within a given thread. Each thread can register a key value and retrieve that key value.

- `pthread_getspecific`

  Retrieves the value associated with a key for the calling thread.

The Tcl thread model requires a separate interpreter for each thread, and allows multiple interpreters per thread.

The `pthread_setspecific` and `pthread_getspecific` are used internally by the Tcl thread extension (version 2.6.5) to see if an interpreter has initialized the Thread Specific Data structure yet.

As part of `libmilter` providing a clean context for each message, it destroys data associated with the `pthread_*` calls, causing the Tcl interpreter to believe that it needs to initialize the ThreadSpecificData structure multiple times for a thread. This involves allocating new memory.

When a conversation is complete, the associated interpreter is destroyed, and the thread extension cleans up one ThreadSpecificData structure, though it may have created several.

This seems to be the mechanism behind the memory leaking.

4.1.4 The fat lady ain't singin' yet

Making `libmilter` and Tcl work together is a work in progress. Like Thomas Edison, I've started by trying dozens of ideas that didn't work. Unlike Thomas Edison, I haven't found the one idea that does work.

The most success to date has been to add a command to the thread extension to explicitly clean the ThreadSpecificData structure, and invoke that from the Tcl code that is processing an email conversation.

This has reduced the memory leakage from hundreds of megabytes / hour to merely thousands of bytes per hour. By restarting the TclMilter every 24 hours, it doesn't swamp the email system.

The new code in the thread extension looks like this:

```
static int
ThreadInit(interp)
    Tcl_Interp *interp; /* The current Tcl interpreter */
{
...
    TCL_CMD(interp, THNS"deinit",    ThreadDeInitObjCmd);
...
}

static void
DeInit(interp)
    Tcl_Interp *interp;          /* Current interpreter. */
{
    ThreadSpecificData *tsdPtr = TCL_TSD_INIT(&dataKey);
    ListRemove(tsdPtr);

}

static int
ThreadDeInitObjCmd(dummy, interp, objc, objv)
    ClientData  dummy;            /* Not used. */
    Tcl_Interp *interp;          /* Current interpreter. */
    int         objc;            /* Number of arguments. */
    Tcl_Obj    *CONST objv[];    /* Argument objects. */
```

```
{
    DeInit(interp);
    return TCL_OK;
}
```

5 The Future isn't quite Now

I've used several mail filters in the past. Despite the problems with memory leakage, I'm having more success at controlling email with my homegrown Tcl filters than with mailScanner, greyList and others.

It's fast and easy to add a short Tcl script to perform some new test when I need one. The email environment changes fast enough that yesterday's solution won't protect you from today's problem.

However, writing email filters is not my paying job. Work on the `libmilter` project is a spare time project, and once the code reached a level of useable (if not releasable) I had to move on to other projects.

It is my intention to return to this project. The ease of developing custom milters in Tcl is too useful a technique to ignore.

The C Raster Image Manipulation Package

Andreas Kupries ActiveState Software Inc. 409 Granville Vancouver, BC CA
andreask@ActiveState.com

ABSTRACT

This paper provides an overview of a new image manipulation and processing package for Tcl, the C Raster Image Manipulation Package, or `CRIMP` for short. We will have a quick look into its history, internal organization and implementation, plus current and possible future features and directions to work in.

1. OVERVIEW

`CRIMP`, the C Raster Image Manipulation Package, is a new package for image manipulation and processing in Tcl.

Note that no mention was made of Tk. Its need for an (interactive) X11 display makes the scripting of image processing on head-less servers quite awkward to set up. Not impossible, but definitely not trivial either.

Thus one of `CRIMP`'s goals is to be independent of Tk and avoid that bit of unpleasantness. Another goal was easy extensibility, i.e. the ability to add more functionality quickly and without hassle.

With regard to the available functionality it doesn't contain much yet due to its very young age, and most of what is present is very basic, however I hope to rectify that in the time to come.

The remainder of this paper is structured as follows: In the next chapter an anecdotal overview of the history of this package is provided, such as it is. After that, in chapter 3, a general overview of its design, implementation, and features is given. This is followed by chapter 4 talking about build issues, and lastly chapter 5 discussing possible applications and future directions for the package.

2. HISTORY

`CRIMP` started with my desire to gain more understanding of the algorithms going into image processing in such diverse areas as the post-processing of photos (red-eye reduction, contrast enhancement, pyramid blending, ...) and document analysis (page recognition, binarization, rectification and dewarping, OCR, ...).

Permission to make digital or hard copies of all or part of this work for personal or classroom use is granted without fee provided that copies are not made or distributed for profit or commercial advantage and that copies bear this notice and the full citation on the first page. To copy otherwise, to republish, to post on servers or to redistribute to lists, requires prior specific permission and/or a fee.
Tcl '2010 Oakbrook Terrace/Chicago, IL, USA
.

I was aware of pixane[4], which was not free, and tcl.gd[5] which was focused on drawing charts and not the kind of things I was interested in. Then there is tkImg [6], which is focused on I/O, and bound to Tk [13] as well.

In the end I based it on Andrew M. Goth's "Critcl Image Processing" work found on the Tcler's Wiki [1], with heavy modification of the internals for better caching of values.

Searching around while writing this paper I found a few more, none of which fit exactly my wants either. All are shown in table 1 on the next page.

It still feels a bit like how everybody writes their own OO system for Tcl. Water under the bridge.

Despite the stated goal of Tk independence the current sources are tied to Tk, simply to allow me to see what the algorithms do while I am developing, without having to leave Tcl/Tk.

The connection is however quite thin, and easily severed. It is enough to remove the files matching the glob patterns `read-tk.crimp` and `write-*-tk.crimp`, and to possibly rebuild the binary part, if `critcl` [3] is not used in interactive mode.

In the future one of the things I have planned to do is splitting these Tk dependent parts into a separate package. Right now this will however require either a complete overhaul of the build system, or work on `critcl` [3] to enable the proper handling of package-specific stub tables. One of my side-experiments in this area is the conversion of the `genStubs.tcl` application found in the Tcl [14] sources into a set of packages `critcl` [3] could use to generate the necessary C code just from `.decl` files.

Beyond that nothing much can be said about the history of the package, given that it is only a few months old[1], and very much a work in progress.

3. DESIGN & IMPLEMENTATION

First, images are values. This design decision is inherited from the "Critcl Image Processing" code [1] `CRIMP` is based on.

While this is a disadvantage memory-wise, with the intermediate results of operations piling up even for things were in-place processing would be possible, it makes for much easier semantics too, with processing pipelines constructed easily. And going back to memory, most intermediate results are likely to be reclaimed quickly, i.e have only a very short life with a refcount > 0.

A semi-issue with the representation as values is that they have a string representation, naturally, and thus are acces-

[1] The work started June 25, 2010

Name		Author	License	Notes
pixane	[4]	Evolane	QPL	non-free binaries
tclgd	[5]	Karl Lehenbauer	BSD	chart drawing, → libgd
tkimg	[6]	Jan Nijtmans	BSD	Tk bound, focus on file I/O
megaimage	[7]	George Peter Staplin	BSD	basic ops + chart drawing, abandoned
(tcl)image	[8]	Jim Garrison	GPL	I/O, scanner & OCR bridge; No repository/files
tclmagick	[9]	Rolf Schroedter & David Welton	BSD	→ ImageMagick / GraphicsMagick
imgop	[10]	Emmanuel Frecon	BSD	→tkimg, pure Tcl, `exec` ImageMagick
tkpng	[11]	Michael Kirkham	BSD	Tk bound, PNG I/O only
LRIPhoto	[12]	David Zolli	OLL	

Table 1: Other image handling packages

sible to all Tcl commands. Doing this is not recommended however as with images shimmering is quickly expensive in both time for the (re)construction of representations and memory used. It is best to use the accessor commands provided by the package instead, to obtain such information. They know the internal structure and can pull the various pieces of data out of it without requiring shimmering.

Here the original internals were modified and refactored, with the original list representation replaced by new Tcl_ObjType's specifically geared towards storing image types and images.

For a deeper look into the internals of the representation see figure 1 below. I am not going into the image types shown there here, save for table 2 on the next page providing a short overview of what we have and may get in the future.

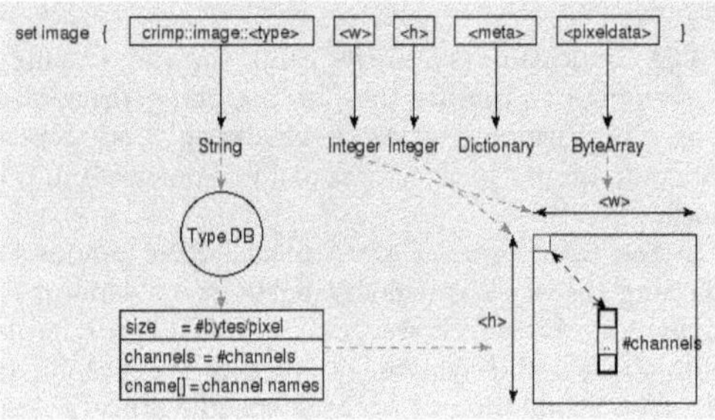

Figure 1: Image representation

Continuing on to the functionality the package is organized into two layers and five main categories. At the bottom the primitives implemented in C, and then a Tcl layer on top of that which implements the policies and heuristics for their easy use [15]. See figure 2 below for a visualization of this structure.

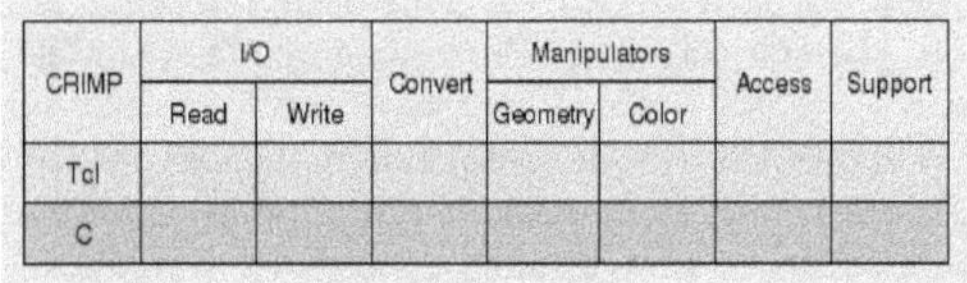

Figure 2: Package structure

Of the five categories both Support and Conversion are relatively small and bounded in size, i.e. with little to no opportunity for extension. C support is the Tcl_ObjType's for the images and image types, the Tcl layer contains commands to handle convolution kernels and function tables, see table table/support on page. Further, the conversion between image types is bounded by the set of types supported and the feasability and/or sensibility of conversion. See table 3 below for an overview.

→	rgba	rgb	hsv	grey8
rgba		X	X	X, split
rgb			X	X, split
hsv	X	X		split
grey8	join	join	join	

Table 3: Image type conversions

For accessors we have the basic ones for extracting the data found directly in an image, see again figure 1, and then higher level ones, image histograms and statistics. This area is thus quite small as well right now, but should have more potential for extension than the two discussed before.

The last two categories, I/O and image manipulation will be the big ones, also with the most potential for extension, with manipulation rating higher on both than I/O. The formats currently supported by the latter are shown in table 4 below. A few other relatively simple formats, like Windows BMP, should be implementable in Tcl as well, however for the more important formats, like PNG [17] and JPEG [18], I expect to not only require C, but also the use of external libraries. Going there might force the use of Tcl 8.6 as well, where the function `TclLoadFile()` is public [19]. A related issue still not clear at this point in time with respect to this, i.e. external libraries, is how to handle the differences between regular use as package, and use within starkits and -packs.

Format		Language	Read	Write
Tk	[13]	C	X	X
PPM	[20]	Tcl	X	X
PGM	[20]	Tcl	X	X
strimj	[16]	Tcl	X	

Table 4: Supported external image formats

A very condensed overview of the currently existing manipulation and support commands can be found in the tables 5 and 6 on the next page.

While this may look like a lot it should be noted that these are all still very basic. The only place where we are already going to higher levels are the commands for the creation of image pyramids.

Name	Colorspace	#Channels	Data/Channel	Data/Pixel	Notes
rgba	RGB	4	1 Byte	4 Byte	
rgb	RGB	3	1 Byte	3 Byte	
hsv	HSV	3	1 Byte	3 Byte	
grey8	Greyscale	1	1 Byte	1 Byte	
grey16	Greyscale	1	2 Byte	4 Byte	Rudimentary
float	Float.Point	1	4 Byte	4 Byte	Rudimentary
grey32	Greyscale	1	4 Byte	4 Byte	Future
bw	Black/White	1	1 Bit	1 Bit	Future

Table 2: Image Types

rotate	90° (counter)clockwise, half turn
flip	horizontal, vertical, diagonals
matrix	Arbitrary projective transforms
resize	crop, cut, expand, up- & downsample decimate, interpolate
alpha	blend, over, set, opaque
binary	add, subtract, difference multiply, screen, max, min
blank	
montage	horizontal, vertical
morph	erode, dilate, open, close gradient, igradient, egradient tophatw, tophatb
filter	convolve, rank
remap	general, invert, solarize, (de)gamma thresholds
pyramid	gauss, laplace, generic
wavy	effect, inherited
psychedelia	effect, inherited

Table 5: Manipulation commands

kernel	make, transpose
table	identity, invert, solarize, (de)gamma thresholds (above, below, in-, outside) gauss, linear, stretch, log, sqrt, eval
map	s.a.

Table 6: Manipulation support commands

Image processing is a large field and we should be able to add to this package for years to come. Some of the possibilities will be addressed in chapter 5.

4. BUILDING

Going forward I have to address a few issues with building this package. While the inherited use of `critcl` [3] has made this relatively easy, i.e. just run `critcl -pkg crimp.tcl`, it is not all roses.

First, it is necessary to hack the package underlying it a bit. It comes with the C files for the Tcl/Tk 8.4 stub declarations to avoid the need for an explicit stub library to link against. `CRIMP` however is based on Tcl 8.5, so we need its stub tables and C files. While a fairly easy replacement having to do it is a barrier to use. It would be, IMHO, much better if critcl could infer the correct version to use from the `package require Tcl ...` statement found in `CRIMP`'s sources.

Then comes the issue of the application not having an explicit `exit` command. Which means that when we use `critcl -pkg` to build `CRIMP`'s shared library for distribution the application will **not** exit, but enter the eventloop started by the `package require Tk`.

Beyond these bugs we have a number of smaller annoyances, namely the need to explicitly list the Tcl files used by the package (via `critcl::tsources`), instead of infering them from the executed `source` command, and, similarly, the need to explicitly use `critcl::config tk 1` to signal that this is a Tk package, instead of infering the same from the `package require Tk`.

5. FUTURE DIRECTIONS

Compared to the short history shown in chapter 2, I hope that the future of `CRIMP` is much longer and enduring. It is certainly filled with lots of work needing to be done.

Here I will mention only a few things I consider to be interesting, and otherwise refer to the ticket system reachable through `CRIMP`'s Wiki page [2], both for getting a list of existing ideas, and as the place where more can be entered, hopefully even with implementations.

1. The C level primitives currently have a great deal of redundancy in them, like replicating code for RGB and HSV, etc. stuff which is formally different, yet identical in code.

   Cleaning this up should be a medium-sized project. It is not trivial IMHO, because of the opposing tension to have the whole code of a primitive in a single function, to enable compilers to perform lots of optimizations, like loop unrolling and such. Which is something we really should preserve.

2. Most image processing tasks are what is called "embarassingly parallel". Thus an "easy" path to higher performance should be to slice an image and then dispatch the parts tiles, stripes) to many threads which can then make easy use of today's multi-core processors.

   This requires more refactorization of the C layer, moving the actual functionality into functions which are separate from the API functions. With that in place we can then add the slice'n'dice code and the thread-management.

3. Better algorithms, either faster, or conserving memory. For example, the current convolution filter primitives are implemented in the spatial domain. An FFT based implementation should be faster, especially for large kernels.

That said, FFT is a useful primitive in its own right, and should be exposed, not just used for convolution.

4. Another venue to explore is dynamic code generation, in various forms.

   Our use of `critcl` [3] already allows a bit of this, although it requires an external compiler, which is not present everythere. Even so, when we come to implementing the binary morphology operators we can already follow Leptonica's [27] route which is to generate C code for a number of important structuring elements (SEs) for full performance, and falling back to a general implementation for anything outside of that set.

   With a truly integrated compiler we would be able to do one better, generating C code for any SE, which then gets compiled to machine code. Then add caching. Another possibility, skip C and the compiler and use a general IR instead, like the input for LLVM, essentially a portable assembler.

5. Higher level operations for the processing and analysis of photos, like

   (a) Fully automatic contrast enhancement.

   (b) Fully automatic panorama stitching. This alone will require operations like SIFT[2] keypoint[24] extraction and matching, computing projective transforms, RANSAC [25], etc.

   (c) Construction of 3D information, lots of overlap with the previous point, plus bundle-adjustment, Levenberg-Marquardt [21], generally "Structure from Motion" algorithms.

   This then goes on into the wider field of photogrammetry and mapping.

   (d) Face detection and recognition.

   (e) General object detection and recognition.

   (f) Generally computer vision [22].

6. Higher level operations for the processing and analysis of documents, like

   (a) Page segmentation (text/image areas, fore/background).

   (b) Detection, analysis and removal of document warp.

   (c) OCR

   (d) Barcode detection, recognition, and extraction.

In conclusion, the Fossil [26] repository containing **CRIMP**'s sources can be reached via the package's Wiki page [2] and is open to all and sundry to provide ideas, code, bug reports and -fixes, etc.

APPENDIX

A. REFERENCES

[1] Andrew M. Goth, Critcl image processing. `http://wiki.tcl.tk/26052`

[2] Andreas Kupries, CRIMP. `http://wiki.tcl.tk/crimp`

[3] Jean-Claude Wippler, Steve Landers, CriTcl. `http://wiki.tcl.tk/critcl`

[4] Evolane, pixane. `http://www.evolane.com/software/pixane/`

[5] Karl Lehenbauer, tclgd. `http://code.google.com/p/flightaware-tcltools/`

[6] Jan Nijtmans, tkImg. `https://sourceforge.net/projects/tkimg/`

[7] George Peter Staplin, megaimage. `http://whim.linuxsys.net/files/megapkg_rev_2415.tar.bz2`

[8] Jim Garrison, tclimage. `http://sourceforge.net/projects/tclimage`

[9] Rolf Schroedter, David Welton, tclMagick. `http://tclmagick.sourceforge.net/`

[10] Emmanuel Frecon, imgop. `http://www.sics.se/emmanuel/?Code:imgop`

[11] Michael Kirkham, tkPNG. `http://www.muonics.com/FreeStuff/TkPNG/`, `https://sourceforge.net/projects/tkpng/`

[12] David Zolli, LRIPhoto. `http://wfr.tcl.tk/LRIPhoto` (French)

[13] Various, Tk. `https://tcl.sourceforge.net`

[14] Various, Tcl. `https://tcl.sourceforge.net`

[15] Jean-Claude Wippler, Poli-C. `http://wiki.tcl.tk/polic`

[16] Richard Suchenwirth. Strimj. `http://wiki.tcl.tk/strimj`

[17] PNG Homesite. `http://www.libpng.org/`

[18] JPEG Committee Homepage. `http://www.jpeg.org/`

[19] Kevin Kenny, TIP 357. `http://tip.tcl.tk/357`

[20] Jef Poskanzer, Portable any map. `http://en.wikipedia.org/wiki/Portable_anymap`

[21] Wikipedia, Levenberg-Marquardt. `http://en.wikipedia.org/wiki/Levenberg-Marquardt_algorithm`

[22] Wikipedia, Computer Vision. `http://en.wikipedia.org/wiki/Computer_vision`

[23] Wikipedia, Computer graphics. `http://en.wikipedia.org/wiki/Computer_graphics`

[24] Wikipedia, SIFT. `http://en.wikipedia.org/wiki/Scale-invariant_feature_transform`

[25] Wikipedia, RANSAC. `http://en.wikipedia.org/wiki/RANSAC`

[26] Richard Hipp, Fossil SCM. `http://www.fossil-scm.org`

[27] Dan Bloomberg. Leptonica. `http://leptonica.org/`

[2]Or other feature detection algorithm

MikroConf: A framework for building command-line interfaces, and specific application for the administration of Linux-based network devices.

Stergiakis Alexandros <alsterg@gmail.com>

September 28, 2010

Abstract

In this paper we present MikroConf, a framework for building Command-Line Interfaces (CLI), and the application of it in the administration of Linux-based network devices. MikroConf introduces a number of innovative features that are unique even to commercial-grade products. It is written in Tcl and C, and exploits many of Tcl's capabilities to provide an a rich and consistent interface to users and developers alike.

Introduction

It is typical for large and complex software projects to incorporate a Command Line Interface (CLI) for configuration and/or administration purposes. Such interfaces exploit a more user-friendly, and robust human-computer interaction paradigm, compared to other configuration methods, such as configuration files, shell CLIs and command-line parameters. In the case of network devices, it has become a requirement for vendors to provide a CLI in conjunction with a GUI. MikroConf is the best free/open-source candidate for this application.

Strictly speaking, MikroConf is both a framework for buidling CLIs and the specific application for it in the administration of Linux-based network devices. In the rest of this paper we always use this name to refer to the latter use, however, all of the features covered herein can be applied into any other application.

MikroConf introduces a number of innovative features for the user of a network device:

- It supports (in a safe manner) in-line scripting in the Tcl Programming Language. Regular configuration commands and Tcl commands can be intertwined on the command prompt.
- It supports an event-based configuration paradigm. Tcl procedures can be registered to be invoked when certain events occur (e.g. link up/down).
- Automation of repeated tasks via parameterized macros (Tcl procs).
- Command output can be captured, filtered, manipulated, emailed etc.
- Usability features such as: ANSI terminal colors and highlights, full screen editing of configuration, and others.

These features enable administrators to be more productive, and achieve more robust device configurations.

From the point of view of the developer, MikroConf offers a number of features that eases extensibility and integration:

- It features a modular architecture. New device functionality is introduced in the form of MikroConf modules, which can be easily written in Tcl or C. Dependencies are handled automatically.
- There is clear separation between the declaration of command syntax and its enforcement code (command handler).
- XML description of command structure, syntax and hierarchy, authentication/configuration modes, running-config sections etc.
- The highest possible flexibility in specifying command syntax, described as a deterministic finite automaton.
- Server-Client architecture and transport protocol independence. Multiple concurrent user sessions are supported.

This paper describes the design and organization of MikroConf's framework, its unique features, and how Tcl has been used to implement this design.

The MikroConf Architecture

MikroConf's architecture is divided into the framework and a number of application-specific modules. The MikroConf Framework (or simply Framework) is the backbone on which MikroConf modules (or simply modules) are attached to implement the various configuration subsystems. For example, there can be a module for IP configuration, and another one for dynamic routing.

The goal of the Framework is to make life easier for the developer, by providing a clear API that he can use to easily implement new modules. The API automates most of the common tasks involved in module writing and operation. Examples of such tasks are:

- Module (un-)registration and inter-module dependency handling.
- File system monitoring.
- Command, configuration/authentication mode (un-)registration.
- Logging.
- Dependencies with external binaries, kernel, busybox, or library features.
- Input/Output and error reporting and handling.
- Running external programs and daemons.

A MikroConf Module is a pluggable component that enables configuration of a specific aspect of the system. It is universally identified by its name and its version number. It consists of a set of Tcl source-code files and a set of XML files. These two sets of files help separate the configuration enforcement code, from the aspects that pertain to the interaction paradigm. Simpler modules would most likely have a single source-code file and a single XML file that together constitute the whole module code.

The XML files, also called *Specs files*, define what we call in MikroConf, *Module Specifications*. That includes:

- New configuration modes defined by the module
- New authentication modes.

- New commands and paths.
- The structure, syntax and description of each command.
- New running-configuration sections and entries.

The exact structure of a Specs file is described by a DTD document, included in MikroConf's sources.

The Tcl source-code files, are collectively called *Configuration Enforcement code*. They are comprised mostly by callback procedures, which are called at various occasions, such as when:

- The module is first loaded
- A command that belongs to the module is executed
- Another module is requesting an exported service
- The module is unloaded or reseted.

In case where many source-code files are used, one of them is the entry-level file, also called *Module file*. This file is loaded first, and loads any other source-code files as necessary.

High-Level Design Choices

During the design and implementation of MikroConf we made a number of important decisions, that have deep and long-lasting effect on MikroConf. In this section we discuss and justify these high-level design choices.

Use of Interpreted Language

Applications for embedded systems are traditionally written in a compiled language, and in particular in C. This practice is justified by the following facts:

- C is suitable for low-level system programming, which traditionally is needed for deeply embedded systems. Such embedded systems don't feature a complete operating system, but instead the embedded software must tackle with the hardware directly.
- C produces compact code with very few library dependencies, resulting in small flash and memory footprint. The C standard library is quite small comparing to the standard libraries of other languages like C++.

- Historically C compilers produce code that runs fast. However, newer compilers for other languages produce equally fast code.
- C (like any compiled language) produces binary code that "hides" the source code on the target device. This is desirable for Intellectual Protection, as well as for minimizing exposure to patents and copyright threats of other parties.

With the advent of Linux and the increased capabilities of the hardware, many of these factors have become invalidated. In particular:

- It becomes possible now to use C for the low-level system programming, and an interpreted programming language for other parts of system programming, that don't require low-level access to the hardware.
- The extra overhead of interpreted languages becomes bearable, as embedded systems have grown in hardware resources, from a few hundreds of kilobytes of memory and flash, to a couple of megabytes.
- The processor speed has also been increased, making possible to run the slower interpreted programs with sufficient speed.
- Interpreted languages have been improved in technology. It is now possible to compile interpreted code to bytecode that runs in a comparable speed to C programs.

Based on these facts, and contrary to the tradition, we decided to use a combination of compiled and interpreted languages for MikroConf. C is used for the parts that need low-level system programming, and for the rest Tcl, a high-level interpreted language. This combination gives us the following advantages in comparison to using pure C:

- Easy debugging and patching. The code can change on the fly without recompilation on the embedded system.
- Tcl is a glue language. This promotes re-usability of existing system-level components (external programs), by glueing them together with a thin interpreted language code layer.
- Speeds-up development process. Programming in Tcl is much more easier and efficient than in a compiled language. Studies have shown that there is a 1-10 correspondence between Tcl and C code, in terms of lines of code. In other words, one line of code of Tcl,

would take ten lines of code if it was written in C (in average).

- Since less code is being written, it is easier to spot logical bugs in the code.

Use of Tcl

It turns out that Tcl is particularly suitable for the task, for the following reasons:

- Its syntax naturally resembles the customary user interface paradigm used in CLAIs, which is: word1 word2 word3 ... So Tcl code and device configuration commands look the same. Which means that both can coexist naturally on the same command prompt.
- The majority of Linux system configuration is performed via text commands or text files, which makes Tcl a good choice, because everything in Tcl is text and it has superior text processing capabilities.
- It's easy to learn, both for developers (writing modules) and users (in-line scripting).
- The standard Tcl interpreter is quite small comparing to some other interpreted languages, around 700kb, and there exist a number of different minimalistic TCL implementations, which are less than 100kb.
- It turns out that the question mark and tab characters don't have any special meaning in Tcl, and hence they can be used by MikroConf without breaking interoperability with Tcl.

We found in Tcl a number of build-in features that were particularly helpful for the development of MikroConf:

- The ability to rename and delete commands.
- Variable, command and execution traces.
- The build-in mechanism for finding and loading Tcl modules.
- The Tcl Virtual File System.
- Tcl threads and interpreters.
- The ability to customize error handling.
- The catch-all mechanism for commands that are not recognized.
- It's standard library and many other libraries and extensions.
- The Safe interpreter security mechanism.

Maximizing Outsourcing

To minimize development effort, one important design goal for MikroConf was to maximize exploitation of what it is already offered by the FOSS community. The idea is to utilize existing FOSS projects and mechanisms that are included in a typical Linux-based firmware, both for configuration enforcement (set) and information retrieval (get). And since each individual FOSS project uses radically different approaches for set and get, a glue language like Tcl, comes very handy to integrate all these heterogeneous components together.

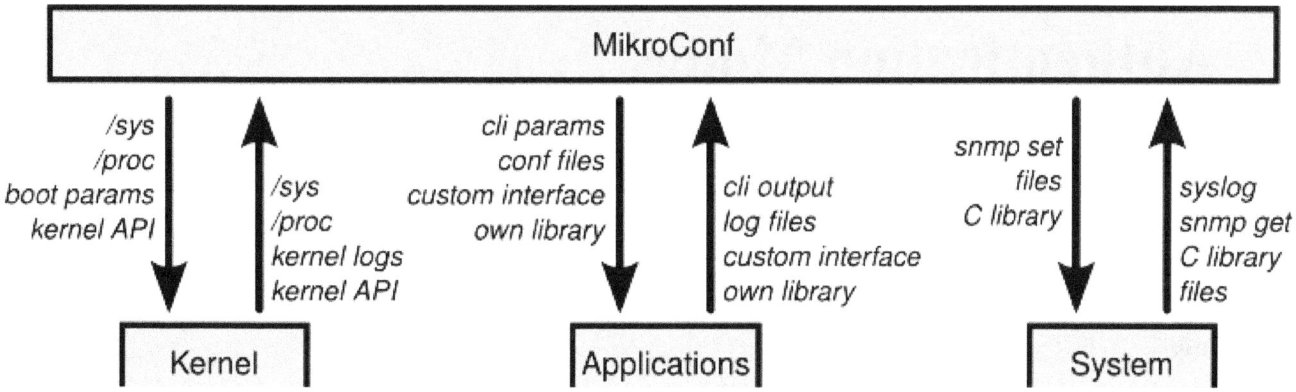

Set Method	Examples
External Program Execution (exec)	Interface configuration (ifconfig)
Kernel Virtual Filesystems (/sys, /proc)	IP forwarding, Security options
Kernel Boot Parameters	Console settings, Password recovery, Module parameters
CLI program arguments	Busybox DHCP Client (udhcpc)
Application Configuration files	DNS Server (dnsmasq)
System Configuration files	Timezone (/etc/TZ), Static IP-Hostname mappings (/etc/hosts), DNS Settings (/etc/resolv.conf)
SNMP SET	Not currently used

Table 1: Configuration enforcement methods.

Get Method	Examples

Syslog	Debug messages (`debug ...`)
Program Output	Interface Configuration (`show interfaces`), Logged-in Users (`show users`)
Kernel Virtual Filesystems (/sys, /proc)	OS info
Low-level APIs through Tcl binary extensions	Checking POP3 mailbox (`mail check`)
SNMP GET	Not currently used

Table 2: System information retrieval methods.

Authentication Modes

MikroConf supports arbitrary number of authentication modes organized in a tree hierarchy, with increasing privilege level from the root to the leafs. Therefore the authentication mode on the root is the less privileged of all. The side figure gives an example tree of authentication modes. It consists of four modes: user, inspector, admin and priv, with corresponding privilege levels: 0, 5, 15 and 15 respectively.

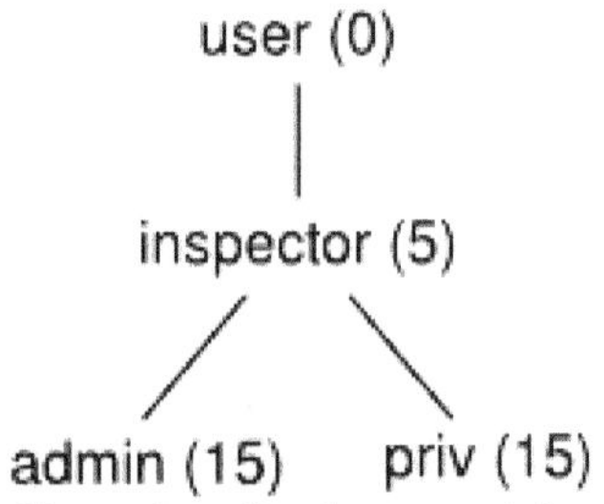

Drawing 2: A tree with four authentication modes.

When a User logs-in to the system, he automatically enters the root of the tree. In order to move to an other authentication mode, he has to traverse the complete path that connects the two modes.

Certain commands can be made accessible only to authentication modes of certain privilege level or higher. Due to the organization of the authentication modes in a tree structure, this is the same like saying that certain commands can be made available to subtrees of the complete tree of authentication modes. Switching mode requires the execution of a MikroConf command, which of course must be visible in the authentication mode we are switching from.

Different MikroConf Sessions can be artificially confined within different subtrees of the complete tree of authentication modes. When this feature is used, then a session enters directly on the root of its subtree, and cannot escape to authentication modes above its artificial root. We will see why this feature is useful when we talk about Background Sessions in a later paragraph.

An authentication mode is declared by some MikroConf module which is called the owner for this authentication mode. Thereafter, other modules can make use of this authentication mode, as long as the owner module remains loaded.

Configuration Modes

Configuration Modes are in many ways similar to Authentication Modes. They are organized in a tree structure, and moving around along the tree paths requires execution of commands. Sessions can be confined in sub-trees of the whole tree of configuration modes, and upon session establishment they always enter to the root of their tree.

Every configuration mode dictates the minimum privilege level required in order for its commands to be executed. Individual commands within a configuration mode can optionally impose a more restrictive privilege level, but not a less restrictive one.

The module that initially declares a configuration mode is the owner of this mode. Other modes can then expand it with their own commands. Hence, a configuration mode can be collectively defined by many MikroConf modules, each of which defines a segment of it. However, the owner of a mode should always remain loaded, as long as other modules rely on it.

Configuration Enforcement

In the previous section we enumerated the methods that we are using to apply configuration directives in a MikroConf-enabled device. In this section we further elaborate, and discuss the assumptions that we make, the overall design of our configuration enforcement approach, and some of the internals of the implementation.

Design Choice: One way flow of configuration

In MikroConf, when setting configuration, actions are taken to enforce it on the surrounding software environment. However, when showing configuration with the `show running-config` command, the software environment is generally not queried. The answer will be based on what

MikroConf things is the case, which of course depends on the configuration commands that have been successfully applied so far.

Conversely, if there is a bug in MikroConf and a configuration command is accepted but not enforced, or if the underlying system configuration changes via other means, then `show running-config` will show a configuration that does not correspond the "real" system configuration. We can say that the running-config shows the intention of the administrator, and not the actual system configuration. In the optimal case where there is no software bugs, the two should be match. This is not necessarily the case for other show commands, that typically display the output of external programs, which accurately reflect the actual system configuration.

This one-way flow of configuration greatly simplifies the design and implementation of MikroConf modules. Otherwise, module writers would have to query the underlying system and/or parse complex configuration files in order to derive the necessary information to generate the running-config. Running a program with some arguments or writing a complex file, is far easier than parsing the output that a program generates or a complex configuration file. Parsing would most certainly need regular expression matching and/or parsing based on grammars (with scanner and parser).

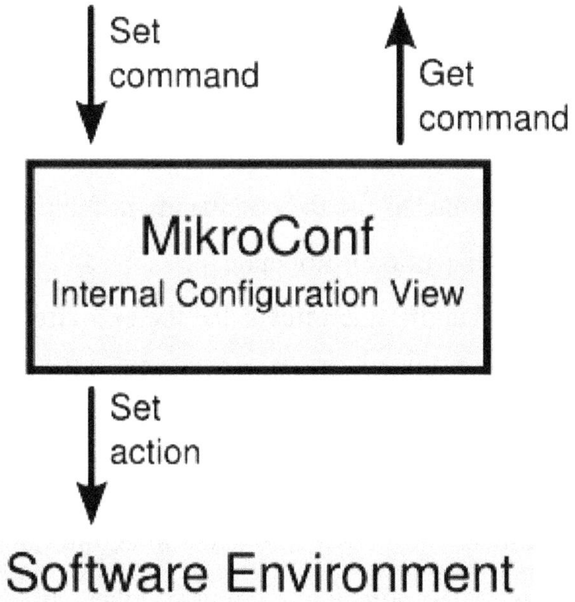

Drawing 3: The flow of running configuration directives.

A side effect of this decision is that all configuration must go through MikroConf. **No manual configuration is allowed, or by any other means**, at least for a subsystem that a MikroConf module exists and is loaded.

MikroConf's *Internal Configuration View* is essentially Tcl variables, arrays and memory objects that store the running configuration in the format that is most convenient to MikroConf module. The running-config is generated based on this data. The startup-config on the other hand is merely a regular file on the file systems.

Design Choice: Active generation of running-config

One approach in generating the running-config, is to merely remember the issued (and successfully executed) commands, and listing them when the running config is requested. We call this passive generation of the running-config, because it doesn't involve any Tcl code that generates dynamically the running-config.

This approach has many flaws. One problem is that it is difficult to match the positive and negative forms of a command. Remember that the two forms don't need to have the same syntax, and a negative command can cancel many positive ones at once. Therefore, merely recording commands and listing them, has the problem that it is not possible with the information available to match positive to negative commands and vice verse.

In any case, an approach must give satisfactory answers to the following questions:

1. One question is in what order to list the commands in the running-config. Merely listing them in reverse order of execution is not enough.
2. A second issue is how to handle side-effects that the execution of a command can have on other, previously executed commands. For example, turning off RIP dynamic routing, should also remove all other RIP-related commands.
3. Sometimes the negative form of a command must be displayed, instead of the positive form. An example is the `no shutdown` command under interface configuration mode.
4. Sometimes a positive or a negative command takes effect by default, but is not necessarily listed in the running-config.
5. And finally, any MikroConf module must be able to include commands for listing in any place in the running-config, and at run-time.

The approach that we follow in MikroConf enjoys all this versatility.

There are two elements that together construct the in-memory representation of the running-config: The *Running-config Section* (or simply section) and the *Running-config Entry* (or simply entry). The in-memory representation is a tree structure, consisting of sections that include as children other sections and/or entries. At each branch level on the tree all sections and entries are ordered based on an *Order Number* assigned to them.

Each section has a name, a parent section, and an order number. Each entry has a parent section, an order number, and a callback Tcl procedure. The callback Tcl procedure when executed returns text that is displayed verbatim on the running-config.

When the running-config is requested, the algorithm visits all sections and entries in the tree, starting with the root and progressing to the leafs in a depth-first fashion. At each branch the section or entry with the smallest sequence number that hasn't been visited before is selected first. When an entry is encountered, its callback procedure is executed and the returned value is concatenated at the end of the "working" running-config. When all the tree nodes are visited the algorithm terminates, and we have the complete running-config.

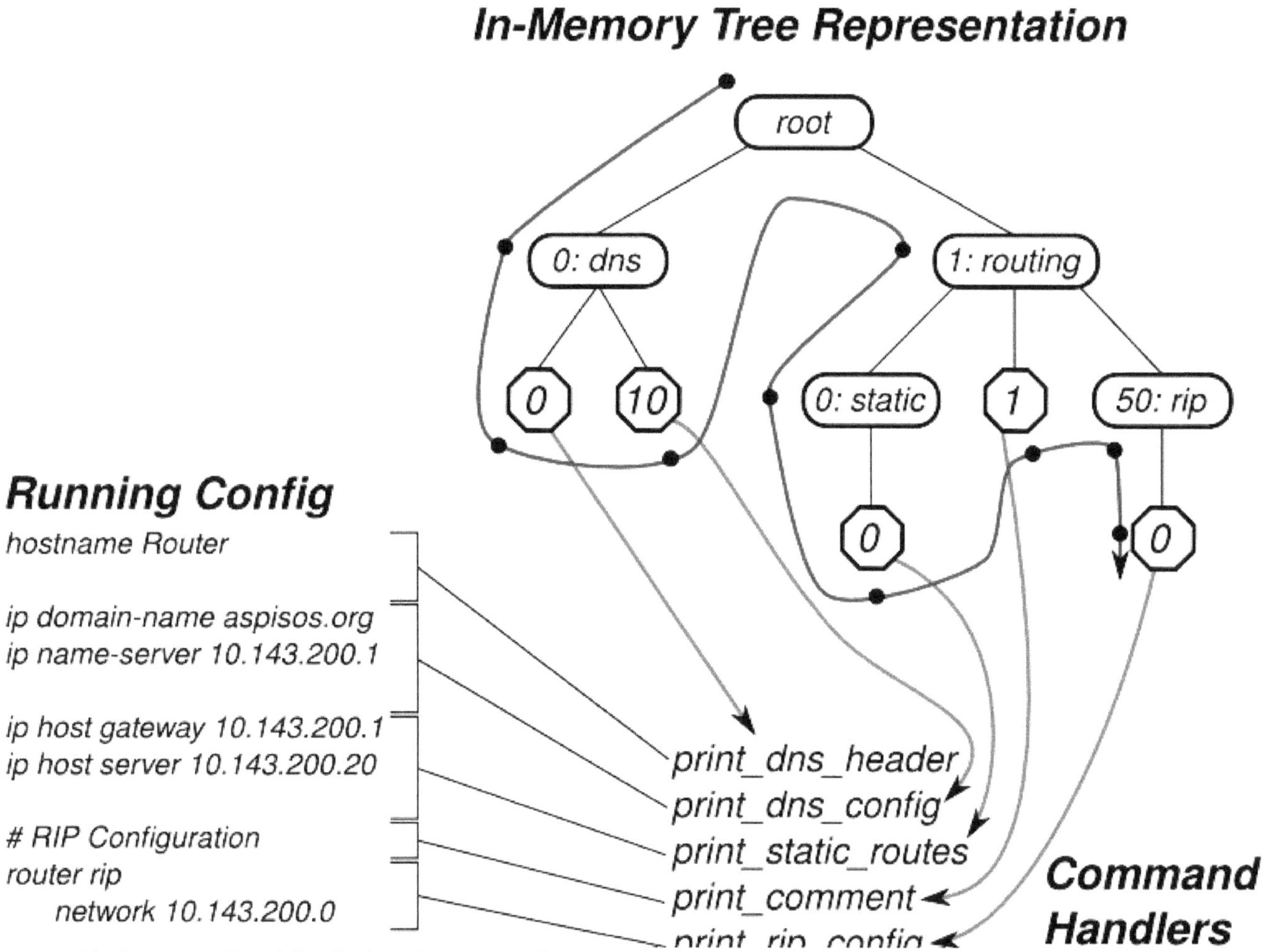

Albeit versatile, this design has one disadvantage: Normally the syntax specifications for MikroConf commands reside on a separate XML file (or many) that accompanies a MikroConf module. With this design, a module's Tcl code also needs to be aware of the syntax of the individual commands, since the commands have to be generated back from the Internal Configuration View.

Design Choice: Apply anew on boot

As configuration commands are enforced on the software environment, files get written and initialization scripts can change. These system files reflect the running configuration, but they are not kept for next reboot. Instead, the startup-config is applied on boot and all configuration enforcement operations are preformed again.

At first glance, this doesn't seem a good design, as the boot time increases. Keeping those files would reduce boot time, because we wouldn't have to go through the normal command-execution/command-enforcement loop of MikroConf.

However, there is a very good reason for doing so, which also simplifies MikroConf's design. The problem arises when the hardware settings of the underlying device change between two boots, or a MikroConf module is removed or get updated. When the system reboots, some configuration files on the file system will not reflect the changed environment, and this can cause hidden configuration or misconfiguration on the device.

On the other hand, if the startup-config is always applied on boot, and no system-level configuration files are kept between reboots, then such changes in the hardware or software environment will most likely cause an error in the execution of some of the commands in the startup-config. MikroConf will reject the erroneous commands, and the system will remain in a stable state.

Design Choice: Incremental Configuration

From what we have discussed so far, it must be clear that the running-config and the underlying system configuration must be synchronized at all times. A configuration command must always be reflected back to the operating system. This is an Incremental Configuration approach, because it allows for single independent commands to be executed and take effect immediately.

We also considered a non-incremental approach that seems to simplify the design, but we ruled it out on the basis of failing user's assumptions. In the non-incremental approach we would enter configuration commands at some point in time, and at some later point we would enforce them all at once by entering the special command `submit`. Then the internal view would be synchronized with the operating system. This approach makes module coding easier, because we don't have to worry about the interactions between different commands. All command handlers assume factory settings before they are executed.

For example consider the case: (it does not apply to MikroConf, but demonstrates the point)

```
Router(config)# service password-encryption
Router(config)# enable password foobar
```

In this simple example we enable password-encryption before we specify a password to be encrypted. When the `enable password` command is later entered, it has to take into consideration the possibility that password-encryption was previously requested, and hence the password must be encrypted. With the non-incremental approach the `enable password` command would always be executed first, and hence such conditional checks would not be necessary. There are other more complex examples where the benefits of non-incremental configuration become more apparent.

Information Retrieval

Most of the times the show commands will simply print verbatim the output of external programs. Other, less often used methods, are to parse configuration files, query the /sys or /proc kernel filesystems, or get the required information via a system-level API with a binary Tcl extension. Last, it is also possible to use SNMP GET where-ever applicable.

Except for the `show running-config` command, all other show commands should always reflect the actual configuration of the system, and not the perceived one.

Debugging Information

The `debug` command enables logging of extra debugging information, via the standard MikroConf logging mechanism. This information is most often used for troubleshooting purposes. Responsible for collecting the debug information is the module that owns the particular debug command executed. For instance, the `debug kernel` command owned by the *base* module is responsible for collecting extra kernel debug information and sending them over to MikroConf's logging buffer. From there these messages will be sent to all active user sessions that have their logging threshold to *debug*. A module logs debug info via the standard MikroConf logging mechanism, which sends the logs to MikroConf's log buffer, as well as to the terminal of every active user sessions (granted that their log threshold permits it).

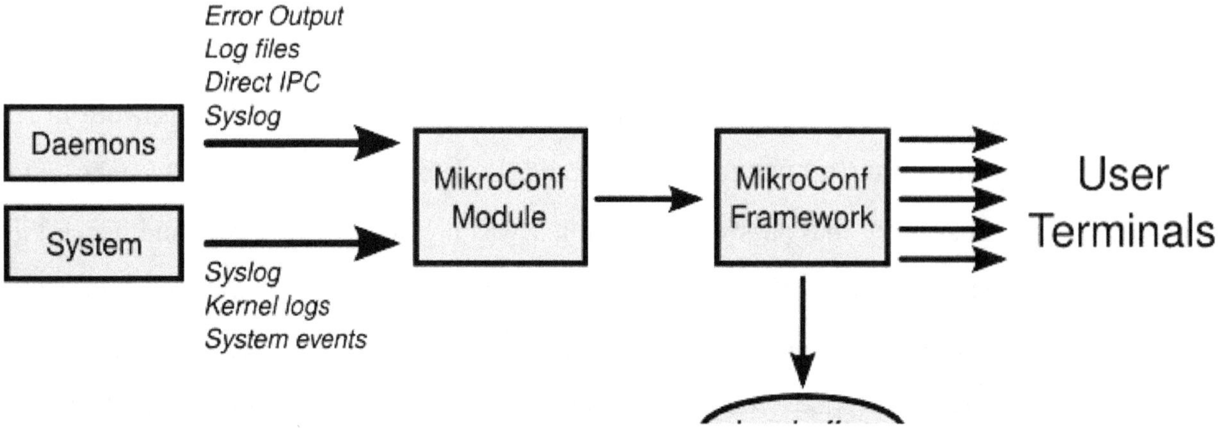

Getting extra debug messages, might require patching of external applications, or special compilation flags, or command line arguments. In any case, these messages can be sent from within the application to syslog and from there MikroConf will pull them, or alternatively they can be sent directly to MikroConf via a IPC mechansim, such as message queues.

Incidentally, MikroConf is using a message queue to pull the syslog messages directly from the syslogd busybox applet.

User-Interface Independence

Since MikroConf modules already go into the length of implementing configuration enforcement procedures for the CLAI, it is desirable to make these procedures accessible also to other possible front-ends, via a appropriate generic interfaces. Three such possible administration interfaces or front-ends are: Web-Gui, NMS, and SNMP. MikroConf is designed to allow all three of them to be layered on top of MikroConf's configuration enforcement code, so that much of the work done for the CLAI can be reused for these interfaces as well.

One important design feature of MikroConf that enables this abstraction, is the separation of the code that handles the user interaction (which is specific to the interaction paradigm), from the code that enforces the actual configuration directives. Each MikroConf command has a corresponding command handler. Command handlers do not receive the words that make-up the command-line one-by-one and in the order they appear. Instead the command-line is broken down into its components, these components are then recognized and passed-on to the handler in the form of a dictionary. The handler can then check the dictionary for the desired information in a convenient manner, without the need to do any parsing of its own. This makes possible to make syntactic changes to a command, without updating the respective command handler, as long as the dictionary remains the same.

An RPC mechanism can be used to export the command handler functionality to remote processes, that follow different interaction paradigms.

Process Architecture

In this section we outline the architecture of MikroConf on a process level. In the following discussion we assume that the reader is familiar with many of the terms used in the context of Unix-like Operating Systems, such as: Process, Daemon, Shell, login process, Interprocess Communication (IPC), Unix Domain Socket, and FIFO (or named pipe).

MikroConf, on a process level, is divided on the *MikroConf Daemon* (or simply the Daemon) and the *MikroConf Shell* (or simply the Shell). At any given moment, only one MikroConf Daemon can be running, while multiple MikroConf Shells can connect to it.

The MikroConf Shell is a normal shell like bash or ash, only that it gives the MikroConf CLAI to the connected user. It is spawned by login after a successful authentication over the network (telnet, ssh, ...) or a local (serial, ...) connection.

When a MikroConf Shell first starts, it connects to the MikroConf Daemon via a Unix Domain Socket, in which the Daemon is constantly listening at. Via this connection it requests for a new session to be allocated to handle the incoming connection. If the Daemon grands the request, it sends back an acknowledgment (with some additional information) via the same socket connection.

The socket connection is maintained throughout the existence of the session. If it breaks for any reason, then both parties know that the session has been terminated, and the Daemon will clean-up any session information, whereas the Shell will simply exit.

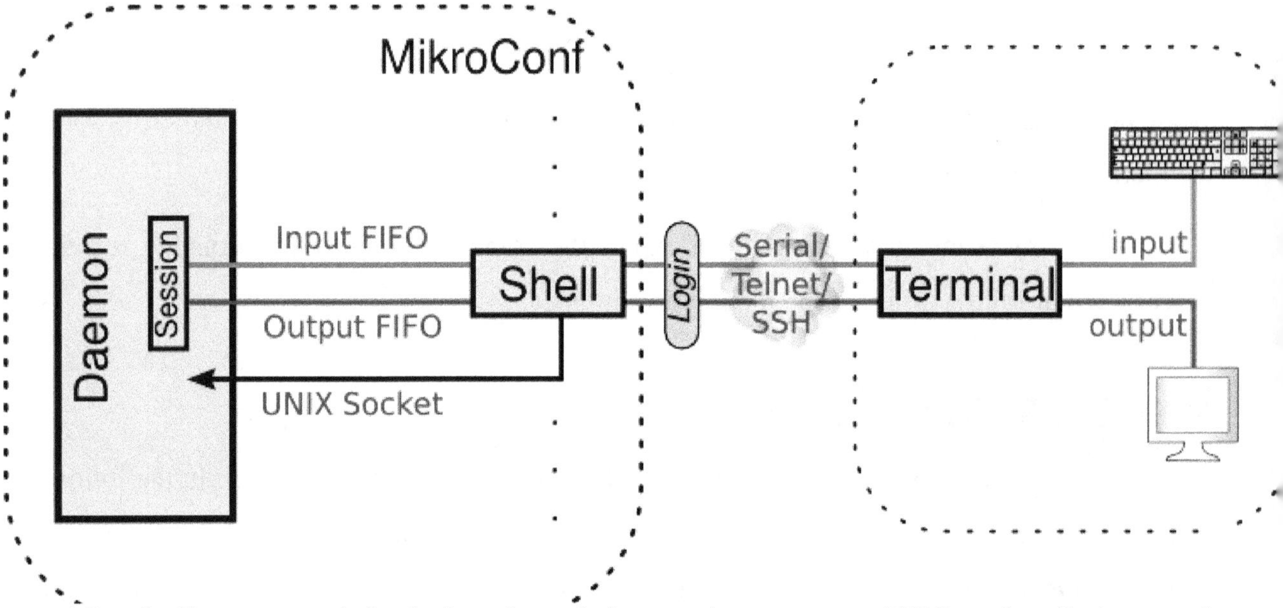

After the Daemon sends back the acknowledgment, it creates two FIFOs to handle input and output from/to the Shell. The Shell redirects its standard input (stdin) to the Input FIFO, the Daemon reads the input from there and processes it. The Daemon writes any session-specific output to the Output FIFO, from which the Shell reads it and redirects it to its standard output (stdout). This way we have a continuous stream-oriented connection from the remote user to the Daemon, for both input and output.

It might sound complex, but in actuality this is a very simple and elegant design, involving simple and standard IPC mechanisms. Most importantly it makes MikroConf connection-protocol unaware. MikroCon doesn't need to "speak" the various communication protocols that can be used to connect remotely to a device. It will work with any remote shell protocol, so long as there is a server implementation for it in the firmware.

Thread Architecture

In the previous paragraph we outlined the architecture of MikroConf on a process level. Now we will see how a MikroConf Daemon process is organized internally in threads. In this discussion we assume that the reader knows the non-exclusive list of terms: Event loop, Threads, Multi-threading, Synchronous and Asynchronous message passing, and Unix pipes.

Processes, Threads, Interpreters

MikroConf is a multi-threaded application, and it builds heavily on the threading infrastructure provided by Tcl. Therefore, before we go ahead and talk about MikroConf's internal architecture, we need to summarize Tcl's threading model. For a more in-depth discussion of Tcl's threading model, please consult external resources.

A Tcl application can initialize and use many Tcl interpreters at the same time, organized in a tree hierarchy. They can communicate by message passing, either synchronous (returned value is waited upon) or asynchronous (returned value is not waited for). Initially, there is only one interpreter, the Master interpreter, which is the root of the tree and can create other child interpreters as needed.

A multi-threaded Tcl application has many threads, each one of them hosting a interpreter tree. Threads can also communicate with each other via synchronous and asynchronous message passing. Such a message has as source an interpreter in one thread, and as target the Master interpreter of another thread. A multi-threaded Tcl application initially starts with one thread, the Master thread, that can later create other threads. The thread organization is flat, not tree-like as the interpreters.

Each Tcl thread has a single event loop which is shared among all hosting interpreters. Any interpreter can send a job to be executed on the event loop of its thread, or to that of other threads. If the job is sent synchronously, then the sender waits for the job to be completed before execution resumes in that interpreter. If it is sent asynchronously, then the execution continues immediately, and result is not waited for. At any given moment (assuming that the event loop is not empty), there is a job being executed, while the remaining ones are waiting for their turn.

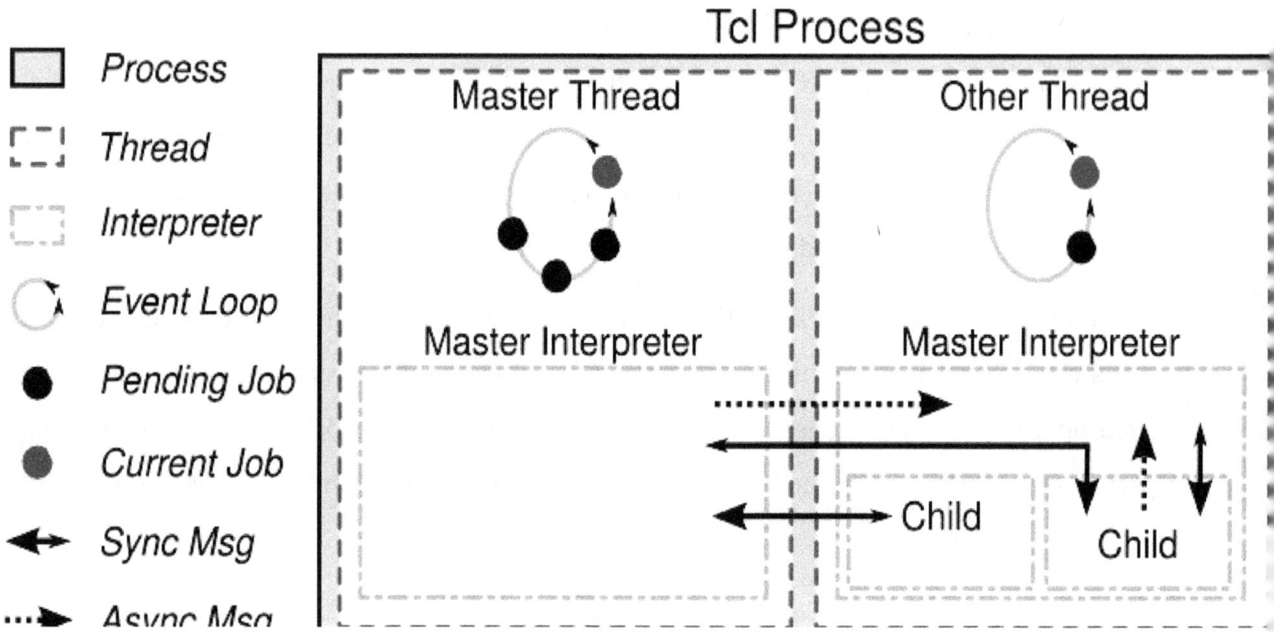

Master, Session, and Slave

As aforementioned, MikroConf relies heavily on Tcl's threading model and interpreter architecture. We start with a *Master Thread* that hosts the *Master Interpreter*. These two alone implement the MikroConf framework.

For every incoming user connection, a new Tcl thread is created to handle it. This per-session thread is called *Session Thread*, and its initial (or master) interpreter is called *Session Interpreter*.

A Session interpreter handles user interaction for its session, among other session-specific things. Each MikroConf Session is identified by a unique *Session ID*, which is essentially the thread id that Tcl returns for the respective Session thread.

Each Session interpreter creates a child interpreter, which we call *Slave Interpreter*. User commands and scripts are safely evaluated within this Slave interpreter.

The next Figure visualizes the information flow. User input that comes through the Input FIFO is read by the Master interpreter and passed on to the respective Session interpreter with the use of a Unix pipe. The Slave interpreter can only access the input stream indirectly via the Session interpreter.

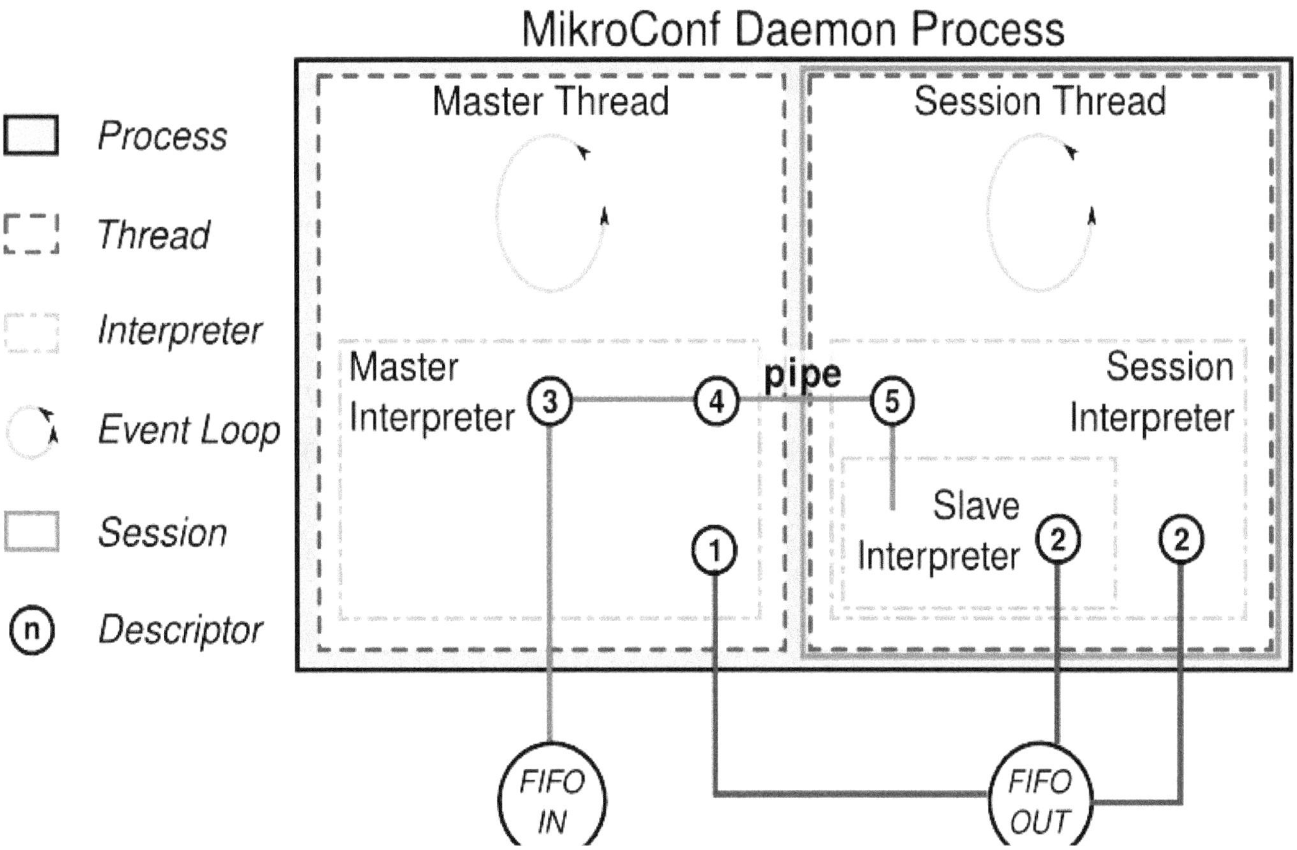

As far as the output stream is concerned, both Master and Session threads maintain a direct connection with the Output FIFO. The Session interpreter shares the file descriptor for the Output FiFO with the Slave interpreter.

Next we give the rationale for the most important aspects of this design, in a FAQ fashion:

Why we need a per session thread

We need a separate Tcl thread for each user session, because we need a separate event loop for each session. The reason we need a separate event loop is that we don't want user actions in one session to block the whole MikroConf application (including other parallel user sessions). This would be the case if we had a single thread (and therefore event loop) for the whole MikroConf application.

For example, with the current design this simple endless loop executed in a user session does not block the MikroConf framework itself or any other parallel user sessions, even though it blocks the Session thread it is executed in (or better say, it puts it in runaway state):

```
Router> while {1} {puts "endless" }
```

Why we need a Slave interpreter for each session

We need the Slave interpreter for two reasons:

1. To enforce restrictive security policies on what Tcl code the user can execute on the command line. The Session interpreter cannot be used for this purpose because it needs full Tcl access, as it handles user interaction and other low-level stuff.
2. To hold any user defined procedures, variables and any other session state created by the user. We don't want to contaminate the Session interpreter with user defined state.

Therefore, command line is evaluated in Slave, where security policy is enforced and user state is isolated. User interaction and other stuff are handled by Session.

Why input stream has to go through the Master interpreter

First of all we need to remind the reader that it does not make sense to open a FIFO for read by many threads, as it becomes non-deterministic which thread receives what part of the input. However, a FIFO opened for write by many threads is ok, since all written data will eventually end-up on the other end of the FIFO, albeit possibly mixed-up.

Having the above in mind, the reason why we needed the input to go first via the Master interpreter is because we want the Master to intercept special keystrokes and enforce them in his execution context. The primary keystroke that is intercept is the break key sequence, which breaks any executed command. If the user prompt is blocked due to evaluation of a user script, Master is the only interpreter/thread that can interrupt the evaluation of the script prematurely. The same applies for other bocking cases.

Why we need to have two direct connection to Output FIFO

We need one connection from the Master in order to print messages and logs asynchronously. And we also need one from the Session, obviously for allowing the user and the Session interpreter to print messages to the terminal.

Background Sessions

One special type of session in MikroConf is the *Background Session*. This is like a user session but without any user connected to it. Instead of being user-driven, it is event-driven. MikroConf uses backgrounds sessions to evaluate event-handlers and to apply the startup configuration on boot.

At any given time there is one background session active, that is used to evaluate event handlers. This background session is called *Events Session*.

Security Policy

As aforementioned, a Tcl *Security Policy* is enforced within the Slave interpreter of each session. A security policy defines what Tcl commands are accessible to the user of the session, and with what functionality each. The policy depends on the authentication mode the user is currently in. More privileged modes have access to more Tcl commands and of less-constrained functionality.

We define three security policies:

- **Background**: This is for background sessions.
- **Privileged**: This is for user sessions in privileged mode.
- **Default**: This is for user sessions in user mode, and for any other session type for which a security policy is not explicitly defined. This is the most constrained polity.

For each security policy we make some changes on the Slave interpreter, which constitute an offset from Tcl's Safe Interpreter Base. The Tcl Safe Interpreter Base is a security policy build-in to Tcl that is considered (by the Tcl developers) safe for most applications. As of Tcl 8.5.1 it is defined as depicted in the next table. Of course it is subject to change in future versions of Tcl.

Command state	**Build-in Tcl commands or procedures**
hidden	file socket open unload pwd glob exec encoding fconfigure load source exit cd

visible	tell subst eof list pid time eval lassign lrange fblocked lsearch gets case lappend proc break variable llength return linsert error catch clock info split array if concat join lreplace fcopy global switch update close for append lreverse format read package set binary namespace scan apply trace seek while chan flush after vwait dict continue uplevel foreach lset rename fileevent regexp lrepeat upvar expr unset regsub interp puts incr lindex lsort string
visible alias	clock

Table 3: The Tcl Safe Interpreter Base.

The actions that we take to modify Tcl's safe security base are:

- **Hide**: We hide additional Tcl commands.
- **Expose**: We expose previously hidden Tcl commands.
- **Alias**: We redefine the functionality of a Tcl command, usually by adding constraints in it or special functionality.

Policy	Action	Commands/Procedures
Background	hide	clock chan interp rename package
	expose	
	alias	unknown proc gets read fileevent fconfigure flush
Privileged	hide	clock chan interp package
	expose	cd exec file glob load open pwd socket
	alias	rename proc unknown gets read fileevent fconfigure flush
User & Default	hide	clock chan interp package
	expose	
	alias	rename proc unknown gets read fileevent fconfigure

Table 4: MikroConf's Security Policies.

You will find the rationale for these decisions documented inside MikroConf's sources (policy.tcl).

Note that we disallow renaming, deleting, or overwriting build-in Tcl commands. These actions are only possible for user-defined commands. User-defined commands must start with a capital Latin letter, underscore or number. This is to avoid name collisions with MikroConf commands, which could cause a lot of trouble to the administrator. This could also have security implications (e.g. install malicious versions of MikroConf commands).

Logs

MikroConf has a central logging mechanism, which aggregates logs from many sources, and handles, stores, and reports them centrally. Namely the event sources are:

- Syslog, the GNU/Linux system log facility. (From syslog we also get kernel log messages that are sent by klogd)
- Output from external applications (like daemons).
- Messages logged in external log files, belonging to other applications.
- Messages logged by the user from on the command line.
- Messages generated by MikroConf itself.

Each log message is associated with the usual syslog properties: the time it was arrived, a severity level, a facility, and a process name. Except for the messages that were pulled from syslog, all the other messages are reflected to syslog as well. This is done so that we can use busybox's syslogd applet to send over the messages to a remote syslog server.

Log entries are stored in a memory mapped file which resides on the file system. The memory mapped region is written in a cyclic manner: when writes reach the end of the region, they continue from the start of it. These two properties (regular file & cyclic writes) gives us a persistent cyclic log buffer. Such a buffer offers two advantages:

1. The logs are persistent across reboots. If a MikroConf router crashes unexpectedly, then after boot we can still find the error messages associated with the crash.
2. The log buffer always holds the newest/latest messages. Therefore, we don't have to deal with log rotation manually.

Of course, for the log buffer to be persistent, the corresponding log file must reside in a persistent file system. If this is not the case then the firmware vendor must write an event handler for the LOG_BUFFER UPDATE tag/event, that is generated when the log buffer changes. This event is rate limited. The event handler should copy the log file to a safe place, in a persistent file system. The firmware vendor must also create an event handler for the SERVER BOOT tag/event, to restore the log file from the safe place, back to its original place where MikroConf expects to find it. This event is generated on boot, before the log buffer is loaded.

Events

MikroConf's event architecture allows for the following:

- A style of aspect oriented programming which makes the source code more understandable and clear.
- Easy and straightforward customization from firmware developers, with no need for knowledge of MikroConf's internals.
- Facilitates the implementation of MikroConf's event-based configuration paradigm.

An *Event* is a combination of two strings: a *Tag* and event *Name*. It can be emitted from anywhere within the Framework or MikroConf Modules.

A generated event is received by the *Event Dispatcher*, which looks for any registered *Event Handlers* for this tag/name combination. If handlers are found, they are executed in the order they were registered. The dispatcher also passes on to each handler any parameters provided at the moment of generation. Multiple event handlers can be associated with a single tag/name combination.

Am Event ID uniquely identifies the exact binding, which can be later used to unregister the event handler.

Event handlers can be executed synchronously or asynchronously. In the former case they are executed **right after** the generated event, whereas in the latter, it is executed when the event loop becomes idle.

Blocking

An important requirement in MikroConf is that the user should be able to break from any executed command by pressing the break key sequence. This requirement affected MikroConf's design a lot, since we have to look at every place where blocking can happen, and figure out a way to interrupt it at user's request. All the possible places where blocking can occur are:

While executing an external program

Sometimes an external program can be long-running. Take for example a VI session. Those programs should be executed with the *ptyexec* command that can be interrupted at any time.

While evaluating a Tcl user script on Slave

As we have seen, the Slave interpreter is where user scripts are evaluated, and during evaluation the prompt is not available. We distinguish two cases of here:

1. A user script runs indefinitely, but without being blocked at any command (that is, it is in a runaway state.
2. A user script has blocked at some command waiting for some something (e.g. some input from a **blocking** channel).

None of these cases are addressed at the moment. This is an area that needs further investigation.

While waiting for user input from the terminal

We provide a non-blocking version of gets, called sgets, that does not block the event loop of the Session, when it is used to receive input from stdin. It works by emulating gets on a non-blocking channel, as it is the case for the input stream of a session. Therefore, when a command handler prompts the user for some input using the sgets procedure, the user can break out of it.

While executing the body of a command handler

There are times where some Tcl code can block, such as when waiting for a network event to occur. For these cases where blocking is a possibility, we provide a solution in the form of two commands: `timeout` and `blocks`. The former will interrupt execution of its body after a predefined number of seconds (it uses the SIGALARM signal to wake up), whereas the latter will execute its body in a different Tcl thread. The two commands can be used in conjunction, in which case the `timeout` command should be in the body of the `break` command, and not the other way around.

URL Types

Certain MikroConf commands accept a special URL type argument, which enables access to local and remote locations. For example the `copy` command can be used to copy the running-config from a remote/local location and then apply it.

```
Wrap# copy ftp://ftp.example.com/pub/running.config running-config
```

To provide such functionality we make use of Tcl's Virtual File Systems mechanism. We use urltype Tcl VFS to create mappings for URL types to local directories, as well as Tcl VFSs which export specific network protocols.

The following URL types are currently supported:

URL Type	Location/Protocol
temp://	Maps to local directory: /tmp
flash://	Maps to local directory: /mnt/flash
system://	Maps to local directory: /
nvram://	Maps to local directory: /tmp/nvram
bootflash://	Maps to local directory: /mnt/boot
slot0://	Maps to local directory: /mnt/pcmcia0
slot1://	Maps to local directory: /mnt/pcmcia1
ftp://	Maps to the FTP protocol.
http://	Maps to the HTTP protocol.
webdav://	Maps to the WebDav protocol.
null://	Anything copied here is goes to the bit bucket.

Table 5: Tcl Virtual Filesystems.

More URL Types will become available in the future, such as nfs:// cfs:// shttp:// tftp:// scp://

Another example of MikroConf command that uses URL types is `dir`:

```
Router> en
Router# dir temp://
Directory listing for temp://*
Perm  Bytes        Access      Modified    Name
drwe  4096         2008-05-22  2008-05-22  1/
drwe  4096         2008-05-22  2008-05-22  2/
-rw   5563         2008-05-22  2008-05-22  3
```

```
Router#
```

The Specs File Structure

The *Specs file* is an XML file that adheres to the following DTD specification:

```
<?xml version="1.0" encoding="UTF-8"?>

<!ENTITY end SYSTEM "xml/end.xml">
<!ENTITY exit SYSTEM "xml/exit.xml">

<!ELEMENT module (confmode*, authmode*, mainconf*, tree+)>
    <!ATTLIST module name NMTOKEN #REQUIRED>

<!ELEMENT confmode EMPTY>
    <!ATTLIST confmode name NMTOKEN #REQUIRED
                                    string CDATA #REQUIRED
                                    parent NMTOKEN #REQUIRED
    >
<!ELEMENT authmode EMPTY>
    <!ATTLIST authmode name NMTOKEN #REQUIRED
                                    string CDATA #REQUIRED
                                    parent NMTOKEN #REQUIRED
                                    privilege NMTOKEN #REQUIRED
    >
<!ELEMENT mainconf EMPTY>
    <!ATTLIST mainconf name NMTOKEN #REQUIRED
                                    parent NMTOKEN #REQUIRED
                                    order NMTOKEN #REQUIRED
    >

<!ELEMENT tree (path | command)+>
    <!ATTLIST tree conf NMTOKENS #REQUIRED
                        priv NMTOKEN "0"
    >

<!ELEMENT path (desc?, no?, (path|command)*)>
    <!ATTLIST path name NMTOKEN #REQUIRED>

<!ELEMENT command (syntax?, desc, exec, print*, no?, argument*, grammar?)>
    <!ATTLIST command name NMTOKEN #REQUIRED>

<!ELEMENT syntax (#PCDATA)>
<!ELEMENT desc (#PCDATA)>
<!ELEMENT nodesc (#PCDATA)>
<!ELEMENT exec (#PCDATA)>
<!ELEMENT print (#PCDATA)>
    <!ATTLIST print section NMTOKEN #REQUIRED>
    <!ATTLIST print order NMTOKEN #REQUIRED>

<!ELEMENT no (syntax?, desc, argument*, grammar?)>

<!ELEMENT argument (desc, nodesc?, type)>
    <!ATTLIST argument name NMTOKEN #REQUIRED>
<!ELEMENT type (#PCDATA)>
```

```
<!ATTLIST type name (exact|list|dlist|fixed|any) #REQUIRED>
```

Table 6: The DTD document that describes the structure of a Specs file.

In the following paragraphs we describe one-by-one the use of these XML entities.

Authentication Modes

An authentication mode (authmode) is declared with the XML element `authmode`. No two MikroConf modules should declare the same authentication mode. Although any module can use modes declared by other modules. Authentication modes form a tree hierarchy, with the user necessary to be in the parent authmode in order to switch to the child.

The `authmode` element accepts the following XML attributes:

- `name`: The string that uniquely identifies the new authentication mode.
- `string`: The string to be displayed on the command line when user is in this mode.
- `parent`: The name of the parent authentication mode.
- `privilege`: The Privilege Level the new mode will be associated with. It must be in the range of 0-15, where 15 is the maximum possible authority status.

For example, the two build-in authentication modes User and Privileged are defined with the following two XML elements:

```
<authmode name="user" string=">" parent="root" privilege="0"/>
<authmode name="priv" string="#" parent="user" privilege="15"/>
```

As you can see both User and Privileged authmodes have as parent the special "root" authmode. This is not really an authmode, but represents the root of the tree.

Configuration Modes

Configuration modes (confmode) are defined into two steps. In the first step, they must be declared in a similar manner to authentication modes as we saw above. Like authentication modes, they have `name`, `parent`, and `string` XML attributes with same function. Just like authentication modes, a configuration mode is always declared by a single MikroConf module, which is called the *owner* of the confmode. Other modules use it freely as long as the owner module is loaded.

For instance, the declarations for the Entry and Global Configuration modes are:

```
<confmode name="entry" string="" parent="root"/>
<confmode name="global" string="(config)" parent="entry"/>
```

The second step is to create *Command Trees* for the previously declared configuration mode. A Command Tree appears in the Specs file with the `tree` XML element, and it can host any number of `path` and `command` elements. We will discuss these elements on the next section.

For the two aforementioned confmodes there are three Command Trees specified in *base* module:

```
<tree conf="entry" priv="0">
  ...
</tree>

<tree conf="entry" priv="15">
  ...
</tree>

<tree conf="global" priv="15">
  ...
</tree>
```

As you can see, the `conf` attribute associates a command tree, with a previously declared configuration mode. The `priv` attribute, on the other hand, says that all the commands (and paths) contained within this tree are accessible to uses that have the specified privilege level or higher.

You might have also noticed that a configuration mode can be spitted in many Command Trees which can exist in the same Spec file. This is handy to categorize commands based on the required privilege level. It is also possible for Command Trees to exist in different Specs files (belonging to different modules) and collectively define a single configuration mode. This design allows for instance the *rip* module to register commands that appear in the *interface* configuration mode (which is owned by the *interface* module).

Beware that before a configuration mode is defined by a module, no other module can register Command Trees for it.

Running Configuration Sections

The internal representation of the running-config is a tree structure, that comprises of *Sections* and *Entries*. A running-config section is declared with the XML element:

```
<mainconf name="..." parent="..." order="..."/>
```

For example, *base* module defines the followings:

```
<mainconf name="register" parent="root" order="0"/>
<mainconf name="auth" parent="root" order="10"/>
<mainconf name="terminal" parent="root" order="20"/>
<mainconf name="line" parent="root" order="40"/>
    <mainconf name="console" parent="line" order="10"/>
```

The name attribute is the name of the new section; parent is the name of the parent section; and order is the *Order Number* of the new section. Obviously, no two MikroConf modules should declare the same running-config section. Although any module can use sections owned by other modules.

Paths, Commands and Arguments

Commands are declared in the module's *Specs file*, which is an XML file. Commands can be added or removed at any time during a module's lifetime.

Any valid MikroConf command can be broken down to the following parts:

- The command path
- The command name
- Command arguments

Take for example the following three commands:

```
ip host gateway 10.143.200.1
ip domain-name aspisos.org
ip name-server 10.143.200.1
```

They all share the same path, which is `ip`. They have different command names: `host`, `domain-name`, and `name-server`. And, of course, they support different arguments, which is everything that follows after the command name.

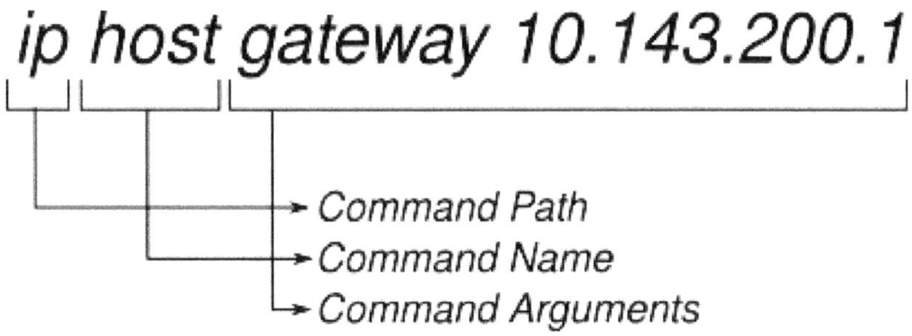

Drawing 9: Break-down of an example command, in its constituents.

The definition of the ip path in the above example could be:

```
<path name="ip">
   <desc>IP Configuration</desc>

   <command name=" host" > ... </command>
   <command name=" domain-name" > ... </command>
   <command name=" name-server" > ... </command>

</path>
```

A `command` XML element defines the entry-point for a MikroConf command. It accepts a `name` attribute which is the word you need to enter on the command-line to access the command. It also accepts a number of child-elements, which we discuss hereafter:

<syntax>

This element is optional. If present, its body describes how the command arguments can appear on the command line. In other words, it defines the *Command Syntax*. Notice, that the declaration of the arguments themselves is done by another element, the argument element, which we discuss later. If this element is absent, then the command will not accept any arguments at all; which is of course a valid option.

The syntax is described by a regular expression, which internally is processed as a deterministic finite automaton. The states of the automaton correspond to the argument positions on the command line. The arcs from each state are the arguments that are valid for the corresponding position. The command's arguments are the elementary blocks of the regular expression (the symbols accepted by the automaton). This design gives maximum flexibility and control over how arguments can appear on the command line.

The regular expression in the body of this element is represented by a nested Tcl list, which forms a syntax tree. The following structures are legal to appear in the regular expression:

Expression	Description
{S x}	Atomic regular expression. Everything else is constructed from these. "x" is the name of an argument of the command, as declared with the `argument` element.
{. A1 A2 ...}	Concatenation operator. Accepts the concatenation of the regular expressions A1, A2, etc. Note that this operator accepts zero or more arguments. With zero arguments the represented language is epsilon, the empty word.
A1 A2 ...}	Choice operator, also called "Alternative". Accepts all input accepted by at least one of the regular expressions A1, A2, etc. In other words, the union of A1, A2. Note that this operator accepts zero or more arguments. With zero arguments the represented language is the empty language, the language without words.
{& A1 A2 ...}	Intersection operator, logical and. Accepts all input accepted which is accepted by all of the regular expressions A1, A2, etc. In other words, the intersection of A1, A2.
{? A}	Optionality operator. Accepts the empty word and anything from the regular expression A.
{* A}	Kleene closure. Accepts the empty word and any finite concatenation of words accepted by the regular expression A.
{+ A}	Positive Kleene closure. Accepts any finite concatenation of words accepted by the regular expression A, but not the empty word.
{! A}	Complement operator. Accepts any word not accepted by the regular expression A. Note that the complement depends on the set of symbol the result should run over. See the discussion of the argument over before.

Table 7: Regular expression syntax rules.

The following picture depicts the deterministic automaton for the syntax of the `telnet` command.

Command "telnet" :
. {? {. {S user} {S USER} } } {S HOST} {? {S PORT} }

Drawing 10: Break-down of an example command, in its constituents.

<desc>

This element is mandatory. Its body is the help text that appears when the user presses the question mark. It is advised to be less than 80 characters long.

<exec>

This element is also mandatory. Its body is the name of the command handler. If it is not given with an absolute namespace path, then the handler is looked up in the private namespace of the module.

Moreover, if additional arguments are provided in excess of the handler name, then these arguments are passed verbatim as the first arguments of the command handler, (before the standard API arguments).

<print>

```
<print section=" ..."  order=" ..." >
```

This element is optional, but it can also appear multiple times. With every instance it registers a callback procedure to be executed when generating the running-config. In other words it registers a running-config entry.

The `section` attribute specifies the running-config section this entry should attach to, and the `order` attribute specifies the *Order Number* for the entry. If an entry with the same order number already exists, then the order of execution of the two entries is unpredictable. The section a `print` element refers to must be previously defined with a `mainconf` element.

<no>

This element is optional. If present, it enables the negative form of the command. It can have its own `syntax`, `desc` and `argument` child elements, which have the same function as those for the command element.

When syntax is present, it defines the syntax for the negative form of the command, which can be different from that of the positive form. The element `syntax` can involve arguments declared either under the `command` or `no` elements. If an argument appears with the same name under both `command` and `no`, then the one under `no` takes precedence.

Finally, the element `desc` specifies the help text for the negative form.

<argument>

```
<argument name=" ..." >
```

Every instance of this element registers an argument for the command. There should be exactly one instance for every distinct argument name that appears as symbol inside the `syntax` element. The symbol name used in `syntax` and the `name` XML argument of this element must match.

The `argument` element must have as child elements one `desc` and one `type`. Optionally it can also have one `nodesc` element. The `desc` has exactly the same function as we have seen so far, only that this time is for the argument. The `nodesc`, if present, specifies the help text for the argument when the negative form of the command is used. If not present then help text for the positive version is printed in both positive and negative forms.

Finally, the `type` element specifies the type of the argument. For instance, it can specify if the argument accepts one of a finite number of fixed strings, or an arbitrary string. It has the form:

```
<type name=" ..." > ... </type>
```

The `name` XML attribute can be set to one of the literals: `exact`, `list`, `dlist`, `fixed`, and any. Depending on what it is set to, the body of the element takes different meaning. We will see each one of the cases separately:

```
<type name=" exact" />
```

In this form, the argument accepts only one word, which is the string specified in the name XML argument of the argument element. Command Completion and Abbreviation will consider this word as an option, and In-line Help will display it as well.

An example use of this argument type is the command:

```
show running-config [all]
```

show is a path, and running-config is the command name, and all is a keyword that can be implemented as an exact type argument.

```
<type name=" list" >item1 item2 item3 ...</type>
```

The argument accepts a finite number of words that are specified as a Tcl list on the body of this element. Command Completion and Abbreviation will consider these words as alternatives, whereas In-line Help will only list the name of the argument element and its associated help text.

An example use of this argument type is the command:

```
log {debug | info | ... | critical | alert} message
```

The alternatives of the second argument are known in advanced, therefore we can implement them with an argument type of list.

```
<type name=" dlist" >tcl_procedure_name</type>
```

This is similar to the list type above, but with the difference that the list of strings is actually generated dynamically at run-time. It is done so by calling the tcl_procedure_name procedure, which is expected to return a Tcl list. If tcl_procedure_name is not in an absolute namespace path, then it is looked for in the private namespace of the module which owns the command.

As with the `list` type, Command Completion and Abbreviation will consider all the dynamically generated words as alternatives, whereas In-line Help will only list the name of the `argument` element and its associated help text.

An example use of this argument type is the command:

```
interface {name0 | name1 | ...}
```

We don't know in advance all the available interface names. We can compute them, however, at run-time when the command is being edited or executed. The `dlist` argument type is the solution to this.

```
<type name=" fixed" >
   word1 {help text for word1}
   word2 {help text for word2}
   ...
</type>
```

This argument type explicitly lists all the words that the argument accepts, along with their help message texts. The body of the element must be a valid Tcl serialized array. Command Completion will consider the words as valid alternatives, whereas In-line Help will display them along with the corresponding help messages.

This argument type exists solely to simplify the command syntax. It is equivalent to using multiple `exact` argument types, set as alternatives in the command syntax. However, this will enlarge the automaton that corresponds to the command syntax (one state per `exact` argument), whereas with the `fixed` argument type we have a single automaton state for all keywords.

```
<type name=" any" />
```

This argument type accepts any string as valid word. It is used for user supplied values that cannot be confined within a finite number of alternatives, such as for the case of an email address.

The syntax of the command should not allow two different arguments of type `any` to compete for the same argument position, because in this case it is indecisive to which argument the word should map to. Nevertheless, it is ok to combine argument types with finite number of alternatives, with a single argument type of `any`.

Beware that multiple types for the same argument are not supported. You will need to define different arguments of different types to accomplish this.

Conclusions

In this paper we presented MikroConf, a framework for building Command-Line Interfaces (CLI), and the application of it in the administration of Linux-based network devices. We covered MikroConf's design and implementation aspects the pertain to Tcl.

References

1. MikroConf Router Configuration Interface, http://mikroconf.sourceforge.net/
2. The Tcl Programming Language, http://www.tcl.tk/
3. Small Tcl, http://wiki.tcl.tk/1363
4. Tcl Modules, http://www.tcl.tk/cgi-bin/tct/tip/189
5. Tcl Script Cancelation, http://www.tcl.tk/cgi-bin/tct/tip/285.html
6. tcldoc Documentation Generator, http://tcl.jtang.org/tcldoc/tcldoc/tcldoc.html
7. taccle Parser, http://wiki.tcl.tk/11425
8. fickle Scanner, http://wiki.tcl.tk/3555
9. Tclx, http://tclx.sourceforge.net/
10. Memchan, http://memchan.sourceforge.net/
11. tcllib, http://tcllib.sourceforge.net/
12. TclTest, http://www.tcl.tk/man/tcl/TclCmd/tcltest.htm
13. TCL Modules, http://www.tcl.tk/cgi-bin/tct/tip/189
14. Tcl Binding to Tcl Virtual File System and urltype,

15. TclVfs, http://sourceforge.net/projects/tclvfs

16. Tcl Virtual File System, http://wiki.tcl.tk/2138

17. Tcl SNMP Tools, https://sourceforge.net/projects/tcl-snmptools

18. Tcl Inotify, https://sourceforge.net/projects/tcl-inotify

19. Tcl POSIX Message Queues, https://sourceforge.net/projects/tcl-mq

20. Tcl Syslog, https://sourceforge.net/projects/tcl-syslog

21. Tcl PAM Authentication, https://sourceforge.net/projects/tcl-pam

22. Tcl mmap Interface, https://sourceforge.net/projects/tcl-mmap

23. The uClibc Project, http://www.uclibc.org/

24. The uClibc++ Project, http://cxx.uclibc.org/

25. The busybox Project, http://busybox.net/

26. The linux-pam Project, http://www.kernel.org/pub/linux/libs/pam/

27. The tDOM Project, http://www.tdom.org/

28. Tcl's Build-in Memory Introspection, http://wiki.tcl.tk/3248, http://wiki.tcl.tk/3248

29. The Net-SNMP Project, http://www.net-snmp.org/

30. The GNU Project, http://www.gnu.org/

31. The Linux Kernel, http://www.linux.org/

32. The Expect Project, http://expect.nist.gov/

33. Elliotte Rusty Harold, W. Scott Means, “XML in a Nutshell, 3 Edition”, O'Reilly

34. Simon StLaurent, Michael Fitzgerald, “XML Pocket Reference”, O'Reilly

35. Bouglas R. Mauro, Kevin J. Scmidt, “Essential SNMP, 2 Edition”, O'Reilly

36. Tony Stubblebine, “Regular Expression Pocket Reference”, O'Reilly

37. John E. Hopcroft, Rajeev Motwani, Jefrey D. Ullman, “Introduction to Automata

38. Theory, Languages, and Computation, 3rd Edition", Addison-Wesley

39. Flemming Nielson, Hanne Riis Nielson, Chris Hankin, "Principles of Program Analysis", Springer

40. W. Richard Stevens, "TCP/IP Illustrated, Volume 1: The Protocols", Addison-Wesley

41. Ethan Cerami, "Web Services Essentials", O'Reilly

42. The Etch Protocol, http://en.wikipedia.org/wiki/Etch_(protocol)

43. The SOAP Protocol, http://en.wikipedia.org/wiki/SOAP

44. The CORBA Protocol, http://en.wikipedia.org/wiki/CORBA

17th ANNUAL TCL/TK 2010 CONFERENCE
Chicago (USA)
11-15 October

TK II

Fri October 15, 2010 09:00-10:45

TclA Publications

Enhanced Tcl/Tk Widgets for EDA Applications

Gaurav Bansal, Roshni Lalwani
DFTVisualizer Group, Mentor Graphics Corporation
{gaurav_bansal | roshni_lalwani}@mentor.com

Abstract

Considering the huge designs required to be navigated and analyzed in the Electronic Design Automation (EDA) applications, there is need to enhance the underlying Tcl/Tk widgets to optimize both the performance and memory consumption.
This paper talks about enhancing the MtiHierarchy widget (part of the Mtiwidget package) and Text widgets in a way that eliminates the performance overheads due to the magnanimity of the data in the EDA applications and also providing various useful features.

1. Introduction

DFTVisualizer is a Tcl/Tk based rich graphical user interface (GUI) which provides a debugging environment to the EDA tools of Mentor Graphics. It is built upon various open-source mega-widgets like MtiWidgets, MtiWaveWidget, Text Widgets.

The biggest challenge in handling huge amount of the data is when it has to be edited in runtime through the GUI. An addition or deletion of a column would take something close to half an hour while handling a typical design which has more than 10M gates. This was a serious limitation for a GUI.

In addition to enhancing the performance of the existing features, supplementary features had to be added in the application to meet the new developments being done in the backend EDA tools. Features like sub-columns and frozen-in-place tree column, did not have an inbuilt support in MtiHierarchy widget.

Similarly it was required to enhance available text widgets to provide a transcript window which is not just a mirror of the command line output, but also provides features like visual differentiation between various types of information as well as hyperlinks so that the user can open the reference documents/files by clicking on the link, start the debugging process by clicking on the errors reported by the tool, etc.

Section 2 below covers MtiHierarchy Widget, highlighting work done to enhance the performance and add new features. Section 3 outlines the enhanced text widgets which support smart hyperlinks.

2. MtiHierarchy widget

MtiHierarchy widget is a part of Mtiwidgets, which is a Tcl/Tk based open source package providing various useful capabilities like Hierarchical Tree interface, docbar, toolbar, pane manager, tabbed pane interface, etc.

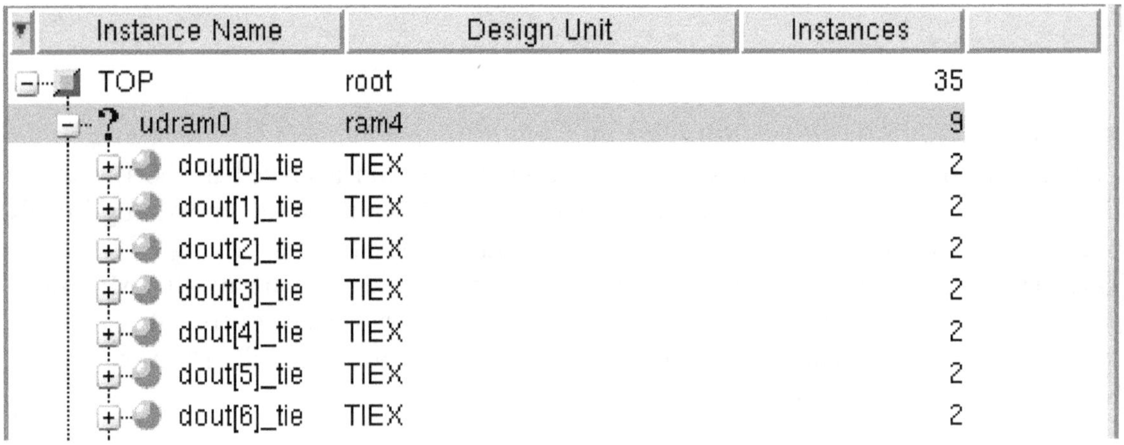

Figure 1 – MtiHierarchy widget

MtiHierarchy widget provides the Hierarchical tree interface as seen in the image.
But with exponential increase in the complexity and size of EDA designs, there was a need to enhance MtiHierarchy widget to avoid associated performance overheads. The approaches for each enhancement along with its limitations and possible solutions to its limitations are discussed further.

a. Callback support to improve the performance

The protocol for displaying hierarchical tree in MtiHierarchy widget involves sending information of each instance (row) from the EDA tool to the widget. Information is passed to the MtiHierarchy widget in the following format.
<name> <app data> <label> <tag> <icon> <label> <tag> <icon>...
The "name" is the unique id of each instance (e.g. memory address) and "app data" is a general purpose field for storing any application specific data. The information to be displayed in each column is sent in a set of three parameters i.e. <label> <tag> <icon>.

The conventional approach to displaying a data in widgets is to pass the information for the entire tree/block irrespective of how many instances are actually displayed in the visible portion of the widget. The widget stores the data for each instance as an "item" (object of data-structure wTreeItem_t) where the data in <name> field is stored in "item->name" for that instance. Data in the <app data> is stored in the "item->appData" and "item->data" stores the sets of <label><tag><icon> of all column corresponding to that instance.

In Figure 1, the data set passed to MtiHierarchy widget for the "TOP" instance is shown in Figure 2.

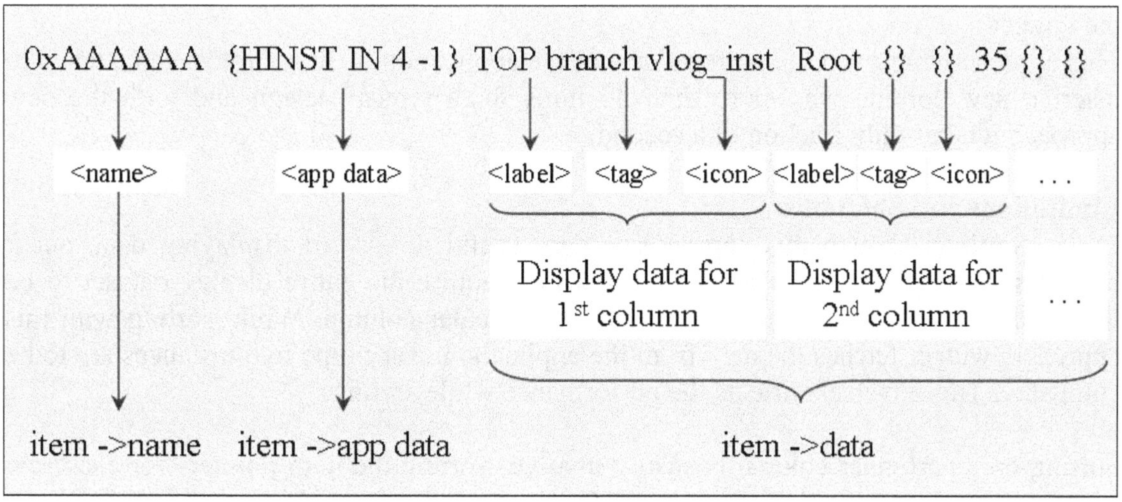

Figure 2 – Protocol for displaying hierarchical tree in MtiHierarchy widget

Widget uses "item->data" for that instance to display the information in each column. Now if the user were to insert a new column in the widget consisting of a tree with 10M instances under top instance. The conventional approach would require iterating over the entire tree and append a set of <label> <tag> <icon> to the list of each instance in the "item->data" field. This is what caused a major performance overhead.

Considering that only about 50 instances are in visible region at a time and the display data is easily retrievable for each instance, given that the widget has instance's <name> and <app data>, an alternative approach is implemented where the information is split into static data (<name> and <app data>) and the dynamic display data (sets of <label> <tag> <icon>) such that the widget stores only the static data and requests the dynamic display data from application as and when required.

For the 50 instances in visible region, the widget requests the display data from the application by passing their <name> and <app data>. So wherever the widget was using the field "item->data" (sets of <label><tag><icon>) to display any instance, now it gets the display data from the application at runtime as:

```
if (treePtr->callback) {
          wtcl_callbackForItemData(treePtr, item);
          list = Tcl_GetObjResult(treePtr->interp);
} else if (item->data){
          list = (Tcl_Obj*) item->data;
}
```

The new approach does not require any modification of the data at the widget side. So addition/deletion of a column does not require any iteration. The new data for the column is provided by the backend application when display data is requested for an instance by the widget.
This approach improved the performance of the application by many folds. Time taken to insert a new column was more than 30 mins for a typical design and with the new approach it takes only fraction of a second.

Limitations and Solutions

1) Sorting: Though this approach is very useful in case of displaying data, but it becomes inefficient when using features which require the entire display dataset to be involved, for example, sorting the tree on a particular column. While sorting with this approach, widget fetches the data from the application every time two instances are to be compared. This adversely affects the performance while sorting.

Sorting on a particular column basically involves sorting the item pointers for each row based on the <label> field of the column. Conventionally, the widget compares the labels of the relevant columns stored in "item->data" and sorts the item pointers. With the new approach we pass the column and the parent instance to the application which returns the list of sorted item->name of its child instances. We have to order the item pointers accordingly.

So we create a hash table with "item->name" as the key and "item" pointer as the value. From the sorted list of item->name returned by the application, we get the corresponding item pointer from the hash table and place them in a sorted array.

With this approach sorting is at least as fast as before for the columns with strings and is faster for columns with numerical values.

Algorithm for sorting

```
if (flag set for backend sorting) {
  entry=Tcl_CreateHashEntry(itemName,item->name,&status);
  Tcl_SetHashValue(entry, item);
}

// Call the application function with parameters like sort
// column name, and parent id and app data, direction of
// sorting, etc

// The application returns the list of sorted item->names

// Iterate over the list and for each item->name get the
```

```
// item from the hash table
if (entry = Tcl_FindHashEntry(hash_itemName, tokens)){
        item = Tcl_GetHashValue(entry);
        // Re-arrange the fields item->parent->firstvis,
        item->siblings, item->nextvis, item->visIdx, etc
        as per the sorted list of items got from the
        above step
}
```

2) Find/Search: With no display data stored in the widget, doing a search for an instance name in the hierarchy tree will again require fetching the display data for each instance and will be more expensive. In order to avoid the overhead of fetching data for each instance from the application we pass the details of the parent while searching at a particular level. At the backend we search for the required pattern in the sorted list associated with the parent and return the relative position (if found) of the matching instance to the widget. The widget calculates the absolute index by adding the parent->visIdx + relative position returned by the application.

b. Sub column support

In EDA applications an instance has some properties which are organized and best viewed as a set of sub-properties. For example we need to classify faults into various categories which have further sub-categories. These can be best displayed as a column of category with sub-categories as sub-columns. From a GUI purpose the view should be such that sub-columns display when a column is expanded in-place to see its sub-categories and collapse it back to see just the category.

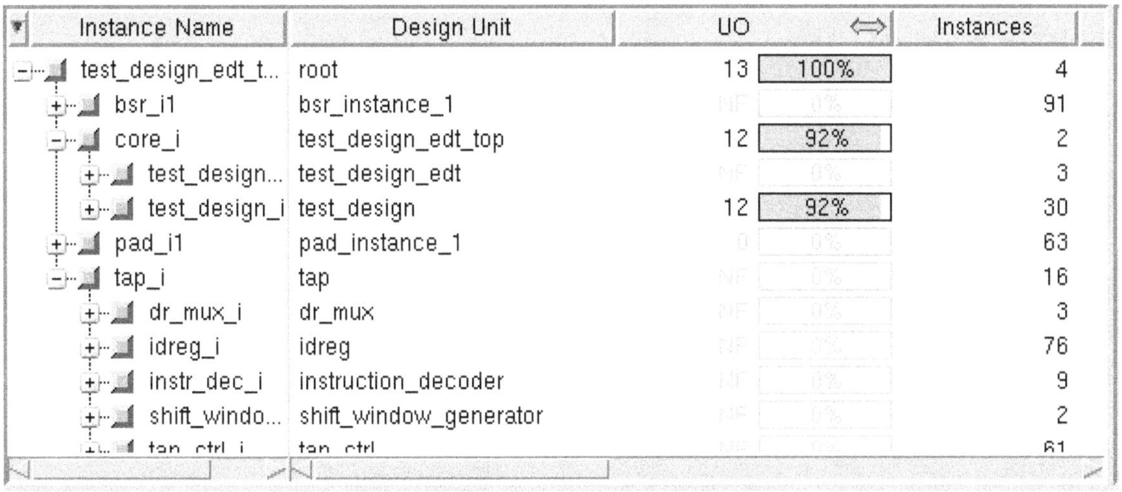

Figure 3 – MtiHierarchy widget with expandable columns

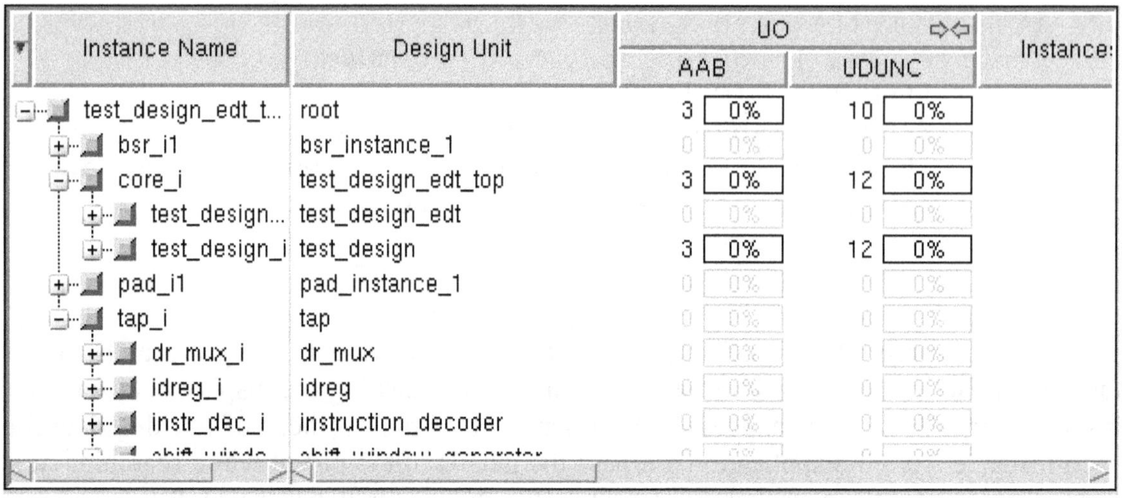

Figure 4 – MtiHierarchy widget with sub-columns

MtiHierarchy widget does not have an underlying support for displaying sub-columns. The available infrastructure in the widget is to create a header button and a column and grid them in the same column. With this available infrastructure there are two approaches that can be followed to display sub-column in widgets.

1) Create sub-columns and pack them inside the column. This will also require that we create a frame for header instead of a header button and pack the header and sub-headers inside the header frame.

Note that the protocol for display data remains the same as before except that the <label> for a column should now be a "list of labels" for a column with sub-columns such that the display data passed to widget for a column with sub-columns will be:

<label1 label2 label3> <tag> <icon>
where label1 is the label for 1st sub-column, label2 is the label for 2nd sub-column, etc.

Brief overview of the changes required for implementation of sub-columns is as follows:

Provide APIs for sub-column addition, deletion, move, configure, hide, show, cget, index, rename, drawmode, etc. on the same lines as available for columns in class mtiwidgets::Hierarchy in file mtihierarchy.itk.
e.g. we would need to provide APIs for sub-column addition as

```
$_hierWidget column subcolumn add "$column" "$subcol"
$_hierWidget column subcolumn delete "$column" "$subcol"
```

For these operations we would require keeping a map of the name and number of sub-column, just like we do it for columns, and update the variables accordingly.

E.g. For addition of a sub-column we need to keep a map of the number of the new sub-column, its name, parent, etc.

So while adding a sub-column specify the parent column and keep a map of the sub-columns and its parent columns.

```
itk_component add subcol$_subcolNum {
      wvalueWidget  $itk_component($column).$subcolumn \
      itk_component(tree) \
      -parentColumnNum $column_index] .........
#Update the global variables to map the subcolumns-columns
properly
lappend subcol_list $_subcolNum
set _subcol_col_map [lreplace $_subcol_col_map $colIdx
$colIdx $subcol_list]
lappend _subcolParent $col_number

#Generate the corresponding sub headers
subheader add $_subcolNum $col_number
```

To be able to make column expandable/ collapsible we need to provide a clickable icon on the header button. This will require making changes to class mtiwidgets::Colbutton in the file mticolbutton.itk.

We need to define two options: 1) –togglestate to specify the state of the expandable column so that the icon can be updated accordingly. 2) –togglecommand to specify the function to be executed when the icon is clicked.

```
::itcl::body mtiwidgets::Colbutton::_toggleMode {} {
     if {$itk_option(-togglecommand) != ""} {
          uplevel "#0" $itk_option(-togglecommand)
     }
}
```

Function associated with –togglecommand is defined by and in the class mtiwidgets::Hierarchy in the file mtihierarchy.itk as.

```
$hdr configure -togglecommand [::itcl::code $this
_notifyCol_expand_collapse $col]
```

The function in widgets further calls the function in application so that the application can add/delete the sub-column as required.

```
::itcl::body
::mtiwidgets::Hierarchy::_notifyCol_expand_collapse {col} {
     # Notify application about expand/collapse
}
```

This approach has the limitations that since the sub-headers and sub-columns are in different frames/grid cells, there will be algorithmic approach to make their widths align with each other. So whenever we map the sub-columns we have to explicitly make the width of sub-column equal to that of sub-headers.

```
$subcolumn configure -width [winfo width $subheader]
```

Also, since we pack the sub-headers and sub-columns, the user does not have a fine control over the widths of individual sub-column. So when we increase/decrease the width of a column, all the sub-columns increase/decrease proportionally.

2) In order to address the limitations of the previous approach, alternative approach can be considered. Create a placeholder row below the headers to hold sub-headers, if required. When sub-columns are created, create a frame to occupy the 2 rows which will contain the sub-headers and the sub-columns. Grid the sub-headers in row 0 and sub-columns in row 1 of this frame. This will provide the user a lot more control over the sub-column as compared to the previous approach. The only thing that we need to take care is that the headers of the other columns make their row span as 2 so that the headers are the same height as occupied by the header and sub-header combined.

c. Making tree column frozen in place (non-scrollable)

In the current implementation of widget, all the columns are scrolled horizontally with the scrollbar. Since the tree column is the most important column and all the data in the rest of the columns is associated to the instance in the tree column, keeping the tree column frozen while scrolling would provide the user a much better interface. Also, since the design names in many designs are very long, it provides a very convenient way to be able to see the full names of the instances without having to increase the width of tree column.

Usually the horizontal scrollbars are associated with changing the xview of the canvas. So to provide the scrolling to rest of the column, we would require two canvases, one that contains the tree column and the other that contains the rest of the columns. The two canvases will have their own scrollbars that will alter their xviews. So when we scroll the 2nd canvas, only the columns inside that canvas scroll, keeping the tree column frozen. The scrollbar associated with the canvas containing the tree column can be used to scroll the instance names in the tree horizontally.

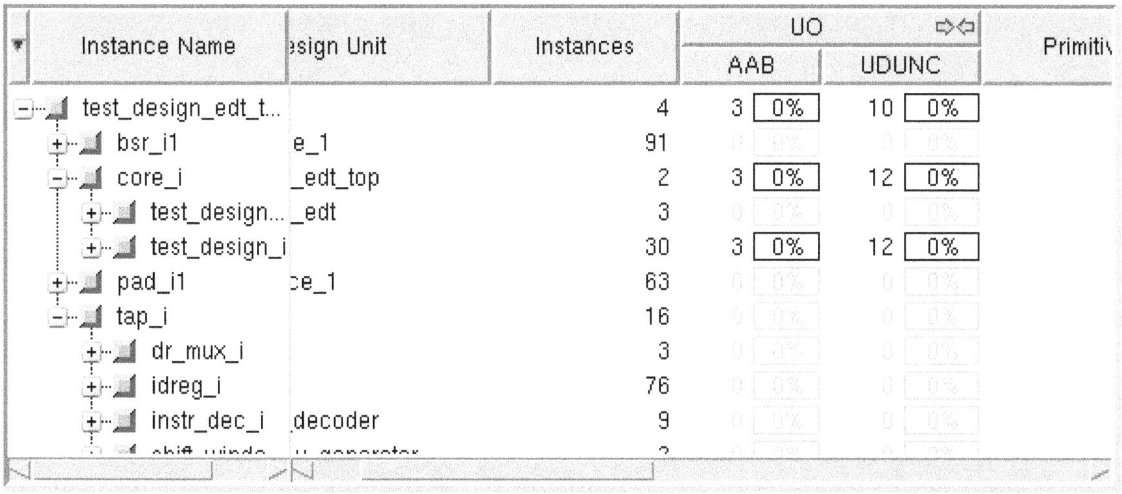

Figure 5 – MtiHierarchy widget with tree column frozen in place

Brief overview of the changes required for implementation of this feature is as follows.

The components of MtiHierarchy widget are in the following hierarchical order:
Clipper (a frame) → Canvas → Sfchildsite (a frame) → Columns

So we create two canvases and grid them inside the clipper as column 0 and column 1 of row 0. We place the scrollbars for both canvases in column 0 and column 1 of row 1 under them.

We configure the 1st scrollbar to alter the xview of the column 0 such that it scrolls the instance names of the tree column and not the column itself. 2nd scrollbar is configured to scroll the xview of the 2nd canvas so that the rest of the columns scroll past the tree column.

```
$sb1 configure -command [::itcl::code $column0 xview]
$sb2 configure -command [::itcl::code $canvas2 xview]
```

One thing that we need to take care of is that now the index of column grid in the 2nd canvas is two less then the earlier index, as the columnspan of the tree column is 2. So if we grid the first column in 2nd canvas, it was the 3rd column in the earlier configuration.

One of the issues faced during this enhancement was that since the header button of the tree column and rest of the column are in different grid systems, it was required to algorithmically align the heights of the headers. So if we have expanded a column in the canvas 2 such that it has sub-column, it requires that we increase the height of tree header so that headers align themselves.

```
itcl::body ::mtiwidgets::Hierarchy::_headerButtonResize
{col} {      ...............
     #Get the height of header 1

     # If it has sub-columns then the effective height we
     should consider is 2X

     # Check if there is any height difference in the
     # header rows

     # If tree header is smaller then increase the height
     # of its grid row by extra padding

     # If the tree header is bigger then decrease the
     # padding
}
```

3. Enhanced Text Widget

The current implementation of text widgets is useful for providing an integrated transcript window that mirrors the shell window of the DFT tools. This means that all messaging, commands issued, error messages, which are shown in shell window of the DFT tool can also be seen in transcript window with the underlying text widget. The Enhanced text widget highlights the error messages, commands and the warning messages in a red, black and green color respectively. This text highlighting is to help the user to point out the problematic line easily to debug the issue related to DFT.

Some of relevant text like files names, instance names, Design Rule Violation ID and lines numbers are also made available as hyperlinks. So the user can clicks on the hyperlinks to get to the relevant file or to the relevant information in other windows of the tool to debug the issues very quickly. The snapshot with the transcript window with above features is shown in Figure 6.

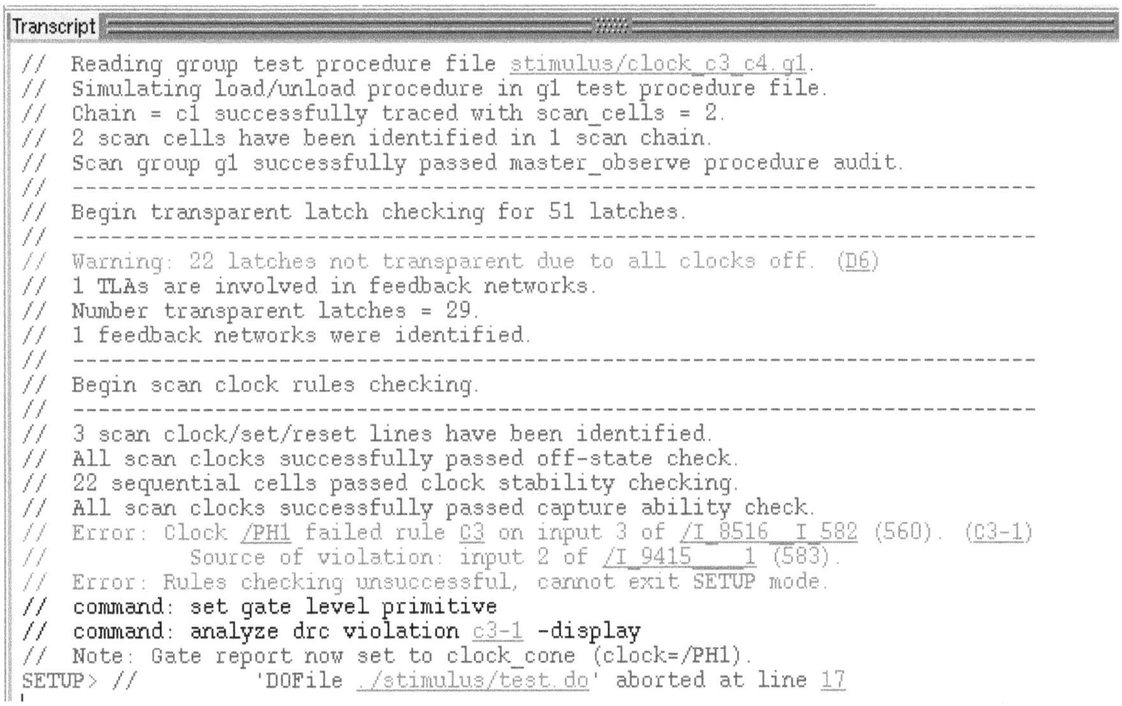

Figure 6 – Enhanced text widgets with hyperlinks

To highlight the (Error/warning/commands) message lines with different color the text in widget has to be parsed line by line to classify the same as error messages, warning messages and commands. To display file names, instance names and Design Rule Violation IDs as hyperlinks, the text in the widget has to be parsed word by word to mark them as hyperlinks.

One of the limitations of providing this enhancement was that, for EDA applications, the size of the log files could be very large. Parsing a big file had performance overheads which made the GUI busy for quite some time. The solution was to provide incremental parsing of the file such that only the portion of the output in the visible region of the widget was parsed.

Algorithm for incremental parsing

```
1. Load the plan text from file in to the text widget
   (read & write in chuck size of 256k). This will done
   only for first time
2. Calculate the boundary lines (B1, B2) of visible area
   of text widget. Start line = B1 and last line = B2.
   The algorithm for boundary calculation is shown below.
3. If  (text between { B1,B2} is not already parsed) {
        for ( line = B1  line <= B2  line++ ) {
            If(line starts with pattern (Error/Warning/..)
```

```
            Highlight the line in (red/green/..) color.
            Parse the same the line word by word
          If (word is a filename/Instance name/Design
              Rule Violation ID)
            Mark it as a hyperlink
      }
  }
```

Algorithm for boundary calculation

The boundary calculation is done based on the visible area of the text. If the text between the visible area is already parsed then the boundary calculation method returns null else returns the boundaries.

```
1. set {frac1,frac2} [$widget yview]
2. set N total number of lines in the text widget
3. set start = N * frac1
4. set end   = N * frac2
5. Set buffer = 10
6. set start = start - buffer
7. set end = end + buffer
8. if {start < 1.0 }
      start = 1.0
9. If { end > last index }
        end = last index
10. foreach {pS pE} [$w tag ranges tagParsed] {
      if { [$pS <= $start] && [$pE >= $start] }
         set start $pE

      if { [$pS <= $end] && [$pE >= $end] }
         set end $pS

      if { [$start >= $end] }
        return NULL

   }
11. $widget tag add tagParsed $start $end
12. Return $start,$end
```

4. Bibliography

TCL wiki, http://wiki.tcl.tk

The State Controller Pattern: An Alternative to Actions

William H. Duquette
Jet Propulsion Laboratory, California Institute of Technology
William.H.Duquette@jpl.nasa.gov

ABSTRACT

A GUI application must enable and disable widgets as the state of the application changes. Bryan Oakley's notion of "actions" aids this by associating widgets with user actions; widgets associated with an action can be enabled and disabled as a group. This paper suggests a different pattern in which widgets are associated instead with the conditions for which they are enabled, thus greatly simplifying the problem of triggering widget state changes as the application state changes.

1. The Problem

As has often been noted at the Tcl Conference over the last few years, it is trivially easy to write a quick-and-dirty GUI using Tcl/Tk; the difficulty lies in giving the GUI all of the little professional touches. One of those professional touches is to make each GUI control be "grayed out" when the action it invokes is currently invalid.

For example, MS Word has a table editing toolbar. Some buttons on it create new tables; these will be enabled when the insertion point is in normal text, where a table can be inserted. Other buttons modify part or all of an existing table; they will be enabled only when the insertion point is within a table, or perhaps when some portion of the table is selected.

Anyone who has tried to create a polished GUI has had to address this issue; and has usually found that it is more work than seems reasonable.

2. The "Actions" Pattern

In his 2004 conference paper, "Actions: A Simple Implementation", Bryan Oakley describes the Actions pattern, his way of making the problem more tractable. [1] His insight is that there are often multiple ways to invoke any given action the user might wish to take. In a word processor, for example, the user might wish to copy the selection to the clipboard. He can:

- Enter a key command, **Control-C**
- Press the **Copy** button on the toolbar

- Select **Edit/Copy** from the Edit Menu

But although there are many input vectors, there is a single action underlying all of them: copy the selection. If there is no selection (or if the selected object cannot be copied), all of these vectors should be disabled. When something is subsequently selected, all of them should be enabled. Moreover, it should be possible to toggle them all at once. This is called setting the *validity* of the action.

The Actions pattern therefore has these characteristics:

- Each distinct action the user can do is represented as a `proc`-like pseudo-object in the application. For example,

```
action define copy {} { event generate [focus] <<Copy>> }
```

- Each action's validity can be set:

```
action enable copy
action disable copy
```

- Each action can be invoked, which causes the action's body to be executed:

```
action invoke copy
```

  If the action takes arguments, they are passed along with the action name.

- Each action can be associated with any number of buttons, menu items, key commands, and so forth:

```
button .toolbar.copy -command {action invoke copy} ...
action associate copy .toolbar.copy

.menubar.editMenu add command      \
    -label   "Copy"                \
    -command {action invoke copy}
action associate copy .menubar.editMenu "Copy"

bind all <Control-c> [list action invoke copy]
```

- Setting the action's validity automatically enables or disables all related GUI controls.

- In Oakley's simple implementation, actions are managed by an "action manager" singleton; as he notes, they can also be implemented as explicit Tcl objects using an object framework like Snit.

As a result, the application logic responsible for setting action validity is nicely decoupled from the actual widgets that invoke those actions. This pattern has a number of advantages:

- The application logic is clearer, as it is written in terms of meaningful actions rather than arbitrary widgets.
- The application logic is shorter, as there are typically many fewer actions than GUI controls.
- The application logic is more stable with respect to GUI changes: the appearance of the GUI and the number of GUI controls per action can be completely changed without changing the application logic at all.
- The set of actions provides a vocabulary of commands that can be used to script the user interface, for test purposes or even for user scripting.

I refer to this as a pattern rather than as a library, because it usually makes sense to tailor the action manager implementation to the application.

3. Actions vs. Conditions

The reason why actions simplify the program logic is shown in the following diagram, which partitions the set of GUI controls in the program by the actions that they invoke:

a1	*a2*	*a3*	*a4*	*a5*	*a6*	*a7*	*a8*
g1 *g2* *g3*	*g4* *g5*	*g6* *g7* *g8*	*g9* *g10* *g11*	*g12*	*g13* *g14*	*g15*	*g16* *g17* *g18*

In the diagram we have eight actions, *a1* through *a8*, and 18 GUI controls (menu items, buttons, etc.), *g1* through *g18*. By relating the controls with the actions, we now have less than half as many entities to enable and disable.

Now, it is likely that some of these actions are enabled and disabled under precisely the same conditions. Group the actions by these conditions, *c1* through *c4*:

c1			*c2*		*c3*	*c4*	
a1	*a2*	*a3*	*a4*	*a5*	*a6*	*a7*	*a8*
g1	*g4*	*g6*	*g9*	*g12*	*g13*	*g15*	*g16*
g2	*g5*	*g7*	*g10*		*g14*		*g17*
g3		*g8*	*g11*				*g18*

Suppose that instead of associating the GUI controls with the actions, we associate them with the conditions for which they are valid. We now have fewer sets of GUI controls to deal with, and they are tied directly to the program logic (the condition) that sets their validity:

c1	*c2*	*c3*	*c4*
g1 g2	*g9*	*g13*	*g15*
g3 g4	*g10*	*g14*	*g16*
g5 g6	*g11*		*g17*
g7 g8	*g12*		*g18*

This is essentially what the State Controller pattern does.

4. Notional Application

This section describes a notional application, to be used in examples in the remainder of the paper. The applications on which I am currently working have the following flavor:

- They are time-step simulations, in which the user prepares a scenario consisting of a number of entities of different kinds, and then allows simulation time to elapse, possibly intervening between time steps.

- They are document-centric. The scenario is a document that can be opened and saved.
- The application has distinct states; the user's actions are constrained by the current state.
  - **PREP:** Scenario Preparation. In this state the user can edit anything.
  - **PAUSED:** In this state, many aspects of the scenario are fixed. The simulation can be asked to starting running forward.
  - **RUN:** In this state, the user can watch the simulation execute, but cannot do much else other than pause it or return to PREP.
- Each entity has a set of attributes (i.e., a record structure). Consequently, the application has a browser for each kind of entity, allowing entities of that kind to be viewed, created, edited, and deleted.
- The application manages one simulation model at a time.
- The application has multiple windows, allowing multiple views on the model. All windows are identical in their capabilities (as with multiple editor windows on the same document). In particular, all of the various browsers are available as tabs in each of the windows.
- The application has a modular architecture based on Snit widgets. [3] Each window contains a variety of components, each implemented as a Snit widget.

Our notional application is a simulation of cars, roads, and gas stations:

- Roads and gas stations must be created and edited during PREP.
- Individual cars can be created and edited during PREP and while PAUSED.

5. State Controllers

The Actions pattern partitions the set of GUI controls by the actions they invoke. The basic notion of the State Controller pattern is to partition the set of GUI controls not by the actions they invoke, but by the conditions for which they are valid.

A state controller is a Snit object that controls the `-state` of some set of objects according to a `-condition` expression. If the condition is true, the `-state` of the objects is set to `normal`; otherwise, it is set to `disabled`. The API is straightforward:

`statecontroller` *`name`* `-condition {`*`expression`*`}`
: Create a new state controller with a given condition.

`name` `control` *`object ?key value ?key value...??`*
: Ask state controller *name* to control the `-state` of the named *object*. The optional arguments represent a dictionary of values to be used in the `-condition` expression.

  If *object* is a list of length 2, then the first token is assumed to be the name of a Tk menu widget and the second is the label of a menu item.

`name` `update` *`?object...?`*
: Ask state controller *name* to update the `-state` of all of the objects it controls. Optionally, it can update only the named objects.

Once the state controller has been created and the GUI controls have been associated with it, all that remains is to invoke the controller's `update` method on events that might cause the controller's `-condition` value to change.

Note that there is no command to forget a controlled object. If a controlled object no longer exists, the state controller silently forgets it.

5.1 Example: Adding an Entity

In our notional application, road and gas station entities can be created only while the simulation is in the PREP state. Each kind of entity has a browser, and each browser has an "Add" button.

First we define the state controller; its condition, of course, is simply that the simulation state is PREP:

```
statecontroller inprep -condition {[sim state] eq "PREP"}
```

Because this condition applies to GUI controls in different components, we define `inprep` at application scope.

Next, in each browser we ask `inprep` to control the "Add" button:

```
# Associate a widget with the statecontroller
button $win.add -text "Add" -command {...}
inprep control $win.add
```

When the simulation state changes the simulation notifies the `inprep` object:

```
inprep update
```

The controller then sets the `-state` of all controlled widgets in one fell swoop. That is all there is to it. The advantages are plain:

- Instead of defining "addroad" and "addstation" actions we define a single state controller.
- Associating the GUI controls with the state controller is no more work than associating them with an action.
- Instead of having code in every browser to subscribe and respond to simulation state changes, we call `inprep update` once when simulation state changes..

5.2 Example: Editing or Deleting an Entity

Each entity browser also has Edit and Delete buttons, which are valid only if the simulation is in the "PREP" state *and* an entity is selected in the browser. Pressing the button pops up a dialog used to edit the entity's attributes.

This is a difficult case to implement with the Actions pattern, because we can have multiple instances of a particular browser. For example, we might have two windows open, each displaying the gas station browser. Different gas stations might be selected in the two browsers, so that the Edit button is valid in one but not in the other. As a result, we would need to have two actions (or, more generally, *N* actions), one for each gas station browser. This is doable, certainly, but it smells funny: we have two "actions", but only one real action being performed.

The State Controller pattern takes this in stride. All we need do is to parameterize the state controller's `-condition` with the name of the browser:

```
statecontroller inprepWithEntity -condition {
    [sim state] eq "PREP" &&
    [llength [$browser selection]] == 1
}
```

We might also need to add a method to the browser widget itself; but as we are using Snit this is straightforward.

The value of `browser` is specified when a widget is controlled:

```
button $win.edit   -text "Edit"   -command {...}
button $win.delete -text "Delete" -command {...}

inprepWithEntity control $win.edit   browser $win
inprepWithEntity control $win.delete browser $win
```

Now, `inprepWithEntity` must be updated on two events: when the simulation state changes, and when the browser's selection changes:

```
# When sim state changes (In the "sim" module):
inprepWithEntity update

# When selection changes (In the browser component):
inprepWithEntity update $win.edit $win.delete
```

Changes to the browser's selection only affect the widgets that are part of that browser; consequently we ask the controller to update them specifically. The controller then evaluates its condition for those widgets alone. This is a minor performance hack, and can reasonably be omitted.

The menu items for editing and deleting entities only depend on the simulation state, and so can be controlled by the `inprep` controller.

5.3 Widgets with Unusual States

Most Tk widgets have two values for `-state`: `normal` and `disabled`. A few have additional states, such as `readonly`. If `normal` and `disabled` are not the correct pair of states for a given widget, the easiest solution is to wrap the widget in a `snit::widgetadaptor` and let the wrapper translate `normal` and `disabled` into the desired pair of values.

6. Triggering State Controller Updates

It is unpleasant to sprinkle calls to a state controller's `update` method around the code to catch all of the events that make a state controller's `-condition` change. The code is clearer if the module that defines the state controller can also subscribe to all of the relevant global events, which implies the need for a non-GUI application-level event mechanism. Although Tk virtual events can be used to do this job, they are unsatisfactory. Instead, we use a mechanism we call the `notifier`. Any module can send notifier events at any time, without declaration:

```
notifier send ::sim <State>
```

Here, `::sim` is the module sending the event and `<State>` is the event being sent. (Events can also include arguments.) Any number of modules can subscribe to this event from this sender:

```
notifier bind ::sim <State> inprep {
    inprep update
}

notifier bind ::sim <State> inprepWithEntity {
    inprepWithEntity update
}
```

This allows the definition of the state controller and the global calls to `update` to be co-located:

```
statecontroller inprep -condition {[sim state] eq "PREP"}
notifier bind ::sim <State> inprep {inprep update}
```

This combination appears often enough that our implementation of `statecontroller` supports it directly:

```
statecontroller inprep \
    -condition {[sim state] eq "PREP"} \
    -events    {::sim <State>}
```

7. Combining State Controllers with Actions

Suppose that instead of using a singleton action manager, as described in Section 2, each action was implemented as a Snit object with a `-state` option. One could then implement a three-tier architecture: GUI controls are associated with action objects, and action objects are controlled by state controllers. This preserves the use of actions as a kind of scripting language for the application. In our application domain, however, we have approached it differently.

We have the notion of an *order*, a user input that changes the simulation model. Looked at another way, any change that needs to be saved as part of the scenario document is made by an order. In our example, we would have orders to add, edit and delete roads, gas stations, and cars, along with many other operations. Like actions, orders are a kind of managed pseudo-proc. Unlike actions, orders are non-GUI.

Orders provide the application with the same scripting ability as actions, and at a level better suited to the application domain. (They also provide a basis for multi-level undo/redo.)

The primary variable that determines whether an order can be validly sent or not (assuming its parameters are valid) is the simulation state, and consequently the order manager handles this explicitly. Each order "knows" the simulation states in which it is valid. The order manager subscribes to the "`::sim <State>`" notifier event, and sends the "`::order <State>`"

event when order validity changes. Thus, we can write state controllers like this:

```
statecontroller orderValid \
    -condition {[order valid $order]} \
    -events    {::order <State>}

statecontroller orderValidWithEntity \
    -condition {
        [order valid $order] &&
        [llength [$browser selection]] > 0
    } \
    -events {::order <State>}
```

When we associate a GUI control with the latter of these state controllers, we need to specify the name of the order along with the name of the browser. Thus, we can edit the list of states for which the order is nominally valid as part of the order definition, and all of the GUI controls will be enabled and disabled accordingly, with no other code changes.

In short, instead of using actions to mediate between state controllers and GUI controls, we are using state controllers to relate orders to GUI controls.

8. Key Commands

Oakley's action manager implementation disables key bindings by making `action invoke` a no-op when the action is disabled. Because a state controller can control many widgets invoking many different operations, it has no notion of an `invoke` method. In order for a state controller to control a key binding, then, it would be necessary to define the key binding as an object with a `-state` option. It would be easy to implement a Snit type that wraps key bindings in this way, but to date we have not felt the need to do so.

9. State Controllers in Practice

The example in Section 3 suggests that a complex application could require many fewer state controllers than actions to do the same work, while greatly reducing the application logic in the GUI components that have controlled widgets.

In the most recent release of the project on which I am currently engaged, the main application has approximately 75 orders. These orders are invoked by approximately 150 GUI controls **per application window**. The state of these 150**N* GUI controls is managed by just 8 state controllers defined at the application level. The code in the components that contain these GUI controls is limited to the following:

- Associating the controls with the relevant state controller

- Invoking the state controller's `update` method when the component's state changes (only if needed).

We add new state controllers very rarely, and the rest of the time we do not think much about them; they just work.

In short, enabling and disabling GUI controls is no longer more work than seems reasonable.

10. References

[1] Oakley, Brian, "Actions: A Simple Implementation", 11th Tcl/Tk Conference, http://www.tcl.tk/community/tcl2004/Papers/BryanOakley/oakley.pdf.

[2] Oakley, Brian, "Actions", http://wiki.tcl.tk/11505

[3] Duquette, William H., "Snit's Not Incr Tcl", http://www.wjduquette.com/snit.

11. Acknowledgements

This research was carried out at the Jet Propulsion Laboratory, California Institute of Technology, under a contract with the National Aeronautics and Space Administration, during the development of the Athena Stability & Recovery Operations Simulation (Athena) for the TRADOC G2 Intelligence Support Activity (TRISA) at Fort Leavenworth, Kansas.

Copyright 2010 California Institute of Technology. Government sponsorship acknowledged.

TileQt and TileGtk: current status

Georgios Petasis

Software and Knowledge Engineering Laboratory,
Institute of Informatics and Telecommunications,
National Centre for Scientific Research "Demokritos",
Athens, Greece
petasis@iit.demokritos.gr

Abstract

This paper is about two Tile and Ttk themes, TileQt and TileGTK. Despite being two distinct and very different extensions, the motivation for their development was common: making Tk applications look as native as possible under the Linux operating system.

1 Introduction

In this paper we describe two extensions, TileQt and TileGTK, which aim to provide native look to Tk applications that use Tile/Ttk under the Linux operating system. Ttk is the best effort so far in providing Tk widgets with native look under all major operating systems. Among these, Microsoft Windows and Apple OS X offer a native widget set, and a suitable API, that applications can use in order to natively draw widgets. Wisely, Ttk fully exploits these APIs, allowing Tk applications to look exactly as native applications under these two operating systems.

The situation is very different for the Linux operating system, though. Under Linux, there is no native API that can be used by applications in order to draw widgets. Instead, the Linux desktop is mainly dominated by two environments, KDE [6] and Gnome [5], which are based on two different toolkit libraries, Qt [3] and GTK [4] respectively. These two libraries follow a quite different approach in implementing widgets, making the two libraries incompatible with each other. Both Qt and GTK support styled widgets, following again a different approach on customising the visual appearance of widgets. What is common between the two however, is the difficulty for third-party software to access their style API: both assume that applications use one of the libraries as their widget implementation basis, frequently mixing widget styling details with their internal implementation details.

Both TileQt and TileGTK try to use (and in some cases abuse) what is available as public APIs in the respective widget toolkits. The public APIs usually target either style development (so as new widget styles or themes can be developed) or new widget development (so as new or composite widgets can be developed). Despite the different scope of the public APIs, both TileQt and TileGTK try to use the available public APIs in order to draw widgets, a job that is usually performed by the toolkit internal (and thus not exported) functionality. This is why the development of both extensions followed a similar path: the sources of Qt and GTK were studied, in the detail required to understand how each library draws its widgets. Then, each extension tries to reproduce, as much as possible, the drawing behaviour of the corresponding toolkit, but organised in the framework defined by Ttk. Of course, it is not always easy, or even possible, to reproduce the internal drawing operations of another toolkit, mainly because the public API is not sufficient for this purpose. Typical examples are the scale/slider widgets from the Qt toolkit. These widgets seem as an ad hoc addition to the library: instead of following an approach that decomposes these widgets into elements, the widgets are drawn as a whole, by a single function in the context of an object of a specific

C++ class. An approach like the aforementioned one is difficult to be reproduced without simulating a large part of the toolkit. Thus, in such cases, both TileQt and TileGTK follow a different approach:

- Instances of widgets are created by using the public API of the widget toolkit.
- The properties of these widget instances are modified to match the Ttk element that must be drawn.
- The widget instances are drawn on an offline (not visible) pixmap.
- The pixel metrics of the widget instances are used in order to locate the widget part/element that corresponds to the desired Ttk one.
- The located part/element is copied onto the window that must be drawn by the Ttk element.

Of course, deviations from the expected behaviour are expected, when a public API is used for purposes other than the ones it was designed for. It is not uncommon to receive a wrong answer for a query on a theme property not frequently requested by the widget toolkit when drawing a widget, or to need a property that cannot be retrieved from the toolkit theme. In such a case, usually there is no alternative than to improvise. And when properties are guessed, their value can never be correct for all cases and for all themes, leading to visual inconsistencies and unsatisfied users.

The rest of this paper is organised as follows: in chapter two the problems of interfacing a toolkit library to Ttk are presented, followed by a brief presentation of the TileQt and TileGTK extensions, along with the supported Ttk widgets by each extension. Finally, some open issues and future directions are presented in chapter three, which concludes this document.

2 Mapping between Ttk and other widget toolkits

TileQt and TileGTK are quite different from each other, implementation wise. However, the problems of interfacing Ttk to another toolkit library (that being Qt, GTK or any other library) are exactly the same, and seem to be independent of the target toolkit library:

- Understand the internals of the library that must be interfaced. This is a time consuming, but feasible task, if the library sources are available. Thankfully, the sources of both Qt and GTK are publically available, along with sufficient documentation.
- Understand how to initialise the library from a hosting application. Both the Qt and GTK libraries assume that they are in control of the application, and that their "main" function will be executed, which will usually initialise the library and install a never-ending message loop. Of course, calling a function that never returns is not a desirable action, thus it is important to find a way to initialise the library without calling functions that will block (i.e. because the event loop is started and its termination usually means the termination of the application).
- Understand how the toolkit library locates themes, and how themes are loaded and used in order to draw widget elements.
- Find a way to map Tk drawables (windows, pixmaps, etc.) to the drawables of the toolkit library, and vice versa. This is an important step, as each library expects its own structures while using its API. This task may be difficult to be achieved, if the implementation is limited only to the public API of the library (targeting portability), as all libraries tend to hide platform-specific structures under abstraction layers, in order to ensure portability across multiple operating systems.

- Find a way to map Ttk widget states to the ones supported by the target toolkit library. This mapping is not always straight-forward, and mapping differences usually result in visual differences.
- Identify which widgets can be drawn directly (i.e. widget elements can be mapped between Ttk and the target toolkit library, through its theme API), and which widgets have to be drawn as a whole, followed by a segmentation step so as to identify and extract individual elements. Widgets belonging to the latter category are always difficult to be supported correctly, as it is not uncommon the pixel metrics of elements to be erroneously declared by the theme, especially since they are rarely needed (as the widget is drawn as a whole by the toolkit). This is quite common in Qt: being written in C++ it is easy for a theme to just subclass another theme, draw the widget differently, but never update the methods that return size information for the various elements.
- Ensure thread-safety. This can be an easy task if the target toolkit library is already thread safe (i.e. Qt where widgets can be created and drawn by any thread), or more tricky if it is not (i.e. GTK, where widgets must be created/drawn only by the thread the library was initialised).

And of course, an extension that is a Ttk theme must cope with the large number of available themes for the interfaced library. It is common that some themes work as expected, while others don't, due to various reasons: from using a new widget layout (i.e. scrollbars) to reporting erroneous pixel metrics for elements.

2.1 TileQt: a Ttk interface to the Qt widget toolkit

TileQt is a Tile/Ttk theme that aims to use Qt styles for drawing Ttk widget elements. Historically, it was the first C/C++ extension that attempted to provide a Ttk theme, based on the Ttk public API, without being part of Ttk. Its development started around 2003, supporting only Qt 3.x at that time. As a first attempt, several obstacles had to be overcome, ranging from initialising Qt and loading the style along with Tk, to building the extension with TEA/autoconf, which has limited support for locating the C++ compiler or Qt libraries. Several attempts were made by the author to build a robust build system for TileQt, from plain autoconf scripts, to a combination of Tcl scripts that locate components and then drive configure. The fact that all of them failed was the main motivation for switching the build system to CMake [1], which currently is able to support all the build requirements of TileQt. Also, TileQt was extended to support Qt 4.x in addition to Qt 3.x, when KDE 4.x was released: TileQt aims to provide support for both Qt 3.x and Qt 4.x, as well as Tile in Tk 8.5 and Ttk in Tk 8.5/Tk 8.6. In general, supporting both Tile and Ttk is easy, with the exception that TileQt cannot be built with the latest ActiveTcl 8.6 beta 2 distribution, due to an outdated version of "ttkDecls.h". Instead, a newer version must be retrieved and used, from the Tk CVS server, hosted at SourceForge [2].

TileQt has not been maintained for quite some time now (the last ChangeLog entry dates back to December 2008), but the source code compiles under an up-to-date Linux distribution (tested with Fedora 13 and the latest 8.6 beta from ActiveState [7]). Invoking one of the TileQt demos produces the output shown in Figure 2, while the Ttk elements and widgets supported by TileQt are shown in Figure 1. As it is evident from both figures, TileQt currently lacks support for scrollbar and scale widgets under Qt 4.x, as the implementation has not been updated from the Qt 3.x era. Looking closely at Figure 2, more display inconsistencies can be detected, such as faint white traces at the round corners of entry widgets, and offsets by one or two pixels on notebook tab rendering. However, these inconsistencies are not so important or noticeable by end users, at least compared to the complete lack of support for scrollbars, an essential widget for many applications. Finally, a problem seems to exist regarding thread safety of TileQt with recent Tk versions: the basic demo script (demo.tcl) of TileQt crashes when a second interpreter is initialised, so as to display a Qt theme selection dialog, which suggests important changes in recent Tk/Ttk versions that TileQt must take into consideration.

Widget	Qt 3.x	Qt 4.x	Widget	Qt 3.x	Qt 4.x
Background	☑	☑	LabelFrame	☑	☑
Button	☑	☑	NoteBook	☑	☑
CheckButton	☑	☑	TreeView	☑	☑
RadioButton	☑	☑	Progress	☑	☑
MenuButton	☑	☑	Paned	☑	☑
ToolButton	☑	☑	SizeGrip	☑	☑
Entry	☑	☑	ScrollBar	☑	☒
ComboBox	☑	☑	Scale	☑	☒

Figure 1: Widgets supported by TileQt under Qt 3.x and Qt 4.x.

Figure 2: TileQt running under the Gnome Desktop, in an up-to-date Fedora 13 Linux distribution.

2.2 TileGTK: a Ttk interface to the GTK widget toolkit

TileGTK is a Tile/Ttk theme that aims to use GTK styles for drawing Ttk widget elements. TileGTK is a recent extension, compared to TileQt, as its development started on August 2008. However, since both extensions were developed by the same author, TileGTK shares the same approach as TileQt: its development started from the TileQt sources, adapting names with search and replace, and slowly porting the widgets from Qt to GTK, one by one. The CMake-based build system was also inherited from TileQt. Of course, the development of TileGTK involved an extensive examination of GTK and GLib sources, in order to understand how GTK draws its styled widgets, revealing a significantly different approach than Qt. A major cause for this difference is the fact that GTK is written in C, instead of the

C++ employed by Qt. Of course, interfacing to a C library has some advantages, like the ability to use the library through a stubs interface, which TileGTK employs: reusing the GLib facilities for loading dynamic libraries, TileGTK is linked only to GLib. GTK is located and loaded dynamically, when the TileGTK extension is initialised from Tcl. And assuming that Tcl will add dynamic loading of arbitrary shared libraries in the (hopefully near) future, TileGTK can drop linking to GLib, allowing binary distributions of TileGTK to be distributed under the BSD license, to match the license of the sources.

Again TileGTK has not been actively maintained for some time now (the last ChangeLog entry dates back to August 2009), mainly because the usage of the Linux operating system by the author has been significantly diminished, compared to previous years. However, the source code still compiles under an up-to-date Linux distribution (tested with Fedora 13 and the latest 8.6 beta2 from ActiveState). Invoking some of the TileGTK demos produces the output shown in Figure 4, while the Ttk elements and widgets supported by TileGTK are shown in Figure 3. As it is evident from both figures, TileGTk currently lacks support for the treeview widget, as the implementation has never been written. Looking closely at Figure 4 (and Figure 3 for gray-coloured checked items), reveals several visual inconsistencies for some widgets. For example, the arrow for comboboxes and menubuttons cannot be drawn through the available public API, thus a generic arrow is drawn instead, borrowed from the scrollbar widget. Despite the fact that the scrollbar widget can be split in elements, and elements can be drawn by using the public API of GTK, there are visual differences in the arrow background shapes (they are not round, like the ones shown in the native GTK scrollbar visible at the right top corner of Figure 4). Scale and progress widgets are also drawn wrongly: scale grips are drawn larger than the native ones, suggesting a segmentation error while decomposing a widget drawn as a whole by the GTK style engine into elements. Similarly, the filled area of progress widgets overlaps with the widget borders. Finally, there exists a white line, drawn just below the raised tab in notebook widgets. In addition, the problem of thread safety observed in TileQt is also present in TileGTK: the basic demo script (demo.tcl) of TileGTK crashes when a second interpreter is initialised, so as to display a GTK theme selection dialog.

Widget	GTK 2.x	Widget	GTK 2.x
Background	☑	LabelFrame	☑
Button	☑	NoteBook	☑
CheckButton	☑	TreeView	☒
RadioButton	☑	Progress	☑
MenuButton	☑	Paned	☑
ToolButton	☑	SizeGrip	☑
Entry	☑	ScrollBar	☑
ComboBox	☑	Scale	☑

Figure 3: Widgets supported by TileGTK under GTK 2.x.

3 Conclusions, Open issues and Future directions

Maintaining an extension such as TileQt and TileGTK is not an easy task. Widget toolkits tend to evolve over time, sometimes introducing incompatible changes (i.e. Qt 4.x vs Qt 3.x), or deprecating useful functions. Apart from the constant monitoring required, there is also the issue of themes: there are too many of them floating around. It is not uncommon to fix a drawing error in one theme, with a change that breaks another theme, leading to a dead end. A promising idea is, of course, to prioritise themes: default themes of popular Linux distributions (such as Ubuntu or Fedora) should have priority over the rest of available themes.

Another aspect is the distribution license of generated binaries. The source code is distributed under the BSD license, but BSD does not cover the produced binaries. Both TileQt and TileGTK need to link with toolkit libraries (Qt, GLib, GTK) that are covered by the GPL license, which is transferred to the produced binaries. The fact that GTK is written in plain C, allowed TileGTK to access almost all GLib and GTK functions through a stub table. The only functions used directly are the ones related to shared library loading, offered by GLib. Once these functions are replaced by equivalents offered by Tcl, then linking to GTK will only happen at runtime, offering the possibility for TileGTK binaries to be delivered under a different license, such as BSD.

Finally, integration with the dominant Linux desktops, Gnome and KDE, is still an issue. Retrieving the theme, currently used by the desktop, is not always easy (especially for Gnome), while the retrieval of the colour scheme can be even more problematic. Regarding the latter, Qt and KDE provide more facilities towards this goal, while GTK doesn't. Under GTK, the missing functionality is attributed by parsing GNOME configuration files, and despite not being an elegant solution, it seems to work for the time being. Future work on both TileQt and TileGTK should focus on implementing the missing widgets (i.e. scrollbars under Qt 4.x) as well as fixing the visual problems that can be observed under popular themes.

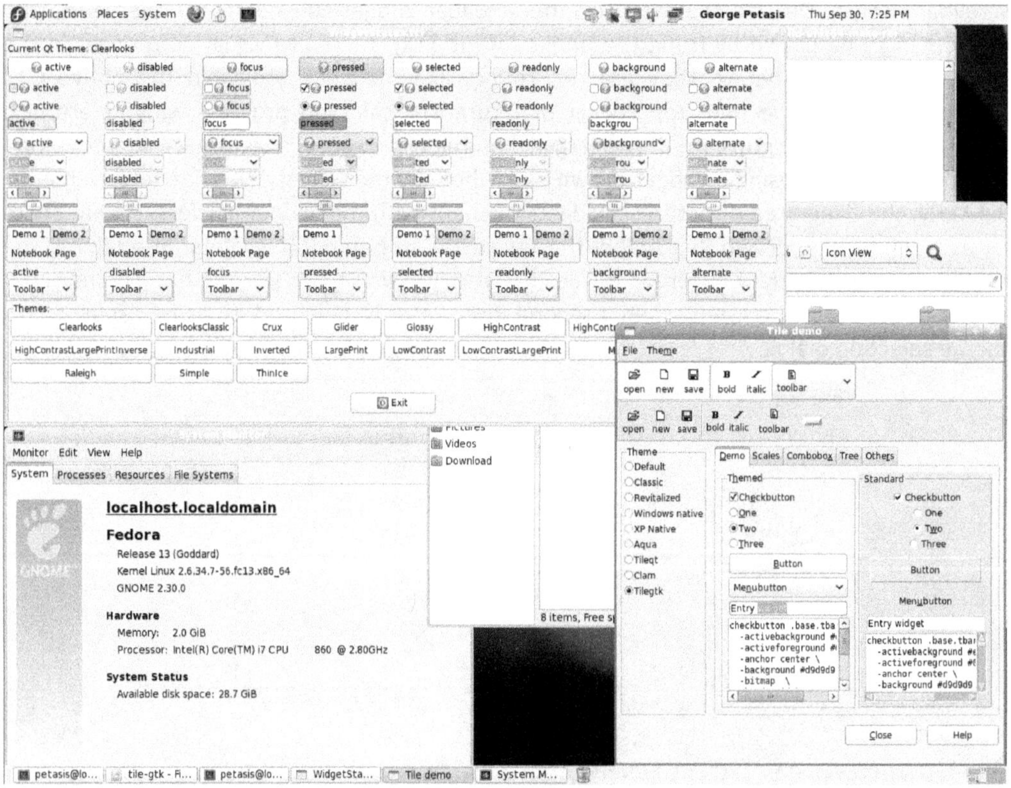

Figure 4: TileGTK running under the Gnome Desktop, in an up-to-date Fedora 13 Linux distribution.

4 References

[1] CMake – A cross-platform make: http://www.cmake.org/

[2] Tk Toolkit CVS access: https://sourceforge.net/scm/?type=cvs&group_id=12997

[3] Qt – A cross-platform application and UI framework: http://qt.nokia.com/

[4] The GTK+ project: http://www.gtk.org/

[5] GNOME: The Free Software Desktop Project: http://www.gnome.org/

[6] The KDE Community: http://www.kde.org/

[7] ActiveState – The Dynamic Language Experts: http://www.activestate.com/

17th ANNUAL TCL/TK 2010 CONFERENCE Chicago (USA) 11-15 October

TK III

Fri October 15, 2010 11:15-13:00

TclA Publications

Tcl/Tk guidelines for improved automated regressions - a case-study

Saurabh Khaitan, Madhur Bhatia, Tushar Gupta
Mentor Graphics Corporation

Abstract:
Automating regression flow for any GUI application always poses a lot of challenges. The automation demands recording and replaying the user interactions with the GUI often with timing synchronization between operations. There are some commercial and open-source solutions available which provide interactive test capabilities which can capture user sequences. Such testing applications access the internal objects of the application through the hooks provided via GUI toolkit. For automating the GUI based tests for our emulation product Veloce, an enterprise application based on Tcl/TK, various testing solutions were evaluated. Automation of GUI testing was supplemented by other methods like tcl script regressions, custom test applications and specific logging wherever required. The paper presents a case-study of various issues encountered in developing good automated regression flow for emulation GUI, and presents some coding and development guidelines for Tcl/Tk applications in general for suitability for development of automated regressions.

GLOSSARY:
AUT- Application under Test
GUI – Graphical User Interface
VP – Verification Points are used by automated regression tools to check the states of GUI.
Waveform Widget – Widget to view waveform signals
Path browser – Widget to traces signal connections in a design.

1. Introduction:

With the increase in the size and complexity of applications over time the need to ensure functional compliance over releases is increasingly felt. This can be guaranteed by creating extensive and stable automated test suites. The difficulty in creating such regression suites multiplies manifolds when GUI testing is involved.

Even a small size application creates excessive permutations and combinations of sequence of steps that are too large to test manually in consistent manner. Specially when the applications are continuously evolving, keeping in pace to test each feature is a cumbersome task. Even elaborated manual testing processes are error prone and there are chances of test scenarios being left out. Automated GUI testing tools have the capability to automate this task for you and it helps you to improve the quality of your application. It also cuts down the "time to market" for the tool if deployed in early stages.

Earlier GUI automation tools were analog, which means they recorded the mouse movements using co-ordinate movements. This was a very poor automation technique and required tremendous maintenance efforts every time there was a minor change in the AUT. Modern GUI automation tools are smarter and are "object-based". These tools are closely integrated with the AUT and recognize the control in graphical applications like buttons, menus and text input widgets. This technique is more robust and requires no changes in the regression suites with changes in GUI design or screen resolution so we will use "object-based" tools.

While developing automated regression suites we encountered many issues that were resolved in the process. We discovered that if the planning and strategies are done in the early stages most of these challenges can be met easily. In this paper we discuss the guidelines that are followed to develop robust and reliable regression suites. These guidelines are captured in the following sections:

- Guidelines for developers (Section 2)
- Testing strategies for QA engineers.(Section 3)
- Limitations and their workaround (Section 4)

The guidelines suggested for developers are to be applied at the initial stages of development and are discussed in detail in the following sections. The testing strategies for QA engineers are to be used at the time of automated regression suite development. At the end the paper summarizes some limitations that we encountered even after following these guidelines. The paper also discusses the workarounds used to plug these limitations.

2. Guidelines for Developers:

To facilitate the development of robust and reliable regressions, the developers need to provide hooks to various GUI objects. Apart from this, the developer also may be required to create infrastructure to dump extra information for regressions. We list below some of the techniques we use to help building regressions for our tool.

2.1. Use of global arrays: Global arrays can be used to store widget names so as to provide access to internal GUI components. There can be multiple arrays and each of them may have handles to widget instances related to specific feature or module.

Another way to provide hooks is by providing access through functions for all the relevant widget instances.

Providing access to various widgets will help the test writer emulate the exact user behaviour. For example, if there is a button that calls a function, test writer can invoke the button rather than call the function directly if he has the access to the button.

2.2. Direct use of internal functions: We also found that direct invocation of functions in tcl script to perform a GUI operation to be useful in verification of the code. A sequence of such functions use, can emulate a complex user operation that is not easy to capture in a GUI regression tool. Therefore, while developing an application, developer should design his code in a way that code is encapsulated into small functions that can be used in the regressions to emulate complex user sequences.

The script shown below illustrates use of sequence of functions along with use of arrays, to perform a complex user action of creating an annotation file, adding signals to it, and saving the file.

```
project open -prj_file_path veloce.prj
createAnnotationFileWin

addNetToAnnotationWin top.AIn[1:0]
addNetToAnnotationWin top.BIn
addNetToAnnotationWin top.w1[9:6]
addNetToAnnotationWin top.YOut
addNetToAnnotationWin top.ZOut

$annotationWin(fileTypeCB) invoke
$annotationWin(fileTypeCB) selection set
1
$annotationWin(fileTypeCB) invoke

saveAnnotationFile
```

In the code above a complex user action is getting mimicked by calls to functions `createAnnotationFileWin` to create an annotation window, `addNetToAnnotationWin` to add multiple nets to the opened window, and finally saving the file using the function `saveAnnotationFile`. All these functions are internal functions and the GUI users are not aware of them.

2.3. Use of environment variables: For regressions, the use of environment variables can help to eliminate user interactive controls and provide behaviour suitable for regressions. This behaviour can be actions like printing the message to log files which can be used for automated verification. The coder should be judicious in the use of environment variables. If the checks are placed in the part of the code which is excessively used it can cause a performance penalty. Let's look at a sample code to understand the use of environment variables.

```
proc medmessageBox {args}
{
    ...
    if (![info exists
::env(MED_REGRESSIONS)]}
    {
        if {![batch_mode]}
        {
            tk_messageBox
                -parent $par
                -message $msg
                -type ok
```

```
                -title $ttl
                -icon $icon
        }
        else
        {
            med_message $msg
        }
    }
    else
    {
        med_message $msg
    }
    ...
}
```

In the code above we can see that with the use of environment variables like MED_REGRESSION the part of the code which will be active in regression mode is selected.

2.4. Use of algorithmic functions: The algorithmic functions in the code can be written in the manner that they can be used independently through the script to perform the tasks and test them. This will enable efficient test creation to test these functions in specific. With the use of environment variables they can be used to dump extra information for regressions.

For instance in our application we have a function `findpath` that is used internally to search a hierarchical path in a tree and update the tree to point to the path if it is found. Since this function can work as a standalone function, it is used in automated regressions. With help of environment variables it is able to print the status for regressions.

```
proc findpath {fullpath separator tree}
{
    # sanity checks
    ...
    #tree search algorithm
    ...
    # tree update
    ...

    # code for regressions
    if {[info exists
::env(MED_REGRESSIONS)]}
    {
        if {$found}
        {
            set msg "path found"
        }
        else
        {
            set msg "path not found"
        }
        echo $msg
    }
}
```

In the code above the standalone function findpath is powerful enough to perform complex GUI operations like tree search, tree update. In regression mode this will dump extra debug information for verification.

2.4. Text representation of graphical display: Many times screen display, may have a text representation. For example waveform display can be efficiently represented as text file. Application developer can make sure that a way is provided to dump this type of display in a file which can be used in script based automated regression for verification. In our GUI we also have ways to dump display in schematic and path browser to a file. We also dump trees into text file for verification.

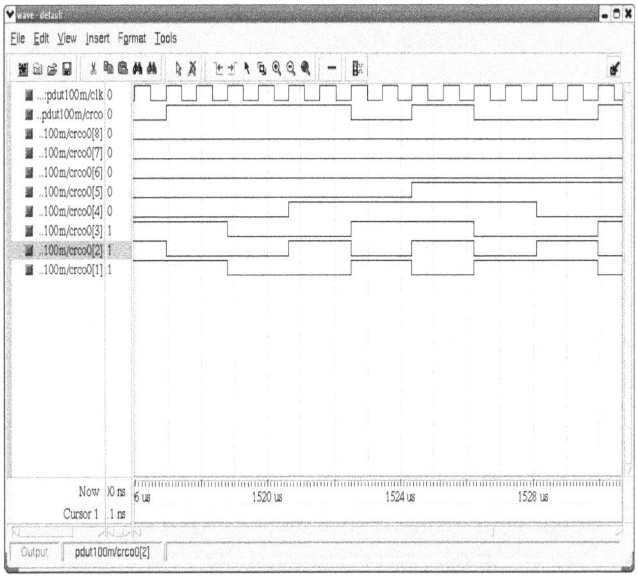

Figure 1: Waveform Widget

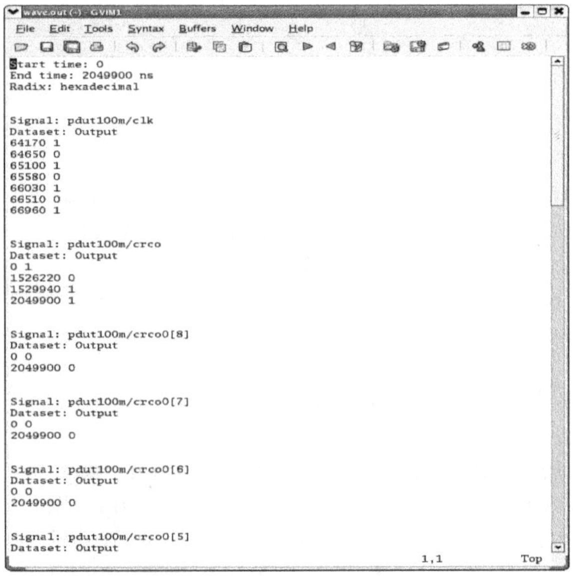

Figure 2 : Text representation of waveforms

The Figure 1 shows a graphical representation of waveforms as it is visible to the user. For regression purposes we are using a text dump of the waveform display as shown in Figure 2.

3. Testing strategies for QA Engineer

While creation of automated tests we developed some strategies which were very useful in making the regression suites resilient. To make the regression suites robust it is recommended that "Object based" GUI automation tool be used. Some guidelines that we followed are:

3.1. Use of Verification points: Just recording the user inputs to the GUI and re-playing them will not cover the testing requirements of GUI applications. It is of utmost importance that the state and the different properties of the numerous controls and widgets in the AUT are also checked. For incorporating these checks we used the concept of verification points. Verification points are checks introduced in the tcl script recorded through the GUI testing tool. These checks verify the current state and properties of the controls and widgets of the AUT after desired sequence of events. These checks are very important in ensuring the functional compliance of the AUT.

To illustrate this further lets take a scenario where a user is interested in checking the state of a widget. This can be easily done by querying the value of properties of the widget. In order to test the enabled state of a widget ($widget) the code will look like:

```
test compare [property get $widget state]
"enabled"
```

When we use Verification points these compare calls are inserted into the tcl script recorded by the automated GUI testing tool. Sample Code for checking state and image of a new_file button looks like:

```
# Verification Point 'newfile'

test compare [property get
[findObject
":vsim.dockbar.tbf0.standard.tb.button_0"
] state] "normal"

test compare [property get [findObject
":vsim.dockbar.tbf0.standard.tb.button_0"
] image] "__new_icon"
```

Here the automated testing tool inserted two property get calls, which then compare the returned value with the expected value. This technique is very useful in checking the functionality and state of the GUI.

3.2. Use of Global procedures: Creation of procedures for standard sequences in GUI has multi-fold advantage. Primarily it helps QA engineers to cut down on the time required for creation of tests as the same code can be leveraged across test suites and reduce maintenance overhead. It also helps in stabilizing the regression suites across incremental software releases. If there are any major changes in the application controls in the GUI code all the tests that are accessing that control of the AUT will start failing. With use of global procedures this can be achieved by changing at one place. The verification points which are part of the global procedures can also be shared across tests making testing of the states of the widgets in the AUT more exhaustive. Sample script using global proc:

```
proc main {}
{
        snooze 10

        #sourcing all global scripts
        source [findFile scripts
        "clean.tcl"]
        source [findFile scripts
        "analyze.tcl"]
        source [findFile scripts
        "close.tcl"]


        # global procedure - clean_all
        clean_all

        # global procedure - analyze
        analyze

        #global procedure - close_proj
        close_proj
}
```

In the sample script above it can be seen that we are calling three global procedures – clean_all, analyze and close_proj .We can see that usage of global procedures makes the test look very concise and manageable.

3.3. Synchronization points: Object based GUI testing tool insert time synchronization (snooze commands) to imitate user actions. This approach can make the regression suites unreliable at times. Consider a case when the test was recorded on a fast machine and is re-played on a slower machine, in such cases the test may fail. To avoid such scenarios we used the concept of synchronization points. While recording test the user can select to insert waitForObject statements. These statements wait for the given object to exist and be accessible thus eliminating the race condition created on slower machines. Sample Code:

```
waitForObjectItem ":vsim.#mBar" "File"
invoke activateItem ":vsim.#mBar" "File"

waitForObjectItem
":vsim.#mBar.#mBar#file" "New"

invoke activateItem
":vsim.#mBar.#mBar#file" "New"

waitForObjectItem
":vsim.#mBar.#mBar#file.#mBar#file#new"
"Project..."

invoke activateItem
":vsim.#mBar.#mBar#file.#mBar#file#new"
"Project..."
```

In the sample code above three synchronization points (`WaitForObjectItem` calls) were inserted to wait for the existence of the item before invoking clicks on them. The synchronization points can be used effectively in this manner to synchronize the automated tests.

3.4. Offline debug: It is very important for a GUI automation tool to provide its users with a way to debug the failures in an offline mode. This helps the QA engineers to debug the failures in the regressions. Modern GUI automation tools provide environment variables which when enabled will capture the state of the GUI when a failures occurs. So whenever a Verification point fails or GUI behaves unexpectedly the current state of the GUI is captured as screenshot by the automation tool. This screenshot can be viewed later in offline mode after the regression is over. This is a very useful for debugging of regression failures.

4. Limitations & their Workarounds

While the guidelines mentioned above enables the user to automate the testing of majority of the AUT, but still there are some limitations that exist with using the object based GUI testing tools. We have captured the limitations encountered and suggest some workaround to overcome them:

4.1. Custom widgets: Automated testing solutions are equipped to recognize and support standard Tcl/ Tk widgets. If the application uses custom widgets then the automated testing tool will fail to recognize the new widgets. There are two ways to solve this problem. The first and the robust solution is to work with the testing solution development team and get the support for the custom widget integrated in the GUI automation tool. This will at times require the user to share his custom widget code with the automation tool development team. The second solution is to use the conventional analog-style testing. This will enable the user to even create tests for custom widgets. Of the two solutions proposed the former solution is more robust and reliable.

4.2. Drag and drop: The testing solution that we employed for our test creation was not capable of capturing Drag and drop operations of the user. There are many black box GUI testing tools that are VNC based and capable of capturing DnD operations.

4.3. Canvas widget: Canvas widgets used in the AUT are similar to drawing canvasses. These widgets do not have properties like other standard widgets such as buttons. Thus it is not possible to create Property Verification points for canvas widgets as was done successfully for other widgets. To verify these widgets we used screenshot verification points. In screenshot verification screenshots of the canvas widget is captured at the time of test creation which is used as a reference image for consecutive runs. An example of the screenshot captured can be seen in Figure 3.

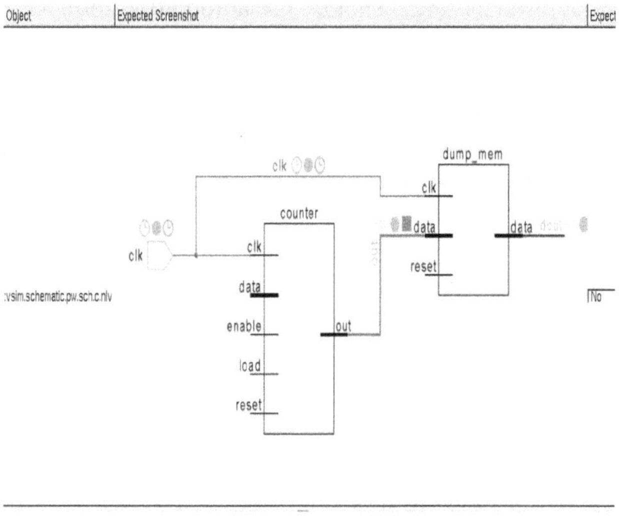

Figure 3: Screenshot Verification point

There is also an option of adding mask to remove unwanted portion of screenshot from these image comparisons. Other way of verifying canvas widgets is using textual dump of graphical display with the help of developers as discussed in detail in Section 2.4.

5. Conclusion:

Following the strategies elaborated above we were able to create robust regression suites for our Tcl/Tk based application. Initially some changes were required in the GUI code to align it to guidelines mentioned before but once the test suites were created it helped in eliminating the arduous process of manually testing the GUI. This not only enabled us to reduce the testing time for our GUI applications but it also caught issues which sometimes creep into subsequent patches of the software. The GUI automation testing tool that we used was Squish from Froglogic. When the tool is in the development phase if basic guidelines mentioned in the paper are followed majority of the GUI testing can be automated. Following the strategies discussed in the paper while test creation stable and robust automated regression can be developed.

6. Bibliography:

1.http://en.wikipedia.org/wiki/GUI_software_testin g

2.Squish, http://www.froglogic.com/download/book4

TkGecko: Another Attempt for an HTML Renderer for Tk

Georgios Petasis

Software and Knowledge Engineering Laboratory,
Institute of Informatics and Telecommunications,
National Centre for Scientific Research "Demokritos",
Athens, Greece
petasis@iit.demokritos.gr

Abstract

The support for displaying HTML and especially complex Web sites has always been problematic in Tk. Several efforts have been made in order to alleviate this problem, and this paper presents another (and still incomplete) one. This paper presents TkGecko, a Tcl/Tk extension written in C++, which allows Gecko (the HTML processing and rendering engine developed by the Mozilla Foundation) to be embedded as a widget in Tk. The current status of the TkGecko extension is alpha quality, while the code is publically available under the BSD license.

1 Introduction

The support for displaying HTML and contemporary Web sites has always been a problem in the Tk widget, as Tk does not contain any support for rendering HTML pages. This shortcoming has been the motivation for a large number of attempts to provide support from simple rendering of HTML subsets on the text or canvas widgets (i.e. for implementing help systems) to full-featured Web browsers, like HV3 [1] or BrowseX [2]. The relevant Tcl Wiki page [3] lists more than 20 projects, and it does not even cover all of the approaches that try to embed existing browsers in Tk through COM or X11 embedding.

One of the most popular, and thus important, projects is Tkhtml [4], an implementation of an HTML rendering component in C for the Tk toolkit. Tkhtml has been actively maintained for several years, and the current version supports many HTML 4 features, including CCS and possibly JavaScript through the Simple ECMAScript Engine (SEE) [5]. Despite the impressive supported list of features, Tkhtml is still missing important features found in contemporary Web sites, such as complete JavaScript, Flash or Java support. Thus, several approaches that try to embed a full-featured Web browser and instrument it through various means have been presented. For the Windows operating system it is quite easy to embed and instrument Internet Explorer using COM, either through Tcom [6] or Optcl [7]. Under Unix, a similar effort has been made by the Entice project [8; 9], which embeds Firefox through the TkXext [10] extension for X11. The extension presented in this paper, TkGecko, is more similar to the latter set of approaches. It does not implement another HTML renderer, but tries to reuse an existing one. Aiming at supporting a wide range of operating systems and, at the same time, ensure high degrees of compatibility, the rendering engine of the cross-platform and popular Web browser Firefox was chosen, known as Gecko [11].

It is not the first time that the embedding of Gecko in Tcl/Tk has been attempted. An earlier project under the same name (TkGecko) existed nearly a decade ago, company-sponsored, whose results and progress remain unknown as it was a closed-source project. The main sources of information regarding this earlier attempt are a paper presented at the 7th USENIX Tcl/Tk conference [12] and references in the Tcl Wiki [13]. However there is nothing common of the TkGecko presented in this paper and the earlier approach except the name: the two projects do not share any code, while the newer TkGecko is an open source project, distributed under the BSD license and whose source code is publically available at SourceForge [14].

The rest of the paper is organised as follows: chapter two provides an overview of the TkGecko extension, along with an example of how the extension can be initialised and used in order to render a Web page. Chapter three briefly presents the widget subcommands, along with the facilities for accessing the DOM tree of the rendered page. Finally, chapter four concludes this document and presents some future directions.

2 TkGecko: Embedding Gecko in Tk

Mozilla's Gecko rendering engine is not a simple piece of code. Being the essential element of many products (including Firefox, Thunderbird, Camino, Flock, SeaMonkey, k-Meleon, Netscape 9 and many others), Gecko is a cross-platform, standards-compliant and feature-complete rendering engine. Its complexity is evident not only by the size of its source code, but also by the effort required in order to embed it in a C++ application. Embedding and communication with the Gecko engine is performed through a protocol known as XPCOM [16], a cross-platform component object model, similar to Microsoft's COM. There is documentation on how Gecko can be embedded in C++ applications [16], but there are several problems when such an embedding is attempted:

- Stability of the API: the public API is more fluid than stable, and currently there are several embedding APIs available. Despite that TkGecko being less than a year old, a novel embedding API has been presented already [17], making the embedding process a moving target.
- Complexity of the API: several classes have to be implemented, as functionality is scattered among many interfaces that usually interconnect with each other.
- Thread-safety: the threading model followed by the Gecko engine internally is unknown, making difficult to ensure thread safety if the host application also uses threads.
- Dependence upon toolkits: under some platforms (especially Linux), the Gecko engine relies on widget toolkits (such as GTK) for rendering content and widgets. This poses many additional problems, as the toolkit must be also initialised by the host application, its message loop initialised, and native windows must be mapped as windows of the toolkit.

TkGecko implements a large percent of the classes required, offering access to a wide range of features from the Tcl/Tk programming language. Its source code is a mixture of static code and code dynamically generated through SWIG [18] in order to handle the number of the interfaces that must be exposed as Tcl commands. Despite its complexity, though, building TkGecko from sources is not so difficult (provided that a Development XULRunner SDK is available) as it is handled by the CMake build tool. Regarding the aforementioned problems the stability and complexity of the API have been coded with the hope that the used API will not be deprecated for a while. Dependence upon the GTK toolkit is something that affects only Linux, and the current implementation initialises GTK and initiates its event loop in a separate thread automatically by the TkGecko extension, while Gecko is loaded and initialised in the thread that also runs GTK. Finally, thread-safety is still a target to be reached: despite the code has been developed with thread-safety in mind, stability in a single-threaded host application is still an issue after prolonged use.